Praise for the Bestselling

ALASKA BEAR TALES

"*Alaska Bear Tales* is a compelling collection of stories about mankind's adventures and misadventures with Alaska's ursine residents, some funny, others fearsome."

—*The Milwaukee Sentinel*

"This is a book full of stories that will keep the reader from putting it down until the last page has been turned."

—*The Indianapolis News*

"Few people have ever seen a bear up close, and most—after reading this book—would prefer to keep it that way."

—*The Everett* (Washington) *Herald*

"*Alaska Bear Tales* will plant hairy tracks a foot long in readers' memories and leave them hearing things in the brush and looking over their shoulders every time they step out of the house."

—*The Homer* (Alaska) *News*

ALSO BY LARRY KANIUT

Alaska Bear Tales

More Alaska Bear Tales

Some Bears Kill

Cheating Death: Amazing Survival Stories from Alaska

Instant Sourdough

DANGER STALKS THE LAND

ALASKAN TALES

OF DEATH AND SURVIVAL

LARRY KANIUT

ST. MARTIN'S GRIFFIN ❧ NEW YORK

With gratitude I dedicate *Danger Stalks the Land* to those in the acknowledgment section, with the hope that they and you readers experience a long and safe life.

Library of Congress Cataloging-in-Publication Data

Kaniut, Larry.
Danger stalks the land : Alaskan tales of death and survival /
Larry Kaniut.
p.   cm.
Includes bibliographical references (p. 317).
ISBN 0-312-24120-8
1. Survival after airplane accidents, shipwrecks, etc.—Alaska.
2. Adventure and adventurers—Alaska.   3. Accidents—Alaska.
4. Escapes—Alaska.   I. Title.
G525.K25   1999

917.9804—dc21   99-33504
                                                                                      CIP

Design by Maureen Troy

First Edition: November 1999

10   9   8   7   6   5   4   3   2   1

Call me danger. Call me death. Call me rugged terrain,
hypothermia, or severe turbulence. Call me anything you want.
But know this. I seek to kill. To maim. To destroy.
I stalk the careless. I lay in wait for the unprepared.
I look for the ignorant. I waylay the unsuspecting.
I devour the weak. I pursue the complacent.
And I embody death. I go by many names and
I'm clothed in many forms. Some of these are avalanche,
ice, drowning, midair collision, crevasse, freezing,
steep terrain, grizzly. The bottom line is this . . .
if I find you, death follows in my footsteps because . . .
I inhabit the Land of Death.

—LARRY KANIUT
November 1998

ACKNOWLEDGMENTS

This book is a tribute to all whose stories fill its pages. I cannot thank them enough for generously sharing their experiences and reviewing the completed materials. Family, friends, and media people contributed to this book's completeness, for it was they who provided leads to the contributors.

Thank you to my competent, dedicated, and insightful agent, Stephany Evans, who took up the challenge of representing me and did so with determination and flourish . . . truly a dynamic lady. Thanks to Marc Resnick, my St. Martin's editor, to whom I owe so much—it has been a learning experience and I am extremely grateful for your leadership and flexibility in allowing me huge parameters.

And thank you especially to my editor-in-chief—my sweet, wonderful wife, Pam, who edited every story and provided ongoing encouragement and support.

CONTENTS

DANGER STALKS THE LAND

TOO LITTLE, TOO LATE

BY LARRY KANIUT

I can't get out. I don't want to stay here in this water.
I don't want to drown.

The GI struggled in the waist-deep muck of upper Cook Inlet not many miles north of Anchorage, Alaska. He had ventured too near the mudflats while duck hunting with friends and now expended energy in a desperate effort to free himself from the gluelike glacial silt that held him tightly in its grasp. He knew that the tide was due to change; if he failed, the inlet's cold, glacial waters would cover him within a few hours.

A short time later an airboat roared to the GI's aid. Three rescuers helped him break down his shotgun to use as a "straw" should the tide come in sooner than they could extricate him. Their efforts were futile.

The GI panicked and begged them to shoot him so that he would not suffer the death of drowning. They refused and left him in the mud as the gray-brown waters washed over his head, another victim claimed through carelessness.

That's the story the newcomer heard in 1966. He was a gung ho outdoors kid fresh from Oregon. Buoyed by visions of adventure, he gobbled up anything he could about the Last Frontier. I know because I was that kid.

After thirty-two years' embellishment it's time to chronicle the facts. In November 1988 I drove to Palmer, Alaska, to interview one of the key players in that tragic story. Lynn Puddicombe warmly welcomed me into his home and told me about his experience.

It is a sad story that serves as a warning to prospective hunters. Steer clear of the forbidden banks of the inlet; practice caution before entering that land of death.

For decades duck hunters have frequented the flats on Knik Arm north of Anchorage. A common bond connects those waterfowlers—get up early, savor the hot coffee, down some food, put on the hip waders, head for the blind, bag some birds, and go home. September 17, 1961, started out as such a day. However, it ended much differently.

A father and his sons enjoyed the day, hunting geese from their Coffee Point cabin near the hay flats. Forty-four-year-old Merle "Doc" Puddicombe enjoyed the outing with his teenaged sons Larry, Lynn, and Joe. Because there is often little water to run and an airboat has a shallow draft, the men were using the family airboat. It was a dry-run Banks Maxwell drive, fourteen-foot wood-and-fiberglass hull, with a sixty-five-horse Continental power plant.

In the midst of the hunt they heard an airplane, looked up, and saw it coming in just over the blind. The men figured it was one of many pilots they knew and didn't think much of it.

The pilot swung around, opened his door, and hollered at the men. Something about "stuck in the mud." They couldn't understand it. He made another pass. He shut down power and came in at idle. He pointed down the inlet and shouted, "Man stuck in the mud!"

Doc and the two older boys burst into action.

The low tide required some effort to work the boat free and into the water. By the time they freed the boat, the tide had started coming in. A foot bore tide was racing up the inlet, and Doc shouted over the roar of the engine, "It doesn't look good, but I still think we can save him."

The hunter was standing dead center in Wasilla Creek on the lower end of Palmer Slough, 150 to 250 yards from either shore. He was surrounded by mudflats.

They couldn't tell how deep the water was but assumed it was ankle- to knee-deep. They pulled up to him and Doc stuck a pole in. Larry and Lynn jumped out of the boat, landing in ankle-deep water. The hunter was mired crotch deep in muck, water lapping at his waist. The rescuers knew then that it was pretty bad.

The mud is soft when the tide is out. When the tide comes in and moving water hits the mud, it hardens up like cement. As long as a person keeps moving, there is no danger of getting stuck.

Larry and Lynn thought their stoutness was an advantage. Larry was twenty-one years old, six feet, and 180 pounds; Lynn was seventeen, six feet three, and approaching 200 pounds.

They learned the trapped hunter was Sp5 Roger J. Cashin, a thirty-three-year-old soldier stationed at Fort Richardson in Anchorage. He had been hunting with three fellow soldiers. At first they'd laughed at him because he was stuck. They were sitting on the shore thinking it was pretty funny.

Once they saw the water coming in and realized the seriousness of the situation, they went into action. One took off to phone the Rescue Coordination Center at Elmendorf Air Force Base in Anchorage. He had to go all the way across the hay flats at least one and a half miles.

His other two friends shouted encouragement from the bank but were afraid to venture out into the mud. A large quantity of driftwood covered the beach. If they'd known what they were doing, they could have built a trail to him and gotten him out.

Doc gave Cashin's two friends a gas can and told them to build a signal fire on the bank. One of them lit a match and dropped it onto the brush, then poured gas onto the flame! Although it blew him up the bank, at least they got a fire going.

Cashin had been stuck long enough to fire all his ammunition. He had used the three-shot signal to attract attention. Hunters in the area didn't hear his shots, and even if they had, it's not likely that they would have paid any attention because evenly spaced shotgun reports are common.

Freeing Cashin would have been easier if he'd been wearing hip boots. His choice of footgear would be a major factor in his chances of rescue. Unfortunately he wore regular army boots that lace up about halfway to the knee. Veteran hunters fear wearing ankle-tight hip waders that can't be removed.

Initially the rescuers tried to free Cashin with the boat. Doc revved the airboat while Cashin held on, but the boat pulled straight up. Next they used the boat's lift for leverage. Cashin held on to the side of the boat while Doc fired the motor a couple of times, but that also failed.

Then Larry and Lynn hung on to him, hoping to get some leverage from inside the boat to pull him out. That effort met with failure also.

Their tools were limited, consisting of a machete and two pry bars. The rescuers tried to scoop the mud from around his legs.

There was no way to break the suction on him. They slid the machete down his leg hoping to get hold of the laces and cut them. He was stuck too deep to allow the machete to reach his laces.

Larry and Lynn took turns using the machete and keeping the boat close while Doc manned the boat. The tide increased in volume.

Recalling other experiences motivated the rescuers to work frantically. They remembered shooting and wounding ducks that fell into the soft mud. The birds beat their wings and disappeared into the muck. They'd seen several moose stuck in that same area. Although moose appear strong enough to get out of anything, they couldn't escape that inlet goo.

Doc had always told his sons, "Never go out in that mud. If a moose can't get out of there, you should think about what you're going to do."

Time flashed by as the men worked feverishly. The teenagers were near convulsions from the paralyzing ice-cold, glacial water. Because the water was getting deeper, they abandoned digging.

They tried to get leverage by running an oar through Cashin's belt and over the gunwale then lifting up, trying to pry him loose. It was hopeless, but they refused to give up.

Larry and Lynn put an oar across their shoulders and Cashin held on to it. They tried to lift him out. It didn't work.

Doc stayed in the boat. He reminded the boys to keep moving, sometimes yelling at them. He'd shut down the engine. The boys kept one arm on the boat whenever they could. They kept working, trying to keep from sinking.

Larry got hung up in the mud a couple of times, and Lynn pulled him loose. They kept their hip boots on, moving enough to pop them out of the mud if they started sinking.

Cashin had a tough time standing. He'd been there so long that he must have been numb.

Next the boys bent down and put one of Cashin's arms over each of their shoulders. They bowed their necks underneath his shoulder in his armpits and tried to stand up. They could see it hurt him too badly. Their efforts were futile.

They exhausted every idea they had. There was nothing more they could do.

The water rose higher and higher. Before long the water was approaching Cashin's chest as the boys bent over him in knee-deep water.

When the Puddicombes hunted the flats, they always knew the exact size of the tides. That day they expected a small tide. Soon the water started running out.

Lynn told Larry, "This guy's gonna make it." Doc watched the tide and the boys held Cashin up.

They were overjoyed for a second as the water started receding. But all of a sudden the wind shifted, and they felt a strong wind in their faces. That's common on the mudflats. The wind picked up hard and came across the inlet. When the wind does that, it takes the tide.

The tides on upper Cook Inlet are run by the wind. Where a normal twenty-five-foot tide stops without a wind, the wind piles the water up another five or six feet, resulting in a thirty-foot tide! The wind can also bring the tide in an hour earlier. Tricky thing.

By then water was underneath Cashin's chin. The rescuers were desperate. They took apart a shotgun and told Roger, "If the tide comes over your head, pinch your nose and breathe through this barrel." But he never used the shotgun for breathing. He didn't want any part of it. It seemed he didn't think he could survive anyway.

Meanwhile a big Hercules flew up and down the river. The military was looking for Roger. When the emergency message finally reached Elmendorf, somehow the location of the stuck hunter was given as the Knik River. Two planes and two helicopters were searching the wrong area—they were flying over the Knik River instead of the duck flats!

Pandemonium reigned with the incoming tide. The ice-cold water kept surging into the area. There was a lot of noise and commotion.

One pilot flew over to the Knik trying to motion the military to come over to the duck-flat side. Another pilot flew down the inlet and found Roy Knapp. Roy arrived, parked his boat nearby, and built a huge fire.

About that time another pilot in his new Super Cub flew over. He attempted to land in the grassy, shallow water near the scene and flipped his plane over.

Roger was still alive. Doc was worried Cashin might panic and grab one of the boys. But Roger wasn't panicked.

Roger remained calm. He never got tripped up. He never panicked. He never cried. He didn't scream and ask to be shot. The boys were amazed at his reserve. He looked at Lynn and said, "I don't want to stay here. I don't want to stay in this water."

Lynn replied, "Well, I hope you don't have to either."

When it became apparent that the Puddicombes couldn't help him, Roger took his wallet out and said, "Give that to my wife. Please tell her I love her."

Reluctantly the men realized there was nothing they could do.

When the tide went over his nose, Roger tipped his head way back.

Lynn held the back of his neck. Roger didn't yell; he didn't scream. He just went limp.

He died before the water went over his nose. Maybe it was shock. The boys held Roger for a minute. They noticed his hair floating at the surface. No bubbles came up. One minute he was breathing with them; the next minute he was gone.

Doc told his boys the soldier knew there wasn't anything they could do. In spite of their failure, the rescuers felt good because they had done the best they could.

The rescuers did so much in so short a time, it seemed as though they had all day to save Roger. But when it was all said and done, they'd worked with Cashin no more than thirty minutes . . . possibly as little as fifteen.

Since Lynn had been in the water the longest and was on the verge of hypothermia, a pilot flew him to Palmer. He was met by his mother and younger brother Craig.

On the next shallow tide, officials set out to recover Cashin's body. They put ropes around him and tried to pull him out. They thought they would put a belt around him and take pressure up in the helicopter; however, the nylon rope broke when the helicopter attempted to hoist his body from the mud.

Doc Puddicombe received a letter from the U.S. Army, Alaska, a few days after the incident, commending him and his sons for their very determined effort to rescue Sp5 Roger J. Cashin.

Epilogue

It didn't have to happen. It was a senseless death. Had Roger Cashin's hunting buddies responded early on instead of taking the situation as a joke, Cashin would be alive. Doc Puddicombe was disturbed about that until the day he died.

People said the Puddicombes could have saved Cashin. Each skeptic had his reasons. People said, "Why didn't you remove his legs with a chain saw?" If the army was there with a doctor, the Puddicombes could probably have removed his legs and pulled him out. (How many people could survive having their legs cut off? Would a doctor ever let someone do that? Probably not.) Most people hunting geese do not carry a shovel or a chain saw!

One rumor stated that Cashin asked his rescuers to shoot him. That never happened.

Under the circumstances the military couldn't have done any more than the Puddicombes had done, even if they had arrived immediately. Their equipment was inadequate. The only thing that will get someone out of the mud is high-pressure water, and that process wasn't in use at that time.

Now rescue groups are equipped with portable compressors to deal with the problem. Helicopters can set down even if the water is deep or hover above the water.

The fire department and rescue units flush them out. The jet pump effectively blows away the muck.

Roger Cashin's death saved a lot of lives through the years. He didn't die in vain. A lot of people woke up to the dangers that mudflat country presents.

It was much worse before the 1964 earthquake. The cut banks were thirty feet high. Bore tides with six-foot heads sloshed up the slough. They rumbled into the hunting area sounding like a train in your living room. Locals joked about it: "The train's coming."

When it roared in, big slabs of mud fell from those mud banks and smacked the water. All night or all day long it sounded like cannon fire echoing up the slough.

Now water comes in and fills the whole area up, even on a small tide. A thirty-three-foot tide will sneak up on you and steal your boat. It's quiet because there are no banks anymore—just tapered, shallow shoulders. (Many people who hunt the mouth of the Little Susitna don't realize that its conditions are similar to upper Knik Arm's . . . under the right conditions a twenty-eight-foot tide will fill the area in ten minutes, completely covering the numerous tide guts.)

During the terrible ordeal and up to the very end Roger Cashin's attitude was remarkable. A rescuer stated, "It was a privilege to have known him. I wish we could have saved him."

For Roger Cashin to die, everything had to happen perfectly. And it did.

Though his situation was impossible, Roger Cashin never gave up. Another man who refused to quit was Randy Cazac.

NEVER GIVE UP

AS TOLD TO THE AUTHOR BY RANDY CAZAC

Look at all the blood. What happened?

Since 1971 I've wanted the details of Randy Cazac's hunting accident. Even though he was a former student, I never learned the specifics of his experience until recently when I called and asked him if he'd share his story. He kindly agreed, and on December 2, 1998, I met him at his Anchorage home where he told me the following.

By the time I finished cleaning the ptarmigan, it was around four o'clock in the afternoon. Ron and Skip had been gone for about an hour. I got up from my seat on a sleeping bag and walked a few steps to the other side of the road to stretch. While I stretched, I suddenly went spinning around and my ears went numb with a buzzing sound. I was stunned and confused. Trying to get a feeling for what was going on, I looked around. Nothing seemed out of the ordinary. Then I looked down. I saw blood gushing from my left leg. I immediately fell to the ground.

There was so much blood that the first thought I had was "Oh, man, I'm going to die!" I rolled onto my side and covered the holes in both sides of my leg with my hands. I lay there for some time. After a few moments some of the shock must have worn off because I figured Ron and Skip were too far away to hear the shot and that if I was going to have any chance to live, I'd have to do something myself.

I dragged myself about thirty feet to the gear, leaving a massive blood trail. I managed to get my knife out and cut free a sleeping bag from my pack. I crawled inside it and removed my belt with some difficulty. I tied my belt above the wound in an effort to stop the bleeding. I then rolled over onto my side again and covered the wounds with my hands to try to stem the flow of blood.

While lying there, I could finally get some understanding of what had happened. Apparently the wind was blowing with sufficient force to blow over our gear. The .270 rifle leaning against the packs had fallen over and discharged (somehow managing to hit me thirty feet away).

I remember being scared and weak, but I honestly don't remember any great pain. I was afraid to go to sleep for fear I'd die. So I forced myself to stay awake.

While I waited for Skip and Ron to return and with darkness falling, the wind picked up in intensity and the snow began to build up around me.

Who would have dreamed something like this could happen when my friends and I planned the trip? On Tuesday, April 13, 1971, Skip Krysak, his brother Ron, and I decided to get away for a while and do a little hunting. Skip had just returned on leave from the navy after SEAL training and was eager to get out into the woods. I was still in high school at Dimond High in Anchorage, Alaska, but it sounded like a good idea to me. A friend of my mother's offered us the use of his cabin north of Cantwell and we accepted.

Back then the Parks Highway didn't go all the way through to Fairbanks, just to Mt. McKinley Park, as it was then known. And the road wasn't maintained beyond Cantwell in the winter. This left us with the option of taking the railroad to an adjacent area and snowshoeing in to the cabin.

We took the train north that morning and got off approximately seven or eight miles north of Cantwell. We hiked across the frozen Nenana River to the road. Because we had only two pair of snowshoes, we took turns. One of us hiked on foot while the other two used the snowshoes. That proved to be quite a chore with the deep snow. Later, when we reached the road, the snow was perhaps only a foot deep, which made going much easier.

A handful of cabins were spread over several miles in this area, and we had only a vague description of the one we were looking for. It would take some effort to find the right one. We hiked into the first couple we came to and came up empty.

On our way in, we ran into some flocks of ptarmigan and shot several.

Some of the snow was chest-deep. Since it had been my turn to go without the snowshoes the last stretch, I was exhausted. It was getting on toward late afternoon and the wind increased, so we thought this would be a good time for me to rest. Meanwhile Skip and Ron would look for the cabin. While they were gone, I'd have time to clean the ptarmigan.

We stacked all the gear beside the road and leaned the rifles and shotguns against the gear.

They took the snowshoes and pressed on in the direction they were most likely to find the cabin. Since the wind was howling pretty good, I wasn't looking forward to camping out. I hoped they'd get lucky and find the cabin. That's about when the shot rang out and I found myself badly wounded by the .270.

About forty-five minutes later I heard something like "Look at all the blood. What happened?"

Skip and Ron ran over to me. I weakly explained what had happened and told them someone needed to get back to Cantwell and get help.

By that time I was so weak I'm sure I was also a little delirious. However, I told them which way to go. Probably knowing he had one shot to save me, Skip didn't want to believe me. He repeatedly asked me about the directions. Finally knowing they had to get started, they decided Skip would head toward Cantwell and Ron would stay with me.

Ron opened up our other sleeping bags, laid them out, and stuffed me and my bag into another one. He then crawled in beside me and pulled them back over us. By now it was completely dark and the wind was gusting to fifty miles an hour and drifting snow was all around us. I told Ron, "No matter what, keep talking to me. Don't let me fall asleep." He told me later that I was in and out of delirium while we waited, and he just kept bringing me back to some level of consciousness.

Meanwhile Skip ran nearly seven miles back toward Cantwell in the snow, never knowing for sure whether he was headed in the right direction. Nearly two hours later he saw a light. He hiked an extra three hundred yards through chest-deep snow after missing the turnoff into the man's driveway. Skip got the man out of bed and they immediately got into his pickup and drove up the road for us. When they got to where we were, they almost didn't see us because we were nearly covered with snow.

When they located us, they loaded me into the back of the pickup and drove me back to Cantwell. We went straight to the home of a missionary whose wife was an RN. Thank God. While she packed the wound and finally stopped the bleeding, her husband called on the radio (there were no phones then) to Air Rescue. Air Rescue said they could not come to get me because of the high winds, and they didn't see the weather coming down anytime soon. I heard this and figured that was the ball game. The missionary then called another local resident, pilot Frank Wright. He told Frank what was going on.

Frank told him to meet him at the strip and he'd do what he could. They carried me out to the truck on a blood-soaked mattress. The RN came with us. We headed to the airstrip where Frank was waiting with his Cessna 180. He'd removed the rear seats to accommodate me. They loaded me into the plane and Frank gave the missionary instructions regarding takeoff. He told the missionary if the wind was gusting too high, to signal him with a flashlight. He would then shut down and try again. These kind people risked their lives just to get me to the hospital. (I wish I could remember their names. They were such good people.)

When we took off, it was blowing hard but Frank decided to go for it. We bounced, shook, and wobbled like no plane ride I'd ever taken. But we got off the ground. On the way up the poor RN got airsick and bagged it.

While in the air the pilot asked me if I wanted to go to Clear Air Force Base or Fairbanks. I asked him what was in Clear. He said just a doctor. I knew I needed hospitalization so I told him Fairbanks. It was twenty-two minutes more flying time but we made it.

Frank had called ahead for ambulance service and was advised two ambulances were en route, one military and one civilian. When we landed, a military ambulance awaited. They quickly loaded me and headed out. En route they asked me if I wanted to go to the civilian or the military hospital. I asked them for their opinion and it was unanimous—civilian.

When I got to the hospital, they whisked me into the emergency room and started emergency procedures immediately with the IVs. They had a whole team ready to go. As they began treating me, I discovered that my femoral artery had been completely severed. It was now ten hours after being shot, and they were obviously amazed that I was still alive.

While I was on the examining table, the Alaska State Troopers came in and interviewed me about the accident. They told me they would reach my parents for consent for treatment since I was a minor. About an hour later they came back in and interviewed me again, which I thought was kind of strange.

I found out later, after the first interview, they had taken my driver's license and gone to the address on it. They waited outside for an hour for someone to come home. Trouble was, my parents lived at a new address. The Troopers called my parents at four o'clock Wednesday morning the fourteenth to tell them I had been in a shooting accident, that I was in Fairbanks Community Hospital's emergency room.

This delayed needed surgery another hour. My mother called right away and told them to do whatever was necessary. They even let me talk to her for a minute and she said she would be up on the next plane. By then I was so weak all I remember saying was, "Hurry, Mom."

The medical staff swung into immediate action readying me for surgery. Sometime during this period I was either sedated or finally fell unconscious.

My parents didn't know how badly I was injured, but when my mother finally got there, she was informed that I was in intensive care and that the situation was critical. They told her they had little hope for my life and even less for the leg.

The femoral artery had been completely shot away. I had been without circulation in my lower leg for almost ten hours before I got medical attention. My heart had stopped in the operating room and all my veins were collapsed. But a visiting Hindu anesthesiologist had found a vein in my armpit and had managed to get my heart pumping again.

They had taken me out of surgery once. They thought they had all the bleeding stopped. But it started again, and they had to take me back in for further surgery to tie off the bleeders that they had missed.

While on the way to intensive care I had quit breathing and they had had to perform an emergency tracheotomy in the elevator. They wanted to amputate my leg if the bleeding started again. My father told them, "If he wakes up without that leg, it will kill him."

They pumped blood into me all the next day and night. A doctor, two nurses, and two interns were the first to donate. I was still unconscious.

My parents and several friends who had driven to Fairbanks didn't know from one minute to the next if I was going to live. They were told that if I made it through the night, I would most likely live. Brain damage was a distinct possibility, as well as liver or kidney failure from being in shock for so long and losing so much blood.

About 5 A.M. on April 15 the nurse left intensive care to talk with my parents. She had a grin on her face as she told them she thought I would be okay. She said, "Randy woke up and told me to 'get that damn thing out of my throat so I can talk' " (meaning the trach which only blows air until you cover it, which I didn't know).

About 9 A.M. I woke up again for a few minutes and my mother came in. I talked to her briefly and asked her to get me a copy of *Atlas Shrugged* for a class assignment. Why she started crying and smiling at this request I had no idea.

After this I seemed to get better pretty rapidly. I was receiving tons of antibiotics and they seemed to be working. I even got up on crutches and into a wheelchair daily after about ten days.

After that I started feeling really bad most of the time. About three weeks after I entered the hospital Mom made up her mind to transport me to Anchorage, but the doctor had already beat her to it. He said that the wound would still require seven to ten days to close and that I might as well be in Anchorage waiting it out. They flew me to Anchorage in a basket stretcher, a gurney that they strapped me to. They had removed several rows of seats in the back of the airplane to accommodate the gurney and IV stand, then took me to Providence Hospital.

Dr. Voke took one look at the wound, put me in intensive care, and wanted to operate that night. But since my dad was out of town, my mother asked the doctor to wait until morning. By the time morning rolled around, the doctor had assembled four more specialists to assist him.

The wound was so badly infected they had to remove nearly five pounds of infected tissue. They discovered that the artery that had been spliced in Fairbanks was also infected. They said it was completely exposed and that it was likely to burst. No one told me exactly what was going on at first, but when they put a nurse by my bed twenty-four hours a day, I knew something was up. They finally told me about my condition.

I was getting weaker and weaker again. At one point the nurse was feeding me a piece of toast one morning when my left leg felt cold all over. I told her, "You'd better go get some help." She lifted the cover and it was déjà vu all over again. Blood was going everywhere. The nurse immediately called for help and started to compress the wound. A doctor, then another, showed up and they wheeled me to the operating room and went to work.

The artery was so damaged they couldn't repair it this time. They just tied it off. They had some indications that my body was already rerouting some of the circulation through other vessels because I was getting a pulse in my foot. They decided this was the best hope of saving my leg.

Even though I returned to the operating room every three to five days to remove more dead tissue from the infection, the wound still refused to close. It got to the point where Dr. Voke was running out of leg to save. Then one day after nine of these visits, he decided that was all he could risk and made up his mind that he wouldn't take any more of the tissue. That very same day I remember I woke up and was telling myself, "Hey, I feel better today. And I'm going to make up my mind to feel a little better every day." And for the most part I did.

Each day I seemed to get a little better and a little stronger. My family was there every day. My friends were terrific. They actually had a waiting list every day after school to see me. Everyone was pulling for me. My mother always sat quietly in the corner of my room and got to hear a lot of stories from my friends, which was unfortunate because I'd hoped she'd never discover them.

Then one day Dr. Voke told me the wound had completely closed and that we would be able to graft over it.

From then on it was a progression of successes and failures. We discovered that I had lost the main nerve in my leg. The ankle was paralyzed. I had no knee muscles. I was told that I would never walk again without a full leg brace and without the aid of crutches or canes. I also cried the first time I saw myself in a full-length mirror down in physical therapy. I entered the hospital weighing approximately 172 pounds. The day I saw myself in the mirror I weighed 89 pounds.

Somewhere in the middle of all this I got my graduation ceremony in the hospital—gown and all—while in a wheelchair.

The skin graft took. After two and a half months in the hospital, I went home.

With the help of my family, my friends, physical therapy, and an orthopedic prosthetics maker (who taught me how to lock my leg a certain way and swing it), I was able to get rid of the full leg brace in a few months. I threw away my crutches within five months. I was down to one cane within a year; and after about eighteen months I was walking unaided. The last cane has been a wall hanger now for over twenty-five years.

I am so thankful to so many people who rallied to my support. They were the greatest. I wish I could remember or include every name of every person who helped me.

Epilogue

In reflecting on my accident, I don't think making a tourniquet of my belt to stop the bleeding helped or played a part in saving my life because I didn't get enough pressure. I had applied the thick belt to my upper thigh.

And another thing of interest—when I was sitting there cleaning the ptarmigan, I had been wearing a pistol. I had moved the pistol holster around so that it was between my legs in my lap. When I was stretching and the rifle went off, I hadn't moved the holster. When they found the pistol, they discovered that when the rifle bullet exited my left leg, it hit the pistol and bounced off it . . . otherwise the bullet would have entered my right leg also.

A parting message I leave is to be more careful handling firearms . . . and never give up on yourself.

Determination is a crucial ingredient for survival, one that Billy Mitchell employed.

FIRE AND ICE

*As Emmet began to freeze, Mitchell told him to get into the water
while he attacked the tree with his ax.*

When I first came to Alaska, I gobbled up every adventure story I could. One
of those stories was about Billy Mitchell, who later became a lieutenant colonel
and was discharged from the army for his futuristic ideas. His story is a great
example of the need for caution and preparedness in the bush.

In the summer of 1901, Lieutenant Billy Mitchell evaluated the telegraph line
from Fairbanks to Valdez and determined the slow progress of its construction
was due to working summers only. He recommended year-round work—moving insulators, poles, food supplies, and forage in the winter to prep for summer,
when holes could be dug and poles set.

Pleased by his assessment, superiors charged Billy with reconnoitering the
country and surveying the route for the line. This was unexplored, uncharted,
unmapped country . . . in a word . . . wilderness. The first leg covered four hundred miles between Eagle City and Valdez, where an underwater cable from the
United States ended. This route harbored no human habitations that would
provide sustenance, and only by procuring wild game could the men supplement
what provisions they carried on foot or by dogsled.

Mitchell's orders included sole responsibility for acquiring transportation,
necessitating the purchase of dogs and sleds. He selected each dog himself; his
first choice was a dog named Pointer, a Mackenzie River husky.

Pointer became his leader, and Billy later claimed him to be the greatest dog
he ever saw. Pointer weighed 120 pounds and was perfectly suited for and sure
of the trail, able to find the trail with nose or paws. The dog protected both sled
and team under any circumstance and was so fierce Mitchell had to cut his fangs
off to prevent his chewing other dogs. He and Mitchell became best buddies.

After building a substantial kennel of dogs, Billy took a man named Emmet
to survey the country, checking geography and noting the equipment they'd
need for withstanding the weather. During these reconnaissance missions they
traveled light, carrying no tent. They dug a hole in the snow for fire, and they
often slept in the heat radiated from the fire. Or, they slept in a hole in the snow
under the dogs.

Captain Burnell was working north out of Valdez along the Tanana River, more than 150 miles distant, and Mitchell planned to meet him.

Mitchell and Emmet found Mentasta Pass, followed it south to Mentasta Lake, and crossed it with no trouble. They reached the outlet, the Tokio River, which was fed by warm springs. The surface of the river was slippery and pockmarked with bad ice. The ice was layered in sheets with as much as three feet of open water between the top and bottom layers.

They constantly broke through one or more layers, wetting their moccasins and trousers. Their footwear and pants instantly froze as hard as boards when they exited the water into the minus-sixty-degree weather.

At one spot Mitchell and his entire team and sled plunged through the ice. He found himself instantly in water up to his shoulders. The dogs swam to the edge of the ice and clawed for a hold on the slippery, cold surface. Pointer gained purchase on the ice and clawed himself out. He was able to pull another dog named Hunter from the water, then a second and a third. Finally the entire team, sled and happy musher were safe on solid ice.

Although Emmet avoided the same fate, he broke through at another spot up to his waist. Both men were now drenched.

The struggle they faced was that of surviving the freezing cold: they had to build a fire or perish. Survival in those extreme temperatures dictated urgency. *Got to get a fire started to warm up and dry off.*

A dead tree hung over the river as if provided by Providence. Billy instructed Emmet to begin chopping the tree since he was drier than Billy. Billy drove his team to shore, breaking through the ice along the way. He released the dogs from their harnesses so that each dog could look after itself, rolling in the snow to "sponge" off the damp or chewing at its paws to bite off the forming ice.

Mitchell got two candles from his sled. Using matches carried in a shotgun cartridge to keep them dry, he lit the candles in a sheltered spot. Periodically returning to the sheltered candles the men warmed their hands. They knew that if their fingers got stiff or froze, they were useless. Frozen fingers or hands in that situation meant a slow death by freezing.

Emmet's ax handle was so brittle from the cold that it broke on his first stroke. As Emmet began to freeze, Mitchell told him to get into the water where he could "warm up" while Mitchell attacked the tree with his ax. Halfway through the tree Mitchell's ax handle broke. If ever things looked bad, this was it.

Even Mitchell's tin of kerosene had frozen.

Mitchell returned to the water as Emmet retrieved his second ax and cut down the tree. He stripped its branches off in moments and started a fire.

In the meantime, before Mitchell had been able to turn them loose, three dogs chewed through their traces and got loose. Within seconds the dry kindling and wood touched by a tiny spark became a roaring fire, completely changing the mood of the moment and the possibilities of the men's survival.

They dried out their gear and fed their animals.

The next day they continued south expecting to meet the mail carrier. While running along a steep bank, Mitchell noticed a spot ahead where a sled had broken through the ice. He mushed his dogs up over the bank, where he had seen the top of a tent.

In front of the tent a man sat on his sled, his head tilted forward on his hands. Before the man sat a large black dog. When Billy called to the stranger, he received no answer. He approached the man and found him frozen to death. Beneath him was the mail. The man held a match between his teeth. Between his knees was a box, on which he had tried to strike the match when his hands had frozen.

Four dogs had chewed through their traces and left, leaving the man's faithful dog with all four feet frozen. They placed the mail carrier's body in his tent and laced it up. Then they put the dog out of its misery.

Regardless of the advancements in technology, man is no match for Mother Nature (no pun intended). Where water and extreme cold temperatures are involved and man gets wet in the wilderness, the results are the same: unless he gets a fire going or has some form of heat, his chances of survival are nearly zip.

The technology of the 1990s is light-years ahead of 1900s; however, Mother Nature is the same. The need for vigilance in the outdoors never changes in Alaska . . . as you'll see when you read the next tale by Jack Whitman, "Death's Cold Grip."

DEATH'S COLD GRIP

AS TOLD TO THE AUTHOR BY JACK WHITMAN

Every time I tried to pull myself up onto the shelf, however, another chunk of the thin shelf ice would collapse.

In the fall of 1996, I was desirous of gaining trapping information in the McGrath area. After I called the Anchorage office of the Alaska Department of Fish and Game to ask for some help, a lady suggested I contact Jack Whitman, the McGrath-area biologist. He kindly invited me to "come to McGrath and I'll take you trapping for a few days."

During my stay with Jack, his wife, Natalia, and son, Valya, I gained a great deal of respect for him and the job he was doing for the state of Alaska. Jack shared some trapping stories with me, of which the following is one.

Snow gently piled up through the afternoon and into the evening. The forecast was for the front to pass during the night, the temperature to drop, and the sun prevail—an absolutely perfect combination for wolf hunting with my airplane. I was certainly not up with the big boys when it came to hunting wolves. I could track a pack from the air as well as the best of them, but my prowess at sneaking my Cub into (and then, more importantly, out of) marginal openings in the taiga was not honed by years of hard-won experience.

Anyway, the next morning dawned as promised. Dawn, however, in mid-January in western interior Alaska, doesn't really exert itself until about 11 A.M. While this always gave me plenty of time to gulp several cups of mud and to take care of the previous days' skinning and stretching, it resulted in a relatively short day of trap-checking or wolfing. By departure time the plane had been fueled, deiced, preheated, preflighted, and disrobed of wing and windshield covers.

I departed the frozen river as early as practicable in the minus-thirty-degree temperatures. I had previously worked a pack in the Big River country that had at least two really nice blacks in the pack of eleven. I hoped that with the new tracking snow, I'd be able to cut their tracks, find the pack, and at least have a chance of bringing home a pelt or two. The last time I'd worked the pack, they were only about thirty miles from my house in McGrath.

Tracking snow was perfect, and I was excited about the prospects. The deep snow had resulted in higher than normal winter mortality of the area's moose population, due to both diminished food availability and unusually heavy wolf predation. The Black River pack was composed of several adults, apparently very proficient at killing moose. I stayed a hundred feet or so above the spruce, taking advantage of the new snow and the tracking light, wandering easterly trying to cut fresh tracks.

No more than twenty minutes from home, I crossed over four or five fresh otter tracks. Knowing that the otters at the end of the tracks would be easy to find and, hopefully, to harvest, I stayed with the tracks for what was probably less than two miles and found them busily working a blackfish hole in the ice.

Blackfish are a unique species of small, minnowlike fish that exist in subarctic ponds and sloughs. These waters, with a thick covering of ice and snow for most of the months of the year, generally go down to almost immeasurable parts per million of oxygen. Blackfish have evolved to live in these environs through their ability to utilize free oxygen. The hordes of these small fish jumping out of the water and gulping mouthfuls of air maintains open holes in the ice throughout the winter.

I swung the plane around, setting up for a landing. Ice thickness this time of year was generally not a problem, as long as I missed the blackfish holes and the thin ice around the beaver lodges and caches. As a precaution, however, I taxied my little ski plane across the frozen lake and up into the nearby willows rather than shutting down on the ice. Better safe than sorry.

After the plane was shut down and the engine cover was thrown over the cowling, I pulled out snowshoes and rifle, kicked into the shoes, and headed for the open hole where the otters were catching blackfish. River otter usually run in groups and this time was no exception. They were numerous in this country and pelt prices were reasonably good, but I had never taken more than one otter from a group by shooting.

The blackfish hole was no more than two hundred yards from the airplane, and even in the deep snow, I covered most of the distance in only a few minutes. I slipped out of my snowshoes, sat on one, and stuck the other tail in the snow to use as a shooting rest. I sat and waited no more than thirty yards from the hole.

Within seconds, a large male otter periscoped up out of the hole. Unconcerned at my presence, he slipped up out of the open water onto the ice shelf, at which point I shot. The otter thrashed a bit, flopping back into the water. I stood up, kicked back into my snowshoes, stuck the butt of the rifle into the snow, and started for the now-quiet otter.

Two or three more otters periscoped up to see what the commotion was about, then quickly dove back into the depths. As I approached the hole, it was evident I wasn't just going to be able to grab the otter and get back to the plane, since he was floating in the center of the five-foot-diameter hole.

I got to the hole and slipped out of one snowshoe, which I planned to use to extend my reach. When I put my foot down on the ice without the benefit of the snowshoe to spread the weight, the ice gave way and I plunged through.

The immediate cold was excruciating. Unimaginable. I grabbed the otter and slid him onto the ice. Every time I tried to pull myself up onto the shelf, however, another chunk of the thin shelf ice would collapse. The blackfish activity had created a larger hole than I had suspected, and the fresh snow had disguised the fact that the surrounding ice was so thin. After what was probably no more than three minutes (it seemed like the larger part of an eternity), I was able to pull myself onto reasonable ice, retrieve my floating snowshoes, and hurry back to the airplane.

Yeah, I was cold! No real problem, however. I carried my otter, picked up my rifle stuck in the snow, and returned to the plane. I remember feeling a bit disappointed, knowing I'd have to either make a fire and dry out, or simply return home. My wolf expedition was effectively thwarted for the day.

To save on airplane weight, I hadn't been running a battery in the plane and had to hand-prop the thing. On the second pull through, she started, and I hopped in. We bulled our way through the deep, soft snow on the bank, got back into my arrival track, and had no problems getting airborne once again. I remember glancing at the outside-air-temperature gauge, noting that it showed minus thirty-five degrees. Yeah, I'd better just point toward home.

What I didn't realize was that while I sat relatively motionless in the small cockpit, the inside air temperature was not significantly different from that outside. My thickly insulated coveralls, soaked entirely through, were flash-freezing into a sitting position.

By the time I landed on the river in front of my house and taxied into my parking spot, I was shaking uncontrollably. I pulled the mixture knob and my little plane quieted, then I dropped the door and tried to get out. It wasn't happening. I was frozen in position. I couldn't move. I had shut off the airplane, and without a battery, I couldn't restart the engine. Without a battery or the prop turning, my electronics were inoperative, too. I couldn't radio for assistance.

I finally worked one arm out of my parka and was able to grab the overhead brace. I managed to get myself unstuck from the seat and flop over sideways. No stopping now, as my center of gravity tilted my noggin painfully into the lift strut and I ended up, still in a sitting position, sprawled on the new snow below the airplane. I shivered a minute or two there on the ice, finally tilting myself up into a squatting position. I squat-walked up the bank and into the warmth of the house.

Conclusion

I am constantly reminded how unforgiving this environment is on humans who try to coexist with the brutal elements. Despite one's careful planning and experience, unforeseen dangers are always lurking. I look back on experiences such as this and allow myself a chuckle at how naive my actions were, but am subtly reminded that the outcome of the next outing may not be so humorous.

Certainly Calvin Lauwers's mountaineering adventure was far from humorous.

FAIRWEATHER NEARLY WON

AS TOLD TO THE AUTHOR BY CALVIN LAUWERS

I had a headband on . . . I thrust my head forward against the snow.
I felt a real solid blow to the back of my head.

When I learned that my former student Calvin Lauwers of Anchorage, Alaska, had had a climbing accident on Mt. Fairweather while attempting a climb with two buddies, I asked him to share his story.

The three of us left Anchorage in March of '89. Eric Peterson is a friend from Waterloo, Iowa, who commercial-fishes Alaska in the summertime. Another friend with whom I've done the most climbing is JT, an experienced climber who owns a backpack shop in Colorado.

We chose Mt. Fairweather because it's an impressive mountain and one of the biggest in Alaska. Most of the mountains are inland, but the base of Fairweather is twenty miles from the coast. Mt. Fairweather is just over fifteen thousand feet and more difficult to climb than the west buttress of Mt. McKinley.

After planning a fourteen-day trip, we jumped on Alaska Airlines and flew to Yakutat. We stayed overnight at Yakutat Air Taxi. Because we had so much gear and food, and because we wanted to go as light as possible, we sorted through our gear. We figured our climbing route would involve primarily snow and ice and didn't figure on much rock at all. One of our big debates was whether to take our climbing helmets. It is not uncommon on alpine snow/ice climbs to climb helmetless. In March and April in Alaska it is usually cold enough that there is not much rockfall. We decided that we wouldn't take them.

The next day we woke up and the weather looked good, so we took off in a Cessna 185. On the first trip in, the pilot flew JT and me and a little bit of gear. He then returned and picked up Eric and the remaining gear. The pilot dropped us off on the Fairweather Glacier, which was real foggy.

We packed our gear into individual packs, and even after eliminating gear, we had quite a bit as our packs weighed around seventy pounds. We skied up the glacier a couple of miles, set up our tent, and spent the night.

The next morning we packed up, moved our camp, and looked at the route we'd be climbing. We weren't able to see the entire route, but we could see the bottom part and checked that portion out.

The next day we got up early and started our climb on a jumbled ice field. It was pretty slow going because we encountered a lot of crevasses and house-size chunks of ice. As morning wore on, it was a beautiful, clear day with temperatures in the fifties. That night we camped right there on the ice field.

The following day we commenced our climb. It was extremely warm for that time of the year—daytime temperatures hovered in the fifties. That area traditionally has some pretty nasty weather, and one of the reasons we were giving ourselves so much time was to allow for the weather. But beautiful, clear blue skies greeted us. The biggest problem was that the warmth during the day led to a lot of avalanches. They exploded around us all day, rumbling by on either side of us and sounding like bombs bursting.

We tried to make sure we were climbing in areas that were safe. After that first day we were a little gun-shy about climbing in the daytime because every two minutes we'd hear an avalanche. Therefore we started sleeping during the day and climbing at night, using our headlamps to provide light.

The first few days we encountered good, short pitches, requiring no real technical climbing. We got up next to a big avalanche chute that we had to cross to get to the main route that we wanted to climb. We were there in the late afternoon preparing to climb across. Watching avalanches go down that thing, we decided we'd go to sleep and get up about three in the morning to go across in the coldest part of the day with the least amount of avalanche activity.

We awoke and prepared to cross the chute, stretching out two 150-foot ropes. With lots of room we spread out as far as possible planning to cross the chute as quickly as possible to avoid an avalanche. We got across and felt pretty good about being on the route.

As we looked at it, we noted quite a few spots with some exposed rock, and we thought it might be a little trickier than we had thought from down below. The good weather continued as we climbed.

On the fifth day we were going up a real steep area. There was a lot of ice. It was the kind of place where you wouldn't want to fall. Although JT and Eric swapped leads, at this time JT was leading, with Eric behind him. Our procedure was standard. JT would climb seventy-five feet, put in protection, and belay Eric up to him. Then they would belay me up.

JT climbed up an ice-snow couloir. As he got to the top, he tried to put in some snow pickets for protection, and he just didn't feel safe with them in. So he decided to go over to where he saw some rock and try to throw a sling around the rock to use it for protection.

As JT moved along, he hit a rock and dislodged it without realizing it. Six to eight inches in diameter, it screamed down the mountain toward Eric and me. Eric glanced up just before it got to him, jumped out of the way, and yelled, "Rock!"

All I heard was "Rock!" I thrust my head forward against the snow. I felt a solid blow to the back of my head, and I knew I'd been hit. I lost all feeling in my legs and arms.

I'd fallen and was hanging there by my rope. And yet I wasn't completely suspended, my body hanging over the snow.

My immediate thought was of a dog getting run over, making his final kick before he dies. I was conscious and yet I had no feelings in my legs or arms. As I lay there, I could see my arms and legs flailing all over the place, moving spasmodically, yet I wasn't feeling anything. I knew I wasn't doing anything to make them do that. I couldn't move.

Eric turned and looked at me and asked me if I was all right. My exact words were, "No. I'm dying."

He goes, "Don't joke with me like that."

"I'm serious. I have no control over my body."

As I was talking, I knew I was alive. I didn't think I was going to die. I had lots of flashbacks of earlier days of playing sports and being real active, knowing now that I was going to spend the rest of my life in a wheelchair. It was too much to comprehend. I just couldn't believe it. I was kind of praying out loud, "God, why? Oh, no. I'll be paralyzed."

I'd only been married a short time. I pictured my wife pushing me around in a wheelchair. It didn't sound good.

For one or two minutes I had no control. I wore a headband with thick bunting. Finally I was able to pull it off. The band had a large hole and was covered with hair. I could see tufts of hair and blood on the snow. I was missing a big bunch of hair on the back of my head. Eric looked at my injury, and I could tell by the look on his face that he was worried. The injury was probably more serious than I had thought.

I was beginning to have feeling, first in my legs. It was as though the numbness went away and all of a sudden I could feel my toes. I could feel myself moving. My arms were still kind of limp. As I moved my neck, I began to get feeling throughout my legs and arms.

I knew I shouldn't stay there long. JT yelled, wondering what had happened. Eric told him that I'd been hit by a rock and that he needed to come down.

JT climbed down to where we were. He looked at my injury. He's an EMT and understood immediately the need to get me off the mountain. We decided we'd better move off the pitch. Just below us was a protected ledge where we could rest and work on my injury.

They took my stuff, and I climbed down to the ledge. I was down there alone praying to God, crying almost. Sobbing with joy. I was so happy that I wasn't paralyzed. I figured I was going to be okay.

They came and tended my injury, which was pretty bad. They cleaned it, put some antibiotics on my wound, and wrapped my head in an Ace bandage.

I didn't want to end the climb right then because we'd spent quite a bit of money and time preparing for it. We usually do one pretty good climb a year, so I hated for it to end so soon. Most of the difficulty except right at the summit lay behind us. From where we were to the summit looked really nice; the slope angled out above us and would require steady but not nearly as technical climbing.

I was anticipating that, but they said, "No, way. We're going down. It doesn't matter. Head injuries can be real dangerous. You might not feel the effect right away, but we need to get help if you need it."

So we down climbed that day. I carried a pack, but they took a lot of the weight that I'd had and divided it up between them. We reached our tent site from the night before. We were actually a little above the clouds. It cleared up. You could see the water, and it was a beautiful, clear night looking over the bay. We set up our tent for the night.

While we enjoyed the beauty, JT and Eric gave me a little better medical attention. They took a Swiss Army knife, using the scissors, cut around the wound. After cleaning it out really well, they put on some paper stitches to hold the skin together. Then we wondered what we were going to do miles and miles from anybody. We knew we weren't supposed to be picked up for another seven days.

We had a little handheld radio with a marine-band VHS (the straight VHS operates on a line of sight), which we had taken in case of an emergency. We figured the only contact that we'd be able to make would be with an airplane or, possibly, a boat. Contacting someone was a long shot, but we set up the radio.

Looking straight out at the bay, we called on an emergency channel for anybody who might hear us. A guy picked up our transmission on a boat and said he was fifty miles offshore in the Gulf of Alaska.

He asked where we were. We said, "We're not on the water. We're up on Mt. Fairweather about eight thousand feet. We've got a guy hurt."

The fisherman was completely shocked that a handheld radio would transmit so well. He was more interested in the radio than my injury. He wanted to know what kind of radio we had so he could purchase one.

After he asked us five or six times if we were sure that we were on Mt. Fairweather, we told him it was urgent that we get ahold of the Yakutat pilot . . . to see if he could pick us up the next day. We figured it would take us a day to reach the glacier.

The fisherman said he knew the pilot and that he'd get ahold of him through the marine operator. So he called us back on the radio and told us that he'd talked to the pilot, who would come in the next day.

It was real warm the following day. We got up and descended toward the glacier. That was probably one of the scariest days of the climb because we were climbing in the heat of the day. In spite of the avalanches crashing all around us, we needed to get down to the glacier. A lot of big, big ice chunks were melting and falling all around us. We jumped into crevasses to protect ourselves. Traveling wasn't safe, but we stayed in areas that we thought were safest.

We reached the glacier and skied with our sled to our original campsite. We set our packs out on the glacier to give the pilot visuals to enhance his depth perception, and he was able to land there.

He flew me and just a little bit of the gear back to Yakutat. Even though the weather wasn't real good by then, he dropped me in Yakutat and flew back to pick up JT, Eric, and the remaining gear.

The pilot's wife gave me a ride to the physician's assistant. It was amazing that they didn't have a doctor in Yakutat. The physician's assistant had a lot of responsibility for logging, fishing, and climbing accident victims.

She said medical facilities don't stitch after twenty-four hours because it usually won't help and there's the threat of sewing infection into the wound. Since the gash was three or four inches long, she thought it would help to stitch it up. She said it looked really good and she was impressed with the care I'd received on the mountain. It had already started to heal.

We got on a plane the next day. It was full of commuters going from Juneau to Anchorage via Yakutat. They bumped three people for medical emergency and we three flew back to Anchorage.

I went to North Care where a doctor x-rayed me. He said I was lucky to be alive. He said my initial numbness and loss of feeling was probably temporary paralysis. He said that will sometimes happen for a short time, but with a harder blow you are paralyzed.

I told him the story of how we got ahold of people and how we got out, and he said, "Well, you're a lucky guy."

I haven't had any problems. At first I had a few dizzy spells. Aside from that it hasn't bothered me.

I talked to Eric a couple of days ago. We were planning another climb this year to Fairweather to give it a grudge match; but I think we're going to go to Mt. Deborah or Mt. Logan instead.

Just as Calvin's mountain outing turned ugly, so did Fred Easley's when he was overcome by an avalanche.

LOOK FOR A CORPSE

BY LARRY KANIUT

Vaguely he heard a sound in the distance, one which he did not recognize. At first he thought it was the sound of shovels biting into the snow . . . then he realized there was no rhythm to the sound, just an irregular but steady smooshing sound. With horror Fred recognized the sound as that which results when snow settles!

During my quest for outstanding adventure tales, I read an incredible story in the *Alaska Sportsman* about a man's avalanche adventure. I rewrote the tale and hope you'll marvel as much as I when you read it.

Slowly the three men slogged along in the swirling snow and billowing wind. Their destination was the mine on Lucky Chance Mountain near Sitka, Alaska. It was a Sunday in December 1936. J. Clark Sutherland, an engineer, Otto Hill, a miner, and Fred Easley eagerly anticipated what lay ahead. When the wind ceased, they realized that instead of being on the side of the mountain, they were far down the mountain, nearly at the bottom of a canyon. The air was clear. Not only was it easy to discern their whereabouts, but it was also possible to evaluate the conditions of the snow around them.

Fred immediately recognized a danger signal near him in the snow. He knew from experience that the yellow spot hid a pocket of air below the surface. He reveled in the fact that they had stopped where they had, or they might have ventured out onto the crust of snow and broken through into the cavern below. While contemplating their good fortune, they heard a *schhhwoosh*.

During that moment, the mountainside loosed part of its snowpack and jettisoned it to the canyon below. Fred was completely covered with snow. One moment the three men were talking; the next moment Fred was gone.

Clark and Otto were slammed across the snow by the same wall of snow that buried Fred. Snow covered Clark, who resigned himself to death. Just before losing consciousness he realized two of his fingers were above the snow! That's when he started clawing free.

Clark felt Otto's hand on his boot. Clark dug until he had Otto's head free and discovered that Otto was alive but unconscious. After reviving Otto, the two dug for nearly three hours until they were free from their trap.

In the meantime, Fred, who had heard nothing from his friends and assumed they were dead, figured he was going to have to make it out on his own.

The avalanche struck at 9 A.M., pitching Fred into total blackness, totally encasing him in snow. He sprawled facedown in the snow that pressed against every part of his body. He felt that he was drowning in snow. His lungs screamed for oxygen. He couldn't yell. Panic overcame him. He held his breath for as long as he could, figuring it was his last. His ears pounded. When he could hold his breath no longer and his lungs were on the verge of exploding, he gasped for air.

Perhaps some air had been trapped near his head. Whatever the reason, he gulped a mouthful. Gradually he was able to piece things together. He had been standing near a large boulder when the avalanche hit. The force of the snow knocked him onto his face where he lay at a forty-five-degree angle. His left hand was pinned near his side with his elbow bent. His right arm was straight in front of him, his hand barely touching the boulder. His head was immobile, as was his body because of the tremendous weight of the snow.

Fred experienced anxious moments thinking his back might be broken, paralyzing him, until he joyfully moved the fingers of his right hand.

A myriad of thoughts flashed through his mind. Strangely enough he wondered about the heir to his stamp collection and the prediction of a fortune-teller who had once told him he'd live to be an old man (he didn't consider his current age of twenty-eight old!). But the thought that the shock of his death might kill his mother motivated him to get out.

Slowly he freed his right hand and scooped the snow away from his face. He found his stocking cap and put it on his head. He could barely make out the dark outline of the rock. He had no way of keeping track of time as his watch had stopped.

Even though Fred's movements were severely limited, he had some things in his favor. First, he was warmly dressed. He wore long-handled underwear, blue denim jeans, a wool shirt, three pairs of heavy woolen socks, shoe packs with rubber bottoms, and an oilskin suit—pants and jacket waterproofed with oil. He also wore a pair of homemade snowshoes with long wooden frames. In addition to his stocking cap Fred wore a homemade woolen hat, consisting of two wool socks, which covered his head, extended to his shoulders, and kept his neck dry and warm. He couldn't have been better dressed for his ordeal.

Second, he carried the group's lunches. He had volunteered to carry the men's six-pound lard can containing a dozen sourdough pancakes, six sardine sandwiches, three chocolate bars, and coffee.

Third, Fred had some matches and a pocketknife.

After assessing his situation, he wondered about Clark and Otto. He knew that almost certainly his survival depended upon their welfare. Had they been buried in the slide? Were they digging him out? Had they gone for help? He didn't like the prospect of rescuers' finding their frozen bodies after the snow melted.

Fred found breathing easier, possibly because the snow had not fully compacted around him due to his proximity to the boulder—maybe there was an air pocket between him and the rock.

Although his right pant's leg had frozen to the snow where the oilskin was pulled above the jeans, Fred did not feel cold because he was dressed so warmly.

He called out. There was no answer. From time to time he repeated his cry for help. Vaguely he heard a sound in the distance, one which he did not recognize. At first he thought it was the sound of shovels biting into the snow. He exulted in the thought that his pals were digging him out. But then he realized there was no rhythm to the sound, just an irregular but steady smooshing sound. With horror Fred recognized the sound as that which results when snow settles!

As unnerving as it was to hear the steadily compressing snow above him, he reconfirmed his decision to give it a fight.

By now he had freed both his right hand and his right leg. Gradually he groped snow from beneath him and kicked it behind him with his right leg.

Sometime later, his tomb lightened as a thread of daylight shone through near the large boulder. Could it be? Then he glimpsed blue sky as the crack widened and let in fresh air.

Fred yelled excitedly over and over. He heard an answer, "Hell-ooo." It was too good to be true. He was going to be saved! Or was he hearing things? He had to remain calm. Then he heard the unmistakable voice of his pal Otto: "We'll have you out in a little while."

Soooo . . . his friends were both alive. And they were going to rescue him. Fred satisfied his longing for air with huge gulps, and he rejoiced—he'd be out of this tomb in jig time. He thanked God for air and for his friends above. While Fred rejoiced, he heard Clark tell Otto to get the shovels while he looked for Fred.

No sooner had Fred heard Clark than another *schhhwoosh* trembled his body. With the movement, his breathing hole closed. Another avalanche had covered Fred! Had his friends found him sooner, he could have escaped his doom.

Fred now breathed with greater difficulty. The settling snow began its crunching sound anew, and Fred felt the fear it presented as well as the fear for his companions' welfare. Since they knew he was alive and had a pretty good idea where he was, there was still hope for his rescue unless the second avalanche had buried them.

The second avalanche hit at noon, fifteen minutes after Clark and Otto had freed themselves and had begun searching for Fred. That second slide swept them down the canyon. Clark was tossed free, but his friend was buried a second time. When Clark looked for Otto, he saw his hand protruding from the snow. Clark hurriedly began digging him out. By the time Clark freed Otto, however, it was dark; and both men had frostbitten feet. They had to reach the shelter cabin before they froze. They wanted to inform officials of Fred's predicament so they could recover his body.

Once they reached the safety of the cabin, Clark left Otto to warm up and to regain his strength while he struck out for Sitka to raise help and to telegram Fred's mother of his demise.

Meanwhile the "corpse" was busy trying to dig himself out. Although able to dig only with his right hand the first three hours, Fred had since freed the snow around his body and managed to bend his right knee enough to reach and free the snowshoe. Using his teeth, he eventually gnawed through the wood frame until he'd broken off a piece. He used it as a paddle to shovel the snow.

In time Fred freed his entire body except his left arm, which was trapped by his pack, frozen to the top of his tomb.

In wild desperation Fred set his teeth to the leather pack strap only to give up in frustration when he met with failure. Reminded of his pocketknife, he began an effort to get it. The knife was just beyond his grasp, his fingertips barely able to touch it. The fabric of his pants pocket provided the solution—he could pull on the top of the fabric and gradually ease the pocket and thus the knife upward. Finally he retrieved it.

At length he clasped the knife between his teeth and opened the blade with his right hand. The knife fell from his nervous fingers. He found it in the snow and picked it up. Eventually he cut the strap of the pack.

By now it was late afternoon, and he was hungry. He found the metal lard container crushed and its contents squished and generously saturated with coffee. Nevertheless it was food, and it was welcome to his lips. He inhaled coffee-sodden pancakes and a chocolate bar.

Unknown to Fred, his companions were stumbling away toward safety, frostbitten and bruised, and grieving for the loss of their friend.

Fred ascertained by the darkening that afternoon had evolved into night. He took out his watch and struck a match, but there wasn't oxygen enough for the match to burn. He was unable to see the dial of his watch and discovered it had stopped. He wound it and let it go at that. The ticking provided a companion to mark time with him.

Fred's hands became cold. He had also dropped his knife and his snowshoe paddle and was unable to find either. He decided to hang on to his other paddle at all costs, knowing that its loss spelled certain death for him.

An overwhelming thirst gnawed at Fred. In spite of his surroundings he was suffering dehydration. His lips were dry and chapped. He reached ahead and secured clean snow, which he placed under his tongue. Allowing it to melt slowly into water assuaged some of his thirst.

He felt a need to remove his boots because his feet were soaked. With great effort he removed his footwear and his socks. He struggled to wring the water from his stockings. The chilling cold made his finger movements difficult, and his struggle to get his socks and boots back on was so grueling that he decided not to remove them again.

His eating paralleled his digging. He rationalized that help would arrive. Plus he needed energy to stay warm and to dig. So he ate.

Digging and moving snow became routine. He inched along his tunnel, digging, passing snow along his body, kicking it beneath his feet and scooting forward. Little by little he moled along.

Fred's efforts were compounded by the consistency of the snow. Rather than a light, fine powder, it was hard-packed, wet snow. His digging required jabbing and scraping the crystallized, icelike snow.

Scrape. Jab. Scrape. Dig. Pile. Scoop. Tamp. Inch ahead.

The routine continued hour after hour.

And always the sound of settling snow continued above. *Was it a shovel?* The sound could discourage and cause panic . . . or Fred could use it to inspire his escape.

More digging . . . moving from side to side to scrape and poke, first resting on one elbow then the other. His coffinlike cocoon gave him enough room to turn from side to side, but provided no excess room for exaggerated movement.

While Fred inched along his tunnel toward the surface, Clark Sutherland trudged toward Sitka. Twenty-four hours had elapsed since the first avalanche had struck. Early Monday morning Clark, still suffering from exposure and shock, arrived in Sitka. The town siren screamed across the bay summoning men and women from their daily tasks. Sutherland told his story. He impressed on the townspeople the urgency of assisting Otto and recovering Fred's body.

The wheels of rescue churned. U.S. Commissioner William Bahrt put together provisions and men to rescue Otto Hill and to recover Fred Easley's corpse.

A day and a half of physical confinement and determined digging coupled with the mental trauma of combating cold, fatigue, and near hopelessness had taken their toll on Fred. His strength was sapped by his effort and the cold. His body screamed for relief.

Fred's feet were numb, requiring his attention. He rubbed them to maintain circulation. Every jab at the ice demanded a conscious effort. Cold constantly chewed at his hands, numbing them and creeping up his arms. He wondered how long it would be before the cold made it too difficult to hold his snowshoe paddle. His elbows became raw from alternately leaning on first one and then the other.

Sleep teased him. His eyes became heavy. His body's need for rest battled his mind's resolve to keep digging. He knew that the siren song of sleep would doom him, that if he allowed himself to sleep, his body mechanism would not permit him to wake up. Monday afternoon dragged on. To sleep or not to sleep.

Dig. Scrape. Jab. Scoop. Tamp the snow behind. Inch ahead.

Twelve more hours crawled by. Fred had now been trapped forty-eight hours.

It was Tuesday. Hallucinations confounded his mind. He closed his eyes and beheld a large room, domed and spacious. A crack in the ceiling beckoned him. He opened his eyes and jabbed at the dome overhead, only to hit crystallized ice inches above him. His excitement faded. He was still trapped in his tomblike cavity.

Near noon on Tuesday Fred gave in. He decided to sleep. He reasoned that sleep brought comfort. It relieved his pain. There was no cold. The ache in his elbows subsided. The mental struggle ceased. It would be a peaceful, painless death. He opened his eyes for a final look at his tomb.

Again the crack in the dome captured his attention. It seemed to be widening, almost calling him to another world. He closed his eyes. He heard the compressing snow . . . *kaa-runnch* . . . *kaa-runnch* . . . *kaa-runnch*. It had become rhythmic. But the sound was different. Was he dreaming?

No. A ringing sound of a shovel against rock! Could it be?

The *chunk* of shoveled snow tossed upon snow met his ears. It *was* rhythmic! Yes. Rescuers!

Fred shouted. His muffled, quiet voice met his ears. Adrenaline coursed through his veins. He turned around and dug feverishly in the direction he'd left.

One of the workers had heard Fred's cry and thought it was a fellow worker.

The sound of digging grew louder. Suddenly a *sschhuunk* penetrated the snow. A shovel pierced the snow before his face. The shovel withdrew, taking snow with it; and a hole opened up to the outside world.

With a thrust and a grin Fred lurched from the depths and said, "Gee, fellows, I'm sure glad to see you."

Although the brightness of his new surroundings was blinding, the sky had never looked so blue to Fred. He had never breathed purer, sweeter air. He reveled in the beauty beyond the grave. He looked across Sitka Sound and marveled at his resurrection.

Ten men had been digging for four hours, expecting to recover Fred's body. Sutherland had directed the effort, having designated a fifty-foot circle, telling the searchers that Fred would be found within that circle. Fred emerged from the circle's center. Now his rescuers were spellbound by this living creature standing before them.

Although Fred thought he could walk, his legs would not support him. He was carried on a sled to the cabin where men took turns for sixteen hours massaging him and restoring his circulation before they took him to the hospital in Sitka.

Before long, Fred was back to normal. After a monumental struggle and almost unheard-of tunneling of fifteen feet in fifty-two hours, Fred was finally saved from the jaws of death—beneath two avalanches and a combined twenty-one feet of snow.

Though the townspeople of Sitka had looked for a corpse, Fred Easley had spit in death's eye.

Avalanche is but one danger hurled at Alaska's outdoor participants. Denise Harris and Roger Lewis discovered other dangers.

NEARLY TOO LATE

BY LARRY KANIUT

Their toes and feet turned black with frostbite. The most they slept was twenty minutes. Then they awoke in agony and prayed.

When I read Denise Harris and Roger Lewis's two-part story in *Alaska Magazine*, I knew their story was too good to leave out of this book.

Denise Harris was working at the park chalet in Glacier National Park when she met Roger Lewis. They shared outdoor interests. She had worked with the U.S. Forest Service and he with the National Park Service. They became better acquainted and decided Alaska offered a challenge that was worthy of their attention. They might even have an adventure in the Great Land.

In the spring of 1979 they headed north. They gravitated to Seward, Alaska, where Jack Cogland offered them a job collecting ore samples at his gold mine. They accepted and were flown to Nuka Bay, fifty miles from Seward. The couple took a stray husky-shepherd pup that they named Nuka. John Kenney, a powder man, went along and settled three miles away in a trailer.

On October 31 they arrived at the remote mine site on the Gulf of Alaska side of the Kenai Peninsula.

After collecting samples in Surprise Bay for two months, they realized they were running low on food. One night John invited them to dinner, but they were unable to conquer the thickening ice in the bay to get to his quarters.

They'd had no contact with the outside world. No plane was scheduled to pick them up. Their concerns mounted. Denise and Roger didn't think anyone knew they were out there and were pretty sure no one would be looking for them.

After five days of fighting the ice and realizing their food was nearly gone, the couple decided to leave. They planned to paddle to Portlock, the closest town/logging camp, seventy-five rugged, cliff-hugging miles away by boat. They would load up and leave on December the eighteenth.

That morning the couple left an undated note for John, expressing hope of reaching Portlock or Seldovia by Christmas. They loaded their camp supplies, food, and a .30-30 rifle aboard their two-person Folbot, a collapsible kayak. Next they stowed Nuka. Then they got aboard and, with three inches of freeboard, waddled away from Surprise Bay.

The next day they pulled onto a beach and awaited better weather.

They renewed their journey on the twentieth and paddled steadily, encountering fair to heavy seas. They paddled on and on, hoping to stay afloat and endure the grueling voyage.

Nearing Gore Point at dawn on the twenty-second, they encountered eight-to-ten-foot seas, a howling wind, and riptides. This thin strip of land jutting/slicing into the Gulf of Alaska is home to some of Alaska's fiercest weather. Like much of the gulf coast, the steep cliffs offer little shelter from the elements.

Since continuing on would invite disaster, they landed a quarter mile from Gore Point. Halfway between Surprise Bay and Portlock, they established a camp at the foot of the cliffs 150 yards from the ocean. They were amazed as thirty-to-forty-foot waves hammered the beach.

During the day they moved their kayak farther from the water, then returned to their tent to wait out the storm. Early in the afternoon Roger looked from the tent and saw waves pummeling the beach only eight feet away. Their very survival depended on getting to higher ground.

Denise and Roger flew into action, dismantling the tent and jamming their sleeping bags into stuff sacks before scampering fifteen feet higher up a trough. They sheltered under a cliff in a cavelike opening with rain dropping through a hole above.

Roger placed a foam pad beneath them, wrapped blankets about them, and they huddled together. They kept vigil on their tent, packs, and gear on the beach below. They prayed. As rain continued to fall, Roger elected to cover the opening in the ceiling. He dropped down to the beach to get a piece of plastic from the pack.

Instantly he found himself swimming. He'd been swallowed by a giant wave. Struggling to stay afloat and gagging on salt water, he swam to Denise. He shoved her up through the hole and yelled, "Get out of here."

Roger chucked blankets up to Denise and pulled himself up to her. He was soaked from head to foot; and they had no fire or shelter. Fearing hypothermia, they spread the pad, lay down on it, pulled the wet wool blanket over them, and tugged the plastic over the top as a shield from the rain. They cuddled together.

It was difficult to breathe so Roger made a small hole. They spent a cold, wet night shivering.

The following morning two cold, stiff people emerged from their cocoon. During the night the waves had receded fifty to sixty feet. They saw half of the Folbot below. Along with the other half, the sea had robbed them of flares, a mirror, and binoculars.

Although they'd lost signaling devices, they still had their food pack (dry soup, rice, and beans); gas stove and a quart of fuel; the rifle and five bullets; clothing in the form of pants, sweaters, sweatpants, down and wool hats; wool blankets;

and their tent. Their sleeping bags remained, but they were useless balls of ice.

Without the kayak, their only way out was on foot. They knew the country between them and Portlock was punctuated by steep cliffs and an icy, rock-covered shore (there was no such thing as beach as we perceive it). John had told Roger of a logging road coming into Port Dick, a bay just west of their location on Gore Point. Maybe they could find the road to reach Portlock or Seldovia.

The rock-covered and ice-swathed landscape was devoid of any trace of wood. They desperately needed to find other shelter.

Their only escape route was a snow-covered, steep hill behind them. It seemed insurmountable. They inched their way up the slope. At last, the couple pitched their tent on a thirty-degree slope, bathed in spraying mist from the pounding surf below. Nuka was unable to climb the cliff and they were forced to leave her below. Denise and Roger were happy at daylight the next morning when Nuka bounded into camp.

Their new home provided them with shelter and time to reflect. They rested and planned for four days. Their daily ritual included mixing snow and dried soup, allowing it to soak. Each night they started the camp stove to heat their soup lukewarm. They also tried to dry their socks (holding them over the heat). To save fuel they only used the stove five minutes. That five minutes provided them the only external heat they enjoyed. They cherished and looked forward to that time of the day.

Early in their misadventure their toes began freezing. Because they were un-aware of the danger of thawing frozen flesh, they continued trying to warm their feet. They cut their space blanket into bootie-pouches for their feet. They also made mittens of their blanket.

On the twenty-seventh Roger's hopes rose when he saw a wolf. A good omen, it represented food and a way out. Roger reasoned if the wolf reached them, they could follow its trail off the beach to safety. Raising the rifle to his shoulder and aiming behind the wolf's shoulder, Roger fired. At the crack of the rifle, the wolf bolted. Roger had only wounded it.

Following the wolf, Roger waded through tide pools. A dilemma confronted the man as he pursued the animal. The tide was coming in, and he didn't want to use another bullet to shoot the animal. Afraid of losing the wolf, Roger rushed back to the tent for his sheet-rock ax and knife.

When he returned, the wolf was very much alive. Roger threw rocks until he hit the wolf and it turned its head. Then Roger rushed in and hit the animal with his ax. He held the wolf underwater for two minutes until he was sure it was dead.

The young male wolf weighed no more than sixty pounds, nevertheless it was food. Roger skinned the wolf and took the hindquarter to the tent. He seasoned and fried it until it was brown. They ate what they wanted, and Denise stored the remainder in a jar.

They had seen no search planes. In their weakened and worsening physical condition, convinced that their rescue depended upon them, the couple decided to travel inland over the wolf's trail on the twenty-eighth.

Before leaving, they divided their gear. Denise carried the pack with their food, matches, stove, foam pad, and tent. Roger took the duffel bag with blankets, maps, compass, rifle, wolf hide, and Swede saw.

Their first obstacle was a steep hill thirty yards high.

Denise was wearing knee-length rubber boots, which provided little warmth and were very slippery. As she struggled up the slope, she slipped and fell. She lost her grip on the small pack, and it started tumbling away from her.

Roger ran to recover the bouncing pack. Before he could reach it, the pack took a final bounce off the boulders and plummeted straight down into the ocean.

It was all Roger could do to keep from diving in after it. He reasoned, however, that he would probably not be able to get back to shore even if he got the pack; and even if he did, he'd be soaked again. It was gone—and with it they lost their food, matches, stove, blanket, mattress pad, and tent.

Standing around feeling sorry for themselves would help none. They started up 1,400-foot Gore Peak, slogging upward one step at a time.

The cliffs ahead became even steeper. In a tight spot while gripping a ledge by two fingers, Roger lost control and fell. Thirty feet below he started sliding. Gaining speed, he rocketed toward a precipice that dropped fifty feet to the rocks below. Charged by his will to live and determination not to leave Denise behind, he spun onto his back, dug his heels into the snow, and ground to a stop.

After carefully inspecting his body, he crawled back to Denise. It was a joyful reunion.

From there they worked their way along a cliff all day—travel, rest twenty minutes, move on.

At nightfall they stopped and propped themselves against the steep, timbered slope.

With their remaining mattress pad under them and a blanket over them, they tried to sleep. But there was no sleep. They were wet. They were hungry. They were in too much pain. They removed their boots, noting that their feet continued swelling, sloughing, and turning purple.

Denise used the wolf pelt for a foot covering; Roger used his space-blanket booties and two pairs of socks (which he alternated from his feet to his body trying to keep one pair dry).

The next day was another test of their wills. They encountered hip-deep snow. They'd take a step and fall through . . . sometimes four to five feet. They'd done about all anyone could to survive.

That night they camped under a scrub spruce tree. They dug snow from around its base. Roger cut boughs with the saw to be used as bedding and a windbreak.

They repeated their nightly ritual: removing their boots and placing their feet against Nuka's fur as she lay down.

The temperature dropped to minus ten degrees that night.

The following day they descended Gore Peak and camped on a snowless, driftwood-laden beach. Since they had no matches, they had no fire! A cold, miserable night kept them company.

The next day Roger and Denise walked but a quarter of a mile before encountering a waterside cliff. Their only course was a frozen waterfall fifty yards high and four inches thick at the base.

With the duffel bag slung from his wrist and his belt knife in hand, Roger chiseled footholds, one by one.

It took them until 1 P.M. to cover a hundred feet. As it warmed up after noon, the sun melted the ice surface. The higher they went, the thinner the ice became.

The going was very slick. Near the top Roger sought a stable spot. As he inched toward a bush twenty feet away, he heard, then saw, Denise fall, sliding and bouncing all the way to the beach a hundred feet below.

Denise examined herself. Aside from a scratched hip she was all right. However Denise didn't think she could get back up to Roger. He told her she'd have to—that he couldn't come to her.

She pleaded with him to come down to her; but he refused. He kept working toward the bush, exhorting her to climb back up.

Reluctantly Denise began climbing. She had covered half the distance to him when she slipped and fell again down the same path.

This time she was determined to stay where she was. She yelled to Roger to toss her clothes down. She decided to return to their last campsite and die on the beach.

He refused to respond to her request.

Half an hour passed. Would she try again? Would Roger help her? Finally she started up again. It was more painstaking than ever. She had lost her mitts. She slowly removed ice from a hole and eased upward one hole at a time. Her hands throbbed, but she had no other prospect. Roger urged her on.

Nuka could not climb the ice and went off seeking a different route.

At last Denise was nearing Roger. He extended his hand in joy and relief and guided her to safety. They set up camp for the night. Nuka barked from the distance and wolves howled off and on till daylight. They feared the wolves would kill Nuka.

The next morning they marveled when they heard Nuka bark. Nuka not only survived the night but also found a route to them.

After that the days blurred together. Theirs was a continuous struggle physically. Barriers confronted them—mostly steep ground and ice-covered cliffs. Still Takoma Cove, Sunday Bay, and Taylor Bay lay ahead. The mental anguish also took its toll. The geography, the weather, and their condition eroded their hope for survival.

Their toes and feet turned black with frostbite. The most they slept was twenty minutes. Then they awoke in agony and prayed.

Roger's color left him. He looked lifeless, as though he were dying. They were too weak to talk normally; their conversation was slow, quiet verbalization.

Roger figured nobody would find them before it was too late. Unbelievably, it had been two months since they'd seen another human being. They had seen no search planes. After a week without food they talked about shooting the dog and themselves.

But Denise's determination to see her mother again gave birth to her reasoning, "I'm going to get out of here if I have to crawl all the way."

Roger was shamed by his lack of determination compared to Denise's. He resolved to go on, but his faith was gone.

Some days Roger cut handholds in the ice with his buck knife and progressed a mere fifty feet. Their best day yielded two miles, but their average was a half mile a day. They encountered seven-foot drifts and howling wind, yet miraculously continued on.

At night Roger slept with his arms crossed over his chest and his hands inside his clothes. Denise slept curled up with her back to his.

Some mornings they awakened covered by frozen ocean spray caked to their bedding. They had trouble getting out of bed in the mornings. Cramped and cold, they fought their aching joints, hands, and feet. Often it felt as if their bodies were on fire and they hurt all over. Supreme willpower was needed to force frozen feet into cold, hard, and sometimes snow-covered boots.

After the grueling task of leaving the bed, they slowly repacked the saw, rifle, and bedding into the duffel bag and lurched on till darkness fell.

By the eighth of January they'd gone without food for a week. As a last resort Roger decided to kill Nuka for food. Denise agreed. He did not want to use a bullet and decided to use his knife. Roger called the dog. Nuka wagged her tail while he felt for her heart. Then he jabbed the knife into her chest.

Although Roger's knife broke, Nuka died. The couple skinned and gutted the dog, saving the skin to use as a foot cover. Roger took a bite of the heart, assuming the meat would provide him energy.

He gagged on the raw meat. He couldn't deal with having killed their canine companion and went off to be by himself.

Denise quietly cut off the dog's hindquarter meat and placed it in a plastic jar. She then carried the dog's remains to the surf.

Later the couple ate part of the dog and felt stronger.

By this time Denise had dark circles under her eyes. Dark frostbite splotches covered her hands. Her normal 125-pound, five-foot-six-inch frame was now reduced to a hundred pounds. Her curly, long auburn hair was matted and dirty. This twenty-year-old wondered if she'd ever see civilization again.

Meanwhile thirty-one-year-old Roger had lost thirty-five pounds from his normal 170 pounds. His five-foot-ten-inch frame was stooped. His brown hair was browner and his blue eyes hollow. Surely his former marine and police experience had helped them get this far.

The ninth of January dawned clear and cold. Eagles wheeled overhead. Wolves howled in the distance.

Roger looked toward Taylor Bay. As much as he wanted to focus on the job at hand, his constant pain made it difficult. He saw sheer cliffs to the water's edge. There was no way they could walk the beach. While contemplating their physical agony and the mental anguish, Roger heard, then saw, a Coast Guard helicopter.

It flew over them less than 150 feet away. His joy and excitement was short-lived, as it clattered on by. Emotionally it was worse having it go by than if he hadn't seen it at all. It was 4 P.M. Dusk fell. And with it fell his hopes.

For nineteen days they'd struggled. They'd fought steep, icy walls, roaring seas, and wind. They'd struggled through deep snow. Their stomachs pinched their spines in hunger. They'd endured the frigid fingers of frost. They'd battled mental torment.

He wouldn't quit now!

As hurriedly as he could, Roger put together the saw. He cut spruce boughs and placed three letters in the snow ten feet across . . . SOS. It was grueling work in the deep snow. But he did not quit.

He tied a red sweatshirt on a fifteen-foot pole and jammed it in the middle of the *O*. At that moment he saw a plane fly over. It was a Grumman Widgeon. His duffel bag was twenty feet away. Roger hobbled to it for the rifle. He fired three times into air and fell backward, wanting to keep his eyes on the plane. The pilot tipped a wing toward Roger.

Roger shouted to Denise that they'd been found. The plane circled and climbed higher. The Widgeon's lights blinked. Periodically the plane flew out of sight but returned. Denise and Roger's anxiety grew as they wondered why the pilot didn't signal them. They wondered if they had, in fact, been spotted.

Cold and discouraged, Roger suggested they crawl under the cover to get warm. Denise refused, saying she wouldn't until the plane left or did something.

Roger reasoned the pilot wouldn't waste fuel flying in circles unless he had spotted them.

For an hour and a half the plane circled.

Distant purring grew louder until Roger realized and shouted to Denise that a helicopter was coming for them. The chopper came in straight and low, almost in slow motion, blades fanning the water and churning snow and branches, lights flashing. The light from a huge spotlight snaked along the landscape until it focused on them.

The helicopter hovered above them as a basket lowered earthward. Both tried to get into it. By quickly hoisting the basket, the rescuers signaled that they wanted one at a time to climb aboard.

Roger got into the basket and was lifted up. He could not conceal his joy as he hugged and kissed the state trooper on board.

Before the crew could attempt to rescue Denise, they needed to burn off extra fuel and lighten the load. As they circled, Denise's first reaction was that they were leaving her to die. She didn't know what to do and started crying.

Finally the helicopter picked her up. She was as excited and thankful as Roger had been. She grabbed a coastguardsman, hugged him, and repeatedly said, "Thank you."

Later they met their rescuer, Bill DeCreeft (Kachemak Air Service), to express their gratitude. Roger and Denise spent over a month in the Homer hospital. During this time they lost some of their toes. They felt it was a small loss compared to having their lives and each other. While in the hospital they began making plans to be married. A perfect ending to their miracle journey!

Rescuers found Denise and Roger before it was too late. Another lady whose mental anguish and suffering was no less great than theirs and who yearned for rescue was Cari Britton.

SOLE SURVIVOR

BY LARRY KANIUT

We've had twenty-six crashes through the twenty-sixth of August with eighteen deaths—that's one plane crash a day for this month.

Every year many private aircraft fail to return from flights in Alaska. When I read about one such event and the young woman who spent the night aboard a crashed airplane only a few miles from Anchorage, I tried to imagine her desperation. Although I wanted her words to tell others of the agony and heartache she endured then and since, I was unsuccessful in obtaining a personal interview. I rewrote the story from newspaper clippings.

Rhythmic rattling reverberated off the canyon walls as the olive drab helicopter waddled up the valley. The crew knew there was no such thing as a normal rescue mission—every launch to find or save someone brought something new, different, or unexpected. They were near the 3,700-foot level and on the north side of a ridge near Eklutna Lake, twenty-eight miles northeast of Anchorage. Below, on a ridge of the Chugach Mountains, lay the crumpled wreckage of a Cessna 172 aircraft.

As the MH-60 Pavehawk chopper neared the plane, one of the crewmen noted a face through the window and a hand waving. "We've got a live one!" he exclaimed into his headset mike. The pilot jockeyed the guppy-shaped bird into position for landing.

Inside the 172, Cari Britton felt overwhelming joy. *They came to get me. I'm going to make it.* Tears formed in her eyes and gradually trickled down her cheeks. Her long hours of fear and doubt were over. Waves of relief washed over her.

It was 9:45 A.M., Friday, August 23, 1991. For fourteen hours Cari had lain alone in the twisted aluminum remains of the four-place aircraft. During the long night she had wondered if it would be her casket.

What would it be like finding yourself on a mountain ridge, the sole survivor of a plane crash? Your last memory is of watching sheep off your left wing. You must have crashed and blacked out. You can't move.

Robert Works, your friend who is visiting you and your boyfriend, sits beside you dead.

You repeatedly call for Lloyd, but there is no response.

Darkness comes a couple of hours later, bringing cooler temperatures. You're cold. Can't sleep. Must try to stay warm. You have no food or water. Worse than that, you have no companionship. You think everyone else is dead. And worst of all, you wonder, *What if Lloyd is dead?* You're unable to do anything to help the others.

After a while you realize that Lloyd will never answer you again.

Are there any bears in the area? Will they smell blood and come to the plane?

You're familiar with flying. Yours is a flying family. Your parents have their pilot's licenses and have owned a small plane. You knew about forced landings. Even though you were ready to put your flying knowledge into practice, you were trapped.

It was clear and sunny at 7 P.M. the previous evening when you and three others left Merrill Field in Anchorage to look for Dall sheep. The long daylight hours were dwindling, but darkness was still two to three hours away. Plans were for a weekend hunt. A flight over the area would give the hunters an idea where the sheep were and hence where to establish base camp for their hunt. After that it would be only a matter of time before a sheep-and-hunter rendezvous took place.

For the past year you and your boyfriend, Lloyd H. Jones, twenty-seven, have lived and worked in Anchorage. You were employed as a manager trainee for the National Bank of Alaska; he worked as an administrative assistant at United Parcel Service. You and Lloyd enjoyed being outdoors together and spent a good many weekends there.

Your friend and Lloyd's, Robert Works, twenty-six, of Casper, Wyoming, was a law student who had come to Anchorage to visit you two.

The pilot, Ronald Pritchard, twenty-two, of Anchorage, had his instructor's rating and his commercial pilot's license. The plane, owned by Joseph Wilbur, was operated by Flight Safety of Alaska, an Anchorage-based flight school. The aircraft's records indicated that it was well maintained.

During the night you agonized over your physical pain and discomfort. However, that agony paled by comparison to the mental anguish, knowing your cabin mates were dead . . . and wondering if you would be joining them. And if so, how soon?

You wonder what life will be like without Lloyd. How you'll cope. Then you think of your family . . . what your loss will mean to them. You determine not to give up. You remember the motivation for this flight.

After leaving Merrill Field the Cessna flew over the low ridges of the Chugach Mountains, occupants looking below for white dots. As the plane approached a ridge top, the group watched sheep on the mountainside out their left windows. One moment they were airborne; the next moment, without warning, they were splattered against the ridge. Forty minutes after takeoff the Cessna 172 was down.

The Federal Aviation Administration requires aircraft to carry emergency locator transmitters. These transmitters are activated by a 4-g impact, which sends a signal to overhead satellites. The signal in turn is sent to various agencies.

Sometime after midnight Thursday, the Civil Air Patrol in Anchorage picked up an ELT signal.

The 210th Air Rescue Squadron from Kulis Air National Guard Base at Anchorage International Airport responded to the emergency signal. When they landed to assist the plane's occupants, the chopper was seventy-five yards above the crash site.

Guard Tech. Sgts. Eric Sachs and Patrick Malone left the chopper and hiked downhill to the plane. They discovered Ron Pritchard's body beneath the fuselage. The men tore the plane's door off and found the other two men dead. Sachs and Malone spent an hour freeing Cari from the wreckage, stabilizing her and transporting her to their helicopter.

The mercy flight departed immediately to Humana Hospital, Anchorage, where Cari was admitted. Her condition was diagnosed as critical but stable. She initially underwent four hours of surgery for leg injuries, a back injury (crushed vertebra), and internal injuries.

Her sister Lori Gross arrived from Lyman, Wyoming, to be with Cari, and in short order she was on her way to recovery. Her major hurdle now would be emotional healing from the loss of her boyfriend and friend.

Afterword

The cause of the accident was investigated. Alaska State Troopers spokesperson Janelle Hout said, "It looks like [the pilot] missed the top of the ridge by about three hundred feet."(1)

Joette Storm, spokesperson for the Federal Aviation Administration, said, "Pilots should have someone else do the looking and focus on flying . . . The pilot's decision-making ability is critical."(2)

It is critical in chartering an air-taxi pilot to have some understanding of the risks involved in flying with a stranger, especially during peak air-flight seasons when many pilots are overtaxed by constant stick time and little sleep time. Your life could well depend upon your decision.

Myriad flying predicaments confront Alaskan pilots. More than one such hazard can grab a pilot as Paul Weimer relates in the next story.

A TAIL AND A PRAYER

AS TOLD TO THE AUTHOR BY PASTOR PAUL WEIMER

*I swam and floundered back to the wing and got back up on the plane.
I was soaked. My hands were beginning to get numb.*

What would it be like standing on a sinking aircraft in slushy lake ice during a cold April night in Alaska . . . in temperatures so cold that an inch of ice formed on the water around the sinking plane during the night? In 1986, Paul Weimer found out.

I heard about Pastor Paul Weimer from Dave Beeman of California. I was pursuing Dave's bear tale when he asked me if I'd heard Weimer's flying story. I told him no but that I'd contact him. As it turned out, Paul is the father of a former student of mine. On Friday, November 27, 1998, I met Pastor Weimer at his Dimond Boulevard Baptist Church in Anchorage.

The fifty-six-year-old preacher, a dark-haired, solidly built man with a smile in his heart, was flying his Piper Cub Super Cruiser light plane, constructed with aluminum tubing and covered with cloth fabric. As Paul returned to Anchorage, he engaged in a long-standing practice. He shares his story and convictions below.

Slush ice sucked me into the lake. I fire-walled the plane and pulled my flaps. No response. One second I was in the air, moments later I struggled in watery slush.

That was the beginning of my adventure in Lake Tustumena, which proved to be a severe test of faith. Some people consider my experience the result of a foolish decision. My watery adventure began rather innocently but ended several hours later with some hard lessons learned.

As I approached Lake Tustumena on my way home from Homer on April 17, 1986, I looked carefully at the beach. I wanted to practice low-slow flight, which I've done hundreds of times on beaches in winter conditions.

During the winter of 1985–86 Mel Wick rebuilt a major part of my airplane, including the installation of flaps. Flaps are control devices that produce lift, allowing the plane to fly slower as well as to get off the ground quicker. The addition of flaps meant that the plane would handle differently. It also meant that I would need to learn how to use them in order to fly my PA-12 more effectively. I was still trying to get used to the flap operation of my aircraft when this incident occurred.

Flaps on my airplane slowed the landing speed about eight miles an hour. To get accustomed to the modification, I decided to practice a maneuver that has been very helpful to me through the years. If I'm approaching a long beach and I'm alone, I will sometimes come down and hold the power of the airplane just above stall speed, say forty miles an hour, and fly just a couple of feet over the beach. The plane will stall once in a while, and the pilot acts accordingly, either touching down or adding power (applying gas). This procedure familiarizes you with flying in close proximity to things.

In my neck of the woods the top two to four feet of Alaskan lakes freeze solid in the winter. Tustumena appeared frozen from beach to beach with no open water anywhere. Since I was two-thirds of the way across the lake and had touched my main landing gear onto the lake several times, it appeared the ice was safe. It felt solid. The final time I touched down, approximately a mile from the north shore, I discovered a change in the ice. It was soft.

I immediately felt it. I knew I was in a stall and in trouble. I gave the airplane full power and full flaps to counter the stall.

A stall involves the airflow over the wing. The attitude of the wing as the propeller pulls the wing through the air and the speed determine whether the plane will stay in the air. If you go too slow through the air, the airflow will not support the wing anymore, and it falls. The engine can be running wide open and you still stall.

Power and flaps failed to pull the plane out of the slush. Combined with the stall, the slush simply pulled the airplane into the icy lake. The plane went up on its nose and began to sink.

Sitting at an unusual and precarious position in my shoulder harness and seat belt momentarily confused me. It lasted but a split second before I knew I had to get out of there because water was flowing into the cabin.

I unbuckled my belt and harness. Within the fraction of a second it took to open the door, water was almost to my knees. I grabbed the wing root and pulled myself up onto the right wing. By that time the plane had settled until the water was even with the wing.

The tail was two feet off the slush. I estimate the slush was three or four feet thick. Like a glass full of slush ice, it was completely rotted and there was no body to it.

My weight on the wing accelerated the airplane's sinking, so I quickly scrambled back up the fuselage. The additional weight lowered the tail, placing more of the plane's surface on the slush and stabilizing it somewhat.

My problem was compounded because I was wet, and I had lost my hat exiting the plane. My down vest and Carhartt coveralls were in the cabin of the plane.

I've read a great deal about survival through the years. In thirty years in this country I have foolishly gotten myself into a few situations I wish I had not been in . . . some of them dangerous. I'd learned how to survive in cold weather a little bit, but never anything like this.

I believe the most important thing in survival is attitude. For me that involves knowing the Lord and knowing that I can look right into the probability of death and not worry about it because I know where I'm going.

Of course, I prayed immediately. The Lord gave me presence of mind to realize I had to get my emergency locator transmitter out of the airplane. Even though I didn't know if I could reach it, I took a jackknife out of my pocket, cut a hole in the top of the fuselage, and reached down into water up to near the ceiling. I knew where the ELT was in the baggage compartment and pulled it out. It had been submerged. The activator light was not operating. I didn't know if my beacon was working.

Normally a 4-g impact activates an emergency locator beacon. The beacon transmits a signal on 121.5, the emergency frequency. Satellites overfly the position every ninety minutes. Once a satellite picks up a signal, no action is taken until a second signal is received. Your location can be pinpointed within five miles, though sometimes the reading is affected by terrain such as mountains.

When a pilot is reported missing in Alaska, a flight service station is called to determine his last location. If the response is negative, the Rescue Coordination Center at Fort Richardson Army Guard near Anchorage is informed. RCC then contacts the pilot's employer or other persons familiar with his flying habits before the officials decide on the urgency of the search. Normally the Civil Air Patrol, Alaska Air Guard, and private pilots take part.

I was sixty-five miles south of Anchorage on an isolated lake thirty-two miles long and seven wide. You might say, I was in a world of hurt. My only hope was that my locator beacon would transmit my location and that the Lord would bail me out of my misfortune.

My next thought was to attempt to walk the thousand yards across the ice to the shore where a small cabin sat near the beach. Gingerly I walked to the end of my right wing and tested the ice with my foot. It wouldn't hold three pounds. So I went back to the tail and tested the ice on either side. It was just as bad.

I went back up to the wing root and walked the left wing out to the end. I put my foot onto the ice, four inches below the wing. It was hard, so I walked a little bit farther . . . a little bit more, and a little bit more. With all my weight on that area it seemed stable. I thought I'd try walking.

I got five feet from the wingtip and down I went. It was just slush.

I swam and floundered back to the wing and got back up on the plane. I was soaked. My hands were beginning to get numb.

I looked down through the skylight over the cabin area and saw my down vest and Carhartt coveralls floating near the top. I decided to get those items out. I was unable to free the vest, so I cut it in half with my knife. At least I had half of the vest. I retrieved the Carhartts and wrung out the vest and coveralls as best I could. I sat down on the wing, took my shoe packs off, removed the liners, and wrung them out.

My hands were stiff and I couldn't do a very good job. I put the clothes and boots on and was immediately cold. I wondered, "What am I going to do?"

All of my nice survival gear was stashed neatly under the rear seat out of reach!

It was probably two-thirty in the afternoon. Water had not reached the top of the wing. An area two, two and a half feet wide at the center of the wing (at the fuselage) was not underwater.

I thought of taking the fuel caps off and lighting a match to see if the gasoline would burn. I reasoned that it would not explode since it was surrounded by water. I understand now it was not a good idea.

I had a bottle of matches I had removed from the water. The bottle was watertight, but enough moisture was in the bottle to prevent any of the matches from lighting.

By necessity I stayed on the tail, which became my perch. I made my way back to the tail surface where a wire comes off each side of the vertical stabilizer and connects to the horizontal stabilizer or elevator portion of the tail. The wire runs at a thirty-degree angle, and I hooked one leg over the wire to give myself more support and waited.

I was cold. Terribly cold. Frigid. My body and knees never quit shaking. Every hour I shouted as loud as I could. That relieved me some.

About five in the afternoon I heard the unmistakable and heartwarming sound of a Civil Air Patrol Beaver approaching. He came up from the northwest end of the lake and worked a pattern back and forth. I knew then that my beacon had been working.

I watched him for over two hours as he worked a pattern from a thousand yards to a mile away. Apparently his direction finder was getting a wrong reading from my beacon because he had me placed over on the beach in the hills going up from the lake. He never came my way.

I prayed. I shouted. I did everything I knew how to do. Finally about seven o'clock the Beaver made a ninety-degree turn and headed straight out across the ice toward me. I thought, "Oh, happy day, here he comes."

He crossed approximately two hundred yards to my right and seven hundred feet high, went out across the ice, did a 180-degree turn, and then came back on the same track. When he got to the beach, I heard his voice over the loud-speaker. It was a mile away, so I couldn't understand what he said. Since it was getting late in the evening, I assumed a helicopter would be there within an hour or so.

It turned out the pilot hadn't spotted me at all. He had misread the beacon's signal and assumed that someone was near the beach. The loudspeaker had instructed the person to shut off his transmitter when the pilot came over the top of him.

Nine o'clock came on and it began to get dark. I knew it was going to be a long night.

All the time the plane was settling a little more into the slush. The water was even with the top of the fuselage with very little clear space on the wings. An inch or so of water covered the tail surface I occupied.

I prayed some more. At nine-thirty or quarter to ten it began snowing. It snowed big flakes real hard. Then a little westerly wind came up, and it got colder. I have no way of knowing how cold it was, but before the night was over, the ice on top of the tail where I stood froze over an inch thick at my feet. I didn't jump up and down because that would jiggle the airplane down into the slush.

All night long I tried to convince myself that I could run fast like a deer and make it across the slush to the beach. But my feet felt like clubs and I couldn't do that. The constant shaking exhausted me. I was dehydrated. The time dragged. I looked at my watch and it was 10:05. Two hours passed, and I looked again. It was 10:15. All night long it went like that.

I shouted. I prayed. A lot of verses came to my mind. A verse in Deuteronomy says, "The everlasting God is our refuge and underneath are His everlasting arms." Psalms 91 says, "He will give His angels charge over you keeping all your ways they shall bear you up in their hands." I shouted that one out.

Nobody can hear you, so you might as well act like a fool. I hollered as loud as I could. Every hour or so I yelled some more.

About eleven or so the clouds cleared away and it was a beautiful night. There was a half moon and stars, but who could enjoy it?

I watched a satellite pass over. Whenever I saw a satellite, heard or saw a high-flying jet, I switched on the ELT.

About two in the morning I fell asleep standing straight up. I had draped myself over the vertical stabilizer beacon light, which is about the size of a glass, and dozed off. I could sleep only about three or four seconds because the light was jammed into my side and hurt so bad. But it was good. I guess I did that twenty or thirty times during the night. I never did come close to falling off.

I took my jackknife and cut some fabric off the tail. I wrapped it around my body and held it on with my belt to use as a windbreak. I cut some more fabric for a hat and cut thin strips to tie it to my head. What a relief it was to have a hat.

I wondered why the Civil Air Patrol wasn't flying at night in the fog for someone as important as I was. I began to seriously question why the accident had happened. I said, "Lord, I'm an idiot to do what I did. I was stupid to do that. And I confess that. Now, Lord, forgive me . . . and get me off of here."

I thought maybe the Lord had something for me to do and the devil wanted to stop me. Maybe he's trying to put doubt in my mind. I've preached to people for forty years about living by faith and trusting the Lord in hard times and trials, and here's my test. I prayed, "Lord, I don't know whether I've done something wrong or not, but if I have, I'm confessing to you."

Maybe my airplane's an idol to me. Maybe I love it too much, spend too much time with it. "Lord, if you want to take the airplane away from me, it's all right with me. If you want to rescue me, I'll never fly another hour in my life." Basically I surrendered totally to Him.

I learned some lessons that night about how the Lord works in a practical way with his children.

As the moon came up, I kept watching the angle of my shadow. I kept praying for daylight. I figured if I could survive until daylight, I had a chance. As I looked at the northeast sky, I knew it couldn't be too long before sunrise. A light shade of blue was beginning to develop. It was clear.

I reached down with my left hand for some lake water to drink.

My back and legs hurt terribly from standing in the same upright position. I was bitter cold.

As daylight developed, I could see for a hundred yards across the ice. But the fog came in from both directions and closed off the sky. I said, "God, they can't even hunt for me in this fog. What are you trying to do now?"

It was around six o'clock in the morning, and I'd been standing there for sixteen hours. Then I heard an airplane. I never saw it, but I could tell by the sound that they were back flying the same pattern they'd flown the night before. I shouted to them, "Why don't you come out on the ice!"

Later several airplanes came out. I couldn't see them, but I heard them flying grids. About nine o'clock I heard a helicopter coming up from the west end of the lake. And that was the sweetest sound I ever heard . . . *whop, whop, whop, whop.*

He came over the beach directly in front of me and flew back and forth, back and forth. I could see his light reflecting through the clouds like a weird, clattering ghost. They were convinced I was somewhere near the beach.

I prayed that God would lift the fog. I talked to the fog, "Fog, get out of here!" Didn't do any good.

I prayed, "Lord, you know how long I can stand here. I don't. I'm sure I can't make it through another night; and the airplane won't stay on the surface that long anyway."

I said, "I'm ready to die, but this would be a terrible way to do it to my family and to my church. They'll never find me in this glacial lake full of silt." My plane top was white, the same color as the ice, and nearly impossible to see.

After about two hours of flying around, the helicopter set down on the beach and cut his engines. I heard music. I thought, "Maybe he will hear me if I yell."

The two state troopers in the chopper knew the beacon was right on the beach somewhere. They were frustrated. They thought somebody left a locator beacon in the cabin. The pilot said to his friend, "I won't be happy to leave here until we check that cabin out."

I hollered as loud as I could, "Heeeeyyyyy! Yeeeeeoooowwww!" I did that for ten minutes. It took three seconds for that sound to cross the ice and run a half mile up the beach. The men never heard me.

They went into the cabin and came back out and had some lunch. While they sat there, the sun burned the fog away. The pilot asked his friend, "What in the world is that out there on the ice?"

His friend replied, "I don't know. It looks like a moose."

They gazed with binoculars for five minutes but couldn't figure out what they were looking at, so they decided to check it out when they left.

The finest picture I've ever seen was that big mosquito coming straight across the ice toward me. They ran the shoe of the helicopter right beside the tail of the plane. I stepped onto it and fell into the helicopter. They took me over to the beach, stopped it, opened the door, and asked, "Anyone with you?"

I said, "Yeah, the Lord was."

And the trooper said, "How are you?" He asked me a few questions, gave me some quick energy food, and we headed for Soldotna. My feet were not frozen. When I took my boots off, my ten toes were as blue as any child's crayon I've ever seen. The troopers were concerned because the circulation was gone.

I was deeply moved when the helicopter landed at the Soldotna airport. There stood my friends Marvin Moser, Tim Cooper, Ed Renner, Lee Browning, and Jimmy Miller. Tom Hibpshman and Hope Anderson and Pam Leffel and ten or fifteen other people welcomed me. We went over to a restaurant to get some hot soup.

After that I got into Eddie Renner's airplane and flew to Kenai and asked the Lofstedts at Kenai Air Service what the possibilities were of going out with a ranger helicopter to retrieve my airplane. They said they'd done that a lot of times and headed out right away.

Three hours from the time they took me off the plane, the mechanic stood on my plane's roof, took a couple of tools out of the helicopter, set them on my plane, and immediately they were covered with water as my plane began sinking. He jumped back into the helicopter and the airplane made its final journey to the bottom of the lake.

I don't believe I would have survived another hour and a half on the plane.

I lost five pounds or more in twenty-one hours.

That night my feet swelled up so I couldn't get shoes on. For a couple of days I had to be a little careful of my feet. I couldn't close my left hand, but it's all right now. I don't think there are any ill effects at all from my accident, so I'm thankful for that.

I want to thank the Lord for keeping me.

Epilogue

A news reporter later said I must have been in pretty good shape to survive my situation. I told him, "My physical conditioning had nothing to do with it. Somebody else kept me, and I don't get any credit at all. I want it to be known that God answered my prayers, and I owe Him everything for my life. I was a dead man."

I start every day reading several chapters from the Bible and committing my day to the Lord. I prayed that day about the trip.

Jesus healed ten lepers who were at the extremity of life. One thanked him, and Jesus asked where the other nine were. He stated it was our duty to glorify God. If we fail to glorify God with our lives, we sin.

Danger on the ice runs the gamut—from life-threatening to fatal.

DEATH STALKED THE ICE

BY LARRY KANIUT

He trusted his and his companions' prayers to deliver him.

Several years ago I ran across a story called "The Incredible Journey." It captured the experience of three men, a story that has been lived through the ages in isolated polar regions where man meets Mother Nature at every turn. I was captivated by it and wanted to share it with you.

They left home that morning on a casual hunt, thinking they'd return with game that evening. But they didn't return that evening . . . nor the next. Their casual hunt quickly turned into a fight for life.

Gregory Ayac, Lawrence Mazenna, and Raphael Patunac, Eskimo hunters from King Island, Alaska, were not strangers to the rigors of their land. Theirs was a hunter-gatherer lifestyle. Their lifestyle proved that experience can be a harsh taskmaster, and these hunters had learned lessons of survival from that aged instructor, lessons they'd need in the days ahead.

Their King Island home is an eight-hundred-foot-high, mile-long rock jutting out of the Bering Sea off the Alaskan coast, some ninety miles northwest of Nome. The Bering Sea is the cradle of the storms, birthing some of the cruelest weather known to man. These squat, bronze-skinned natives had adapted to their land and its weather.

It was January 6, 1949. Gregory left his village home that morning in search of game. His mother and three sisters depended on his hunting skills to fill their larder. Born and raised on King Island for all of his twenty-five years, Gregory was enthusiastic about his prospects and more than fit to the task.

Winter stingily granted him only four and a half hours of daylight. He would make the most of it. He hunted the shore ice south of the island.

Successful hunting requires knowledge of the sea and its changing surface. Autumn brings falling temperatures and sea ice. Eskimo hunters rely on experiential knowledge of the causes and characteristics of ice and its mobility. They know the impact of winds and currents upon sea ice. They know that ice cracks reveal information to the educated hunter. They know that their lives depend upon that knowledge.

Being surrounded by the sea on a remote island makes for difficult living, but the sea yields its bounty. Sea birds and mammals are plentiful depending on the season. Birds such as auks, fish ducks, gulls, old squaws, sea parrots, terns, and loons provide eggs as well as flesh. Seals, walruses, and polar bears relinquish their flesh, fat, and hides, which are utilized in many ways.

This day Gregory shot a seal. He dragged it across the shore ice to the beach. There he discovered two polar-bear hunters—Lawrence Mazenna, thirty-five, the father of three motherless children, and Raphael Patunac, twenty-two. Polar-bear tracks had been sighted northwest of the island.

Since Gregory had never killed Nanook, he joined the two men. His outfit included his spear, which doubled as an ice-testing pole, sealskin bag with small snowshoes, dry grass (boot insoles), seal hook and line, oogruk string, and rifle (.250/3000). He wore sealskin pants, parka, and reindeer socks inside his skin mukluks (boots). He carried a squirrel-skin headband.

The trio left land and trudged out onto the shore ice on the bear's track. Not much later the shore ice gave way to open leads with broken, moving ice floes beyond. A lead is an open stretch of water, a crack in the ice that exposes open water. These leads range from a couple of feet to several miles in width.

The hunters knew the safest ice was shore ice, salt water frozen to land. Though floes are large fields of ice, there is great danger in riding a floe that breaks apart and drifts off into the open sea, because it can break up into even smaller floes and carry the occupants away from safety. Falling into the frigid water with outside temperatures at zero degrees could result in drowning or freezing if the victim emerged from the water.

The men jumped from floe to floe like fur-clad gymnasts, testing the ice with their spears. After a while they realized the ice was moving away from the island, and they hastily returned to the lead they'd crossed earlier. They were shocked to see it had widened.

It was too wide to cross. The frothy water between them resembled a river filled with scattered, churning chunks of moving pan ice. While the floe they rode bumped and clawed its way north, breaking up, the men kept moving from scattered floe to floe, seeking a large, stable mass of ice for their safety. Night fell with a cloudy sky and no stars for guidance.

Gregory's partners were dressed in much the same manner as he. They weren't overly concerned and expected the best. Probable rescue was only a day or so away.

When the hunters failed to return the first night, the men's Jesuit priest, Father Thomas Cunningham, used his shortwave radio to alert listeners along the coast. Although Alaskans knew the danger of being trapped on an ice floe, they chose to search for their fellow Alaskans. Weather was too severe for aircraft to participate, however.

All along the coast shortwave radios crackled, "No trace of missing hunters." Binocular-wielding men scoured the ice field from shore. No one knew how long it would be before an air search could begin.

As the morning of their second day on the ice began, the three devout

Catholics prayed. They prayed not for safety and rescue but rather that events would be as God wished. Gregory thanked God for a safe night and another day.

Sixty-mile-an-hour winds lashed the ice, pushing it and its occupants northwest toward Siberia. Wind-whipped salt spray coated their sealskin pants and parkas.

Late in the day their ice flow ground into a larger ice floe and permanently froze to it.

Snow fell on January 8, and the men got their first food when Gregory shot a seal. Raphael skinned the mammal. Regrettably he frostbit his hands in the process. The hunters ate raw seal and carried three to four pounds as they pressed on.

Their journey was reduced to a snail's pace as Lawrence's left foot began freezing. Gregory removed Lawrence's boots, placing Lawrence's feet against Gregory's body; but it was useless—they did not warm up. Lawrence experienced stomach pain and was unable to eat.

To lighten his load and increase his chances of survival, Lawrence left his rifle and hunting gear behind. Gregory removed Lawrence's heavier items from his sealskin pack and dragged it along. When Gregory's shoulders tired, the men stopped to nap.

That night, Raphael and Gregory chipped ice for a shelter. While working, Gregory accidentally thrust his spear through his left mukluk. Knowing the danger of freezing a foot, he hastily sewed three sets of stitches in the boot with his oogruk string.

On the fourth day bitter cold arrived, and death followed. Only the two young hunters rose from the windswept ice. Lawrence could not go on. He asked his younger companions to say a prayer for him and to press on without him. They were reluctant, but he argued that the young ice was dangerous, that time was a factor, that their only hope was to reach solid ice.

Gregory gave Lawrence an extra pair of cotton gloves. Gregory and Raphael knelt and prayed for God's mercy toward their companion. They left him in his ice shelter, protected from the wind and awaiting death. The younger hunters vanished into the vast wasteland of slush, ice, and snow.

Cold followed the hunters into their fifth day with temperatures below zero. Frigid weather dictated urgent rescue, but the hunt was rescinded.

The next day the hunters consumed the last of their seal meat, which was essential for the strength and warmth it provided.

Gregory's left foot grew numb as it started freezing. Slowly, numbness spread from his feet to his body.

Raphael experienced pain in both his hands. Under freezing conditions where proper medical care is unavailable, freezing extremities are a forerunner to death.

The men smoked the last of their cigarettes before trying to sleep for the night. But as their ordeal had already proven, sleep was rare—they snatched fifteen-to-twenty-minute bits of shut-eye.

As he had every other night, Gregory awoke inexplicably and walked in the minus-thirty-degree chill.

January 11, day six on the ice, dawned clear and bitterly cold. Rescuers on-shore stood by their radios awaiting news of rescue. None came.

The hunters saw the high cliffs of Siberia to the southwest, a vast ice field in the area where they expected to see the Diomede Islands, and the faint outline of an Alaskan mountain far away on the mainland.

For five days they had labored over young ice and pressure ridges, sometimes reaching heights of three hundred feet, the piled ice resulting from ice floes mashing together. Temperatures reached one hundred degrees below zero. They had skirted or hopscotched over leads of open seawater on ice pans. They were constantly blown north past the Diomedes, into the Bering Strait—closer to the Arctic and farther from their homeland.

For a couple of days darkness, plummeting temperatures, snow, treacherous ice, and open water compounded to diminish their chances for survival. Their frustration mounted. Because January's wind and water currents traditionally moved ice seaward, the hunters thought their chances of striking land were slim. The anguish they experienced was devastating, but they retained their hope for rescue.

Their feet froze, complicating travel. Moving from ice pan to ice pan became more difficult, necessitating greater concentration to avoid falling into the bone-chilling water.

Gregory led the way. He fell four times into the numbing water. Each time he scampered out and dried his pants with snow. His sealskin pants were his salvation.

The biting cold attacked their bodies. They fell more often and were slower in reacting. Hunger and fatigue gnawed at them. Using the ancient Eskimo practice, they put snow in their sealskin pouches placed next to their bodies, melting it for drinking water.

Plane sightings excited them. However the aircraft never came close enough for them to signal; the hunters were never seen.

The mountain they thought was Cape Mountain grew larger. Believing an Eskimo village lay at its base, the men lurched on.

They struggled through rough, jumbled ice, encountering hip-deep snow. They put on their snowshoes, took them off, repeating the process again and again.

Raphael's frozen feet caused him to fall several times, and Gregory was always there to help him up.

The ninth day on the ice Raphael's hands froze solid. His fingers were cold, stiff stumps. His pain was so great that he pleaded with Gregory to pull his fingers off. Although Gregory was reluctant, he wanted to please his companion and ultimately complied, snapping off several fingers. There was no blood, and Raphael felt better.

Their next obstacle was a wide expanse of open water separating them from what appeared to be the mainland. Gregory encouraged Raphael and hoped the lead would close overnight, bridging the barrier.

On January 16, their eleventh day on the ice, Raphael was too weak to stand. He fell three times trying to rise and Gregory helped him up each time. During the night the lead had closed, and Gregory pointed out the solid ice between them and the shore. He assured Raphael they could make it.

But Raphael could not go on. He started to cry and asked Gregory to pray for him. As Lawrence had encouraged them both, Raphael told Gregory to go on alone.

Reluctant to leave his friend and thinking Raphael wouldn't live much longer, Gregory departed.

Realizing the missing men lacked food, fire, and shelter and confronted bitter cold, the United States Air Force canceled its search. They had flown fourteen missions, covering thousands of miles and assumed the men were by now frigid corpses.

To get a feel for what these men endured, one could place a bare hand in the snow for five minutes . . . or sleep outside without a sleeping bag in thirty-degree temperature. Add a drop in temperature of thirty to one hundred degrees, add two weeks to the time; and imagine snow falling so fiercely that you couldn't see ten feet in any direction (for three days!).

Gregory pushed on toward the mountain landmark. He was thankful to be alive and determined to survive, though willing to accept death if God chose.

Late in the afternoon with darkness pressing, Gregory stumbled onto a wind-blown hillock. Dead grass protruded from the snow. His discovery proved his suspicions that he *was* on land. He'd escaped his icebound ocean tomb!

Hope thrust him its helping hand. *Maybe he would make it!* He lay down on the tundra to rest. He'd start across the frozen tundra the next day.

On the eighteenth of January, his thirteenth day away from King Island, dawn harkened the weary traveler. He hungered for a sign of life, but there was none. Gregory's guiding mountain was still a distant image. But he struggled toward that landmark.

Softer, deeper snow shackled the plucky Eskimo who had defeated the sea. He resorted to his snowshoes and pressed on.

With banshee fury a blizzard struck. Although weakened by hunger, thirst, and a useless left leg, Gregory struggled on into the teeth of the storm, clasping his hunting gear and rifle with a grip of death.

The next day the snow continued swirling relentlessly. Gregory questioned his instincts. He turned toward the coast. He was confused and wondered if he'd been mistaken about Siberia.

That day he reached the base of the mountain. He rested briefly. Then he stumbled onto a spring. He drank the first fresh water he'd had in two weeks.

The tendon in his left heel pulled away from the bone. Where he had been dragging his lame leg, he was now forced to crawl on all fours. He crawled to the lee side of the mountain to get out of the wind. Gregory slumped into the snow to avoid the wind and the frigid cold. He fought death—pulled his hands into his parka, crossed over his chest. Covered by drifting snow, he felt warm and slept.

As day fifteen dawned, Gregory awakened to find himself entombed. Drifting snow had packed tightly around him, and he was trapped. Normally he could have commanded his strength and escaped, but he was exhausted. He kicked his feet and wiggled his arms.

Beyond the immediate life-and-death struggle pitting man against nature, the search for the missing men ground to an abrupt halt again. Hunters from Shishmaref could not battle the blizzard, and no plane flew.

Time dragged on. Minutes turned into an hour before Gregory's legs and arms were free. Force of habit and survival instincts bade him face the howling snowstorm. Summoning all his strength he willed himself to rise. He forced his feet into his webs and lurched off in the direction of the coast, turning his back to the wind.

Not much later Gregory spotted an object. *Was it real or was it a hallucination?* Clearing his eyes, he focused on a shovel propped in the snow. That tool confirmed his belief that people inhabited the area.

He pushed on until dark. He had reached his limits. Gregory didn't think he could take another step. He saw something and wondered if his eyeballs were freezing. *Could it be a cabin?* And only fifty feet away!

His enthusiasm prodded him. Gregory stepped forward but fell on his face into the snow. He tried to rise . . . but fell again. Crippled by exhaustion and with frozen feet and a numbed mind, Gregory determined to rise. He would not quit.

Rising to his knees, he thrust his spear into the snow near the cabin. He crawled into the shelter. There sleep immediately embraced Gregory.

The next day, January 21, Gregory's discovery of English notices on the walls assured him that he was in Alaska.

Two days previously, Eskimo dog musher Alfred Kiyutelluk had mushed from Shishmaref toward Wales. Alfred had spotted snowshoe tracks four miles north of Gregory's cabin. The tracks wound off inland in the direction of 2,325-foot-high Ear Mountain. The snowshoe design differed from that of mainland-Eskimo webs. Alfred suspected they belonged to the missing King Island hunter.

Turning his dog team, Alfred followed the wandering telltale trail—the left track indicated a useless leg. It was obvious the snowshoer had stopped frequently.

With darkness coming and having no overnight gear or food for himself or his dogs, Alfred decided to return to Shishmaref. He jammed a shovel into the snow as a starting point on his return the following day.

When Alfred reached Shishmaref, word spread. Convinced that no man could withstand the howling storm's fury, white trader George Goshaw radioed Mark's Air Force Base in Nome.

The day after Alfred Kiyutelluk's amazing discovery with rescue all but certain, Gregory faced another setback. The storm's intensity halted the search. Planes were grounded. Nothing moved for three days. Searchers waited. Each day lost was another nail in Gregory's coffin. Rescuers expected to find a corpse when the weather eventually allowed resumption of the search.

When Gregory awakened the next day, he built a fire in the stove. He then found a small Primus stove and fuel. There was not enough fuel for constant heat.

He found a sealskin poke with rancid seal meat. In spite of its aroma and taste he ate some. Gregory found bread scraps on the floor and ate them. He also found a pack of cigarettes.

Gregory removed his mukluks and saw black, lifeless feet. Prayers were his only medicine against gangrene.

Gregory rested on a cot.

January 22 was Gregory's second day in the cabin. He had struggled with the idea of leaving the shelter. As difficult as it was to return to the outside world, he knew he would starve or freeze if he remained where he was. He worked up his courage to leave. But by the time he'd made his decision, darkness had fallen. He decided to leave the next day.

However the next day, Gregory repeated the mental debate of staying versus leaving. Time elapsed. It was dark again as he started to leave the cabin.

On the twenty-fourth, his nineteenth day away from home, he decided to leave before darkness trapped him again. He made preparations. Putting his plan into action, he looked out the window. *Was that a wolf drawn to the cabin by the odor of his rotting feet?*

When George Goshaw's radio message crackled over the airways on January 19, it reached Arnold Olanna. Arnold was an Eskimo hunter from the village of Ikpik, nearly fifty miles southwest of Shishmaref.

On the twenty-fourth, Olanna, seeing the worst of the storm had passed, pointed his dog team toward Ear Mountain. He crossed Gregory's snowshoe tracks and followed them. Around noon he reached Gregory's shelter cabin.

What Gregory thought was a wolf was one of Olanna's dogs.

Gregory was one happy hunter. Olanna helped him into his sled and spirited him thirty miles back to Ikpik.

Because the King Islander needed immediate medical attention, Olanna's brother Elliot sped away the next day to procure plane transportation.

Elliot reached Wales after dark and delivered his message to Jim Brooks,

Weather Bureau observer. Brooks worked all night preparing his plane for the flight of mercy.

On the twenty-sixth Brooks landed near Olanna's cabin. Before leaving with the mercy pilot, Gregory gave all his hunting paraphernalia to Arnold Olanna, his rescuer.

After removing Gregory's mukluks and wrapping his feet in a blanket, Jim Brooks flew Gregory to Nome.

Gregory had survived the Arctic's fury for fourteen days on four hours of daylight each day. He covered three hundred to four hundred miles, much of it on frozen feet in subzero weather in one of the harshest lands on earth. Although witnessing his friends' deaths, he never gave up. He trusted his and his companions' prayers to deliver him.

Gregory Ayac's previous hunting experience prepared him well for his ordeal. But it was not enough to save him. His ultimate survival was due to another element . . . his will to live.

Sometimes, however, the grim reaper overpowers that will to live.

DEATH WORE WHITE

BY LARRY KANIUT

DEADLY SNOW

It was the best of news;
it was the worst of news.
While they rode the magic snow,
death stalked and watched them below.
Their machines repeatedly zoomed;
they knew not their impending doom.
Consumed with laughter they played;
but death would not be delayed.
It was wonderful racing up slope;
too soon there was little hope.
Their partner kept watching the show;
then vanished 'neath the deadly snow.

From the pages of Anchorage's two major newspapers come the following stories chronicling the outings of three groups of men who went for fun, but sorrow followed.

With a slicing, almost inaudible *craaaack* the sheet of unstable snow slipped the slope that held it. Oozing slowly, then building, it erupted into an onslaught of unavoidable death. The whirling white wall thundered ominously down the mountain.

The thick mass of heavy, late snow was an accident waiting to happen. It clung to the thirty-eight degree slope atop a crystallized layer that had fallen earlier and frozen—classic sugar snow (slides usually occur on slopes of greater than thirty-five degrees). All it needed to slide was a little additional weight or vibration from sound or wind.

A snowmachine proved the catalyst.

It was 2 P.M., Saturday, December 29, 1990, when white death hung above the five Anchorage men and their snowmachines near Campbell Lake. Curt Falldorf, a fifty-seven-year-old heavy-equipment operator for the Port of Anchorage, his two sons, Dennis, thirty-five, and Larry, twenty-nine, rode with friends Bob Bloom and Marty. They'd been riding for some time when Curt chose to ride up into the bowl. He sat on his machine in the sunny, warm weather, his back to the mountain, watching the others skitter across the snow.

Seeking the thrill and challenge of the slope, his companions sped ever upward, maxed their power, turned as momentum waned, accelerated, gradually built speed, then roared toward the valley floor . . . and repeated the run.

Dennis sped by his father observing his ear-to-ear smile that spoke volumes about his peace with the world.

The men reveled in the fun, the snow's glistening surface seducing them, lulling them with her sweet charm until she overwhelmed them with her deadly power.

Following the tracks of the others, Bob Bloom drove above Curt. He reached his apex, turned, and started down. In moments the snow he rode was moving faster than his machine. He was in the middle of an avalanche and rode it out, "swimming" the surface atop his machine. Hardly had he stopped when a second avalanche, triggered by the first, swept down the opposite side of the bowl. Adding its mass to the first one, it partially buried him. Truck-sized blocks of snow cluttered the landscape.

Larry scanned the avalanche delta and realized immediately that one of the riders was missing—his father. They dug out Bloom, then turned their attention to finding Curt. Larry cut alder branches to use as probes, then people materialized to help.

The Glen Alps parking lot is accessible by vehicle and has long been the staging area for Chugach Park emergencies by official rescue groups such as the Alaska State Troopers and the Alaska Mountain Rescue. Once again the lot housed rescue personnel.

Thirty-six snowmachiners riding in the area, seven Alaska Mountain Rescue members (specially trained for these emergencies), and Alaska State Parks rangers arrived to search. Within an hour dozens of other people also showed up to help dig. Skiers surrendered their skis and poles as tools.

The size of the avalanche area compounded the search. The hard-packed snow and huge blocks of snow made already hard work more difficult and frustrating.

The trooper helicopter ferried rescuers six miles to the scene even though fog threatened to ground the chopper a couple of times.

Two dogs and experts with metal detectors arrived. About thirty-five volunteers armed with ten-foot poles lined up twenty-four to thirty inches apart and probed into the snow, methodically moving a few steps forward to begin each new probe. Their probes did not hit bottom.

Experts noted that half to two-thirds of the bowl had slid. The fissure was eight to fifteen feet thick. Observing two big areas in the bowl ready to slide, they feared another avalanche. Increasing winds did not help.

As darkness fell, volunteers not equipped with radio transmitters were ordered from the area for their safety. As many as fifty-eight volunteers worked, some till 8 P.M.

Peggy Carlson, a relative of Falldorf's, said if anyone could survive the avalanche, it would be Curt.

Curt's wife, Lois, said, "I know a lot about avalanches, and I'm real scared."(1)

The next day avalanche experts blasted the ridge to dislodge the two dangerous snow areas and to prevent a surprise avalanche.

In some places, thirty-foot probes didn't reach the bottom of the avalanched snow. At least fifty people searched until midnight in the lowering temperatures with no success. The 150–250-yard area had been probed four times, but knowing Falldorf could be twenty to thirty feet under the snow, their hope dwindled.

Later Lois Falldorf said, "I don't think any of us who have lived here and survived avalanches has any real hope. . . . I've lived here too long. Too many avalanches. I gave up hope after six or seven hours. All I hope is that he didn't have an air pocket and suffer. You always hope for miracles. But I know better. . . . I'd like them to find him, because it's unfinished. . . . You don't like to think of him up there."(2)

By Monday, December 31, Alaska state trooper Claude Kilpatrick had arranged for sensitive metal-detecting equipment from EBA Engineering Inc. to be used in the search. The magnetometer and an EM-31 conductivity meter are designed to detect metal deep below the surface.

Relatives, thirty family friends, troopers, and engineers spent most of Monday canvassing part of the avalanche debris where they expected to find Falldorf's machine.

Double-tracked machines pulled huge snow scoops through the area, barely making a dent in the snow removal. Searchers tried about everything and considered other devices such as radar. Larry and Dennis Falldorf were determined to find their father and bring him off the mountain before they quit the search.

On Wednesday, January 2, searchers found Falldorf's machine in ten feet of snow. The family agreed to bring in a ground-penetration device from Canada (at a cost of $10,000 to the Falldorf family).

Larry's wife, Dottie Rae, provided chili, string cheese, doughnuts, and coffee throughout the search. The Alaska State Troopers helicopter flew in generator-powered lights provided by the Anchorage Fire Department.

On Friday a local contractor donated a D-3 Caterpillar bulldozer to assist in the search. The Cat crawled the six slow miles to the search site. The machine's appearance gave the searchers an emotional lift. Three bulldozers, operated by Falldorf's friends, worked through the night, each one accompanied by two men walking with shovels and probing.

Other activities included digging fifteen-foot tunnels in all directions near the pit where the snowmachine was discovered.

On Saturday, after seven days of searching, Larry Falldorf directed the search and ran a D-9 Cat.

Five dogs and handlers from Alaska Search and Rescue Dogs worked the avalanche debris, but they had difficulty picking up the scent because of the number of searchers in the area. Twenty army sergeants from Northern Warfare

Training Center in Fort Greeley participated as part of an avalanche-training workshop requirement.

About 3:30 P.M. searchers found Curt Falldorf's body beneath thirty feet of snow. Curt's body was placed on a sled, and Dennis, followed by twenty-five snowmachiners, pulled it over the snow to the Glen Alps parking lot.

Afterword

Larry said his dad had thirty years of experience on snowmachines and the accident was unavoidable. "We all knew about avalanches. It was nobody's fault; it just happened."(1)

Later Larry and Dennis Falldorf second-guessed their activity: "Perhaps we got . . . a little bit careless. . . . But you ride for twenty years and nothing happens . . . how do you know the snow is weak ten feet deep? . . . There was sugar snow down at the bottom that acted like ball bearings."(2)

Dennis said, "We thought we had a nice place there. It turned out we were wrong. . . . When you try to get out into the country and try to be part of it, you get under its control. If you get too worried about it, you'd never get out the door."(2)

When the avalanche survivors discussed their choice of places to ride, they thought it would be safe because it always was before. But when you consider snow depth and water runoff, it is important to take into consideration changing weather conditions. A shallow glacial stream could be several feet higher later in the day depending upon rising temperatures and/or rainfall. You can never trust yesterday . . . even though the area was safe before, today's a new day.

Radio transmitters have saved avalanche victims. However, considering the snow depth where Falldorf's body was found and the compacted snow around him, it doesn't seem likely a transmitter would have helped him.

Before Curt's body was found, his wife had expressed concern about his being found not only to bring closure to the family, friends, and community but also because "he'd hate it if some kids were up there hiking and might come across what's left. That's just not right. This is just some terrible, unfinished business. Besides, I know it's not Curt up there; just his body."(3)

Larry's wife, Dottie Rae, said, "He really liked doing stuff with his boys."(2)

And Lois added, "Curt . . . loved snowmachines. . . . If Curt could have picked a way to die, it would have been on a snowmachine with his kids."(2)

After writing Curt's story in February 1999, I contacted my friend Al Tegtmeier. Al had kindly introduced himself to me a dozen years before, and knowing him has been a privilege. He allowed me to read five manuscripts he had written about his early days growing up in Chicago, his military service, and his work as a police officer in Monterey, California.

Al was a friend and coworker of Curt's. Although seventy years old, Al had volunteered to search for Curt. Because Al was an eyewitness at the scene for a couple of days and has a keen eye for detail, I asked him if he'd read my summary of the newspaper stories and add his comments. I am beholden to Al for his input, which follows.

When I first read about Curt's accident, I recalled he was a shop foreman at A. C. I. Brown and Root-Halliburton circa 1977. I was shop carpenter then, some twelve years prior, and our two shops were a team for some reason. Although retired and busy, I wanted to help in his search.

Several days went by, and I read about the mounting effort to find his body. Finally I called Curt's best friend, Ed Kareen, a welder and coworker. Ed advised me to take a large scoop shovel to the parking lot and ride to Powerline Pass where the search continued.

With my arctic gear, lunch, and shovel, I went to the parking lot. Although it was the wrong lot, I met a volunteer who had a snowmobile and gave me a ride to the scene.

Much hand-shoveling ensued with scanty daylight. For hours a snowmobile pulled a big scoop to enlarge the area and depth where Curt's machine had been recovered via probes that hit and punctured the machine; this allowed the search area for his body to narrow.

The daylight disappeared and work terminated for the day. A loud noise caused all to look and discover two bulldozers approaching.

I received a ride back to my car.

Next morning I went to the main parking lot and rode in with a volunteer. I could see more extensive lighting (temporarily set up) and the two dozers working. A machine had worked through the night (inconvenienced by the track's breaking).

An indescribable amount of snow had been removed and stacked away from the probable location of Curt's body.

Men were measuring the distance from Curt's last seen position, three-hundred-plus feet away. The open area was increasing in size, and the volunteers' need to relieve themselves away from the main activity made it difficult for the search dogs to operate at optimum efficiency, so they were withdrawn.

Women manned two stations for food and drink. One tent was at the site and the other at the main parking lot along with lights and a rest room.

For a while I dug by hand with others, then one of Curt's sons asked me to climb the snow hill and watch the dozer's path. I did this and was joined by a male newspaper photographer and a gal reporter. We chatted as we watched the path of the closer of the two dozers.

While I sat with my shovel, lunch, and apple, the newspeople took my name for an article and departed to meet their deadline. I waved at them, looked back, and saw a dark spot in the wake of the dozer (it turned out to be Curt's gloved hand sticking out of the snow). I opened my mouth to alert all when someone called out.

I hurried down to the snow pile where the driver was looking back at the area he had just cleared. He dismounted the dozer and walked away (it was Curt's son Larry).

Workers surrounded the spot and dug with hands and shovels to free Curt's body. One of the volunteers, overcome with grief and emotion, left. I moved in and used my shovel to move snow back farther.

Curt's helmet face shield was closed and he appeared to be sleeping. I put the shovel down and held one of Curt's legs as other volunteers picked him up tenderly and placed him in a body bag and onto a sled. One of his sons kneeled down and patted Curt.

A group of us pulled the sled out of the steep area and onto flat ground so that it could be hooked to a snowmobile. Before long the camp was dismantled.

Someone offered me a snowmobile to ride out, but I didn't feel comfortable because of my inexperience, so I rode out on the machine Curt's sons rode to pull his father's body on the sled. Friends and family followed in a long, sad line for the trip to the Glen Alps parking lot. The search was over.

I later attended a memorial party at a hall off Dimond Boulevard and Seward Highway. Balloons, smiling faces, and eulogies from family, friends, and co-workers abounded. Curt loved riding snowmachines with his sons, and his passing, though a tragedy, occurred while he was engaged in an activity that he loved.

Powerline Pass, located less than a dozen miles southeast of downtown Anchorage, was so named because an electric power line transverses the valley from Anchorage to Indian Valley and beyond. I know of a number of fatalities and near deaths in that stretch of land, therefore I call Powerline Pass the Valley of Doom (see chapters "Death Stalked the Edge," "Danger Ignored," and "Heroes, One and All").

At the end of March 1994, skiers John McMahon and Tony Stalion slid over the snow in Powerline Pass. It was around 3:20 P.M. The skiers watched two snowmachiners crisscrossing up and down the sides of a steep bowl near Ptarmigan Peak close to Campbell Lake. They didn't know it at the time, but the machiners they watched were Brandon Ford and an unidentified friend.

McMahon thought the activity was "dangerous and senseless. One guy shot up to the top of the bowl and started making his turn to come down when I saw the crack in the snow form. I never saw [Brandon] come up after that."(7)

The slab of snow that shot down the bowl measured nine feet thick where it broke loose from the mountain, a sheet of white death rocketing toward the valley below, building in depth to a height of forty feet where it piled up on the valley floor.

McMahon and Stalion waved down two snowmachiners in the area and rode with them to the scene of the avalanche, arriving six minutes after the accident. There was no sign of Brandon, and the skiers poked into the snow with their ski poles and shouted for him.

Within forty minutes of the accident the Alaska State Troopers and the Alaska Mountain Rescue Group assembled in the Glen Alps lot to help in the rescue effort. A Red Cross van dispensed food and coffee.

A trooper helicopter shuttled rescuers to the accident scene. By five-thirty teams of snowmachiners pulled carts with food, water, and equipment such as ten-foot probe poles, red-flagged sticks, and transmitters from the parking lot up the valley to the avalanche scene.

Initially the searchers randomly probed with the poles until a number of rescuers showed up. Then they lined up side by side and probed in ten-foot intervals.

Volunteers continued to arrive throughout the night. Seventy-five rescue workers slaved into the night looking for Ford buried beneath twenty to forty feet of snow.

About 10:30 P.M. the rescuers found twenty-one-year-old Brandon Ford's body. Ironically the locale was the very same area where Curt Falldorf had lost his life three years previous (his body was found under thirty-four feet of snow a week after his accident).

Paul Bezilla of Mountain Rescue commented on the hazardous conditions of late in the front range of the Chugach Mountains of Powerline Pass: "People should take extreme caution with this stuff."(7)

Earlier in the day authorities had recovered the body of Jeffrey Ransom, thirty-five, of Kasilof. Around 3 P.M. the day before, he and his friend had triggered an avalanche near Lost Lake in the Seward area about 125 miles southeast of Anchorage. Another sad loss.

Kodiak Man Survives Two Avalanches

Tom Abell Sr. was one happy man Tuesday, February 6, 1996. While he and friends rode their snowmachines near Anton Larsen Pass on Kodiak Island, vibrations from their machines triggered an avalanche.

Abell was buried by the mass of snow tumbling over him. Although he wore a full-faced helmet that provided a small area between the plastic mask and his face for air, snow packed around his mouth caused him to black out from lack of oxygen.

Fortunately he wore a beacon transmitter. No sooner had the avalanche struck than Abell's friends turned on their receivers to pick up his transmitter's signal. They zeroed in on his location and rushed to him, arriving two minutes later. After fifteen minutes of digging, his friends Terry Davis and Tom Dooley found him unconscious.

Terry Davis said, "Without the transceivers, we wouldn't have found him in time."(8)

A year before, an avalanche trapped Abell and his friend and riding partner Rick Gunderson. Neither wore transceivers. Although Abell got out alive, his friend died. Chances are his friend would likely have lived had he worn a transmitter.

Abell said, "This time when it happened, I knew everything to expect, and I knew I was in a world of hurt. In three minutes I blacked out, just like the experts say."(8)

He was able to ride his machine out of the backcountry and said, "We weren't being careless."(8)

Snowmachining is a great way to get around and to enjoy the beauty of the outdoors, but when the unexpected occurs, tragedy too often follows. It would be a wonderful world if all avalanche victims survived and lived healthy lives to a ripe old age.

Some adventures are both tragic and sad; and some participants don't reach old age.

Related stories herein are: "Death Wouldn't Wait," "Heroes, One and All," and "Danger Ignored."

A FRIEND IS LOST

AS TOLD TO THE AUTHOR BY JACK PARRET

All it takes to get in trouble in a place like that is a little slip.

Several years ago my friend Jack Parret told me about a hunting experience he had had when he was a young man. It was a story I never forgot, one that I wanted to share with others. I asked him recently to retell his story so I could incorporate it in this book. He readily agreed. Jack acknowledged that he might not have all the facts, but he'd tell the story to the best of his recollection.

Jack is a retired teamster. At five feet nine inches and a solid 190 pounds, Jack has a vise-grip handshake that communicates his strength of body and is a powerful reflection of his strength of friendship and character. On Wednesday, January 20, 1999, we met at Cornerstone Church of God in Anchorage where Jack told me the following story.

In 1953, I was a nineteen-year-old living in Seward, Alaska. My high school buddy and I decided to go goat hunting in the early fall. Although my hunting partner, Willard Mahirun, was only sixteen years old, he was my very good friend.

It was a nice day in August or September. We didn't have any rain or snow, and no snow was on the ground.

The plan was to go hunting where we thought there might be animals and to get above them. Even though I'd never hunted there, it was common to see them from the highway near Crown Point.

Early in the morning we drove my 1950 Ford twenty-five miles toward Moose Pass, planning to stop and hike up the Crown Point Mine trail. Crown Point is just below Moose Pass, right at the end of Lower Trail Lake. A small road just a little bit toward Seward runs back to the foot of the hill.

We parked in a little parking place at the bottom of the hill. Then we got out of the car, grabbed our rifles, and hiked up the Crown Point Mine trail. The Crown Point Mine trail actually starts at the base of Ptarmigan Mountain and then crosses over to Crown Point Mine. We didn't stay on the trail long because we wanted to hunt on Ptarmigan Mountain.

We didn't carry day packs, just our rifles and what we wore.

Even though it's a pretty good hike up the mountain from that point, we were pretty excited because we expected to find goats on the mountain. Our destination was the ridge that runs to the top of the mountain. When you scare a goat, he goes up, so we wanted to get up above the goats.

We got up above the timber on the ridge and continued climbing. After a couple of hours of hiking we reached an area on the ridge where we thought the goats would be.

It took us a couple of hours to reach the top of the ridge, about thirty-five hundred feet in elevation. It was around eleven o'clock. We got in position above the goats. We felt if we hunted down the mountain on top of them, there'd be a good chance that we'd get some shots. We started down the mountain together, then, somehow, we got separated.

Two or three bluffs covered the face of the mountain and resembled a big set of stairs. Each "step" consisted of three or four "risers" of sixty or seventy feet, leveling off for a ways, rising another sixty or seventy feet, leveling off again, and repeating the rise one or two more times—attaining a combined rise of two hundred to three hundred feet.

I endeavored to work my way down to the next level.

The face of the bluff had a narrow crack, which seemed to be the best way down. This crack was ten or twelve feet from top to bottom and a dozen feet wide at the top. I descended through the crack in the bluff—pressuring my feet from side to side against the rock wall on either side of me. In some places there were footholds, places to step. The treacherous footing required some hiking experience. Even though it was dangerous in the crack, it was far more so going over the face of the bluff.

While continuing alone, I realized I hadn't even sighted in my .30-06 rifle. I raised the rifle and bore-sighted it. I removed the bolt and aimed. I looked through the open sights to see if I was pinpointing on the same object through the sights that I saw through the barrel. It seemed like it was pretty well on.

I didn't see any goats while I was down on the face of the mountain and I decided to go back and meet up with Willard.

I don't remember what our plan was, whether it was for Willard to stay above and hope I'd scare some animals to him or if we even had a plan. In any event, I didn't see Willard anywhere. Of course, that started worrying me.

Trying to figure out where Willard was, my mind raced. *What should I do?* I tried to figure out what could have become of him. I thought maybe he'd tried to come down the face a different way. Maybe he'd headed back to the car, which I doubted. And then there was the greatest fear—maybe he'd fallen. I didn't know and I was in a panic.

I commenced hollering and searching for him, moving around on the face of the hill. I spent a couple of hours scrambling over the knobs looking for Willard. I couldn't find him. Because it was getting later, I knew I had to go. I decided to go back up the ridge.

Jack Darrot, forty years later, on a goat hunt in the same area as the accident
CREDIT: *Kyle Young*

All the way back up to the top of the ridge on the hogback, I hollered and tried to get some response. All of my efforts were in vain. Coming back up was an effort. I reached the ridge by two in the afternoon.

I hoped I'd find him on my way to the car, but I didn't. Reaching the car at three or four in the afternoon, I waited for Willard, dozed off, and when I woke up, it was getting dark. Since he hadn't showed up, I started for town.

As I drove to town, I continued wondering what could have become of him. By the time I got home it was dark. After I reached Seward, I had to go tell Willard's folks that evidently something had happened to him. I tried to explain that he never answered me when I hollered.

The men in town were notified that someone was lost. The next day ten or twelve men from town got together and formed a search party. I went along with them to show them where we'd hunted and to help find my friend.

We drove out to Crown Point and hiked up to the area Willard and I had hunted. We spent the entire day looking for Willard.

I was young and active. I could practically outhike any of the guys in the search party. They thought I was overdoing it or something. There was talk about some possible foul play.

The area we hunted wasn't that large, nevertheless it was the third day before we found him. Evidently he had tried to find another way down. More than likely he was trying to get some footing in a rocky area and slipped, lost his balance, and fell. It was reported that he fell a thousand feet. I wasn't right with them when they found Willard, but I wish I had been. All it takes to get in trouble in a place like that is a little slip. To fall a thousand feet would result in major physical trauma that would make it nearly impossible to survive.

They found his rifle. Willard's body hadn't been bothered by any animals or birds.

When something like that happens to someone you've gone to school with and known, it affects you. Willard was a good person and came from good people, a fine family.

Because I was older and with him, I felt responsible.

It is important to stick together. If you do separate, make firm plans and stay with the plan or stay put.

Even though sometimes our best efforts to help a partner are futile, sticking together does provide hope . . . something that Norm Solberg discovered when his friend Steve Hanson made every effort to save him.

WHEN A FRIEND FALLS

AS TOLD TO THE AUTHOR BY STEVE HANSON

I watched him tumble out of sight. He dropped about five hundred feet.
The only thing I could do was holler to him.

A few years ago when I read about the sheep hunter who fell off the mountain, I determined to learn the story. In the fall of 1997, while speaking at Su-Valley High and spending the night with Glenn and Gayne Turner, I learned that they knew Steve Hanson, the fallen hunter's friend. A year later my friend Jim Brenn told me, "You should get hold of Steve Hanson, who has a tremendous story."

On December 3, 1998, I called Steve and taped his story over the phone, only to discover later that my recorder's batteries had died after the first few paragraphs. We arranged for a second try, and my daughter Ginger Risch transcribed Steve's tale, which follows. As you read, imagine the emotion of the storyteller . . . sharing his good friend's anguish while being emotionally torn by the need to be with him and the knowledge that he must go for help.

My friend Norm Solberg had a sheep permit to hunt in the headwaters of Ship Creek, east of Anchorage. The best way to his permit area, Sheep Mountain, was on the Crow Creek trail, a part of the Chugach State Park trail system that connects the Eagle River and Crow Creek trailheads.

It was actually a pretty nice day as we drove to Girdwood early in the morning, parked at the trailhead past Crow Creek Mine, got our packs all set up, and hit the trail. Within half an hour we were above the timberline hiking a well-traveled trail over gravel-sized, brown-gray rock on the gradual uphill climb. We reached the summit of the pass and continued on another half hour before we dropped over into the Eagle River drainage.

Typical Alaska high country of rock, lichen, and low ground cover met our gaze. On our right Raven Glacier oozed over the horizon down into the valley. Various-sized rocks cluttered the area, and Raven Creek's gray, glacial waters cascaded north, slicing down the valley. Far below we saw the verdant green of alder patches and the dark green spruce timber beyond.

To reach the sheep permit area, we decided to traverse the ridge to our left and pushed on, leaving the trail. We side-hilled toward the ridge, crossing a creek that was a little more difficult than we thought because of large boulders everywhere. We negotiated around that section of the creek and kept traversing the ridge. We figured we'd make it over the ridge, but it was slow going. The weather started to turn on us some and it started getting late. Norm and I decided we'd stay where we were and take off the next morning rather than risk getting socked in.

Past experience prepared us to include our lightweight food, sleeping gear, as well as some first-aid things, knives, and cameras.

We had two one-quart water bottles between us. Since we had crossed the creek more times than we'd planned and got stuck on that ridge, we were rather low on water.

We located a flat area free of rocks and set up our camp. Before long we had the tent up and it started to cloud over. We set up some large plastic garbage bags to try to trap some water should it rain and had a nice evening.

The next morning when we got up, we were socked in with fog. We couldn't see a thing above or below us. We planned to go over the mountain ridge but couldn't because of the lack of visibility. We used the time to transfer the water from our garbage-bag tarps into our water containers.

Little did we know what problem the rain-slickened grass was going to cause us within a couple of hours.

About noon it was starting to lighten up below us. Concerned that we were losing quite a bit of time, we decided to pull our camp and go down and around instead of over the ridge. We packed up our gear and broke camp.

The slope was steep and covered with short grass with some scattered shale slides, but there weren't any bluffs or cliffs. It looked real innocent.

Because it was wet, we both had our green Helly Hansen rain gear on. Norm took off first. Norm was about fifty feet ahead of me when all of a sudden I saw him slip down on his butt and start sliding. I thought it was kind of funny.

But then my amusement turned to disbelief as I watched him slide. He knew he had to stop himself and had his hands out trying to catch something. The ground cover was grass a few inches long, and there was nothing to grab. He shot down the mountain with such incredible speed it was as if he were on a water slide.

With his hands out to keep his balance, he caught his foot. That turned him and he rolled sideways, his hands and legs toppling with the force of rolling so many times. Then he started going into somersaults. His backpack catapulted him down the mountain, and he literally bounced head over heels. Parts of the pack came off and equipment began falling from it. His rifle came free from its pack mount.

In disbelief I watched him tumble out of sight. He dropped about five hundred feet. The only thing I could do was holler to him, "Norm, you've got to stop. You've got to stop yourself."

Realizing what had happened, I carefully worked my way down, the whole time hollering for Norm and picking up pieces of the gun mount. I found his rifle and then bits and pieces of clothing. About three hundred feet down the mountain I saw his backpack. Looking farther down, I could see Norm sticking out from a clump of dwarf willows, lying there lifeless. I hollered for Norm but I got no response. (I think the only reason he stopped was because his backpack came off and he was able to spread-eagle more and slow down his fall.)

As I got closer, I heard a faint moan. I was excited to know that he was alive. I knew I needed to determine what shape he was in.

I started talking to him. Norm wasn't responding to me, and I didn't realize he couldn't hear because he'd lost his hearing aid. All of a sudden I heard this beeping. I looked down his shirt toward his stomach and saw his hearing aid. How that ever came out of his ear and ended up there, I don't know. I picked it up and put it in his ear. Then he could hear me.

He kept saying, "My leg, my leg." I felt down his body slowly and felt a bone that wasn't protruding out of the skin; it wasn't a compound fracture, but I could see that he had at least one break in his leg. I was worried about swelling right away and wondered if he might be bleeding inside. Maybe he had severed an artery. A lot of things went through my mind.

I took my Therm-A-Rest pad out of my backpack and took his boot off. Then I wrapped his leg in the pad to stabilize it. I blew up the pad and tied it with the straps so that his legs would stay stable to prevent further injury.

He could start sliding again real easily, so I decided to move him to a safer location. I had to drag him partway up the mountain to a little ledge; it wasn't much but it was better than where he was. I wasn't sure if I should leave him there while I went for help.

I stood just below and held him in place while I got on my cell phone. I was just hoping that I would have a cell station. I got nothing. Thinking I could make a compound anchor system to help hold him in place, I took my parachute cord and laced it in and out of his body. Then I went to the willows below him, which weren't more than two feet high, and wove a web to catch him if he started falling. There was really nothing to anchor him to, but I knew I would have to go for help, so it would have to do. I hoped the net would keep him from falling more; I didn't know what that was going to do to his leg.

He had lacerations on his face. He was coming to more and more. As he groaned in pain, I was able to talk with him about his leg. I gave him a little water and a couple of aspirin. I looked down onto the Crow Creek trail thinking maybe I could find somebody and get Norm help. I got my binoculars out and glanced up and down for any sign of people, but I didn't see anybody. I knew time was running short. I had to get help and get back in time to get him out before dark or he'd end up spending the night alone. I didn't think he'd survive the night by himself.

I set him all up and told him I was going for help. I even checked out his rifle, which seemed to be okay, and I put it beside him. Although we were about a mile and a half from the trail, I thought he could use the rifle to signal or to protect himself from animals.

I wrapped him in his sleeping bag and in my tent and secured him as well as

I could. Then I gave him all my water and a little bit of food. I left the aspirin bottle in case he had pain.

I left my backpack and took my fanny pack, my radio, a little bit of gorp, an empty water bottle, my compass, and my rifle. As hard as it was to leave Norm alone, I went down the mountain, constantly looking for somebody on the trail.

All of a sudden I saw this lone hiker on the trail, so I fired off a shot into the air. I got my binoculars out and looked. He was working his way up the pass, and I figured I could probably get down, cross the creek, and intercept him so he could help us.

I fired off three more shots—a distress signal—and looked again. The guy looked for the longest time in my direction and then kept going. *I've got to go over to him.* So I continued down the mountain.

When I got to the alders, I started putting out flagging so that we could find the same route up to Norm. I got through the alder patch and was getting closer to the trees. Then I heard the roar of the creek. It sounded as if the creek was in a canyon, and sure enough, when I reached the creek, sheer rock walls lined the sides. The only way around it was to go up or down. It seemed as if down was shorter, so I went down about a quarter of a mile and crossed. Just about then I encountered the guy walking up the trail.

I hollered and ran over and he was looking at me real worried like. I laid my gun down and walked away from it. I said, "I need help, there's been an accident."

We sat down, and I got my binoculars out and explained what I had done and what kind of situation Norm was in. I set a bearing with my compass and told the guy where Norm was.

Then I asked him, "Would you go up there and be with Norm?"

He said, "I can't do that. There is nothing I can do for him."

"If I don't make it out before dark and he's up there all alone, I don't know what will happen to him."

"I'm not trained for that stuff."

I said, "All you have to do is be with him, to have somebody there." He would not do it.

Then I said, "Okay, I'll go back up there. Would you run down for help?"

"My pack's heavy, I'll never make it out before dark, there is no way. It's fifteen to seventeen miles out to Eagle River."

"You've got to try and get out and I'll go back up to Norm."

"I'm not a good runner; I just can't make it."

Then I said, "You've got to go up and be with Norm, I'm going."

I made a big four-by-four-foot X out of flagging and laid it on the tundra to mark the spot from which rescuers could depart the trail.

Then I got my rifle.

By this time the weather was clearing and it was dead calm, a beautiful day.

I continued working my way down the trail, checking periodically to see if my cell phone worked. I got an eighth of a mile and all of a sudden I heard three shots coming from Norm's position. Then I heard Norm scream, "Please help me, help me, help me . . ."—I could hear his echo.

I got real worried, thinking that Norm had slipped or something had happened to his leg. *Something is wrong with Norm.* I was freaked. I turned back and caught up with the hiker, who refused to help Norm. I folded my hands together and got down on my knees. "Please, I beg you"—tears ran down my face—"you've got to go up there."

Norm and I have been hunting for years and he's in pretty good shape, a great guy, a friend, a neighbor. Basketball coach for my kids, a teacher, and the guy is a really good friend. *I just can't see this happening.* It was so hard to leave him. I was still worried that I wouldn't get out.

After I begged that guy, I turned around and left, not knowing if he would go or not. I figured he heard the shots and Norm's screaming. Surely he'd go up there.

I went on down the trail and thought there was no way I was going to make it. I had my Vibram-soled mountaineering boots on, but they were really hard to run in, so I took them off and removed the plastic boot liner. I laced up my inner liner and took off my raincoat. *I can make better time running downhill than going up over the pass, maybe it's just a little quicker, maybe it will be easier to use the cell phone.* I put my rifle and raincoat in the brush, took the bare necessities—phone, water bottle, and the bag—and started running for all I was worth toward Eagle River.

I finally got into the trees a bit and turned the corner. Then I saw a cow moose and a calf standing right in the middle of the trail. *She's got her hackles up. Her head's down and she's coming at me.* I ran back and off the trail, down a hill, and started climbing a tree.

She came at me and I thought, *Man, won't this beat all? The stupid moose has got me in a tree and I'm losing precious time.* The cow started backing off before I got very far up and I climbed back down. I made a big swing around the moose and got back on the trail below them and started running again.

As I got closer to Eagle River, the trail turned upriver. I thought, *Ah, man, now where is this going?* I'm thinking, *I'm losing time here.* Finally the trail turned and headed back down toward the river. By now three hours had passed since I left Norm and I wondered, *Am I going to make it tonight?*

I kept trying my phone. *No signal.* And I hadn't run into anybody.

I reached the river finally and all of a sudden the trail disappeared. The year before, big floods had washed away the trail and markers. I crossed the cold, glacial waters of Eagle River hoping I'd find the trail on the other side. When I got over there, I didn't stop to rest but kept on going. I ran and ran and ran, looking for the trail.

I finally got to a rock wall and knew the trail couldn't be there. So I headed up the side of the mountain and came across the trail. It was slow going, up and down in ruts and rocks.

By now it was around seven o'clock and I finally ran into some people. I was breathing hard and trying to tell them what had happened. There were six people—four in one group and two in the other group. One guy was a hiker and knew exactly where Norm was by my explanation. He said, "I will go up there."

I asked, "You will go up there?"

He made a statement and asked a question: "I know this trail, I can travel it in the dark, and you've got it marked?"

I said, "Yeah, I have got a big X at the trailhead where I came out, and once you find that, you will find where I flagged it. You will have to go up to the creek because of the rock wall and then negotiate around all that. I have got it marked."

He promised me he'd go up there.

I turned to the other people and said, "I've got to get down to Eagle River."

One guy said, "Well, we're heading that way, too . . . to the next camp."

One girl spoke up and said, "I'm a runner. I run in marathons and I will go ahead and pick up the torch here. I'll take your cell phone and head down till I hit a signal to get help."

I said, "That would be great."

Another guy spoke up and said, "I'll go with you."

So they left their packs right there and started running down the trail. We took their extra gear and started down the trail behind them. I still kept walking fast, trying to make good time.

I took us another hour to reach the camp where they planned to stay. I dropped off the gear. They gave me a little bit of food and a strobe light: "Take this with you in case a chopper does come up, so they will be able to see you better." Then I continued down the trail.

In the meantime the girl who took my cell phone got within a mile of the visitors' center and finally picked up the signal. I didn't even know that help was on the way until I left the last camp.

About thirty minutes later, at eight-thirty when it was getting dusky, I heard a helicopter coming up the valley. I sprinted from the trail toward the river hoping I would intercept it. Just as I got out to this great big gravel bar at the river's edge, I turned on the strobe light.

The men saw it and hovered overhead before landing. They signaled me and I got on board. They strapped me in and away we went.

They had me explain where Norm was. We followed Eagle River up to the Crow Creek valley to the X I'd made. We saw a tent—the guy who'd said he was going to help Norm had actually set up camp there. We never saw him, probably because of the alders and stuff he was going through.

We headed up to Norm, and the best thing I ever saw in my life was Norm when he sat up and waved at the helicopter. They picked a landing spot and hovered with one of the helicopter skids on a rock. Two guys exited and ran out of the way while the helicopter rose. They climbed up to Norm and were in radio contact with the helicopter. Then they had us lower a gurney.

The pilot was real helpful and suggested we go to where I had stashed my rifle, my rain gear, and my boots. He said, "Well, let's not leave a gun in the park; let's go pick up your gear."

We flew to the site, but while we hovered, the downwash from the helicopter turned the grass and alders into gyrating waves, covering up any sign of anything being there. There was no way we were going to find my gear.

Pretty soon the guys on the ground called that they had Norm ready, so we returned to them. We dropped a line, they hooked the gurney to the cable, and we slowly wound him up to the helicopter. Of course, the thing was spinning around and around. They finally got him up and inside. What a feeling that was. And then we went back down and landed on that rock with one skid hanging in midair and the two medics jumped into the chopper and away we went to Anchorage.

Twenty minutes later, a little after nine o'clock and just before dark, we landed at Humana, where they took Norm right in. It turned out his leg was broken in three places.

The next day my feet were so bruised from running down the rocks and gravel bar with just the liners on that I could hardly walk. I was really sore, and my daughter Jolene, who was a student attending the University of Alaska, Anchorage, and living in Anchorage, said, "Dad, we'll go up there and get your stuff."

I had explained to her where the X was, so she took a couple friends, Molly and Ben, and they ran up there from the Crow Creek side. It took them all day but they actually found my stuff.

Norm was in the hospital for a few days and had surgery. Now he's doing really well.

We talked about it afterward. I think those ELTs or PLBs (emergency locator transmitter; personal locator beacon) are a pretty good thing to have for immediate help. That might have helped us more, but we were pretty well prepared. Like I said, we have been out a lot together and I go up to Denali quite a bit, so when I go, I like to be prepared.

From falling down mountains to falling out of the sky, events threaten man where life hangs by a thread.

MIRACLE MAN

AS TOLD TO THE AUTHOR BY DOROTHY AND GARY FRANKLIN

*One of the nurses . . . told her to say her good-byes to Gary . . . that you
could not talk, wish, or pray a man as sick as Gary back to health . . .
the only thing that could save him would be a miracle.*

Gary Franklin called me during the winter of 1993–94 and wanted my help
getting published. When I met him at a book signing at Loussac Library in
Anchorage, he wore a clear plastic face mask with holes for nostrils, eyes, and
mouth. His face was ruddy. As he extended his left hand, I noticed his right arm
was crooked as if in a sling. I could not see his right hand and learned that it
was sewn into his midsection to provide a warm, moist environment for his skin
graft to heal.

He was recovering from third-degree burns over 52 percent of his body. He
died six times in the hospital. He and his wife, Dorothy, eagerly shared their
story with me in hopes we could find a publisher for a book about their incredible experience with death . . . and life.

Kaleidoscopic reds and yellows splashed the valley. Dark green tongues of black
spruce licked up the sides of the Talkeetna Mountains from the valley floor, and
golden-leafed aspen, birch, and willow bushes pockmarked the landscape.

The green Arctic Tern, tail numbers 64AT, lifted off the sandbar in the middle
of the Talkeetna River and lumbered into the ominous sky. Pilot Gary Franklin
had taken meticulous measures to lighten his plane because of the short takeoff
distance.

Gary had been told the "strip" was 700 feet long; but on walking it he discovered the usable runway was only 550 feet in length. He opted to leave all his
personal gear behind, found three metal gas cans, and drained as much fuel
from the tanks as the containers would hold. Gary had considered his fuel weight
and the length of the strip before determining he could safely get his plane off
with him and his hunting buddy Scott Weber on board.

Just to be safe, Gary walked three-fourths of the distance down the sandbar
and placed a stick to mark a go/no-go decision point on the strip—he would
taxi for takeoff under full power to that point. If he didn't think the plane would

lift off in the remaining distance, he would pull power and jump on the brakes to abort takeoff.

By 11 A.M. the rainstorm they'd waited to avoid had passed. It was now time to get back to Talkeetna. Scott crawled into the backseat of the tandem two-seater, and Gary took the front seat. With the plane pointing downstream, brakes on, carb heat off, mixture rich, and power at full throttle, Gary released the brakes. The plane bounced along the shore for a couple hundred feet, gaining speed. As the Tern reached and then passed the go/no-go point, Gary felt his speed was good enough to get them off.

At the end of the strip Gary pulled back on the stick and the airplane left the ground. The bush pilot's joy was complete—they were airborne. A few seconds later, however, the airplane settled back toward earth.

The Tern dropped, murky waters rising to meet it. The men had little time to think but hoped the bird would regain altitude. It was not to be. Almost instantly the Tern bounced off the water below, momentarily skipped skyward, then veered into the opposite three-foot, gravel cut bank, shearing its right landing gear. The Tern slammed onto the softball-sized rocks on the bar, striking the belly fuel tank. The tank exploded.

The plane skidded across the rough ground thirty feet before stopping in a ball of fire. The intense heat was unimaginable. Still inside the fuselage, the men were surrounded by flames. Gary threw his hands over his face and screamed. Seconds later he came to his senses, realizing he had to get out of the plane.

He reached for his seat belt and released it. He rolled from the plane and hit the ground rolling. Instantly he realized this maneuver would not work to douse the flames. He ran for the river and dived in headfirst. The cold water doused the fire and provided instant relief.

Rising from the water, Gary's immediate thoughts were of Scott. He looked back at the plane and saw it was totally engulfed in flames. He could not see Scott. Gary's heart died.

Then he saw Scott behind the plane, his clothes and body aflame. Gary ran to Scott and yelled, "Scott! Get into the water!"

Scott was in shock. He stood there with his head down staring at the ground and burning alive. Gary reached Scott, noticed a small puddle of water, and pushed Scott into it. Gary got on Scott's back and forced him down into the water. After Scott rose from the water, Gary determined the fire was out and Scott was more lucid . . . somewhat okay for the moment.

Gary then went back to the river and jumped in to feel the coolness of the water as it soothed his burned flesh.

The men took stock of their wounds while watching the plane burn like an inferno. Scott's hands began bleeding. His face and legs were the most greatly injured.

Gary felt his own skin begin to tighten on his arms, face, back, and chest.

The men discussed their situation. Gary suggested they try to reach a cabin

Gary Franklin's charred airplane frame after the accident. Talkeetna River, Alaska.
CREDIT: *Bruce Hixson*

four miles downriver, although Scott was a little leery. Both realized that Scott's injuries were much worse than they'd previously thought; worse than Gary's.

Just then the plane's fire ignited bullets from their rifles, and the men crossed the river to put distance between them and their wrecked plane. They became wet and started cooling off and sought comfort by retrieving clothes from their packs.

Gary told Scott that the soonest a rescue attempt would be made would be the following day. They decided to go to Scott's cabin.

They crossed the river three more times to reach shore, as the sandbar they'd taken off from was in the middle of the river. They reached the cabin and discovered it was locked, and the keys had been lost in the fire. Gary searched for a way into the cabin, ultimately deciding to break in.

Gary noticed Scott standing and shaking in the sunlight in front of the cabin trying to get warm. Realizing his pal was in deep shock, Gary asked Scott where the ax was. Scott told him it was in the shed near the cabin. The storage shed was also locked, and the only other way into it was to crawl under the cabin for twenty feet, drop three feet into the shed, and return the same way. Gary retrieved the ax and approached the front window.

Three-quarter-inch plywood covered the windows. Gary swung the ax at a section of plywood. The ax smashed into the wood, barely denting it due to the ax's dullness. Gary's hands cried out in pain. He looked at his hands for the first time and found the insides were nothing but blisters. The pain was so great that it almost brought him to his knees. He thought, *I cannot do this.*

Gary turned and saw Scott still standing in the sunlight shaking violently and realized, "I had no other choice." With the ax he started chopping at the window until he broke through.

Gary cleared the window, helped Scott inside the cabin, and laid him down in a sleeping bag on one of the bunk beds. Hoping to warm Scott, Gary started a fire in the stove. As he worked, he thought of the irony of having a fire nearly take their lives only to have to rely upon heat to keep them alive.

Gary wrapped Scott's hands in towels to retard the flow of blood. Recalling his survival training that a person in shock be given water, Gary gave Scott a drink every so often.

Four agonizing hours passed, then Scott started vomiting. Gary thought Scott was in bad shape. He decided to leave Scott to try to reach the downstream cabin. Scott wondered if Gary had the strength to make the trip, and Gary reassured him, "I think so. My legs feel good." Gary left around four in the afternoon.

The first mile and a half wasn't too bad. Although there was a fast current, the river was only midthigh-deep. Every hundred feet or so Gary crossed another ribbon of the stream. Two miles downstream, however, the river presented a drastically different face. Here the ribbons ran together to form one large, deep river.

Gary tried to cross the river but its depth and swiftness were too great. The water was at his armpits, and the current swept him downstream. He was halfway across, his clothes quickly became heavy, and in no time he was waterlogged.

He struggled to keep his head above water. At length he reached the far side and struggled onto the bank exhausted. Gary knew that he was in trouble—he was a long way from either cabin, and it was getting dark. Gary pondered his situation. The river was impassable in his condition. It was getting colder. He needed shelter and heat. There was great danger in continuing; but there was also great danger returning across the channel he'd just survived. He felt his only hope now was to retrace his steps to the cabin.

Gary struggled to reach the distant bank, which took nearly all his strength. He rested on the other side for a while before heading back to his pal. Gary was very weak.

When he finally reached the cabin, he was shaking and the fire was out.

Gary checked Scott, who appeared okay. Gary restarted the fire, then searched for bedding to warm Scott and himself. He found a foam pad, which he put over himself—it wasn't warm but provided some comfort.

Gary spent the rest of the time resting and keeping the fire going. When they ran out of water, Gary toted a five-gallon bucket to the stream for more. It was only fifty feet, but in Gary's condition, it seemed interminably longer.

The next day they ran out of wood, and Gary decided to chop more. His hands still hurt from the beating they'd taken breaking through the window shutter; but he gritted his teeth and chopped.

Gary spent a great deal of time thinking about his family, wondering about their suffering.

Around 4 P.M. the next day, Gary heard the first plane fly over. The plane overflew the crash site several times, convincing Gary the wreckage had been spotted. Shortly the plane left. Gary began doubting. Three hours dragged by before Gary heard a C-130 aircraft overhead. It was circling. Gary knew then that they'd been found.

Nearly three hours later Gary made out the chopping staccato of helicopter blades and knew they'd be rescued.

Approximately twenty-four hours earlier, at 5:45 P.M., Tuesday, September 6, 1993, Gary's wife, Dorothy, had arrived home to an answering machine maxed out with phone messages. Dorothy walked into her kitchen and listened to the first message, left at 10:45 A.M. It told her that Gary's airplane was overdue into Talkeetna and the caller wondered whether she had any information on the whereabouts of the cabin where Gary and Scott stayed during their hunting trips.

She knew that Scott had to be back to work on the evening of the seventh. Gary had also told her he'd call her to check on the family when he reached Talkeetna. Since she hadn't heard from Gary Tuesday, Dorothy almost called Scott's wife to see if he had made it back for work. However, not wanting to alarm Scott's wife, Dorothy did not call. Now she was confused. She knew weather was always a factor and could negate their return. Since Gary wasn't due in Anchorage until the fifteenth, she wasn't too concerned; but she was a bit confused as to why he'd filed a flight plan to be in Talkeetna the night of the seventh.

She waded through all the messages and called the Rescue Coordination Center at Elmendorf Air Force Base north of Anchorage. She gave them the latitude and longitude of the hunting cabin (made easier since Gary always left her a map of his hunting area in case of emergency).

Next Dorothy called her friend Lin Mallonee to let her know that she wouldn't be going to work the next day. Lin drove to Dorothy's to be with her. Dorothy spoke reassuringly to Cory, her daughter. Dorothy called Kulis Air National Guard, Gary's place of employment, to see if anyone there knew any more news.

While Gary and Scott agonized physically and emotionally because of their predicament and while Dorothy sought answers, a rescue was under way. News of an overdue aircraft spread among the flying community. The Rescue Coordinaton Center at Elmendorf notified Kulis Air National Guard that they were initiating a search, even though there were no correlated emergency locator transmitter (ELT) reports by satellites or aircraft in the area and no crashed planes had been seen or reported. Based on Gary's flight plan and communication with his friends and coworkers, the search was focused around Scott Weber's family cabin northeast of Talkeetna.

Maj. Al Olsen of the 210th RQS, who was also qualified in the C-130H, volunteered to fly a training mission for the 144th contingent upon procuring someone to perform search and rescue duty officer (SARDO) duties. Col. Dan Nice volunteered to fulfill this duty. Major Olsen and his crew, Capt. Lyle Langston, M. Sgt. John Forbes, and T. Sgt. Gary Lanham, took off in aircraft #473 ("Scars" 73). They received an update about the search site. Major Olsen diverted from his training flight to the search area, arriving around 1700 hours.

While overflying the area thirty minutes later, Major Olson spotted something below on the gravel bar that had been scouted several times previously. It looked like driftwood from his altitude of fifteen hundred feet. However, he reckoned it could be an aircraft frame.

Olsen alerted the Civil Air Patrol, requesting a Beaver to assist. Those aboard the Beaver spotted the wreckage and concluded it might be a burned plane. There was no suitable landing site for the Beaver, so "Scars" 73, the aircraft Gary Franklin normally flew in, which was now piloted by Major Olsen, climbed to make radio contact with RCC requesting a helicopter.

PJs (pararescue jumpers) were contacted; arrangements were made; and 345 departed to the crash site at 1933 hours. Aboard were CW4 Charlie Hamilton, Capt. Jerry Kidrick, Sgt. Tracey Hartless, SMSgt. Hickson, and M. Sgt. Mahoney. The chopper carried no extra fuel and the sun was descending, which intensified the risk.

Within thirty minutes 345 cruised into the search area. A number of cabins dotted the riverbanks below. They spotted the charred remains of Gary Franklin's Arctic Tern and landed near the river. They found no survivors. Upon searching further they observed footprints leading from the wreckage from either wingtip. Next they found a burned glove near a channel of the river where the tracks ended.

Their consensus was that healthy survivors would have responded to the clatter of the helicopter and the ensuing activity. Since no survivors had made an appearance, and rather than leaving empty-handed, the rescuers decided to approach the several cabins in the area in hopes of finding the survivors.

Maneuvering over uneven terrain PJs Hickson and Mahoney took less than ten minutes to reach the nearest cabin. They knocked on the cabin door and heard what sounded like a groaning old woman. One thought the groan said "Come in" and the other thought it was "Go away." They did not wish to arouse a homesteader's ire. Looking at each other and shrugging, they entered the cabin.

Their discovery was horrifying. The rescuers saw what appeared to be two lumps of grayish black, charcoaled something. They had found the grotesquely burned crash victims.

Gary and Scott were in extreme pain. They'd been vomiting for half a day.

Hickson ran to the chopper for assistance. He informed the others that the crash victims were "load and go" candidates—so critically injured that they could not be treated in the field. The chopper had limited fuel, but Hickson assured Hamilton that they could load the survivors in time.

Hamilton manned the machine. Hickson, Kidrick, and Hartless grabbed a Stokes litter and sleeping bags and headed for the cabin.

While the others worked with Franklin and Weber, Hamilton moved the chopper closer to the cabin to facilitate moving the victims and to save time. Hamilton sat the chopper down within fifty yards of the cabin, one wheel on the riverbank and the other above the river.

An expert medic, Mark Mahoney worked quickly while alone. When the others arrived, they positioned Scott in a sleeping bag and placed him on the litter. All four rescuers grabbed hold of the litter and began their trip to the chopper. Uneven terrain pockmarked by small ravines and gullies and the fading daylight compounded their efforts.

They returned for Gary and completed a second difficult trip.

Chopper 345 lifted off on bingo fuel (with little fuel to spare). They had just enough light to navigate the river valley. As the pilot maneuvered his craft through the mountains to Talkeetna, the PJs took their patients' vital signs and administered oxygen. The cabin was too dark and crowded, and the patients' swelling (edema) made it too difficult for the PJs to administer IVs. Experience taught them that their efforts were an exercise in futility—these burn victims were on their way to another world.

Upon arriving in Talkeetna in pitch darkness, the men were hurriedly transferred to the Providence Life Guard craft and rushed to Anchorage.

Since crashing around noon on the seventh nearly thirty-six hours had elapsed before the survivors arrived at Providence. They were immediately admitted into the burn unit.

Probably the cool temperatures on the river, the moisture of the air and towels, along with drinking the proper amount of water, greatly enhanced their chances of survival.

Around 7 P.M. Dorothy was given some misinformation about the missing plane. A guardsman aboard the C-130 that had spotted Gary's plane told Dorothy the plane was not damaged. Dorothy, Cory, and Lin got excited.

Later Dorothy called RCC and was informed that a helicopter was at the crash site. Dorothy was livid. Because of the misinformation given to her earlier, she was not aware of the crash site. After being on hold for ten minutes, she was told to hang up and that someone would get back to her. Hours later Kenai Flight Service called Dorothy asking for an update on her husband.

Since Dorothy hadn't heard from RCC, she called Gary's work first and was told two burn victims were being transported to Talkeetna (giving rise to the assumption that, since Talkeetna was a small town without a hospital, the victims were not in serious condition). She then called Command and Control at Kulis Air National Guard Base, speaking with Gene Ramsey and begging him to tell her what he knew of the crash site.

Not until Bob Gastrock of Kulis Air National Guard Base called her back did she know that Gary and Scott were being transported via life flight to Providence Hospital in Anchorage.

Bob Gastrock called Dorothy's next-door neighbor Carolyn Wells requesting she drive Dorothy to the hospital. In turn, Dorothy called her friend Teri Osterkamp and asked her to meet her at Providence. Lin Mallonee stayed with Cory.

When they reached the hospital, Dorothy was met by Keith Douglas and Mike Heller, both of whom worked at Kulis Air National Guard with Gary. The duty nurse kept them informed about the life flight aircraft's position.

Later the nurse came to the waiting room to tell the group that Gary had arrived. She gave Dorothy his gold necklace and wallet. Once Gary and Scott were stabilized, the nurse informed the group what to expect and that they could see Gary and Scott.

Gary seemed alert. He asked Dorothy if he could get the boat he'd been wanting for some time. He also asked her if she'd hung the picture he gave her before his trip. He wanted her to retrieve his watch from his shirt's left pocket— she dug the shirt from the garbage to find his watch (the discarded shirt had been cut away to treat his wounds).

Gary wanted to see the other visitors, so they filed by one at a time. He made jokes and told everyone he would be okay.

Gary wanted to see his daughter Cory and told Dorothy to ask the doctor when that would be possible. He suggested waiting a few days to assess Gary's recovery.

Dorothy felt Gary would be fine. She did not share the same hope for Scott, whose face was black and who trembled constantly.

Dorothy sat with Gary for an hour before the smell of burnt flesh overcame her. Whenever she became nauseated, she put her head between her knees and the nurses gave her juice to keep her from passing out.

On the morning of the ninth Dorothy left the hospital around 4 A.M. From her home she contacted the family members. She told Cory the truth about her father.

Even though Cory wanted to see her father badly, it wasn't time. Dorothy took Cory to school and encouraged her to make a get-well card for him, hoping it would help her feel that she was doing something for her father. Dorothy returned to the hospital.

Gary's body was so swollen that she barely recognized him. He asked her where she had spent the night, and she broke down. She felt so helpless and scared. Her first husband had died in a small-airplane accident seven years earlier. While she cried, a nurse put an arm around her and comforted her (as many other nurses would do in the days to come).

On the ninth of September, Gary's medical attendees inserted a feeding tube through his nose to his lower intestine. Somehow the tube got coiled up around the back of Gary's throat, causing him to cough and gag. It was difficult for Dorothy to witness Gary's gasping for air, convulsing.

On the tenth the medical attendees removed Gary's breathing tube, allowing him to speak. He requested food and plenty of chocolate milk. Dorothy was thrilled to hear him. Gary told Dorothy to take a hundred dollars from his wallet and get chocolate milk.

Gary wanted to be with Scott so much that he requested he be able to room with Scott, who was scheduled for his first surgery the thirteenth of September.

When Dorothy arrived at the hospital with daughters Cindy, twenty-five, and Tina, twenty-three, on the thirteenth, Gary had eaten most of his breakfast and was resting well. He sent Dorothy to the store for ice cream and more chocolate milk. He talked and joked with his daughters.

Later that day Gary had his first skin graft. The surgery lasted nearly eight hours and went well. Dorothy and Tina stayed with Gary until 10:30 P.M., when they left for Anchorage International Airport to pick up Dorothy's father. (Tina and Cindy were scheduled to leave early the next morning.)

When Dorothy arrived at the hospital the next day, she was surprised to learn that the doctor had had to insert a tube to Gary's stomach to remove some excess from the feeding tube. Gary was upset about another tube.

Dorothy's father saw Gary in the hospital for the first time on the fourteenth. When he entered Gary's room, Gary's parents were present. It was so difficult seeing Gary in his condition that Dorothy's father left immediately.

Gary's next scheduled surgery was for his left arm on the seventeenth. Dorothy went to be with him at 4 A.M. and on the way to the hospital observed the northern lights brighter than she'd ever seen them. Burn nurses Kathy and Scott took Gary at 6:15 for his tubing before his 8:30 surgery. Kathy (from the surgery unit) debrided (peeled skin) from Gary's face while he was in surgery. Gary did have some fluid in his lungs after surgery, but it was nothing to be alarmed about, they said. In recovery they removed the breathing tube.

The next day Gary told Dorothy, "Get me out of here. They are doing nothing but making me worse." He did not remember the surgeries he had been through nor what was going on around him (was he hallucinating?). He was combative with the nurses, although he rested well when Dorothy was in the room.

Gary's mother, Della, noticed that his left foot was very swollen. When a burn nurse, Ruth changed the dressing on his leg, she noticed the extent of the swelling.

They called in a specialist to do an ultrasound of Gary's left leg. They then discovered that Gary had a blood clot in his leg caused by the femoral arterial line's having been in his leg for too long. They immediately started him on heparin (blood thinner). This started a whole other chain reaction.

Dorothy was upset that day and called her friend Lin to come sit with her while Gary had his dressing changes. In the meantime burn nurse Ruth came to the waiting room after changing the dressings and told Dorothy that Gary had kicked her to keep her away from him. She knew something was really wrong. Gary had been a good patient up to that point.

At 4:30 P.M. that afternoon Dorothy went into Gary's hospital room with their oldest daughter, Tracy. Gary was having difficulty breathing and wanted Dorothy to take the oxygen mask from his mouth in order to tell her something.

The nurses would not allow anyone to remove the oxygen mask. Then Dorothy noticed that Gary's oxygen level was low. Dorothy asked his nurse Ruth what to look for if a piece of a blood clot had broken off and lodged in Gary's lungs. Ruth replied, "Shortness in breath, lowering of blood pressure."

Gary displayed those very symptoms. His blood pressure was 71/50. Ruth started to administer dopamine, a drug to elevate blood pressure. She called in a few other nurses and escorted Dorothy and Tracy from the room. Within a few minutes the loudspeakers declared, "Code 99. Room 2026."

The implications were clear to Dorothy and Tracy. Gary had stopped breathing. Dorothy sat on the waiting-room floor praying. She couldn't understand why God would bring Gary back to her only to take him away ten days later.

The nurses revived Gary, then called the head doctor, Dr. Hood, who was in surgery with another burn patient. He went into the waiting room and put his arm around Dorothy, assuring her that he would do all that he could for Gary. After reviving Gary, the first thing that they did was to insert a line in his heart to measure the pressure of the blood flow. Dr. Hood had called in four specialists to confer about Gary.

At first the attendees thought a piece of a clot had broken off and traveled to Gary's lungs. They spoke of open-heart surgery to remove the clot, giving him a fifty-fifty chance for survival if they operated. He had hard plastic forms on his arms to keep him from disrupting the skin grafts. Because he was trying to hit people with his arms, they had to tie down his arms for his own safety. They had given Gary a paralyzing drug to counteract his fighting them should they put him in a ventilator.

Dr. Hood had called a "bug" doctor, who had given Gary antibiotics to counter "septicemia." Another doctor reviewed the chest X rays, and a third, Dr. Hummel, reviewed Gary's adrenal level. He noticed the level was low and administered a large dose of cortisone.

At 1 A.M. Dr. Hummel approached the family in the waiting room and told them there was nothing more they could do for Gary. Hummel told Dorothy that Gary's stomach and kidneys had shut down and that he was assisted in breathing by a ventilator. Hummel told Dorothy that Gary's blood pressure was falling rapidly.

Tracy and Dorothy went to Gary's room to see him. It was sad. He looked so fragile, far from the big, burly Gary Franklin his friends and family knew. Tubes hung from him and machines were hooked to him. He was completely surrounded by medical personnel. They worked without speaking. Dorothy's heart broke; she thought she would die.

One of the nurses went to Dorothy and told her to say her good-byes to Gary. The nurse said there was nothing more they could do . . . that you could not talk, wish, or pray a man as sick as Gary back to health. She said that the only thing that could save him would be a miracle. She single-handedly crushed all the hopes that the family had.

Tracy went to work on her dad. She was not about to give up on him without a fight. She hollered at him telling him not to leave her. She reminded him of the father-and-daughter Brownie Banquet that he had flown into town to attend with her. His blood pressure was 75/43 when Tracy entered the room with Dorothy. Within an hour it began to rise.

Whether it was the medication or the coaching of his daughter or all the prayer groups that were called in the middle of the night to pray for Gary, a miracle transpired.

When Dr. Hood arrived the next morning, even he was surprised to see that Gary was still alive. Tracy was still talking to her father; she and Gary's father had stayed with Gary all night.

A few days later Gary was improving remarkably. Fellow workers from Gary's office stopped by to see him. Charlie Brenton and Lloyd Ruiz sat with Dorothy for hours at Gary's bedside one afternoon. On the afternoon of the twenty-second of September the nurses removed the air tube from Gary's right nostril.

Over the next few days Gary became quiet and would not speak. On the morning of the twenty-seventh Dorothy's father and Dorothy went into the hospital early. Dorothy's father was leaving Alaska and wanted to say good-bye to Gary. Dorothy had a really bad feeling.

Gary didn't wake up to speak to them as he had whenever they had come into the room previously. Dorothy took her father to the airport to catch his plane. When she returned to the hospital, she looked at the monitor machine; Gary's heart rate was dropping from one hundred down to the fifties and sixties. She called the nurses, who in turn called in Dr. Hood.

They all tried to get Gary to open his eyes, but he wouldn't. The family minister stopped by to pray with them. He is a retired doctor. Based on Gary's symptoms, he suspected a subdermal hematoma. He suggested a CAT scan be done.

Dr. Hood took Gary down to the CAT scan unit. Incredibly, the blood thinner had started a blood clot on the brain to bleed, creating a buildup of blood and fluid and causing the left side of Gary's brain to swell.

Dr. Kralick was called to perform emergency brain surgery.

The doctors told Dorothy that Gary would probably not be able to speak or that he might enter a coma as a result of the bleeding. They cautioned her that he might be "a little slow."

They drilled two holes about the size of a quarter, one in the front on the left side and the other in the back of the left side of his head. The drainage tube was in the back hole. The other hole was stapled shut.

The families were called in once again to sit in the waiting room. The surgery was a success. Tracy and Dorothy went to see Gary. Tracy held Dorothy's hand and told her she had a good feeling about the surgery. The nurses told Dorothy that Gary would be sedated for up to twenty-four hours and suggested she go home to rest. Dorothy left to visit Cory, calling throughout the night and the next morning to check on her husband.

The next morning when Tracy and Dorothy arrived, the first thing Gary did when he saw them was to give them the thumbs-up sign. Dr. Hood advised Dorothy that Gary might have problems speaking. She asked him if it made a difference that Gary was sounding out words and writing them on a dry erase board. Dr. Hood smiled and told her that Gary was going to be fine.

Since Gary had to have the surgery for the blood in his head, they had to take Gary off the blood thinner to try to stop any further bleeding. On the twenty-ninth they installed a drainage bulb in his head to try to get out as much of the blood as possible. Dorothy elected to have a bird's nest installed in the main vein from the leg into the stomach, which would intercept any clots and keep them from the heart or lungs.

Gary was awake during this procedure and told Dorothy he was watching a cool movie (causing her to wonder if he knew what was going on).

On the thirtieth they performed an echo on Gary's heart through his esophagus, to see if the heart was affected by the bacterial spray. The echo was normal. Dorothy's reaction was to "thank the Good Lord."

On October 3 Cory turned six years old. It was the first time she was to see her father since his accident. Dorothy tried hard to prepare Cory for what she was to see. When Cory walked into the room, she put her arm around her father. Gary told her that he had gotten a little sick but that he was going to be fine.

Cory kissed his cheek and told him she loved him. There was not a dry eye in the room, including Gary's.

Epilogue

A few years after I met Gary, I read the April 1998 issue of *Guideposts* magazine, which included a one-page expression that Gary's hunting partner and accident companion, Scott Weber of Anchorage, had written. Titled "The Divine Touch," it is reprinted below.

The night before Gary and I flew back to Talkeetna, Alaska, from a hunting trip, my mother had a disturbing dream. Had I known about her dream, I would never have gotten into Gary's two-seater Arctic Tern the next morning.

Gary Franklin and I worked as aircraft mechanics at Kulis Air National Guard Base. We had taken a few days off to hunt moose up the Talkeetna River, in the remote interior of Alaska, where I had use of a friend's cabin.

Seconds after we lifted off the makeshift wilderness airstrip that September morning in 1993, headed for home, an incredible jolt slammed the plane back down. Wind shear! We smacked the surface of the river, losing our landing gear,

Gary Franklin recovering from skin grafts in his backyard. Behind him is the fuselage frame of his aircraft, retrieved from the river.
CREDIT: *Don Franklin*

then skipped like a stone before hurtling across a gravelly sandbar at sixty miles an hour. The belly fuel tank erupted in flames. Instantly the plane was engulfed. As we skidded to a stop, Gary screamed, "Get out! Get out!" and dove out of the door.

Seated behind him, I struggled with my safety belt. I saw my hands catch fire, my skin burning like paper, as I fumbled frantically with the red-hot buckle. *Jammed!* Pain tore through me and I heard myself scream. Hot smoke seared my lungs. I wasn't going to make it out! *Dear God, forgive me my sins . . .*

Suddenly a firm hand took hold of my left shoulder. Gary! The next thing I knew I was standing outside, a short distance from the blazing wreckage. I threw myself on the ground, trying to smother the flames. Gary dragged me to the river and made me lie in the freezing water. Finally he helped me up. We stared at each other, our clothes burned away, our skin charred and raw. We were in desperate need of help.

It would be another day before a rescue helicopter reached us, and months of agonizing treatment before we could resume normal lives. But something Gary told me made the terrible pain more bearable. When I thanked him for helping me out of the plane, he insisted it hadn't been him.

"I was thirty feet away, rolling on the ground," he said. "I never went near the plane."

And while I was in the hospital, my mother told me about her dream.

"Scottie," she said, her voice tight with emotion, "I dreamed you were in danger. I didn't know what had happened, but I knew you needed help. I woke up, knelt by my bed, and prayed for God to protect you."

At last I knew whose hand had pulled me from the flames.

Many adventurers need a helping hand. All of the victims in the following story could have used hands of support.

DEATH STALKED
THE EDGE

BY LARRY KANIUT

A few minutes passed, then I heard a terrifying scream, followed by a loud whump! *Then silence.*

It seems as if I've gathered adventure stories forever. In July of 1991 the *Anchorage Times* carried a piece about Loretta Andress's hiking accident. I contacted her friend and climbing companion Stanley Truelson, who wrote back encouraging me to contact her. He stated, "Even though this experience was traumatic for us and hazardous for Loretta, we're not sure it is so unusual as to qualify for book mention, but you are the judge of that."

That it was not "unusual" is the precise reason I wanted to include her story. I met with Loretta and Stan at Stan's home in Anchorage December 6, 1998. I told them I wanted to incorporate her story with two others to illustrate how easily the casual becomes catastrophic. A month prior to her accident a young man named Chris Flood fell to his death in virtually the same location. And a year later another young man died from a fall on Flattop. Those two stories follow this one.

Loretta and Stan took turns telling me their story. She started.

What began as a pleasant hike ended painfully July 8, 1991. Our party of six included my twin sister, Loraine; our father; two visitors from Indiana; Stan; and myself. We arrived around 1:45 P.M. at the Glen Alps parking-lot trailhead. Flattop Mountain is roughly fifteen miles southeast of Anchorage. After assembling our hiking paraphernalia and after some last minute chitchat, we started the gradual climb toward Flattop's peak.

We traditionally hiked Flattop every year. It's just over thirty-five hundred feet in elevation. The trail weaves through clumps of dark green mountain hemlock and fifteen-foot-high alder brush for the first quarter mile or so. Then the trail leaves the hemlock and alder patches behind and climbs up through the alpine. Rocks cover the ground throughout the hike. When you break over the top, the peak is relatively flat and covers an area the size of a football field. Baseball-to-football-sized rocks litter area.

Flattop is Alaska's most climbed peak, probably because of its easy access from Anchorage. Although it is a steep climb, it is relatively safe. Though a steady mist was making the slope slippery, it was not significant enough to arouse a fear of falling.

On the way up our party formed into two groups. Stan and I were in the lead. As we neared the top, fog settled in and we could see only a few dozen yards. At the top we walked around, then rested while waiting for the others. A short time later and before the others appeared, we decided to go down.

Because of the dense fog, we couldn't see the well-used trail we'd come up. However even though we weren't sure of the exact direction, we knew going down would eventually take us to the car . . . or at least that we could see better below to get our bearings. We were unsure whether the trail was right, left, or straight ahead; so we started edging over to the right. I was partway down the steep slope, picking my way among boulders and cliffs, when it happened.

I started to step across some rocks to find a better way down but changed my mind. As I stepped back, my backpack scraped the rocks behind me, throwing me off balance. My backpack contained a couple of plastic jars of water, a sweatshirt, and some Band-Aids. It stuck out just enough to trigger my fall and send me off the rock and into space.

Stan then continued: Loretta got ahead and was soon out of sight in the fog. A few minutes passed, then I heard a terrifying scream, followed by a loud *whump!* Then silence.

I called, but there was no answer. Trying to stifle the panic I felt, I worked my way down as fast as I could. The footing was difficult in places. Once or twice the drop down was farther than I could stretch my legs, and I had to try going sideways while hanging on with my fingertips. It seemed like fifteen minutes before I caught sight of her at the bottom of a scree slide. She was sitting up, thank goodness, facing downward away from me. I called, "Are you all right?"

Without turning she answered, "No." Later, she told me she had also asked me to look for her shoes, but I didn't hear that.

After another five or ten minutes, I edged beside and just below her, so as not to kick loose rocks on her. Her face was covered with blood from gashes over her eye and on her head. Blood showed below the edge of her T-shirt. She said she couldn't walk and thought her ankle was broken. She was in her stocking feet, her sneakers having flown off during the fall.

Neither of us wore really warm clothes, because we had expected to keep moving and they would be too hot. But sitting still for a long time in that cool, damp weather could cause hypothermia. The sweatshirt in her pack was soaked because the plastic water bottles had broken during her fall. I left her my thin windbreaker and started down for help. I was worried that it would be hard when returning to find her. She called, half-joking, "Take care of the cats for me."

Not knowing which direction to go to find the trail, I first started right. After fifteen or twenty minutes, the fog lifted and I saw a mountain range in the distance, which I soon realized was the O'Malley Range across the Powerline Trail. I was far to the right of where I should have been. After that it was a matter of working back around the side of Flattop to the left. Finally crossing the trail, I could start down toward the parking lot.

Luckily, I passed two separate pairs of ascending hikers. I told each group that Loretta had fallen above, to the left of the trail. Loretta called out after I left, and one of these pairs found and assisted her.

Nothing is so frustrating as wanting desperately to move faster and not being able to. The parking lot was empty of people, although our party's cars were still there. There was no emergency phone, so I headed up the road to a cluster of homes at Glen Alps a quarter mile away. The first house had a steep driveway with a FOR SALE sign out front. Maybe nobody there, I thought, but I tried it anyway, ringing the bell and banging on the door. A woman came out on the deck above and then came down to let me in. It had taken an hour to reach a telephone.

The emergency dispatcher on 911 transferred me to the Alaska State Troopers, who are in charge of emergencies in the park. After fifteen minutes of conversation, waiting, and more conversation, they were ready to let me hang up. At that moment a state trooper who had been in the area investigating a robbery knocked on the door. He drove me back to the parking lot. Within ten minutes we heard the sirens of a fire engine and an emergency medical vehicle on their way.

It seemed frustratingly long while the paramedics picked over their supplies and equipment, selecting what they would take with them. Ten or fifteen minutes later we finally started up the path, just as we hikers had done earlier in the afternoon.

Half or a third of the way up we met Loretta's father, sister, and the two friends coming slowly down. They had reached the top after we had started down on the wrong side and wondered where we were. I was wearing an oversize coat and a baseball cap (lent by the woman at the house and another woman in the parking lot) to keep the rain off my glasses. I took off the cap to help them recognize me in this group of EMTs and a trooper. The first thing I said was, "She's going to be all right."

Loraine immediately turned around to join our rescue party as we continued upward. The trooper started to persuade her that it really wasn't necessary to come along, but when I explained "twin sister," he changed his mind.

The fog had lifted enough to give a good view. I was sure that we had a long way to go up and was doubtful it could be Loretta when Loraine spotted some people in an open area at about our elevation far to the left. I couldn't hold her binoculars still enough to tell if someone was lying on the ground next to the two people standing up, but we soon decided that Loretta was there.

The team cut left and moved slowly around the slope, where the going was fairly easy. I followed more slowly; my legs were not in shape for a second climb

An injured Loretta Andress and Stanley Truelson.
CREDIT: *Loraine Andress*

that day. As we approached the site, a rescue helicopter from the Air National Guard came into view and began hovering near the top of the mountain. It finally moved to an area below where Loretta was lying and landed.

Even before the hikers found her, Loretta had started scooting slowly downhill on her seat. They carried her part of the way, slipping once. They reached a place above the tree line where they could be seen and that was fairly flat for landing the helicopter.

The rest of the rescue was efficient and smooth. Loretta's neck and back were splinted by the time I arrived. Then she was strapped into a stretcher and moved to the helicopter's larger stretcher. Loraine led the way, and I just tried to keep out of the way.

Loretta concluded:

After I stopped rolling and falling, I ended up sitting with my knees bent and my hands to my head. Then I noticed blood dripping from my head. That's the first inkling I had of possibly serious injuries. And that scared me. I had no idea what my condition was. Once I'd been sitting a while, the broken rib made itself very evident. I wasn't comfortable sitting still, so I tried to scoot down the hill.

The helicopter transported me to the hospital. My injuries included a chipped bone in the ankle, a broken toe, broken ribs, shoulder and knee infections. Stitches were taken in my head (for several inch-long cuts) and in my leg (for a gash below the knee) and in one arm. I was released the next day. My minor injuries took about a week to heal sufficiently to allow me to return to work. I was in good spirits. Later I had surgery on my shoulder, an ankle, and a knee that I'd injured previously.

Epilogue

I'd probably hiked Flattop at least twenty or thirty times. My accident had nothing to do with unfamiliarity with the mountain but rather with the fog that blocked the view of the trail. On the top, where all the rocks are, much of the terrain looks the same, but farther down the trail is very definite. We probably did start down in the correct direction but, as we moved along, began angling to the right.

Stan added, "It's best not to guess in a fog."

How could the hikers have known the outcome of their casual hike ... that a single mistake could lead to disaster? And what about the other hikers on the mountain that day, especially those eyewitnesses who saw Christopher Flood fall and bounce down the mountain?

When I learned one of my tenth-grade English students, Mindy Stephenson,

The rescue team taking Loretta out on a stretcher.
CREDIT: *Stanley Truelson*

witnessed Chris's accident, I asked her if she'd want to summarize her experience. Following is the story Mindy wrote in 1992, which she called "Tragedy on the Mountain."

Although June 13, 1991, was a beautiful day in Anchorage, Alaska, clouds had rolled in, covering the trail to Flattop Mountain, a few miles southeast of the city.

On this day my mother, Joanne Stephenson, was celebrating her forty-first birthday. She likes to take the time on her birthday to get out of the house and do some of the activities that she never seems to have time for, so we left home just after noon and headed up the hillside to meet my cousins and to hike to Flattop.

We met Paul Lidren and Robin Chapman in the Glen Alps parking lot, the jumping-off point for the trail that leads to Flattop. Zac, my little brother, my mom, and I rounded out the group.

We four teenagers scrambled up the trail as Mom took her time. It was the first official day of summer. We hiked in short-sleeved shirts and enjoyed the seventy-degree weather. Most of our party wore shorts, T-shirts, and tennis shoes. My mom wore long cotton pants. We were having a lot of fun as we were running and laughing up the trail. We thought we had heard a scream in the distance but we weren't positive.

Twenty minutes into our hike, we saw a lady and a little boy running down the mountain off the given trail toward us. We were kind of surprised because they weren't on the main trail, which Mom had told us to stay on. The lady and the little boy were running down a shale slide toward the bottom of the mountain.

Several hundred yards below us on the trail, my mom had heard the yelling, but it wasn't until she met the lady and boy that she found out what had happened. Mom suddenly picked up speed and waved us down.

She told us there had been an accident up ahead and explained we needed to help if at all possible. The lady was looking for someone with advanced medical training. She and her young boy, who was approximately eight years old, were going to look for help in the parking lot, which was about a mile below the spot where Mom and the lady had met. Mom told us that a young boy had fallen near the top of Flattop Mountain and was seriously injured. He would probably require a doctor or a medical professional.

There were few climbers that day and this lady, who was not with the injured party, just happened to be up top when the victim and his father were ascending.

The major drawback was the location of the accident. The lady said the youth would be extremely hard to find as he had fallen behind a ledge, and unless we chose the correct route to the top, we probably wouldn't see him. The young boy's father was trying to reach him when the lady headed out for help.

We hurried up the trail, tension building. We traveled in the direction of the scream we thought we had heard earlier. We wanted to go around a face of the mountain off the beaten path. Mom was having a fit and eventually made us circle back and meet her to continue up the main route.

Meantime, we came in contact with two other runners coming up the trail. They were in excellent shape. We told them what was going on. We couldn't see the boy or his father down any of the gullies. No one was really sure of the exact location of the accident; the lady only had indicated it was on the back side of a ledge. We searched in vain. It was a horrible feeling not to be able to help or locate the youth.

Rescue personnel began running up the mountains and a rescue helicopter circled time and time again. First, the chopper focused on the back side of the middle mountain, finally working over the upper mountain. After twenty minutes of searching they spotted the boy, and the helicopter landed at the base of the upper mountain.

Another chopper, a Huey, was advancing our way as we sat on the ledge to the right of the victim, approximately five hundred feet above him. The Huey had afternoon winds to contend with and the location of the accident made the rescue very difficult.

A Channel 2 News helicopter circled from high above. The helicopters were loud and they were stirring up dust and creating winds. Time continued to pass. It had been a couple of hours since the accident, and the boy lay motionless at the bottom of a ravine. Several media personnel arrived and talked with our group as we watched the rescue together. My mom was interviewed (and later quoted) by the *Anchorage Times* regarding the accident. The boys and several medical people attended to the youth, including a doctor in a suit who had hurried up the path. Once rescuers knew the location of the boy, they selected a safer route that bypassed a five-hundred-foot steep cliff.

We felt helpless, but worried. What could anyone do to hurry up the rescue? It seemed like eternity before the boy was strapped in the litter and hoisted into the hovering helicopter. The chopper then sped off to the hospital.

We were told that the boy was climbing straight down a rock face when he hit a snow patch, and slipped and fell. Sliding out of control, he hit his head on the way down the rock face. Medical and rescue people think he was unconscious due to his head injuries when he landed in the ravine.

Even though every effort was made to keep the young boy alive, he died two days later at Providence Hospital.

Flattop Mountain is a great hike under good conditions and *if* people stay on the marked trail. I think more trail markers could be added. This particular day in early June the trail was difficult to determine at several points. Also the weather can change instantly on that mountain, and one should always be prepared for windy conditions. It is nice to know this trail in the Chugach Mountains is still as popular today as it was back in the early 1970s when my mom first attempted the climb.

*　　*　　*

Christopher Flood was a wonderful little boy and will be greatly missed. He was the second youngest of five children born to Debby and Jim Flood. Chris actively enjoyed life and pursued baseball and soccer. He was very good with other kids and received several good citizenship awards at Rabbit Creek Elementary School.

When the nine-year-old hiked Flattop Mountain on Thursday, June 13, 1991, he joined his father, Jim; his seven-year-old sister, Jennifer, and her dog; and a Cub Scout friend. They reached the summit of the mountain and started down.

Evidently just below the summit, before 1 P.M., Chris slipped on the rock or snow in a steep couloir. The snow packing the gully accelerated Chris's speed, sending him out of control. He bounced against rocks like a ball in a pinball machine and ended up in the rock heap at the bottom of the snowfield.

His father, Jim, sent Jennifer down the mountain to the Glen Alps parking lot with two hikers, then he climbed into the gully to assist Chris. When his father reached him, Chris's pulse was irregular and his breathing was weak. Chris had suffered massive head injuries and a broken pelvis.

A helicopter from Providence Hospital thundered onto the scene but was unable to reach the lad because of the steep terrain.

Then Capt. Riff Patton showed up piloting a huge Pavehawk helicopter belonging to the 210th Air Rescue Squadron at Kulis Air National Guard in Anchorage. Battling tricky crosswinds, Patton hovered twenty-five to fifty feet off the northwest wall. Paramedic Steve Lupenski descended the ship's hoist on the steel cable to assist Alaska State Troopers and other rescuers on the ground, including Providence Hospital Lifeguard nurses, Alaska State Troopers, Anchorage emergency medical technicians, firefighters, and private citizens.

Working against the clock to stabilize Chris for movement over the steep and rough ground, the rescuers loaded him onto a helicopter, which rushed him to Providence Hospital. Jim Flood rode on another chopper to be with his son.

Even with medical treatment Chris couldn't be saved. Doctors declared him legally dead, however Christopher's family wanted to keep his body on life support pending organ donations.

Hopefully the pain of Chris's loss will heal in time and his donated organs as well as his story will bring longer life to those who receive them.

The dangers that surround us became glaringly evident again the first week in June 1992 when "A twenty-year-old man fell to his death while scrambling along a craggy, steep wall on Flattop Mountain Sunday."(6)

Climbing instructor Greg Thoelke was on the mountain when the fallen hiker's partner approached him. Greg said, "All of a sudden, this kid came busting out of the trees, screaming, 'I need help, my partner's dead, he's fallen off the rocks.' "(6)

Greg commented that the injured man "was way out there . . . To be climbing in the area where that guy was, you need (climbing equipment) and a professional . . . It's just not safe to be in that area without equipment."(6) Thoelke referred to the area as "Chugach crud" and said, "Whole rocks that you think are gonna offer you a handhold just fall apart in your hands."(6)

Thoelke whistled to his partners below, and while they ran for help, he focused his binoculars on the injured hiker.

A doctor climbing in the area made his way to the fallen man and found him dead.

Alaska State Troopers did not identify the victim since next of kin had not been notified.

The popular trail is climbed by eight thousand-plus hikers a year.

During a church group's winter outing on December 31, 1973, an avalanche rumbled down the west face of Flattop in the afternoon. The group's chaperone, thirty-five-year-old Patrick McDaniel, was killed, and several others were injured. Later the location was named Death Gully.

When you leave your driveway in Alaska, you'd better be prepared because danger stalks the land . . . as the kayakers of Blackstone Bay discovered.

DATE WITH DEATH

BY LARRY KANIUT

Where danger lurks, death can't be far behind.

On a weekend where camaraderie and adventure were the main course, the grim reaper served up a rotten egg.

Three Alaskans entertained three visiting friends from San Francisco. The group planned to kayak in Prince William Sound. The outing was an opportunity to see some of Alaska and to get to know each other better. They would take the train to Whittier, their jumping-off point, forty miles southeast of Anchorage. From there a charter boat would transport them, their kayaks, and gear to Blackstone Bay, where they could kayak at their leisure. Blackstone Bay runs thirteen miles northeasterly from the face of Blackstone Glacier to the mouth of the bay. The fjord is a couple of miles wide. They anticipated no problems, as any danger from possible rough water in Passage Channel would be eliminated by utilizing the charter boat.

The group planned to spend a couple of days in the sheltered waters of the bay out of reach of the wilder waters around the mouth and beyond. Once they reached Whittier, they met their charter and quickly made their way to Blackstone Bay.

Picture this. Six kayakers gliding over the green-blue waters of the bay, green-black spruce trees climbing from the salt water up the slopes, and a wall of glacial ice, its face riddled with huge cracks, that dissected the timber and spilled into the bay.

The six pleasure seekers were divided into four kayaks—two double sea kayaks and two single kayaks. Michael Seblusky and his brother Greg manned one of the doubles, and Billy Herzberg and Judy Marantz paddled the other; Beth Phillips and Carol Rothstein each paddled singles.

It was Michael's second kayak trip. An attorney, he had come to Alaska within the past year or so to work for the Public Defender Agency in Anchorage. He had invited his brother Greg and friends Billy and Judy from San Francisco. This trip was the first time kayaking for the three. Carol was Michael's girlfriend, and she had limited experience. Beth was the most experienced of the group, having kayaked for several years.

During their activities on Sunday, the group agreed that the seas were rough. In spite of that, they'd had no problems. When they camped for the night, they were assaulted by powerful winds that pounded their tent. They were not overly eager to spend much more time "camping"—some of the group just wanted to go home.

Their sleeping bags were wet, their food supply low, the wind never ceased, and they got little sleep. All in all it made for a pretty miserable night. Home sounded good.

By Monday morning there had been little change in the blustery weather. The unrelenting wind kept up a steady drumbeat. Gray clouds swept by overhead and a constant drizzle fell on the campers. Pounding seas turned the normally calm bay into a boiling froth.

In some ways it seemed they were trapped on the bay. It wasn't calm but it didn't seem as rough as the day before.

By the time they decided to leave for their appointed rendezvous, they had spent several hours sitting on the beach and glassing the bay with binoculars.

Phillips was aware of the group's lack of experience and limitations and struggled with the decision to leave. She'd kayaked here years earlier in 1984 and 1985 and had made a number of outings in between. The others were novices.

Even though she felt the group lacked the necessary experience to face the rough waters, the more inexperienced in the group felt the water had calmed and they could make it. It would be hard but safe.

The kayakers launched from a cove on the west shore and into the ebb tide and the wind-pushed waves between the shore and Willard Island, a mile distant. Their objective was Decision Point, the north point joining Blackstone Bay and Passage Channel, where the charter boat would pick them up.

Once off the beach, the group recognized the immensity of the waves and the impossibility of their task. They wondered if the waves were that large earlier or if the increasing wind had created bigger waves.

Phillips was the only one who had any control of her craft. She tried unsuccessfully to warn the others to hug the shore in case of problems. They couldn't hear her because of the overpowering winds. The others headed for Willard Island. She followed. Their decision placed them in immediate jeopardy because the seas came from the rear, and they couldn't see the approaching waves.

With her back to the seas, it was impossible for Phillips to see the huge wave that swept toward her and knocked her over. Dumped from her kayak into the frigid waters, she felt its breathtaking and deathlike grip. Beth knew life expectancy in the glacial water was only ten to fifteen minutes. She floundered to the surface looking for her kayak. It was gone.

Her only choice was to swim and drift with the tide downwind to a beach on the island. By the time she neared shore, she was hypothermic and hyperventilating. She crawled onto the rocky shore of Willard Island, dragging herself along until she was able to stand.

Stumbling along the beach, she found a kayak paddle and used it as a crutch. She awkwardly shuffled down the beach and spotted a double kayak floating upside down a hundred yards off the shoreline.

Before long Carol Rothstein came to shore in her water-filled kayak. She shook with hypothermia and Phillips helped her to shore. They embraced and discovered that both were as cold as ice.

Then Phillips noticed objects floating ashore: "I was afraid they were people."(1)

That's when she discovered Greg's body floating facedown near the beach. Then Beth spotted Mike's body floating twenty to thirty feet offshore. She thought both brothers were dead.

She forced herself back into the water to bring the brothers' bodies to shore. Carol was so hypothermic that Phillips didn't ask her to help. Beth said, "I thought I had lost two friends and I was about to lose another."(1)

By then Herzberg and Marantz had reached the shore safely. Marantz was an intern in a San Francisco hospital. They worked as a team and administered CPR for hours to the brothers. Although color returned to their friends' faces, their first-aid efforts failed to bring the brothers back to life.

Phillips then went looking for the kayak that contained a Thermos of hot tea and a sleeping bag. Phillips retrieved both and returned to the group. Marantz crawled into the bag with Rothstein. They poured hot tea down Carol to warm her up, and she began coming around by early evening.

When the group failed to meet their charter at the appointed time and place, the Prince William Sound Kayak Center alerted authorities of missing kayakers. The Coast Guard requested Alaska Department of Fish and Game to respond with a boat.

The Fish and Game boat rescued the group and took them to Whittier, where they received excellent care. Mike and Greg Seblusky's bodies were flown to California.

Epilogue

Beth Phillips admitted the group's haste to return clouded their judgment. She admitted it was a better weekend to camp than to paddle.

Initially Phillips was reluctant to be a part of the outing. In retrospect she thought if she'd stayed home, the others wouldn't have gone. She said, "I feel awful . . . I should not have agreed to go with so many beginners."(2)

Hopefully this pain of loss will be lessened with time and others can escape such agony without thinking that "it could never happen to me."

IT WILL NEVER
HAPPEN TO ME

AS TOLD TO THE AUTHOR BY MIKE WISE

*The next thing I saw was the sky when the rear of the snowmachine
sank into the icy water and the front end pointed upward.*

Larry Wallace, a former student of mine, former chief of police, and current
director of security for Maniilaq Health Center in Kotzebue, invited me to participate in a survival-training workshop in November 1998. The experience reminded me once again that most village travel is done via air or water. Aircraft
is a reliable means of travel used year-round and is usually the quickest. Where
villages are located on waterways, people employ watercraft until ice begins to
form, then mount snowmachines for the winter, traveling great distances as a
city traveler would by car.

The point is, outside the village there are no roads and no "civilization" as
we know it. A person doesn't drive five blocks to a gas station or pull off the
interstate for a sub and soda. The bush country consists of miles of muskeg,
timber, or mountainous country threaded by snowmachine trails. It is not uncommon for a single traveler or a group to cover fifty to a hundred miles to
attend a community event such as a high school basketball game.

During the workshop I met Mike Wise, who agreed to share an experience
that he, his wife and son, and a friend had while traveling the Kobuk River by
snowmachine. This story illustrates the importance of having a partner when
traversing the unforgiving wilds of Alaska.

My wife, Dr. Marilyn Coruzzi Wise, and I were new to Alaska when we arrived
in 1997. We moved to Kotzebue from Rockville, Maryland. It rarely gets cold
in those Washington, D.C., suburbs. Twenty degrees is not that common, and
it always warms up quickly when it does get that cold. Obviously our experience
had not prepared us for really cold weather.

Kotzebue is an Eskimo village of thirty-five hundred located on the northwest
coast of Alaska. Here above the Arctic Circle, winters are cold and dark. Most
nights are accented by the northern lights, most days are dark, with perhaps
only an hour of limited sunlight. By October most streams are frozen and the

ground is covered by snow and ice. By November the ocean is also frozen. In most places the ice is three or four feet thick, although a few places are notorious for either producing thin ice or never freezing. Winter temperatures can dip to minus forty degrees and even colder. Windchills are routinely reported at minus fifty to minus seventy degrees.

Ironically, most locals look forward to freeze-up because it's easier to travel through the bush when the frozen streams serve as arctic superhighways between rural villages. I have great respect for our Eskimo friends who routinely travel through the bush to visit friends in distant villages, go ice fishing and hunting, or come to Kotzebue to see a doctor. Most do so without incident and think nothing of the experience, while folks like us stand in awe of their ability to endure the cold.

Prior to arriving in Kotzebue, my wife was in private practice as an internist and I was a program sales manager for a large computer manufacturer (Digital Equipment Corp.) doing business with the federal government.

While we enjoyed the out-of-doors, we had never developed a good appreciation for the differences between camping out-of-doors near populated areas and traveling through the Alaska bush, where the closest help may be hours away. Survival may depend on your ability to either keep out of trouble or to save yourself when you get into trouble.

This is our first experience living outside a big city and we obviously still have a lot to learn.

We had attended a number of local survival classes here in Kotzebue but felt "that would never happen to me" . . . after all, I didn't plan to leave the marked trail or travel alone.

One class I had attended was a two-hour bush-survival class conducted by a local native man, Lance Kramer. He reviewed the basics—what to include in a survival kit, the importance of never going into the bush alone, always staying on the trail, and telling someone where you were going.

I was also part of an informal group of newcomers who had formed a group to enjoy the outdoors together. We sometimes had an "expert" visit with us to teach us how to "field-repair" a broken snowmachine, build a snow cave, determine our location by looking at the way snow piles up on one side of brush, or observe weather fronts.

While I would never regard myself as a rugged outdoorsman, I felt confident that I could survive most circumstances I might find myself in. I never really thought anything really bad would happen—I didn't take too many chances, followed the rules I had learned, and never went too far out of town. The only real concern I had was falling through the ice. I had heard enough stories about people disappearing under the ice that I really feared that aspect of bush travel more than any other.

Overflow or thin ice is a constant danger for the ice traveler. Overflow is water that lies unfrozen on the surface of the ice, usually under several inches of snow. Because it's often difficult to see overflow until it's too late, we are advised to drive over the ice as fast as possible. When you do hit overflow, it's sometimes possible for your snowmachine to skim over the surface until (or if) you reach solid ice. The general rule is that the slower you go, the more likely you are to get in trouble.

On Saturday, April 10, 1998, we decided to go ice fishing for sheefish along with our good friend Robert Saddoris. We had not ice fished before. I had expected Phil Henry, an Eskimo native, to join us also, but at the last moment he was unable to ride along. I had traveled the route to Kobuk Lake previously and felt comfortable going without Phil, as long as there was at least one other snowmachine.

When we departed Kotzebue, it was a nice day—about ten degrees, clear, and sunny by 8:30 A.M. We were traveling to an ice-fishing area on Kobuk Lake, just offshore from Augie Nelson's camp. From Kotzebue that's about a forty-five minute snowmachine ride—perhaps twenty miles. I had traveled this exact route at least twice before without incident.

My wife and I followed behind Robert about a quarter of a mile. My eleven-year-old son, Stephen, rode on the back of Bob's snowmachine. Marilyn and I were on our green Yamaha 440-cc Venture snowmachine (it was virtually brand-new, with less than eight hundred miles on it). I think Bob's was a Polaris. Bob was pulling a sled with his supplies—fishing gear and survival stuff.

Because I'd traveled this route successfully before, I never suspected thin ice would be a problem. Since I was following Robert, it never occurred to me that we were in danger.

We were well dressed to be outside in the cold. My wife and I each wore at least three layers of clothes.

During our survival class we had discussed clothes and the basic principle and importance of layering. I was wearing three layers on the bottom (blue jeans, sweatpants, and snow pants) and four on top (undershirt, long-sleeve shirt, hooded Gore-Tex jacket, and a thick, heavy Carhartt parka). I wore two pair of gloves, two pair of socks, and Sorel glacier boots. I had no trouble with the cold before getting wet. In fact, I had traveled via snowmachine in much colder weather than that and remained comfortable although somewhat immobile.

I wore my Leatherman knife on my belt (under at least two layers of thick winter clothing) and had strapped my new 35-mm camera around my waist.

I have a well-equipped survival kit and always take it when I travel anywhere outside Kotzebue. In it are chemical heaters, food, dry socks, fire-starting stuff, flashlight and batteries, an extra knife, and my .44 magnum pistol and ammunition. To make sure the kit didn't fall off during our journey, I secured it tightly to the back of the snowmachine with bungee cords.

While bouncing over the ice, enjoying the day, the ride, and the companionship, I followed Robert's tracks on the marked trail as we passed the Little Noatak River. Up until then the trip was uneventful.

About half a mile beyond that point I noticed a lead in front of me. A lead is an opening in the ice that exposes open water. Traveling about 35 first mph when I first noticed the lead, I thought I should slow down and get a good look at it as I approached. My instinct was to stop, but my momentum carried us forward.

The earlier warning I was given during survival class ("go fast, not slow") flashed through my mind. Also, since my friend Robert had just passed through the area without incident I decided to accelerate as rapidly as possible. By that point there was not enough distance to accelerate, and we passed over the lead at probably 25 mph. It never occurred to me that we were passing over anything other than a small break in the ice.

The next thing I saw was the sky when the rear of the snowmachine sank into the icy water and the front end pointed upward. We both fell off the snowmachine when it fell over to the left. For just a moment we were lying on a sheet of ice, but almost immediately cold water rushed over our heads and we both struggled in an area of open water about a hundred feet square.

As soon as I hit the water, I was surprised, shocked, and confused about what had just happened. It took me a few moments to realize that we had just broken through the ice. My first thought was that my wife couldn't swim and I needed to try to help her stay afloat until I could figure out just where we were and what had happened.

As I was trying to get my bearings, I realized our clothes were going to work against us. They immediately filled with cold water and got very, very heavy, especially my boots—it felt as if they had filled up with a hundred pounds of water and were pulling me under the surface, which made it difficult to stay afloat. It was quite a struggle to keep my head just above the water.

I feared that we might get trapped under a slab of ice, or the current, which can be strong under ice, would pull us under the edge. While pieces of ice were all around us, they posed no danger. Fortunately, the usually strong current in that area had diminished sufficiently for us to avoid being washed under the edge of the ice, although I continued to worry about the current. I recall noting with surprise when we got to the edge of the ice that it was quite thick, at least eight inches, and I couldn't understand how ice that thick would break apart as we passed over it.

My wife is a quiet, calm person. She's at her best when she feels under control of herself and her surroundings. This was not one of those occasions. My attention quickly focused on Marilyn when she called out for help and instinctively lunged out toward me. Her weight pulled me under the surface; that was the only time I really felt panicked. It took all my strength to get my head back above the surface.

She quickly realized I couldn't keep her afloat and released her grip, which caused her to begin to slip under the surface. I took just a moment to get a breath of air and then grabbed her by the coat, helped her stay above the surface, and somehow turned her toward the still-floating snowmachine and pushed her toward it.

Only the rear of the snow machine was above water, and we both grabbed ahold of it. Within about two minutes it sank beneath the surface and I began trying to move us both toward the ice edge.

As I was trying to help Marilyn get to the edge of the ice, I continued trying to release my survival kit from the back of the snowmachine, which was already below the water's surface and sinking beyond my reach. As it sank deeper, I was again pulled under the surface as I struggled to save the survival kit. I quickly realized that wasn't such a good idea and gave up the effort, feeling the rear of the snowmachine slip beyond my grasp. The thought of diving under the surface and trying to retrieve the kit crossed my mind, but that quickly faded because I had no idea how deep the water was and feared being drawn under the ice. The kit would have been too heavy to pull back to the surface anyway.

After getting us both to the edge of the ice, I began looking out over the ice to see if Robert had noticed our problem and was returning. I couldn't see him and didn't know if he had noticed our plight. As we clung to the ice edge, I tried to humor Marilyn by saying we came to Alaska looking for a more exciting lifestyle and had now found it. She wasn't humored.

While clinging to the ice edge I tried to help lift Marilyn out of the water but was just too tired and numb to help her much. After perhaps four minutes I looked up again and saw my eleven-year-old son, Stephen, running toward us. I told him not to approach too closely for fear of the ice giving way underneath him (I later realized that was not likely since the ice edge was about eight inches thick). Looking beyond Stephen, perhaps a hundred yards away, I saw Robert removing a fifty-foot rope from his sled. That was a truly wonderful sight.

I don't know with certainty what had led Robert to look back and check our welfare. However, I suspect it was just his good luck that he didn't go into the water before us. He probably missed the thin ice by inches. I was traveling within a few inches of his track. If I had been exactly over his track, this whole incident might never have happened.

Sometime in the past I recalled learning that if you ever fall through the ice, you can protect yourself from being pulled under the surface of the ice by stabbing a knife blade through a coat sleeve and into the ice surface. That way, even if you loose your grip or loose consciousness, you can stay above water. I tried repeatedly to get to my Leatherman, which was attached to my belt (and covered by my bib-type snow pants and parka). But the thickness of my gloves, as well as having two layers of clothes over the Leatherman, prevented me from getting to it. I did take the gloves off my right hand to try to get to it, but still could not reach it.

The edge of the ice we clung to was at least six to eight inches thick. I was quite surprised to see ice that thick right where we broke through. I always thought ice would gradually thin until it couldn't hold your weight anymore. But I guess ice can be thick in one place and thin or absent just a few inches away.

Once Robert arrived, he wisely kept his distance from us, uncertain whether the ice would hold his weight. He tossed the lifeline toward us perfectly and I was able to grab it easily and hand it to Marilyn. I was able to help lift my wife from the water with one hand while she held on to the lifeline as Robert and Stephen pulled. She just held on to the rope. I don't think I could have tied it around her because my hands were numb by that time.

I could not hold on to the rope Robert threw to me—I guess I was just too cold and exhausted. When he realized I couldn't pull myself from the water, he didn't hesitate to walk up to the edge of the ice and offer his hand to pull me out. Once on the ice, I was so cold and exhausted that I could not stand up, but I quickly realized I couldn't lie on the ice (facedown) too long or my wet clothes would have frozen to the surface, so I eventually got to my feet.

Robert removed his warm parka and dry shirt. He gave both of them to my wife, loaded us into his sled and Stephen onto the back of his snowmachine, and drove us back to Kotzebue bare-chested. The return trip took about thirty minutes. While he's never complained, I suspect he had to have gotten about as cold as we did on the return trip. Without his help I'm not sure we would have survived.

By the time we got back to Kotzebue, my clothes, which I had not removed, were frozen solid. They actually stood by themselves when I did take them off. It might seem surprising, but we just went home and warmed up there. While we were hypothermic, we both knew we were not in any medical danger (my wife is a physician and I'm a paramedic). Just by slowly rewarming ourselves we quickly recovered physically.

Epilogue

During the incident, I didn't think we were going to die, but Marilyn was terrified and thought she might not survive. Later, I did fear, and still feel apprehensive, about traveling on ice. Robert later told me that he initially thought we would not survive. Once he saw that the current had not taken us under the ice and we were still moving around in the water, he knew we were still alive (we had only been in the water four to five minutes).

Because I didn't feel in any immediate danger of dying at the moment (only later), I recall wondering if I was taking the incident much too lightly. Only later did I consider how lucky we were to have Robert see us go through the ice and realized that God was looking over us. Robert and his wife go to the same church that we attend here in Kotzebue (First Baptist), and we've talked some about the spiritual aspect of this incident. We both believe God was looking out for us that day and that it could have been so much more dangerous than it really was.

I still enjoy snowmachine travel here in the Arctic but feel anxious when passing over ice. I've learned to speed up and go around leads, keep an extra set of clothes in a survival kit that is waterproof, and I wear my survival kit on my back now.

As we learn from our experience, we gain valued insight that might save our lives or the lives of others we may seek to find . . . as Jerry Olson did.

FUNCTIONAL RELATIONSHIP WITH GOD

AS TOLD TO THE AUTHOR BY JERRY OLSON

Six days without food took their toll on him.

A few years ago I received a phone call from a man who identified himself as the father of a Cathy Olson, one of the students I had taught my first year in Alaska. He had put together a collection of experiences in Alaska's bush and wondered if he could bring his manuscript by for me to look at. I told him that would be fine and was delighted to meet him. Because I had heard stories of Jerry Olson's flying exploits, I eagerly anticipated reading the manuscript. I asked him if any of his own stories were in the manuscript, and he said no.

Over the next few years it became my joy to get to know Jerry better. Though small in stature, Jerry is a giant of a man, one who has achieved greatness because he is willing to go where others do not.

I later told him I thought it would be wonderful to chronicle some of his flying stories and perhaps put together some flying tips for new pilots. Jerry is a modest, quiet man, unassuming but in control of his life. I periodically broached the subject of using some of his incredible stories in a book, and he kindly allowed me to include the following ones.

The first one took place in the early 1970s. Jerry Olson learned that fellow employee Gary Olson had gone on a moose hunt and failed to return. The hunter's wife called the Anchorage Telephone Utility to advise them Gary wouldn't be reporting to work. Then Jerry Olson chose to do something about it, as you will discover from the following Olson adventures that he shares.

Although Gary and I have similar first names and identical last names, we are not related.

I asked my supervisor if I could take the day off to go look for Gary and his son. With permission granted I went out to Lake Hood along with Marv Arend (a friend and fellow employee). By 9 A.M. we were flying across Cook Inlet en route to the Trading Bay area where Gary's wife thought they might be. We searched until dark to no avail.

In the meantime, Gary's wife had called family friend Norm Sommers, who was in Seattle on business. That evening Norm flew back to Alaska via commercial airlines. The following morning he went to Wilbur's Flight Service and chartered a helicopter, which flew directly to where Gary and his son were camped.

Gary had shot a moose on Saturday, and while attempting to take off he had hit a log and sheared a landing gear. He later told me he knew it was Norm in the helicopter because it didn't waver—he saw it coming from quite a distance and in a straight line before it hovered over him and landed.

It is difficult to explain the shame I felt. It was not an ego thing. Here I was a pilot who owned my own ski-equipped airplane that was suitable to land where Gary was camped. I was also a lot closer geographically than Norm when he received the news about Gary.

I had thought I had a functional relationship with God, but here God had to go to Seattle to find a man who could hear Him . . . a man who didn't have an airplane, nor did he know how to fly. I spent a lot of hours the next few months talking to God and apologizing for not being able to hear Him. During those months I gave my airplane and all I owned to God. I also promised I would use all that He gave me to glorify Him, no matter what the cost, as long as I knew it was in His will.

A few years later the Lord started using me and my plane to rescue downed pilots. My success rate was soon known among my fellow pilots. I once got a phone call from a lady whose husband had told her if he was ever missing in his airplane to call a man by the name of Jerry Olson. She told me that her husband was missing. He was flying to Katmai and didn't show up. She wanted to know if I was the Jerry Olson who found downed pilots.

As it turned out, my wife, Susie, and I got in the Cub and flew his route. Because I didn't feel that the Lord would show me where he was and believed he was dead and in the water, I turned back partway along his route and came home. I went to see the lady and explained that her husband was dead. One week later a body (one of three) floated to shore at Kenai—the others and the plane were never found.

In May 1977, I received a phone call about 10 P.M. Merrill Field, Kenai, and Anchorage Center had picked up a Mayday transmission from a pilot identified as Al Huisingh. He was somewhere in the Alaska Range. I was then asked if I would go look for the missing pilot. I knew that all radio transmissions are recorded and kept on a cassette tape for thirty days, so I went to Merrill Field and asked to hear the tape of Al's last transmission. Listening to the conversation, I heard my friend Al state, "Mayday. Mayday. This is Maule–29 Echo."

I heard Kenai tower respond, affirming Al's transmission; then Al continued, "I am at twelve thousand feet in the Mt. Spur area, my engine—"

I thought, "Al is thinking and is not in a panic. He waited to be acknowledged, then continued his conversation saying as much as possible in a short time and not wasting words on details he knew he couldn't finish."

I then began wondering why his transmission stopped so abruptly. His last words were "My engine." Was he going to say, "My engine quit"? If his engine had quit when he was at twelve thousand feet, he could certainly transmit longer than he had. I concluded that either he glided behind a mountain where his radio was blocked or he was trying to say, "My engine is on fire!" Logic told me that a fire burning up the wires would explain the short transmission. But his voice was too calm for a fire, so I concluded that he had glided down behind a high mountain.

That was as far as my logic could take me. The rest was up to God. I knew in my heart that God wanted me to go get that pilot . . . and that He would show me where to find him. That was a confirmation that Al was alive because I have never found or even looked for a fatality. In my case it seems that God is more concerned with the living than the dead.

No snow was left in Anchorage and my plane was on wheels. However I knew that in the Alaska Range, winter's snow was stacked up. I would need skis to land wherever Al had set his airplane down. I then drove out to the Lake Hood strip and taxied my plane onto a grassy area next to the runway. There I removed the wheels and replaced them with skis. I then went home and called Jim Brenn, a personal friend, to ask if he'd like to go with me. We agreed to wait for daylight, then I took a short nap as I had not yet gone to bed.

Jim and I met at the plane just as the sun rose over the Chugach Mountains east of Anchorage. Using the grass for our runway, we took off towards Point McKenzie, then nosed the plane toward the Alaska Range. From left to right, beautiful, towering, snow-covered mountains glistened in the early morning's sun and filled the windshield.

Where was Al in such a vast area? I could see Mt. Spur off in the distance, but the circumference consisted of hundreds of square miles. I glanced at my compass, which read 245 degrees. I then said, "Lord, I don't know where Al is, but you do. I will stay on this heading until You tell me to turn or I run out of gas."

I was not tempting God with that statement, I was just fulfilling the promise that, "I would use all that He gave me to glorify Him, no matter what the cost, as long as it was in His will." I was sure He wanted me to go get Al Huisingh.

We flew into the Alaska Range about five hundred feet above the terrain while maintaining our original heading. About one hour into our flight, I overheard a conversation between a military C-130 and Elmendorf Coordination Center. The C-130 stated that he was picking up an intermittent signal from an emergency locator beacon. But the signal was so weak and broken up that he couldn't get a fix on it.

I interrupted the radio conversation and asked his location, explaining I was on a search. When the pilot gave me his location, I realized he was directly above me, flying at twenty thousand feet.

As the conversation ended, I was approaching a ridge running perpendicular in front of us. I then climbed a few hundred feet to fly over it. Just as I cleared the top, I heard a locator beacon blaring in my headset. I looked down and there was Al about four hundred feet below, waving to me. If someone had put a map I front of me and drawn a straight line from Point McKenzie to the missing pilot's location, and I had followed that line, I could not have gotten there a minute sooner.

Another pilot in the area radioed to report the find.

From the air Al seemed to be okay. But I couldn't be sure. After notifying Search and Rescue via radio that I had the downed pilot spotted, I decided to land next to Al's upside-down airplane on a steep and short incline.

I analyzed the ground below for the safest-looking area to land, banked, cut power, pulled my flaps, and settled in over the snow. I dodged in and out of house-sized blocks of ice that looked like snow-covered dumplings, touched down, and taxied to a stop.

Upon landing we found Al to be in good shape with no injuries. He was in good spirits. He could probably have done just fine without the soup we gave him. But I'm sure it tasted good after spending the night on the edge of Hays Glacier.

I knew it would not be possible to take off from there with anybody else in the plane due to weight, altitude, deep snow, steep incline, and short distance. Jim and I talked it over and decided that Jim would stay with Al and give him a bowl of hot soup out of a Thermos. Then Jim could fly out with Al on the Search and Rescue helicopter.

I waited until the helicopter was in sight, then took off solo and headed for Anchorage.

After landing on the grass at Lake Hood I was too tired to take time to put the wheels back on my plane and taxi back to my tie-down. I radioed the tower of my situation, then left the plane illegally parked and went home to bed. After a few hours' sleep I went back to Lake Hood to check on my airplane. During my absence the traffic controller had called airport security and had them bring out two enormous cement blocks to secure my plane, a nice gesture.

I thought about several scriptures from the Bible that support my belief that we must have a functional relationship with God if we are to fulfill our individual potential. God chose men to accomplish His bidding.

We are not all pilots, so we can't all rescue lost pilots; however, when we surrender our wills to God's, he will enable us to do things thought impossible.

The following is another story about Jerry. He would never have written a story like this about himself because he's too modest. However I kept after Jerry until he allowed me to read and rewrite the story that his friend Ed Bruce had written.

The annals of flying in Alaska are filled with stories—many are funny; some are dramatic. This one falls into the latter category.

Mike Carlton was a thirty-one-year-old commercial pilot, father, and salesman when a friend asked him to ferry a Cessna 180 to McGrath, Alaska.

Mike waited for good weather, and on Saturday, March 12, 1988, he drove to Anchorage Flight Service Station for a weather briefing. He preflighted the plane, topped off his fuel tanks, finalized his pilot responsibilities, and departed by 9:30 A.M., advising departure control that he'd be in radio contact.

Visibility was good for as far as the eye could see. To save time and fuel Mike took a shortcut. He knew that once over the ridge and on the back side of Ptarmigan Pass, he'd have a straight shot to McGrath.

Nothing out of the norm weather-wise appeared as the 230-horsepower engine purred along. But weather in the form of invisible winds sometimes surprises the unsuspecting aviator.

As he approached the Alaska Range, Mike experienced some turbulence, but it was nothing he hadn't handled many times before.

Flying over the first ridge, Mike suddenly encountered a violent wind blast that shook the aircraft. Instantly his plane metamorphosed from a flying machine into a dancing victim. Like a piece of straw in the wind, the plane danced around the sky, bouncing and gyrating, jerked and pushed in all directions simultaneously.

Severe wind turbulence ruled the sky.

He fire-walled the throttle, but the engine failed to provide the necessary lift. *I only need forty feet In altitude.* But the power wasn't there.

His only hope was to turn around and get out of the turbulence. He muscled the controls, gripping the yoke and dancing his feet across his rudder pedals. A strong gust knocked him toward the right canyon wall, which his right wing barely missed. Mike began a turn. But the combination of strong winds and downdrafts negated his efforts to control the aircraft. The rapidly approaching ridge was just ahead, and he couldn't avoid it. Before he knew it, the 180 slammed into the mountain.

Mike lay in extreme shock inside the demolished plane. Alone and without food he was desperate. He hoped the impact had triggered his emergency locator beacon to alert authorities of his location.

While he wondered about his plight, winds increased in volume and intensity. A strong blast struck the fuselage and launched it over the ridge. It plunged down the steep slope, plummeting until it came to rest in the snow.

Although Mike survived the wild ride, he lost consciousness. When he regained consciousness, he joyfully discovered that he had no broken bones and his only injuries included a scalp cut and aches and pains. He assessed his situation: the wingless fuselage was right side up; the radio equipment was unusable; he couldn't find his ELT (he was uncertain whether or not it was transmitting); he had no food (other than two beaver carcasses intended to feed Iditarod sled dogs) and his canteen was empty; and he had an engine cover, a bundle of dirty clothes, matches, and a white gas stove. Other than those items, Mike had the clothes on his back, his boots, the plane fuselage, and the aviation fuel in its tanks.

The temperature was around zero degrees. No one needed to tell him the importance of maintaining his body heat and avoiding hypothermia or, worse yet, freezing limbs or digits.

Hurricane winds whipped the shelter and Mike was uncomfortable in the metal-skinned plane. His side was cold. Although he used the bundle of clothes and the engine cover for a sleeping bag, he tossed and turned trying to keep warm.

He was comfortable in the knowledge that his nonarrival in McGrath would generate a search.

He survived the night, but clouds obscured the sky. Mike knew he needed to lure a search plane to his locale if he was to live. He hoped the clouds would blow out so he could signal.

He heard search planes for a few days, once spotting a red-and-white one before it vanished in the clouds, depressing him. He periodically made his way to the ridge crest to look and signal in the event of an airplane's appearance.

The next couple of days Mike tried to keep warm and prayed for his delivery.

Mike didn't eat snow because he knew it required more heat for his body to melt it than his body could produce to replace the heat. His cooling body would increase the possibility of hypothermia, so he melted snow with a catalytic heater and aluminum foil (the stove worked well on white gas, but when it was gone, the airplane fuel didn't work as well).

Mike thought he was fifteen miles from the valley floor and considered walking out. However he knew that once he reached the valley, he'd still be miles from civilization as no roads crossed this section of Alaska.

His senses were pitched for an oncoming aircraft he hoped would arrive.

During the fifth night the winds subsided and Mike realized the weather was changing. He saw breaks in the overcast, a good sign for being spotted from the air, but clearing skies meant falling temperatures.

Though weakened from lack of food, Mike felt it was better to die trying than to await certain death. Planning to walk out the next morning, he put together a few articles of survival gear—canteen of water melted from the snow, engine cover, matches, and highway signal flare.

He looked at pictures of his wife, four-year-old daughter Apryl, and two-month-old son David before leaving the plane at daylight. He pushed slowly down the mountain in waist-deep snow, conscious not to overheat his body or to produce sweat, which would dampen his clothes and chill his body.

While returning from a speaking engagement in Sitka, Alaska, in Dick Crow's Aero-Commander, Jim Brenn, a friend of Mike Carlton's, read the headlines in the *Anchorage Times* that Mike Carlton was missing and down in Rainy Pass. Jim thought of Mike, a former fellow pastor, and of Mike's wife, Linda. He thought about the rugged range of mountains appropriately named the Alaska Range and was familiar with the unpredictable weather in the area of Rainy Pass . . . the extreme winds and cold of winter that had taken more than one man's life.

*   *   *

Traditionally friends and officials in Alaska launch immediate search and rescue activities, weather permitting. Alaska Air/Sea Rescue Coordination Center at Elmendorf Air Force Base in Anchorage took the lead coordinating the search effort after being notified by the FAA about an overdue aircraft with last radio contact in the Rainy Pass area. These are highly trained professionals in rescue operations. Assisting Elmendorf was the Civil Air Patrol squadron of Anchorage.

Information about the missing pilot was sketchy. Although Elmendorf didn't know the level of the pilot's flying skills, they had a radio transcript of his weather briefing.

Private aircraft joined the search, and on Sunday, the first day of the effort, the weather was clear and crisp with ninety miles of visibility.

Personnel, equipment (fuel, food), and an emergency medical unit were moved to Puntilla Lake as the base of operations. It was a hundred air miles northwest of Anchorage with no road access and twenty-five miles from the mouth of the Rainy Pass entrance.

Search and rescue operations continued through the night; Civil Air Patrol units, C-130s, and helicopters from Elmendorf Air Force Rescue Squadron flew grid patterns.

Search parties covered the ground on snowshoes and skis, but there were no sightings. No emergency locator transmitter signals had been picked up from the downed aircraft.

Most aircraft had covered every inch of the Rainy Pass area. Searchers knew that every hour in the cold was another hour in favor of the grim reaper.

Search protocol called for the planes to fly specific marked grids, check them off, then return to base for fuel and food, a hot drink, and catch-me-up on the latest information.

On the fifth day of the search for Mike Carlton, Jerry Olson awakened troubled. Jerry, forty-nine, had acquired a reputation as one of Alaska's best Super Cub pilots. He dressed quietly so as not to awaken his wife, Susie. It was 3:30 A.M. Jerry brewed coffee and again experienced the tug to look for Mike Carlton. Jerry didn't know him but had heard about the fellow pilot on the evening news. Jerry felt Mike was still alive.

That day at work Jerry thought about searching for Carlton. When Jerry reached home, he told Susie he had a burden for the missing pilot and decided to take off the next day from work to search.

Jerry drove back to Anchorage and placed a note on his supervisor's desk informing him of his intentions on behalf of the downed pilot.

When Jerry returned home that night, he picked up the phone and heard his friend Jim Brenn say, "Jerry, the Lord spoke to me to find Mike. Let's go find him and bring this man home." Neither man had previously discussed Carlton's situation, and that call from Brenn confirmed Jerry's desire to go find Carlton.

Jerry agreed to meet Brenn the next day at Jerry's Super Cub, where Olson routinely preflighted the plane, topped off his fuel, radioed ATIS (the Automatic Terminal Information Service) for weather, ground control for clearance to taxi, and the tower for permission to take off on a northwest departure for Puntilla Lake. They flew for half an hour in the dark with the sun coming up at their backs.

Olson leveled off at twelve hundred feet in calm, clear air with unlimited visibility. All around them well-known mountains thrust their heads up from sea level—Mt. Susitna, Beluga, McKinley, Foraker, and Hunter. They left the Susitna River and followed the Yentna toward Rainy Pass, crawling over the landscape at 100 mph.

Since both men were lost in thought, neither spoke for the next hour and a half before arriving at Puntilla Lake.

The lake-ice runway at Puntilla Lake showed the wear and tear of six days of use. Jerry and Jim walked into the lodge, were welcomed by search crew members, drank some coffee, and listened to accounts of the previous five days' futile searching.

Jerry's flying expertise told him that the searchers were flying too high to effectively spot a man and his crashed plane on the ground. He thought they might well have already overflown Carlton.

They were given an assigned grid and left the lodge. Jerry refueled his Cub from barrels of gas on-site and took off. He turned his radio to 121.5, the international emergency frequency, and listened while covering his grid. There was no news of the downed pilot.

Following one canyon after another, they covered half their grid without results. They observed a number of bedded moose and caribou traveling in herds over their long-established migration routes.

Having completed their grid search, they returned to the lodge where they warmed up and refueled. Jerry determined to search an area twenty miles to the west that he'd felt strongly about for a few days.

The Super Cub nosed into the first canyon. Seeing nothing, Jerry began a steep climbing turn to clear a ridge to his left. Instantly he felt warm and experienced a tingling sensation. He was calm inside, but keyed up . . . a feeling similar to returning home from a long absence. He knew Carlton was close.

(Later Jim Brenn said, "When we were within half an hour of finding Mike, my heart started racing and pounding in my chest like a kid in a candy store. I just knew we were very close to him and I pounded on Jerry's shoulders from the backseat: 'He's here. Close by. I know he's here.' ")

Mike Carlton moved slowly across the winter landscape for a steady six hours. Six days without food had taken their toll on him. He'd only covered two miles since leaving the plane. His knew he couldn't turn back. He saw no wildlife and the snow deepened as he left the protection of the ridge. He was disgusted that he hadn't taken the time to include snowshoes in his gear before leaving town, chastising himself for taking things for granted.

As he struggled into his seventh hour, Mike felt pain with nearly every step. He now battled not only the elements but also daylight. He felt he was at least six hours away from his destination. He kept asking himself if the logistics of his efforts would allow him to make it.

Exhausted and all but lost in thought, he nearly fell over when he heard the unmistakable strong throbbing of an airplane engine. He looked up and joyously watched a red-and-cream-colored Super Cub clear the ridge before him.

Mike quickly dropped his gear, pulled off his red jacket, and waved it frantically. He reached for the flare but couldn't find it.

Above, Olson banked the plane, initiated a steep turn, and looked down at the same time. Right beneath his left wing stood Carlton. Jerry later jokingly said, "I wagged my wings to let the person know that I had seen him, so he wouldn't throw his arm out of joint waving."

Olson climbed steeply to gain altitude while looking for a landing spot. Then he spoke into his plane's headset, "To any aircraft engaged in the Carlton search, this is Piper niner two seven niner Delta. My location is twenty-five miles west of Puntilla Lake, and three miles up the second canyon on the right. We have found the missing pilot . . . he is alive . . . and appears to be in pretty good shape . . . I intend to land and pick him up. . . . I will drop off my passenger, who will snowshoe to a lower elevation where there is more room to land. Any aircraft receiving this call, acknowledge."

A pilot acknowledged Jerry's call and assured him he would contact Elmendorf Air Force Base, Civil Air Patrol, and Anchorage Flight Service with the happy news even if it meant shouting all the way to Anchorage.

Jerry then turned toward the only landing spot in the area, a flat ledge two hundred feet long that hung over a sheer hundred-and-fifty-foot cliff.

It was beyond Carlton's expectations that the plane could land. There was no place large or safe enough. Yet as he watched in awe, the Super Cub maneuvered into position to land on a ledge. Mike heard the engine's power reduced and saw the flaps lower on the trailing edge of the wings as the plane settled earthward.

Mike Carlton watched a performance seldom witnessed.

Long hours of flying skill guided Jerry's hands over the controls of his aircraft. His feet walked the rudder pedals as he approached touchdown. He knew there was no turning back once committed to the landing. But he exuded confidence and sank the tail into four feet of powder, a maneuver he'd used often. The dragging tail acted like a brake and reduced forward motion. The Cub stopped within fifty feet of touchdown

Olson exited the cabin and hollered to Carlton two hundred yards below, "Are you Mike Carlton?"

Mike responded immediately, "Yes. Who are you?"

By now Jim Brenn had moved up behind Jerry's shoulder and called to Carlton, "Jim Brenn."

Carlton recognized his friend Jim Brenn and suddenly remembered feeling that God had told him, "I will send a friend to get you."

Jerry and Jim untied the snowshoes from the plane struts, put them on, and snowshoed to Carlton.

Later Jerry said, "To witness that reunion was worth every dollar I ever spent learning to fly."

Jim Brenn took a Cup-A-Soup to his friend and added hot water to rehydrate the soup. Jim said later, "When we reached Mike, he was a walking dead man. He was hypothermic. Tears rolled down his cheeks and froze on his cold, partially frozen skin, but there was a dim spark of life in his eyes. He muttered unintelligible words when I approached him.

"I had to pry his lips open to force the soup into his throat. Within thirty seconds he was revitalized. It took us thirty minutes to get him to the plane. We loaded him into the plane, then Jerry started it."

The ledge's width did not allow space to turn around and to utilize the entire length, so Olson was forced to use the remaining area in front of the plane. With nowhere else to go and not enough airspeed and lift generated to be airborne before he reached the cliff, Jerry drove the plane over the cliff. Brenn watched in horror as he saw the plane disappear from sight.

Jim Brenn said, "Jerry took off and the tail feathers disappeared over the precipice, going straight down. A few moments later I heard the roar of the engine, and shortly after that I saw the nose and wings coming up out of the canyon about two or three hundred yards away, rising almost straight up. What a grand and glorious sight!"

Jim then snowshoed to the valley below to await pickup by a rescue plane. He said, "When the Civil Air Patrol plane landed forty-five minutes before dark, it hit a hole and went over on its nose. We were able to pull it out of the hole with no further calamities."

Jerry landed and picked up Jim because the other plane couldn't take off with the extra weight of the passenger.

Jim said, "Jerry and I had seen wolves that day. They were in the same area and would probably have gotten Mike that night."

Pilots and rescue personnel at Puntilla Lake had heard of the rescue and greeted Olson and Carlton warmly when they arrived. Medical staff examined Mike briefly and sent him to Providence Hospital in an Elmendorf helicopter. His family greeted him with glee. He was kept overnight for observation and released.

The following Sunday was extraordinary at Abbott Loop Christian Center when Pastor Wayne Coggins asked Jim Brenn and Jerry Olson to relate their rescue efforts. Brenn finished with the details and Jerry spoke. He said he had been told that the media had incorrectly reported the names of the rescuers. Jerry said, "Yes, they had the wrong name. It was our Lord."

As unbelievable as some adventures are, others seem just as miraculous.

IN THE FACE OF DEATH

BY LARRY KANIUT

The flesh on his foot was nearly burned off.

In the Great North, man constantly confronts danger, be it weather, topography, or animals.

How close to the brink of death can a man come and survive? Many old-time Alaskans found out. One was King Thurmond. In 1914 he was savagely mauled by a brown bear on the Chickaloon Flats. He lived alone in a cabin twenty miles from Anchorage on the south shore of Turnagain Arm.

He stepped outside his cabin and a bear grabbed him, chewed on him, and disemboweled him. When the bear had finished with him, King knew there was no hope to save him, so he took his life. He was later found on his bed with a wound to his left temple from a single shot of a Colt revolver.

Another tough Alaskan mixed it up in a hand-to-paw fight (see "One Tough Trapper") with a wolverine on his trapline. The beast shredded his face. He made for his home cabin, found a lantern, candle, mirror, needle, and thread and sewed his face up. Not pretty but practical.

Cynthia Dusel-Bacon survived a black bear mauling at the expense of her arms (her story follows).

Greg Brown stood toe-to-toe with a brown bear and eventually killed it with his damaged rifle. His intestines protruded from his abdomen, and he used a sail needle and nylon to suture his wounds, recovering completely.

And then there was Dick Wroworth. Unless Dick told you, unless you witnessed his struggle, or unless you've been mauled by a bear, you'd have trouble understanding the near-death experience he had in 1927.

Dick's home territory was the Upper Klutina River country near Copper Center in south-central Alaska. He ran a trapline in winter and often worked for the Alaska Road Commission in the summer.

Dick was a rawhide-rough Canadian who'd been shell-shocked and gassed in France during World War I. He was a tough cookie.

Sometime in late October or early November 1927, Dick was near his campfire when a large brown/grizzly bear stalked him. The brute killed one of his dogs before it knocked him senseless and into his campfire.

Dick landed on the fire where he remained unconscious for fifteen hours. We can only imagine the physical agony and mental anguish he suffered when he regained consciousness. His foot and leg were in terrible condition from the burns—the flesh on his foot was nearly burned off.

As severely injured as he was, his only hope for survival was his trapping cabin. With great effort he struggled to reach his closest line cabin. Miraculously he made it, rested, and dressed his wounds as well as he could.

His line cabin lacked the food staples he needed for long-term survival, so he pushed on to a second cabin. When he reached it, he continued administering first aid to himself and ate what he could. He was miles from his nearest neighbor.

A very sick man, he had been bedridden alone in his cabin for over a month when a native stopped by to visit him. Dick was practically helpless and in serious condition.

The native struck out for Copper Center in search of help.

At 4 A.M. on December 13, John and Nelson McCrary and Paul White left Copper Center accompanied by nine dogs pulling two sleds. They arrived at Dick's camp fourteen hours later after experiencing many narrow escapes on the river ice.

The men did what they could for Dick and loaded him into one of the sleds and pulled for civilization. They arrived in Copper Center the morning of the fourteenth at 10 A.M.

It was touch and go for a while. Some thought Dick would lose his leg. But Dr. Peterson of Kennicott pronounced that Dick's leg might be saved, though he'd lose some toes.

When you read about King Thurmond, Cynthia Dusel-Bacon, Greg Brown, and Dick Wroworth, it is easy to wonder and to ask yourself, how much can a man or woman endure?

"COME QUICK! I'M BEING EATEN BY A BEAR!"

AS TOLD TO THE AUTHOR BY CYNTHIA DUSEL-BACON

Bears usually will kill humans only when surprised or super hungry.

—Capt. Robert Penman, Alaska Department of Public Safety, personal interview, Anchorage, February 1977

I first heard about Cynthia Dusel-Bacon over a local radio newscast on August 13, 1977. She had been frightfully mauled by a bear while working for the United States Geological Survey somewhere up north, around Fairbanks. My interest in her experience led me to write her at the University of Stanford Medical Center.

This courageous lady sent me a tape with her story. She was more than eager to offer her experience in hopes of helping others avoid a similar situation, and she wrote in her letter (typed by holding a stylus between her jaws), "I couldn't be more pleased about your efforts to amass all available information about bear maulings in Alaska. I can't think of a greater contribution one could make to educate people about the potential danger of a bear encounter. I believe very strongly in what you are doing."

A short time later I received her tape and her story.

The summer of 1977 was my third summer in the Yukon-Tanana Upland of Alaska, doing geologic field mapping for the Alaskan Geology Branch of the U.S. Geological Survey. I began working for the survey in the summer of 1975, making helicopter-assisted traverses in the highest terrain of the six-thousand-square-mile Big Delta quadrangle. The second summer, as our budget did not provide for helicopter expenses, the project chief and I found it necessary to map the geology by backpacking, usually a week at a time. Last summer we were again funded for helicopter transport after an initial month of backpacking. All five geologists in our group, after being transported by air to the field area, usually mapped alone. I personally felt quite comfortable.

Every summer in the upland area we saw bears. The first one I saw was walking slowly along on the far side of a small mountain meadow, and I froze. It didn't see me and disappeared into the forest. Another time I was walking through a spruce forest and saw a black bear moving through the trees some distance away. Again I was apparently not noticed. The second summer while I was backpacking, I encountered a small black bear coming along the trail toward me. I had been busy looking down at the ground for chips of rock when I heard a slight rustling sound. I looked up to see the bear about forty feet in front of me. Startled, it turned around and ran off in the other direction, crashing through the brush as it left the trail. This particular experience reassured me that what I had heard about black bears being afraid of people was, in fact, true.

I See My First Grizzly

During my third summer, I saw my first grizzly, but only from the air while traveling in the helicopter. Although other members of our field party had seen them on the ground, I felt myself fortunate to have encountered only black bears. Grizzlies were generally considered to be more unpredictable and dangerous.

All three summers I had hiked through the bush unarmed, as it was the belief of our project chief that guns added more danger to an encounter than they might prevent. A wounded, angry bear would probably be more dangerous than a frightened one. She had therefore strongly discouraged us from carrying any kind of firearm. We all carried walkie-talkies and radios to keep in constant touch with one another and with our base camp. And we were warned against surprising bears or getting between a mother and her cubs. Whenever I was doing field mapping, I always attempted to make noise as I walked so that I would alert any bears within hearing and give them time to run away from me. For two summers this system worked perfectly.

Last summer we were scheduled to complete the reconnaissance mapping of the Big Delta quadrangle. Since it covers such a vast area, we needed helicopter transportation to finish traversing all the ridges by mid-September.

At about 8 A.M. on August 13, 1977, Ed Spencer, our helicopter pilot, dropped me off near the top of a rocky, brush-covered ridge approximately sixty miles southeast of Fairbanks. I was dressed in khaki work pants and a cotton shirt, wore sturdy hiking boots, and carried a rucksack. In the right-hand outside pocket of my pack I carried a light lunch of baked beans, canned fruit, fruit juice, and a few pilot crackers. My walkie-talkie was stashed in the left-hand outside pocket, complete with covering flap, strap, and buckle. I was to take notes on the geology and collect samples by means of the geologist's hammer I carried on my belt, record my location on the map, and stow the samples in my rucksack.

Standard safety procedure involved my making radio contact with the other geologists and with our base camp several times during the day, at regular intervals. The radio in camp, about eighty miles south of the mapping area, was being monitored by the wife of the helicopter pilot. Plans called for me to be picked up by helicopter at the base of the eight-mile-long ridge on a designated gravel bar of the river at the end of the day.

Nice Narrow Trail

After noticing, with unexpected pleasure, that I was going to be able to use a narrow trail that had been bulldozed along the crest of the ridge, I started off downhill easily, on the trail through tangles of birch brush and over rough, rocky slides. The ridge was in one of the more populated parts of the quadrangle, as a few small cabins are about fifteen or twenty miles downstream along the Salcha River, and a short landing strip for airplanes is about ten miles from the ridge. Fishermen occasionally come this far up the river, too, so the bears in the area have probably seen human beings occasionally. This particular morning I wasn't expecting to see bears at all; the hillside was so rocky, so dry-looking and tangled with brush, it just didn't seem like bear country. If I were to see a bear that day, it would more likely be at the end of the day, down along the river bar and adjoining woods.

I descended the ridge slowly for several hundred yards, moving from one outcrop of rock to another, chipping off samples and stowing them in my pack. I stopped at one large outcrop to break off an interesting piece and examined it intently. A sudden loud crash in the undergrowth below startled me and I looked around just in time to see a black bear rise up out of the brush about ten feet away. My first thought was "Oh no! A bear. I'd better do the right thing." My next thought was one of relief: "it's only a black bear, and a rather small one at that." Nevertheless, I decided to get the upper hand immediately and scare it away. I shouted at it, face-to-face, in my most commanding tone of voice. "Shoo! Get out of here, bear! Go on! Get away!" The bear remained motionless and glared back. I clapped my hands and yelled even louder. Even this had no effect on the bear.

Instead of turning and running away into the brush, it began slowly walking, climbing toward my level, watching me stealthily. I waved my arms, clapped, yelled even more wildly. I began banging on the outcrop with my hammer, making all the noise I could to intimidate this bear that was just not acting like a black bear is supposed to. I took a step back, managing to elevate myself another foot or so in an attempt to reach a more dominant position. But as I did this, the bear darted suddenly around behind the outcrop, behind me.

My sensation was of being struck a staggering blow from behind. I felt myself being thrown forward and landed facedown on the ground, with my arms outstretched. I froze, not instinctively but deliberately, remembering that playing dead was supposed to cause an attacking bear to lose interest and go away.

Instead of hearing the bear crashing off through the brush though, I felt the sudden piercing pain of the bear's teeth biting deep into my right shoulder. I felt myself being shaken with tremendous, irresistible power by my shoulder, by teeth deep in my shoulder. Then it stopped and seemed to be waiting to see if I was still alive.

I Tried for My Radio

I tried to lie perfectly still, hoping it was satisfied. "I've got to get at my radio in the pack, I've got to get a call out," I thought. My left arm was free so I tried to reach behind me to the left outside pocket of my rucksack to get at the walkie-talkie. The strap was buckled so tightly I realized I couldn't get the pocket open without taking off my pack. My movement caused the bear to start a new flurry of biting and tearing at the flesh of my upper right arm. I was completely conscious of feeling my flesh torn, teeth against bone, but the sensation was more of numb horror at what was happening to me than of specific reaction to each bite. I remember thinking, "Now I'm never going to be able to call for help. I'm dead unless this bear decides to leave me alone."

The bear had no intention of leaving me alone. After chewing on my right shoulder, arm, and side repeatedly, the bear began to bite my head and tear at my scalp. As I heard the horrible crunching sound of the bear's teeth biting into my skull, I realized it was all too hopeless. I remember thinking, "This has got to be the worst way to go." I knew it would be a slow death because my vital signs were all still strong. My fate was to bleed to death. I thought, "Maybe I should just shake my head and get the bear to do me in quickly."

All of a sudden, the bear clamped its jaws into me and began dragging me by the right arm down the slope through the brush. I was dragged about twenty feet or so before the bear stopped as if to rest, panting in my ear. It began licking at the blood that was by now running out of a large wound under my right arm. Again the bear pulled me along the ground, over rocks and through brush, stopping frequently to rest, and chewing at my arm. Finally it stopped, panting heavily. It had been dragging me and my twenty-pound pack—a combined weight of about 150 pounds—for almost a half hour. Now it walked about four feet away and sat down to rest, still watching me intently.

Here, I thought, might be a chance to save myself yet—if only I could get at that radio. Slowly I moved my left arm, which was on the side away from the bear, and which was still undamaged, behind me to get at that pack buckle. But this time the pocket, instead of being latched tight, was wide open—the buckle had probably torn off from the bear's clawing or the dragging over the rocks. I managed to reach down into the pocket and pull out the radio.

"Come Quick! I'm Being Eaten by a Bear!"

Since my right arm was now completely numb and useless, I used my left hand to stealthily snap on the radio switch, pull up two of the three segments of the antenna, and push in the button activating the transmitter. Holding the radio close to my mouth, I said as loudly as I dared, "Ed, this is Cynthia. Come quick! I'm being eaten by a bear." I said "eaten" because I was convinced that the bear wasn't just mauling me or playing with me, but was planning to consume me. I was its prey and it had no intention of letting the "catch" escape.

I repeated my message and then started to call out some more information, hoping that my first calls had been heard. "Ed, I'm just down the hill from where you left me off this morning . . .' But I got no further. The bear by this time had risen to its feet; it bounded quickly over to me and savagely attacked my left arm, knocking the radio out of my hand. I screamed in pain as I felt my good arm now being torn and mangled by claws and teeth.

I realized I had done all I could to save my life. I had no way of knowing whether anyone had even heard my calls. I really doubted it, since no static or answering sound from someone trying to call back had come over the receiver. I knew I hadn't taken time to extend the antenna completely. I knew I was down in a ravine, with many ridges between me and the receiving set. I knew there was really no chance for me. I was doomed. So I screamed and yelled as the bear tore at my arm, figuring that it was going to eat me anyway and there was no longer any reason to try to control my natural reactions.

I remember that the bear then began sniffing around my body, going down to my calves, up my thighs. I thought, "I wonder if he's going to open up new wounds or continue working on the old ones." I didn't dare to look around at what was happening—my eyes were fixed upon the dirt and leaves on the ground only inches below my face. Then I felt a tearing at the pack on my back and heard the bear begin crunching cans in its teeth—cans I had brought for my lunch. This seemed to occupy its attention for a while; at least it let my arms alone and gave me a few moments to focus my mind on my predicament.

"Is this how I'm going to go?" I remember marveling at how clear my mind was, how keen my senses were. All I could think of as I lay there on my stomach, with my face down in the dry grass and dirt, and that merciless, bloodthirsty thing holding me down, was how much I wanted to live and how much I wanted to return to Charlie, my husband of five months, and how tragic it would be to end it all three days before I turned thirty-one.

It was about ten minutes, I think, before I heard the faint sound of a helicopter in the distance. It came closer and then seemed to circle, as if making a pass, but not directly over me. Then I heard the helicopter going away, leaving me. What had gone wrong? Maybe it was just a routine pass to transfer one of the other geologists to a different ridge, or to go to a gas cache to refuel, and not an answer to my call for help. No one had heard my call.

The bear had not been frightened by the sound of the helicopter, for having now finished with the contents of my pack, it began to tear again at the flesh under my right arm. Then I heard the helicopter coming back, circling, getting closer. Being flat on my face, with the remains of the pack still on my back, and both arms now completely without feeling, I kicked my legs to show whoever was up above me that I was still alive. This time, however, I was certain that I was to be rescued because the pilot hovered directly over me.

Silence

But again I heard the helicopter suddenly start away over the ridge. In a few seconds all was silence, agonizing silence. I couldn't believe it. For some completely senseless, heartless, stupid reason they'd left me for a second time.

Suddenly I felt, or sensed, that the bear was not beside me. The sound of the chopper had undoubtedly frightened it away. Again I waited in silence for some ten minutes. Then I heard the helicopter coming over the ridge again, fast and right over me. I kicked my legs again and heard the helicopter move up toward the crest of the ridge for what I was now sure was a landing. Finally I heard the engine shut down, then voices, and people calling out.

I yelled back and tried to direct them to where I was lying. But the birch brush was thick, and with my khaki work pants and gray pack I was probably difficult to see lying on the ground among the rocks. Ed was the first to spot me, and he called the two women geologists down the slope to help him. Together they managed to carry me up the hill and lift me up into the backseat of the helicopter.

I remember the feeling of relief and thankfulness that swept over me when I found myself in that helicopter, going up and away over the mountain. I knew that my mind was clear and my breathing was good and my insides were all intact. All I had to do was keep cool and let the doctors fix me up. Deep down, though, I knew the extent of my injuries and knew that I had been too badly hurt for my body to ever be the same again.

They flew me to Fort Greely, an army base in Delta Junction, about an hour's trip. There, emergency measures were taken to stabilize my condition. I was given blood and probably some morphine to deaden the pain. An hour or so later I was flown to the army hospital in Fairbanks and taken immediately into surgery. For the first time that day I lost consciousness—under the anesthesia. My left arm had to be amputated above the elbow, about halfway between elbow and shoulder, because most of the flesh had been torn from my forearm and elbow. To try to save my right arm, which had not been so badly chewed, the doctors took a vein out of my left thigh and grafted it from underneath my badly damaged right shoulder, through the torn upper arm, and out to my lower arm. This vein became an artery to keep the blood circulating through my forearm and hand. Four surgeons continued working on me for about five hours, late into the evening. They also did some "debriding"—that is, removing hopelessly damaged tissue and cleaning the lacerated wounds of leaves, sticks, and dirt. I stayed at Fairbanks overnight and then at three o'clock Sunday afternoon was flown to San Francisco.

By this time our branch chief had managed to notify my husband, Charlie (also a geologist for the U.S. Geological Survey), of my accident. They were waiting for me when I arrived at the San Francisco airport at one o'clock Monday morning. I was taken immediately by ambulance to Stanford Hospital and put in the intensive care ward.

Another Amputation

Then began the vain attempts to save my right arm. For more than a week I held every hope that the vein graft was going to work. But a blood clot developed in the mangled arm and circulation stopped. The pulse that had been felt in the right wrist and the warmth in my fingers disappeared and the whole arm became cold. Although another amputation was clearly going to be necessary, the doctors felt that they should wait until a clearer line of demarcation between good tissue and bad tissue became evident. Then they would amputate up to this point and save the rest.

But before that line appeared, I began to run a high temperature. Fearing that the infected and dying arm was now endangering my life, the doctors took me immediately into the operating room, found the tissue in my arm to be dead almost to the top of my shoulder, and removed the entire arm.

As if this were not trouble enough, my side underneath the right shoulder had been opened up by the bear when he tore out and ate the lymph glands under my right arm. This area was raw and extremely susceptible to infection. It would eventually have to be covered by skin grafts, skin stripped from my own body. But before the skin graft could be done, tissue would have to be regenerated in the wound to cover the exposed muscle and bone. I stayed for weeks in the hospital, absorbing nourishing fluids and antibiotics intravenously and eating high-protein meals of solid foods. Slowly, new flesh grew back to fill the hole, and the plastic surgeon was able to graft strips of skin taken from my upper right thigh to cover the raw flesh under my right shoulder. The thigh skin was laid on in strips like rolls of sod, kept clean and open to the air for many days, until it "took." Those operations hospitalized me for a total of six weeks.

It Had Been August 13

During my long days and weeks in bed I had lots of time to review my experience and ponder some of the questions that had puzzled me on that un-lucky day of August 13. Why didn't I simply bleed to death after the bear had torn both my arms to shreds and chewed through the main arteries in each? My doctor explained that because I had been in excellent physical condition and my arteries were young and elastic, the blood vessels constricted and cut off the flow of blood quickly after the flesh was mangled. Even the open ends of the arteries closed themselves off and kept me from losing all my blood, and my life.

Had my call for help over the walkie-talkie really been picked up? Or was the helicopter merely making a routine run over the area when Ed spotted me on the ground? I learned later that my first call for help *had* been heard by the helicopter pilot's wife, Bev Spencer. She understood it clearly and immediately radioed her husband that I was in trouble. She gave him what little information I had been able to transmit about my location, and he started right toward my ridge. He had also heard my call, but not clearly enough to be sure of the message. But why did he leave my ridge after he flew over me the first time? And where did he go?

Actually, Ed hadn't been able to spot me from the air the first time, and realizing that he couldn't fly the helicopter and look for me at the same time, he decided to pick up another geologist first.

The second time over he did spot the bear, and hence, me, from the air, but he also saw that the terrain was too rough for only two to get me up the ridge to a landing spot, so he flew back to pick up a third geologist from another area. Finally, with two assistants, he made his landing and led the successful search and rescue. I only wish I'd known why that helicopter kept leaving me again and again, though. I didn't need that additional mental torture.

Why Was I Attacked?

But why did the bear attack me in the first place? I see three possible reasons: (1) the bear may have been asleep in the brush and I startled it; (2) the bear may have seen me as a threat, not only to itself but also to any offspring that might have been nearby; or (3) the bear was very hungry. I do not even consider a fourth possibility, one that has often been suggested as a reason for discriminating against women in similar situations—namely, the possibility that wild animals, particularly bears, are often attracted by the scent of menstrual blood of women at times of their periods. For the three summers I worked out in the bush, I was never approached by any wild animals, and my periods came and went regularly. On the day of the attack I was not menstruating.

Regarding the first possibility, which I believe is the most likely one, the bear may have been asleep in the brush and woke up startled when it heard me chipping on rocks. It should have had plenty of time to collect its wits, however, as it stared at me and circled me before charging. Although the terrain seemed rather unsuited for a comfortable lair—large, rectangular blocks of broken-off rubble covered the ground and were almost covered by birch brush—this hidden spot may have seemed ideal to the bear.

It is also possible that the bear was instinctively fearful for the safety of a cub in the area. I never saw any other bear that day, but the helicopter pilot, after he left me off at the Fort Greely hospital for emergency treatment, asked Fish and Game officials to find the bear that had attacked me so that it could be checked for rabies. They did and shot what they believed to be the guilty one—a 175-pound female. They reported the presence of a year-old cub in the area, but left it to take care of itself. If the mother encountered a strange creature in its territory and simultaneously noticed the absence of its cub, it could have reacted violently out of rage or fear for its cub. Given that I saw no cub, it may have felt, in sudden panic, that I had something to do with its disappearance.

As to the third possibility, extreme hunger of the bear, the postmortem analysis of the bear's stomach revealed only a few berries and some "unidentifiable substance" that may have been parts of me. I hadn't noticed any blueberry patches on the ridge, so the bear could have been tired of hunting for berries and decided to try for larger game, since it came upon me, either unexpectedly or deliberately, at a distance of only ten feet.

One fact is certain: that bear wanted me for dinner—my flesh and blood—and once having tasted it, did not intend to let me get away. But I did get away. Furthermore, I'm up and around again. The bites on my head have healed and my hair has grown back to completely cover the scars. My right side is covered with new skin, my left stump is strong and has good range of motion. I'm fitted with artificial arms and am ready to resume my interrupted careers as wife and geologist.

It will be difficult for me to operate a workable arm on my right side, where I have no stump, and to manage the use of the arm and hook on the other side, where I have no elbow. But with practice I know that I will eventually be able to make my prosthetic devices and my feet and mouth do many of the things my hands did for me before.

I plan to continue in my job with the U.S. Geological Survey. Both Charlie and I have loved our work there, and our colleagues have been tremendously supportive of me throughout the ordeal. I'd like to stay with the Alaskan Geology Branch, perhaps specializing in petrography—the examination of sections of three-hundredths-of-a-millimeter-thick wafers of rock under the microscope to determine their mineral composition and texture. With only minor adaptations to the microscope, I should be able to do this work as effectively as I was able to do it before my accident.

I am determined to lead as normal a life as possible. I know that there are certain limitations I can't get around, having to rely on artificial arms. But I'm certainly going to do the best I can with all that I have left. And that's a lot!

Where Cynthia's fight with death involved a bear on a rocky slope, Dennis Gum faced death on North America's highest mountain.

AGAINST ALL ODDS

AS TOLD TO THE AUTHOR BY DENNIS GUM

I went under the frigid, blue water a foot or so and surfaced gasping for air.

In the annals of climbing, few people have broken through a snow bridge, fallen fifty feet into a mountain crevasse, and survived the bone-chilling ice water gnawing at them. For six hours Dennis Gum faced death at the bottom of such an ice-walled tomb . . . and beat the odds.

It was my good fortune to have Dennis Gum contact me and share his story.

Camouflaged crevasses pockmarked the glacier. The threat of busting through a snow bridge into chasms below hung heavily upon us. Swirling snow, swept by a blinding blizzard, plagued our every step, compounding our fear and confusion. The whiteout conditions engulfed us while we snowshoed across Kahiltna Glacier on Mt. McKinley in search of base camp, every nerve-racking step like walking through a minefield.

We broke through snow bridges several times. Each time I dove forward, crawling toward safety beyond the crevasse. Every time I stepped on a snow bridge and it gave way, my heart sank. Sometimes the snow merely settled six to twelve inches beneath my snowshoe. When it gave way, I didn't know if it was going to stop or not. All I could do was move forward as fast as possible.

Tension reigned supreme. It was driving us nuts! I can't say I was scared, but my anxiety level was at an all-time high.

We knew we were close to the hill that led up to base camp, but were not sure exactly how close due to the whiteout.

Suddenly Stacy jumped to the other side of a crevasse and yelled, "Stop! Don't come this way!" He had made a small hole the size of a Frisbee on the trail. As I peered toward the hole, I could see darkness below.

The cloud cover had caused the surface of the Kahiltna Glacier to soften and become perilous. We had been traveling since midnight, and it was now five o'clock in the morning of July 6, 1996.

I recalled the previous day when I clung to the side of the headwall totally exhausted, and one of the guides, Stacy Taniguchi, asked, "What do you say you and I go back down to Talkeetna and take Rocky and Lou Ann to dinner?" I had pushed myself to the point of collapse, and my rope team and I had just caught up with the rest of the climbers. I hadn't been able to sleep and was exhausted before we started the carry up the headwall to the 16,200-foot camp.

Earlier, Chris Morris had stuck his head into my tent at the 14,200-foot camp and said, "Denny, you can sit this one out and make a carry tomorrow."

I lay on my sleeping bag exhausted from the altitude sickness that had robbed me of my sleep and said, "If the others are going up the headwall, so am I." As I sat on the side of Mt. McKinley at 15,500 feet and was being asked to turn back by Stacy, I was making one of the toughest decisions of my life.

Don't get me wrong, unlike some other climbers, I wasn't driven to make the summit at all costs, but I am not a quitter. I valued the experience and the opinion of Stacy, and if he felt I needed to descend, then descend I would. We unclipped our fellow climber, Venezuelan Ramon, from our rope and said good-bye to the others. Stacy and I descended, while the other eight members of our team ascended the headwall and the fixed line. Unbeknownst to me, the real adventure still lay ahead.

Since first coming to Alaska with the military in 1980, I had been drawn to Mt. McKinley's rugged walls. It was always financially beyond my means; however, thanks to a program instituted by Mike Gordon, owner of Chilkoot Charlie's, I was able to take part. Mike sponsors a police officer or fireman/paramedic to participate in Mt. Mike's Upward Quest to raise money for a designated charity. This year, the charity was the Holy Rosary Academy. Chilkoot Charlie's, Anchorage Cold Storage, the Anchorage Police Department Employees Association, and the Alaska Mountaineering and Hiking had contributed financially to assist in making a dream come true.

After being selected as the designated climber for 1996, I began training immediately and shed twenty pounds. I knew it would be challenging, but little did I know how physically demanding it would be for this forty-four-year-old, out-of-shape, would-be mountaineer.

Our group met at a bed-and-breakfast in Anchorage on June 20 for our equipment showdown and to meet the other team members. The guides, who were all highly recommended, worked for Mountain Trip Adventures out of Anchorage. Chris Morris was the lead guide, assisted by Stacy Taniguchi and Shawn O'Fallon. I was impressed and surprised at the quality, experience, and physical conditioning of the other climbers.

The other six climbers were from Massachusetts, Indonesia, England, Venezuela, Pennsylvania, and Texas. They had extensive climbing histories, with several members having climbed Everest, Aconcagua, and the Alps. I was also climbing with both a marathon runner and a former member of the British SAS. Their climbing credentials dwarfed mine.

On June 21 we flew out of Talkeetna for the Kahiltna base camp on the South Fork of the Kahiltna Glacier at 7,200 feet, and thus the adventure began. Over the next two weeks, we shuttled our gear to camps at four levels—8,000; 10,000; 11,000; and 14,200 feet.

Dennis Gum at eight thousand feet on Mt. McKinley.
CREDIT: Dennis Gum

One might hear novice climbers say, "Oh, you're climbing the West Buttress. That's the highway and the easy way to go." Climbing any route on McKinley is challenging, hard work and it's dangerous. There is no easy way. That climb was by far one of the most physically demanding experiences of my life.

Each day followed a routine. We climbed uphill for six to ten hours with a heavy pack and sled. The temperatures ranged from ninety to one hundred degrees on a sunny day to minus twenty to thirty on a cold and stormy day, not including the windchill. The winds vary from nonexistent to violent, capable of blowing one off the mountain.

At the 14,200-foot camp I began to have difficulty sleeping because I was experiencing one of the many symptoms of acute mountain sickness—shallow breathing interrupted by a large breath to make up for the oxygen shortage (this periodic breathing is also known as Cheyne-Stokes breathing). The large breath invariably wakes you up, thus you get little or no sleep.

I made a carry to the base of the fixed line on the headwall at 15,500 feet and was beyond exhaustion from a lack of sleep. The guides and I discussed my situation, deciding that Stacy and I would descend the following day.

We left shortly after 11:30 A.M. on July 5 and headed down the mountain. By 6:50 P.M. we had descended to the 8,000-foot camp, fired up the stoves for hot drinks and grub, and awaited the freezing of the snow on the lower glacier to facilitate travel.

Due to the warm temperatures, the lower glacier was extremely hazardous, with numerous exposed crevasses and dangerously thin ice bridges on the trail. The warm days resulted in many of the trail's wands falling over (wands are poles stuck upright into the glacier to designate the safe travel route). At 11:30 P.M. Stacy woke me and said it was snowing and we needed to get moving or we might lose the trail.

We left shortly after midnight on July 6, heading for the Kahiltna base camp about four and a half miles away. I was leading the rope team and we were both pulling sleds. The sleds were about three and a half feet in length and about eighteen inches wide, made of plastic or a hard-rubber-type material. They were similar to a child's sled, only more durable with tie-downs around the edge. My sled held about fifty to seventy pounds of gear. We didn't always carry the same stuff because we tried to evenly divide the team's equipment—my large, black nylon bag contained one or two bags of food, possibly a shovel, fuel, tent, stove or other common equipment, and some personal gear.

Usually the last climber does not pull a sled because it hits him in the heels or slides past him. But more importantly, if he falls into a crevasse, the sled could seriously injure or kill him if it landed on him. After we switched and I was the last person, it was not a good idea for me to be pulling a sled. However, I kept it off my ankles by holding it out to the side with my ski pole.

It was snowing slightly, and we were traveling in a whiteout. We had to negotiate numerous hazardous crevasses. The whiteout made it impossible for us to know that we were about a mile from base camp and about a hundred feet from the base of Heartbreak Hill and the crevasse field.

Tension mounted and we continually commented on the stress, wondering whether we'd drop from sight into a hidden crevasse. I had fallen earlier on the way up the mountain and sunk up to my thigh. I extricated myself from that slot (or crevasse), but a second time I fell in up to my armpits. As I dangled in the slot from the waist down, the three rope teams joined to pull me out.

We had traveled now for about an hour when I tested a crevasse's firmness with my ski pole. The snow bridge broke through. Stacy decided it would be safer for me if he led, and we switched positions on the rope.

At 5 A.M. Stacy broke through a crevasse and leaped to the other side.

I moved away from where he had punched through the slot. He told me not to follow him because he had already broken through. You can generally tell where the crevasses are because you can see where the snow is slightly sagging in a line. You always want to cross perpendicular to the crevasse. Of course, you would prefer not having to cross them, but there are too many to avoid all of them.

I tested the bridge with my ski pole. It appeared to be solid, and I took my first step. The bridge collapsed beneath me, plunging me into the chasm. I felt myself falling.

I was not scared, only surprised. I felt the snow and ice rushing past. By the time I figured out what was happening, it was over. The sled landed next to me and not on my head.

I wish I could say that I had had some profound thoughts while falling, but I didn't. In three or four seconds I'd dropped from the relatively safe surface of the Kahiltna Glacier into its cold, wet belly.

My only fear occurred for about ten to fifteen seconds when I splashed into the water at the bottom of the crevasse. I went under the frigid, blue water a foot or so and surfaced gasping for air. The intense cold sent a numbing shock through my system and stole my breath. My first thought was, *Man, I'm going to drown!*

Panic overpowered me. *I'm dead. I'll never get out of here alive. I'm gonna drown.* Fifteen seconds passed before I got hold of my emotions and determined to live.

When I realized my backpack kept me afloat, the rope held firm, and I was not going any deeper, I thought, *Okay, the joke's over. Now let's get out of here.*

I was suspended in the water up to my waist at the end of the rope wearing a Gore-Tex parka, long johns, and shorts. I appeared to be all right; just wet and extremely cold.

Unbeknownst to me, Stacy had been jerked off his feet and dragged headfirst toward the slot by my momentum. He immediately reached back, found his ice ax, performed a self-arrest, and stopped near the edge of the crevasse, just before plunging over the brink and into the chasm with me. He anchored off the rope to allow himself freedom of movement and immediately called down to me to assess the situation.

As I looked way up, my eyes rapidly adjusted to the light in the crevasse. The crevasse was four feet wide, full of water, and narrowed toward the surface. I could see really well and could see where I'd fallen through. I made out the two holes in the snow bridge above, which looked really small because I was so far down.

Above me, Stacy worked to stabilize things, then peered over the edge of the hole. Because of the distance, his head looked tiny. (Stacy told me later that he could not see me well. For me it was like daytime, but for Stacy it was like looking out of a lit window into the darkness.) I could see two small holes at the top where we had punched through.

It was time to get myself out of this slot using my ascenders. This is accomplished by placing the two ascenders on the rope. The ascender can be moved upward on the rope and its teeth will grip to prevent downward movement. One ascender has a foot loop in it and the other is attached to the climber's waist. The climber alternates between stepping up in the loop and sliding up the waist ascender, then sitting down and sliding up the loop ascender. Thus he is able to inch up the rope in a wormlike fashion. I put my ascenders on the rope and attempted to climb out of the hole.

Even though 6-mil perlon cord tangled my step loop, I wanted out of the water *now.*

I stepped into my loop and attempted to stand up. Because of the shortened step due to the tangle, I was not able to stand up straight and went into an *L*

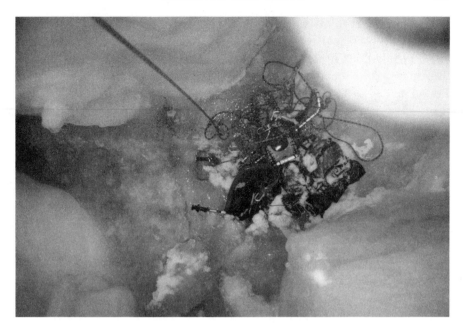

Dennis Gum's gear at the bottom of the hole that he fell into. This picture was taken ten days later, when they returned to retrieve his gear.
CREDIT: *Dennis Gum*

position. This put all my weight on my forearms, and almost immediately they wore out from pulling.

Dropping my pack and taking off my snowshoes, I began to untie the knot and straighten out my ascenders. All of my equipment was floating in the water next to me. I shoved my backpack under me and used it as a small raft to escape the cold water. Because of the parka, sleeping bag, air mattress, and other items all wrapped in waterproof bags, the pack floated. I crawled up on top of the pack and sat on it as if it were a boat.

After getting my ascenders straight, I found I was too weak to do much of anything.

With my back against the ice wall and my left foot resting on a small ice ledge, I was able to pretty much stay out of the water. My right leg dangled in the water.

As the icy water gnawed at my legs, Stacy dropped a line to me, but it was too short. He pulled it back up and tied some additional line to it and then was able to lower stuff to me. Stacy wanted me to open my pack and put my parka on. After telling him that I couldn't do this because I would lose my makeshift boat, he sent his parka down to me. After I donned the parka, he sent down his mittens. Hypothermia was already affecting me because when I couldn't get my fingers in his mittens—either because I didn't think to loosen the wrist strap or they just were too small—I sent them back up.

Fortunately Stacy had the stove in his sled. He had fired up the stove and lowered hot water in his Thermos. As fast as he sent down a Thermos, I drank it and sent it back up. I was so cold I didn't know how hot the water was.

All I could think of was how I needed to force the hot liquids into my belly to keep my core temperature up. He'd fill the Thermos and send it down again. I drank ten or so Thermoses of boiling water. If you asked me afterward how many I had drunk, I would have said five or six. I had no idea. (My watch had stopped, I thought that I had only been in the hole two to three hours max, when in fact it was six hours.) I swallowed the water and involuntarily threw up. My body was saying, *No more water,* but I kept forcing it down anyway.

Stacy's words of encouragement helped keep my mind off my predicament in the freezerlike pit that held me fast.

I was shaking uncontrollably and trying to conserve strength and stay dry. Every time I attempted to use my ascenders, I ended up back in the water. It did not take long to realize this was not a good option.

Stacy had told me earlier that my fiancée, Rocky, had grabbed him by the arm at Talkeetna and made him promise to bring me back alive. My wedding was less than a month away, and even though Stacy intended to keep his promise, he was now worried that he might not be able to.

The hypothermia was taking its toll, and I kept dozing off.

Stacy kept trying with his radio to raise a passing plane or anyone else on the mountain. He was unable to raise anyone at that 5 A.M. hour, which pegged out his anxiety level. He yelled down to me on numerous occasions telling me to hang in there and not give up. He may not have believed it himself, nevertheless it was encouraging to me.

There is a difference between giving up and accepting one's fate. Two hours into the ordeal I accepted that I was not coming out of the slot alive. I did, however, refuse to give up and kept trying to figure a way out. As a last resort, I was going to try the ascenders again or try to climb out with crampons. I was cognitive enough to realize this last option was probably going to result in my swimming again.

As I sat on the slowly sinking backpack, I thought of my fiancée and my children. I thought of how I would miss them and said a little prayer, something along the lines of "God, get me out of here." At any rate, around 7:30 A.M. Stacy said to hang in there, a plane should be flying by soon.

Four planes flew over and Stacy frantically tried to raise them on the radio. None of the planes was on the mountain frequency, and all flew by unaware of the ordeal below them. As the cloud on the glacier lifted, Stacy kept trying his radio. Around 9:25 A.M. his call for help was answered by Joe Reichert, a park service ranger at the Kahiltna base camp. The ranger said he was on his way and would contact the rescue helicopter from Talkeetna. Joe's mother was visiting him at the camp, and he immediately asked her to start boiling water and preparing warm bottles to warm me.

Joe and his girlfriend grabbed ropes and other rescue equipment and began skiing to our location, less than a mile away.

Stacy told me help was on the way, and that a rescue team was skiing down from the camp. He said the Llama helicopter would be here shortly. As I sat in the hole five stories beneath the glacier's surface, I began to realize I might not end up a permanent fixture frozen in the bottom of the crevasse. I did not realize how critical my condition was nor that I was suffering from severe hypothermia.

Above me I heard the familiar voice of Joe, whom I had met at base camp on our way up the mountain. They were going to make a larger opening, and Joe prepared me for falling ice by telling me to cover my head with the parka hood. And fall it did. Large chunks of ice fell all around me. A few struck me, but I was not seriously injured . . . and didn't care because I would soon be rescued.

Joe lowered a rope and asked me to clip it into my locking carabiner on my seat harness. I was not able to open my carabiner since my fingers were like carrots, and I was only able to clip into my locking carabiner with a regular spring-gate carabiner off my hip. I attempted to run the rope through the locking carabiner to my chest harness, but again was not able to effectively use my fingers. Probably due to hypothermia's effect on my mind, I never thought of using a regular carabiner for this task.

Joe and Stacy had put in a pulley system for crevasse rescue and began to pull me up. They'd raised me only a short distance when I heard the helicopter above me. All of my gear, backpack, and sled was still attached to me and was also being extracted.

Since I was only being lifted from the seat harness, I was suspended in the center with both upper torso and legs hanging down. My lower back was killing me.

Realizing I would not fit through the hole in a supine position, Joe grabbed a rope and rappelled into the hole to meet me. He told me I needed to sit up and hold the rope. He dug his crampons into each side of the crevasse and pushed me to an upright position. He handed me the God ring (ring on the end of the helicopter hoist), and I clipped it into my waist harness. He immediately cut loose my gear and all excess ropes. The gear was lost back to the crevasse. I didn't care. I held on to the rope (knocking off and losing my favorite hat), and the Llama pulled us both out of an icy grave.

On the surface I was placed immediately into Stacy's sleeping bag and transported to the Kahiltna base camp where I was placed in the ranger's Quonset-style shelter. Someone took my clothes off and put me in a sleeping bag, probably Joe Reichert.

They placed the hot bottles around me in the sleeping bag to raise my core temperature. Joe's mother kept warming the bottles, which they rotated.

Stacy left the crevasse to climb up Heartbreak Hill to join me. The pilot, Drury, was rubbing my feet and hands. I was so cold all I wanted to do was sleep. I was oblivious of all the activity to save me.

As they warmed me up over three and a half to four hours, I continually had to pee. I don't think I quit peeing for two days.

Stacy and Joe kept waking me and rubbing my hands and feet. After about three and a half hours the PJs (parajumpers) from the 210th Pararescue unit of the Air National Guard in Anchorage arrived and transported me to Alaska Regional Hospital.

Epilogue

I arrived at Alaska Regional Hospital around 3:40 P.M. and was met by my fiancée, who had been notified by park rangers of my condition. I am one lucky individual and owe my life to all those involved, but particularly Stacy Taniguchi, Joe Reichert, and Llama pilot Doug Drury.

My body temperature was in the high eighties to low nineties at the time of the extraction and ninety-six degrees upon arrival at the hospital. If I had remained another fifteen to thirty minutes in the slot, it would have been fatal. No one has ever heard of anyone surviving in a crevasse for six hours after falling into water.

I ended up with some nerve damage in my lower right leg that caused drop foot, though it eventually got back to normal. Drop foot is when the foot slaps down with every step, because you can't control the rolling motion of the foot that you normally get when you walk.

Drinking the boiling water and sitting on the pack kept me alive. My upper lip was swollen, and I had scalded my mouth, tongue, and stomach drinking the hot water. My only other injuries were minor frostbite, severe hypothermia, severe bruising around the thighs, and cold trauma to a nerve in my right leg.

I am thankful just to be alive. After accepting that I was not getting out of the slot, I was in shock that I was safe. I kept saying in the hospital that I couldn't believe I was here. Life takes many unusual turns, some good and some bad. I guess it was just not my time to go.

Men scrambled to help Dennis Gum in the same caring, heartfelt manner that men exhausted themselves to save Gust Jensen.

A BROTHER'S LOVE

BY LARRY KANIUT

*Gust begged him, "Kill me then! Don't let it go on. Please, Nick . . .
I can't stand it."*

In the annals of history, few gunshot victims and rescuers have endured experiences as grueling as those of three Kenai Indians in 1926. History has captured some events that serve as inspiration to others.

In August 1966 my wife, Pam, and I arrived in Anchorage where I had been hired as an English-reading teacher. How was I to know then that a couple of months later I would read about Gust Jensen? How could I have known that one day I would interview Gust about old-time native hunting methods for brown bears. Truly, life spins an interesting web.

Three young men lay in ambush. They had spotted the bear earlier that morning and moved to intercept him. He was far and away the largest animal any of the men had ever seen.

Meandering down the mountain in their direction, the huge beast towered over all the brush he passed. As they watched his distant approach, they realized that this was no ordinary bear. The bear was taller on all fours than alders and willows that normally dwarfed a standing man. They began questioning the power of their rifles, wondering if they had enough firepower to stop this brute. Their respect bordered on fear—a trait uncommon to these rugged Kenai Indians who had grown up in the woods and feared nothing.

Nicholai Jensen, twenty-seven, was the oldest. His younger brother, Gust, was eighteen, and their friend Drafim Delkettie was the youngest at fourteen.

They watched the brown bear to get an idea of his destination, then hastened toward a bear trail to wait in ambush.

Nicholai, Gust, and Drafim spaced themselves out along the trail in the arrangement they felt would result in success. Behind a huge stump and only an arm's length from the passing point of the beast, Nicholai cradled his .30-06. Gust and Drafim crouched several feet off the trail behind alder brush armed with their .30-30s, hearts pounding in their chests.

Each knew the brown bear's tenacity and the power needed to kill such a beast. They knew that a wounded brownie was one of the most dangerous animals on earth. More than one fatally injured brownie had killed its tormentor before it died. Surely this bear was no exception. They treated it with all due respect while they lay in wait.

With its steady, pigeon-toed, shuffling gait the bear moved closer, head down, padding along. Periodically, the men noticed the bear's back, behind and above the thickets it passed. Time crawled as they questioned themselves about their skills and wondered if the bear would cause problems for them or die a quick death.

Closer it came. Silently. They saw it briefly before it dropped into a gully out of sight. Moments later they recognized that familiar smell of a brownie on the breeze. It was almost time.

Thoughts occupied each as he anxiously awaited the approach of the mountain of fur. Only a few yards away, the bear emerged on the trail from behind some intervening alder bushes.

In his crouched position, Gust moved slightly to signal Nicholai. Nick raised his rifle. At the exact moment the bear's head passed in front of him, Nick fired.

His rifle belched fire and smoke. The bullet slammed into the bruin, driving the bear over onto its nose. The men rose as one from their hiding spots and each pointed his weapon toward the bear's head. With hearts in their throats they cautiously edged toward the limp form on the ground. Rifles ready, they watched for the slightest movement. Reason for concern was unnecessary, however, as the bear was quite dead.

Elated, they jumped onto the hulk of brown fur with congratulatory shouts and laughter. They were awestruck by its size. Never had they seen anything like it. The bear's head was half as broad as a man's shoulders. Even though he was near the peak of his strength, Gust labored to lift its head. They dressed the animal and removed the hide.

When they spread the hide out and found that it exceeded fourteen feet in length, their amazement at its size was justified. Later Don Duryea and Nicholai returned to the spot and took precise measurements of the hide . . . a fourteen-foot brown bear. In Alaska's heyday of record brown bears, taken mostly from the Alaska Peninsula or Kodiak Island, the largest bears were around ten feet plus, with some monsters going over eleven feet (one reached thirteen feet six inches (*Alaska Bear Tales*, p. 9).

While cutting and removing the meat from the animal, the men continued to marvel at the outsized bruin and knew that they had accomplished something special.

As they had done with the meat from previous animals they'd shot, they packed the bear in chunks and headed for the beach. They would go to camp, await the tide's rising, load their camp gear, return in the dory to collect the monster, and then row along the beach, retracing their path and collecting the meat from the other animals. All in all it had been an outstanding hunt, and they could be proud to provide for their village.

They had left home five days earlier from Lonesome Bay on the northeast end of Lake Iliamna, Alaska's largest body of fresh water, roughly ninety miles long and twenty miles wide. Their destination had been Cook Inlet, about twenty miles to the east.

Their objective that summer of 1926 was to provide bear and seal meat for the villagers. In those days, few moose and caribou inhabited the country. A severe winter had reduced the village food supply, requiring all able-bodied men to replenish it.

These Indian lads were "men's men," having grown up hunting and providing for the villagers from an early age and fearing nothing. They were accustomed to the rigors of the wild and had the skills necessary to stay alive in Alaska's bush country. They were rugged individuals whose hunting experience prepared them for the task at hand. Their experience in the outdoors tempered their natures, and fear was a subject that was foreign to them.

Carrying sleeping gear and rifles, they had hiked the trail overland past Pile Bay to Old Village, a half dozen miles beyond on the Iliamna River. They'd spent the night at Old Village visiting friends, then pushed off the next morning toward Cook Inlet, where they began their hunt.

The portage trail connecting Cook Inlet and Iliamna Lake rose steeply, then fell off into a verdant valley. Toiling onward they had finally reached Summit Lake, where the trail turned sharply to the right. Having expended a great deal of energy and being soaked in sweaty clothes, they dropped their packs and rested. They ate lunch and drank freely from the mountain springs before donning packs and heading downhill to salt water at Iliamna Bay. From there they'd walked the beach to visit Bill and Don Duryea at Cottonwood Bay. Bill owned a small store frequented by few visitors, as the closest towns were Seldovia and Homer across the water some seventy-five miles.

Nicholai, Gust, and Drafim knew that once they left the Duryeas' they'd be on their own, hunting and enjoying the great outdoors and each other's company until they had gathered as much game as they could transport back to the village.

In the late afternoon Nicholai, Gust, and Drafim had spotted smoke rising from the Duryeas' cabin, where Don greeted them with coffee and dinner. That evening the five sat about the cabin reminiscing and talking long into the night and enjoying the companionship of a shared wood fire and the camaraderie of outdoorsmen who see others seldom. When they finally tumbled into bed, it was with a sense of strong friendship.

After a good night's sleep the three hunters, eagerly anticipating the day, borrowed an old codfish dory and started out into the bay with two sets of oars. Flowing with the tide, they moved along the inlet for six hours, taking turns at the oars so one always got to rest. The slight breeze did not affect them until they rounded the point into Iniskin Bay.

When they reached the beach, they discovered a dilapidated steam bath, a small building whose stove-in sod roof had seen better days. They decided to repair it and use it as a base camp, planning to repair the log walls and patch the roof.

They killed six seals the first two days. On the third day they killed two brown bears. The morning of the fourth day they bagged another brown bear before sunup and had just finished skinning it when they saw the monster bear.

After successfully ambushing it and hauling its meat to the beach, they prepared to return to their village.

At camp Nicholai scoured the beach for firewood while Gust found a piece of cottonwood to whittle. He sat on the bank a dozen feet above the creek and carved a small boat. Standing off to one side and a few feet behind Gust, Drafim jacked live rounds from his dilapidated .30-30 carbine. A heavy piece of twine served as a sling for the ancient weapon that had served his father. Its stock had been cracked and repaired.

As he was exhausted from the day's activities, Drafim's actions were methodical and almost trancelike. With all but one shell removed, he levered the final shell from the magazine and into the chamber. Somehow the twine caught on the lever, causing the trigger to activate the firing pin.

A blast reverberated from the muzzle, shattering the stillness. Instantly Gust tumbled off and down the bank toward the stream. One moment he was busily carving; the next, he was facedown in the creek.

Gust never felt the bullet rip through his back, nor does he remember hearing the report of the rifle. He blacked out from the impact and shock of the bullet and came to when he hit the creek. Gust got to his hands and knees in water a few inches deep. Slowly he forced himself to his feet. In a dreamlike trance he looked about, unable to comprehend his situation.

He saw his shirt covered with blood and blood gushing from his wound into the creek at his feet, trailing red toward the ocean.

Gust's right arm hung limply. The 150-grain bullet had ranged through his right back shoulder, the entrance wound the size of a dime. The bullet had exited the apex of his right arm and chest, leaving a hole the size of a man's fist. Ligaments and muscle tissue were damaged, and his shoulder was shattered.

Gust clutched his arm, mouthing words. But no sound left his lips. Then he passed out again.

Drafim could only stare. He couldn't believe what he saw. How could he have been so careless? How could he have pointed the weapon at his friend? How could it have fired? His open mouth and heart racing, his eyes and mind filled with horror, guilt, and shame. He slowly let the rifle slip from his grasp and fall to the ground . . . and felt his world come to an end.

Drafim jumped down the bank and into the creek. He grabbed Gust and tried to drag him from the water, all the while sobbing hysterically and screaming, "Nick! Nick! Oh, God, Nick!"

When Nick heard the rifle shot, he dropped the firewood he was carrying and stood still. Then he heard someone screaming. Nick sped toward the sound as fast as he could run. When he reached the top of the bank above Gust and Drafim, he looked down and saw the red water of the creek and the two sad figures.

Nick helped Drafim drag Gust to the top of the bank. Gust revived, and excruciating pain rocked him to the core of his being. His body reacted to every heartbeat, throbbing violently. With each pump of his heart, blood geysered from the wound.

Unable to stand the pain, Gust wanted to shoot himself. He called out to Nick, "Give me the gun! Let me kill myself. I can't stand the pain." Nick fought a monumental battle with himself. How could he allow his younger brother to end his life? How could he not? He looked at Gust, thinking he would probably die anyway. It was only humane to put him out of his misery or allow him to do so himself. Nick knew that he had no right to shoot his brother. Nor the conscience to do so. Yet how could he allow his brother to suffer?

When Nick refused, Gust begged him, "Kill me then! Don't let it go on. Please, Nick . . . I can't stand it."

Nick picked up the rifle and tossed it up the bank and into the bushes. He knew they were a hundred miles from a radio—roughly seventy by boat and thirty by land. And he knew, as did the others, that there was little hope of getting a message out in time to save Gust's life. It might be days before they could reach help and more days after that before a plane could come for Gust . . . if he was still alive. The more Nick thought about it, the more determined he became to save Gust's life. And he told Gust as much: "We'll get you out of here."

Gust's loss of blood weakened him and made him less argumentative. He mumbled for water.

Drafim ran to get some while Nick removed Gust's shirt and undershirt. He took off his own undershirt and packed it into Gust's chest wound, then tied Gust's arm against his body.

Moving the boat two hundred yards to water became the next imperative. Drafim and Nick pushed and pushed, shoving the dory across the intervening distance toward Gust's immediate salvation. The wind blew onshore, assisting their efforts, speeding up the tide and hastening the boat's flotation.

While they worried the boat along, Gust regained consciousness and determined to finish what Nick refused to do. He spotted the rifle twenty feet distant and willed to end his nearly unendurable pain. He managed to roll to his stomach before vomiting and passing out. When he awakened, he began the agonizing crawl toward the weapon. Periodic blackouts hampered his journey.

Nick and Drafim took turns running back to check on Gust, noting that he was still alive. But they did not realize what Gust was doing.

Because of, rather than in spite of his pain, Gust forced himself on, crawling ever closer. As weak as he was, he never wavered from his objective. A half hour later Gust had covered half the distance, ten feet. He pushed on.

Forty minutes from the time they started, Nick and Drafim had the boat to water and returned to Gust. In his final efforts before their return, Gust had moved to within a few inches of the rifle, knowing that this would be his final day on earth. As he reached for the rifle, they found him.

Realizing immediately what had transpired, Nick grabbed the rifle and flung it away again. Then he and Drafim carried Gust to the boat and carefully set him in the bow atop a bearskin. They pulled the hide over him for warmth and protection from the elements and water coming over the bow.

They knew that they had miles to go and needed the boat to be as light as possible. Taking only their rifles and water for Gust, they shoved off, each at a set of oars.

They moved into the middle of the bay where the wind kicked up the seas and Drafim wondered aloud if they'd make it. Without breaking his rhythm Nick shrugged and rowed on into the ever-blackening cloud cover ahead.

The sun dropped from sight, and they continued their backbreaking labor, bucking the incoming tide up Iniskin Bay and around the point. Their lack of food began to take its toll, but neither man let up from his rowing.

With Nick behind and stroking hard at a task he had managed his entire life, he felt his younger partner must truly be suffering. But neither let on as to his pain. They changed positions from sitting to standing in order to keep rowing and rest muscles. Drafim's arm muscles swelled and stiffened.

Later in the night Gust groaned. The rowers rowed, rhythmically and machinelike, focusing on rowing and trying to blot out the grueling effort.

Just past midnight and fifteen miles later, they approached Cottonwood Bay. They were rewarded with the changing tide, forcing them into the teeth of its power. The boat became nearly unmanageable as the wind and sea tossed it about in the open water. But they never quit.

Water came over the stern, and they took turns bailing it out.

At sunrise the next morning they pushed through the breakers and pulled their boat onto the beach in front of the Duryeas'. Grinding the boat to a stop on the gravel beach, Nick yelled for the Duryeas.

Expecting the worst, Nick and Drafim pulled back the bear covering from Gust. He'd been silent for several hours, and although he didn't move, he was breathing faintly. His wound had clotted, assuring retention of what blood he had remaining.

Bill and Don helped move Gust to their cabin. While the older men went outside to discuss the situation, Drafim crashed onto the cot and instantly fell asleep.

Old Iliamna Village lay thirty miles away overland. In spite of Nick's exhaustion, he chose to make the trip, figuring he could make it the fastest. Without further delay, food, or drink Nick departed. He set a pace and walked the beach. During his steep hike toward Summit Lake he wanted to stop to rest but feared falling asleep. Onward he pressed.

Evening lights were just coming on when Nick finally started up the last rise to the village. He stumbled to the first house in view and delivered his message. Then he collapsed.

Within minutes Nikita Simeon launched his boat and sped toward Roadhouse (the present village of Iliamna), pushed by an ancient five-horsepower engine. It took seven hours to cover the forty-plus miles.

In Roadhouse, Nikita went to Woody Airways, and Ed Conn wired a message to Anchorage requesting an airplane.

Bad weather prevented air travel. Meanwhile Bill and Don Duryea, assisted by Drafim and Carl Williams, transported Gust over the same trail Nick had taken. The Duryeas had done everything they could for Gust, including changing his bandage and keeping the wound clean. Without medical facilities they could only wait.

Days later the villagers heard the unmistakable drone of an airplane. Before long Roy Dixon was on the water in his float-equipped Stinson. They loaded Gust into the aircraft and left immediately for Anchorage.

When Gust reached the hospital, his temperature was 106 degrees. Nine days had elapsed since his accident. In time Gust healed. His black hair turned white within weeks of the accident. His only permanent damage was a huge scar on his chest.

Nick never regretted his decision to save his brother.

From the shores of lower Cook Inlet to the mudflats of the upper inlet, dangers abound in a multitude of forms.

MY HAUNTING NIGHTMARE

AS TOLD TO THE AUTHOR BY BILL ZEDDIES

*Looking down, I noticed my knees were already noticeably
close to submerging in the mud that had turned to quicksand from
my desperate jarring.*

During the last year of my teaching career at A. J. Dimond High School in
Anchorage, Alaska, I received the following letter and story from a former student. I coached his son in wrestling. It was exciting to think that I could assist
students and others in getting published. Bill Zeddies graduated high school six
years after I started at Dimond.

10-31-91

Dear Larry,

I heard through the "kid vine" that you are putting together another
masterpiece. Like everyone else in town, I have a story for you. I would
appreciate any time you could give to reading and considering this story.
I had a really "great" English-literature teacher in high school, so maybe
there is a glimmer of hope.

Thanks,
Bill Zeddies
Class of '72

I love Alaska. It has been my home for thirty wonderful years. Though I have
experienced many exciting outings in the state, some have been more noteworthy
than others. One day while reading the newspaper I was reminded of such a
disastrously memorable outing several years ago.

"Not again," I desperately mumbled under my breath as my eyes sped across
the headline and the attached story of a young lady's untimely death by drowning. I read that her feet had become stuck in the mud of Turnagain Arm while
she traveled below the high-tide line. She was later covered by the incoming,
silt-laden water of Cook Inlet.

My throat began to knot up as I read on. I get a lump in my throat every
time I read about similar tragic accidents in the Cook Inlet tidal areas. Continued
reading was not really necessary as personal experience has provided the grim,

horrifying details. The haunting nightmare had returned once again like a hundred times in the past, a shocking reminder of the many dangers present in and around Turnagain Arm and Knik Arm, which sandwich Anchorage and create the peninsula upon which the city is built.

Those who tread upon the mudflats around Anchorage often do so with little knowledge of the danger. Others may know of the danger but frequently forget or become complacent. I was among that group as my friends and I headed out in a festive, pre-outing mood on a mid-October Sunday morning in 1976. We prepared to launch an old wooden airboat from the Glenn Highway at the Knik River bridge in the Matanuska Valley a few dozen miles east of Anchorage.

Airboats are powered by an aircraft engine and propelled by the propeller's thrust. Many duck and moose hunters use airboats because of their ability to travel without water, which gives them superiority in shallow water over jet boats and propeller-driven craft. Given a smooth enough surface, airboats are capable of travel on land such as mud, ice, or snow. Usually they are efficient at shallow-water travel, but noisy. They have no brakes or reverse.

When winter sets in, some water-bound lakefront homeowners at Big Lake, Alaska, stranded by ice too thin to travel by land craft, simply fire up the airboat and head to their highway vehicle or other destination.

This old airboat was fire-engine red; the rectangular-shaped rudders mounted behind and on either side of the propeller were painted checkerboard black-and-white. The bright color scheme did not help the performance, but only solicited odd stares from onlookers. It was another dream machine that my dad just had to have, and to be a good son, one I had to endure.

We joked about my shiny, new twelve-gauge automatic as I carefully slid the encased shotgun into the boat (my wife, Louise, had painstakingly purchased the gun as a birthday gift, and I was ordered to take care of it, or else. We also talked about the mud and the rushing water, but not jokingly. The ever-present dangers of the area we planned to hunt were well known to us. We all accepted the danger as fact, but never seriously enough.

The subject of danger always brought to mind a duck-hunting trip near Hayfield Road and the town of Wasilla several years before. On that trip I had left my hip waders behind on a cold, twenty-degree evening in October. Upon being stuck to the ankles in muck, I simply walked out of the hard, stiff rubber boots that I wore. Fortunately they were the kind designed for commercial fishermen; strapless, lined with felt, they did not conform to the feet and legs. Constricting mud, which commonly traps the feet in the more flexible sport waders, does not do so with stiff boots.

Unable to free my boots and determining reluctantly to leave them behind, I had waded the bone-chilling waters of Cottonwood Creek. That long, barefoot, almost unbearable walk up an ice-covered hill to a frigid car almost did me in. After what seemed like hours, shivering bones ceased enough to allow me to start the drive toward my Anchorage home.

That experience alone should have been enough to teach me. However, neither the loss of my favorite boots nor nearly losing my life to hypothermia could keep me from returning to the danger-filled Knik mudflats.

The 4×4 pickup slipped the old boat and trailer ever so silently into the swirling, silt-laden liquid we call the Knik River. The pickup and trailer were then parked above what we assumed to be the high-tide mark (highest point the tide has risen lately). We boarded the boat and left the dark but bustling parking area behind as others prepared to take the same journey using an array of boats, canoes, and airboats.

After a half-mile run downriver and a slight turn to the north, we were speeding up a slowly narrowing slough, a tributary of the main river that led deep into the heart of the area known as the Palmer hay flats.

Soon the engine came to a stop and the boat glided slower and slower until coming to a complete stop on a goo-filled bottom near a solid clay bank. We guarded the boat carefully for a few short minutes until the rapidly receding tide left it high and dry. It would be twelve hours before the high evening tide would float the boat. With the tide out, the only possible escape route would be to hike several hours across treacherous terrain laced with silt-filled gullies. The tide had locked us in like willing prisoners.

We planned to jump-shoot ducks that sat in the creeklike gullies that web the area like roads on a map, widening as they reach for the sea. Most of these trenches start as small crevices and increase slowly in size. Some are area streams, traveling for miles inland. As a general rule, the wider the trench, the more treacherous it is. Little vegetation grows in this area, and that which does consists only of sparse, grain-topped grasses on the high areas that are seldom visited by the salty ocean waters. Trees are nonexistent, except for occasional driftwood logs left by abnormally high-reaching tides.

We left the boat. Ray Uhl and my father, Bill, chose a different direction of travel. Ray was an avid outdoorsman and a longtime Alaskan like the rest of us. He and Dad had worked together at Anchorage Natural Gas (now Enstar) in the early 1960s.

Ray was known for his ability as a bow hunter. I was first introduced to him and his wife, Roberta, when I was a little shaver of seven. Ray and "Berdie" gave me my first longbow and lessons to boot. When I grew to manhood and later married, they became fast friends with my wife also. They held archery titles in Montana and Alaska. Ray once shot a Dall sheep with a longbow, severing the animal's neck with a broadhead arrow that he had manufactured. He was every kid's idol.

I suspected Dad would find a spot to sit on a nearby log and wait for flybys, as was his chosen method of hunting. He wouldn't always admit it, but his health was not what it should have been for a man of about fifty-three. The "old man," as we jokingly called him, had been rode hard and put away wet in his short time here.

Born and raised on a farm in Wisconsin, he had left in his teens to log in Oregon, shovel coal on the railroad, and eventually serve in the Army Air Corps.

After his marriage to Mother, he rode crane hooks to dizzying heights and walked steel beams atop skyscrapers. His crowning achievement was becoming the high-mountain-tramway foreman for the dozen or so air force Distant Early Warning (DEW) sites that closely guarded Alaska's west coast from possible Russian invasion. Every aspect of the remote, isolated DEW line was cold and dangerous. His job required guts, inventiveness, and raw confidence. These cable cars were subject to hurricane-force winds in subzero weather on "nice" days. Our time together was precious.

My old-time school chum and now hunting buddy, Paul Wood, hiked with me for a while. During our high school years Paul and I, though still young, spent many days and nights in the woods or on the water. Our ability to get between a rock and a hard spot was unchallenged by all those who knew us. Paul was ingenious as a young man and reminds me of his intelligence to this day.

Paul was with me on the outing where I lost my boots, and he jumped at every opportunity to harangue me about being stuck. In his usual, carefree fashion he crossed a wide section of ominous-looking gully and kidded me, "See, there's nothing to it." With a laugh on his lips he disappeared over the bank of the opposite gully and into the grasses.

My enthusiasm was high, and though the mud worried me, hope of ducks had an almost hypnotizing effect, and I soon put the fear of danger from my mind. The gully I had been edging was slowly widening, and water was becoming present in its bottom, a likely sign that birds were nearby.

Suddenly a large flock of brightly colored mallard ducks burst into the morning air, reaching for the safety of the sky. The new shotgun took its first-ever, loud, smoky breaths, and a single bird lost altitude, was left behind by his group, and was drawn back toward the earth somewhere over the high bank on the opposite side of the gully from where I stood.

Jubilantly excited but concerned about the wounded bird's being wasted, I briefly forgot the perils of the muddy traps. I started down into the trench before me. Upon reaching the safe high bank on the other side, I sighed, then gave some thought to the ease of the crossing, which gave me great confidence. The green-headed drake flailed in a branch of the gully beyond.

This gully was different, though, even more forbidding. Apprehensive doubt stopped me. Prodding myself, I argued, "It has to be done, and besides, Paul does it." The true sportsman's rules, instilled in me from childhood, reminded me never to leave an animal to suffer and never to waste game.

More carefully than before, I started downward. I reached the wounded bird, then began backtracking. Not ten feet from the safety of the cut bank of the high ground, my feet became mired in the silty goop. Not wanting to lose my boots, I began to struggle. (I later realized I might have avoided my dilemma if I had been able to shed the boots or distribute my weight evenly over the mud's surface.)

I wore cheap, flimsy boots that allowed the mud to push against the sides, thus trapping my feet inside. Something snapped inside my mind as stark realization came to me. I was trapped!

I was hard on myself. I recalled my earlier bout with the mud when I had lost my boots. Now I wondered how I could possibly allow something like this to happen again. In my mind I had gone over everything that had happened the first time. Although Paul had encouraged me many times to disregard the dangers of the area, his advice proved ill-advised.

"Oh, my God! Oh, my God!" I desperately murmured out loud as the situation increasingly worsened. Looking down, I noticed my knees were already noticeably close to submerging in the mud that had turned to quicksand from my desperate jarring. I had no control of myself for ten minutes. Out of control, I wildly jerked my limbs, adrenaline my only guidance. I screamed for help and fired the shotgun, emptying its contents of lead and wadding into the air in a crazed fashion. I fired every one of the twenty shells I carried without realizing I had done it.

Fear of certain death from drowning or hypothermia repeatedly raced through my mind. I shook uncontrollably like a frightened character in an old-time silent film. The world's third-highest tides, traveling at breakneck speed, would fill the gully I was now planted in and cover me up in less than ten hours.

Suddenly something came over me, possibly reality. As I settled into the mud up to my waist, I lost my strength, and I realized that I was going to die. Nothing could be done and that was that. I was weak and soaked in sweat from head to toe.

Looking up, I saw Ray standing on high ground above me, his face pale white and devoid of any expression. He had not heard the shots or noticed my screams. He had just stumbled across me by dumb luck. Realizing the seriousness of the situation, he said he would try to locate our companions and work together to free my lower body from its predicament. For as long as I'd known Ray, he was always coolheaded and did not show much expression under any circumstance.

As he disappeared from my sight, I thought he was the last human I'd see. I was concerned about Dad and knew how shocked he would be when he learned of my misfortune. As I waited, my mind played his arrival like a film, and the hopeless fear on his face was like a nightmare all its own. What would my wife and two preschool sons do? My thoughts then fast-forwarded to the tide that would engulf me later if the mud didn't get me first. My head was well below the last tide mark from that morning's high-flood tide, posted on the clay bank above like a danger sign.

That's when it came to me. I'd stopped sinking. I had reached a depth solid enough to stop my descent. Even though I was up to my waist in the goo and the situation still seemed hopeless, that small tidbit of hope calmly spurred me into thinking about a solution. It was the first time since becoming mired that I'd felt a flicker of hope.

"What if I lay down on the mud with my upper body and crawled out?" I wondered. "It's worth a try." Laying the gun down along with my flotation-type hunting vest, I leaned forward, stopping short. Because I had the feeling that my whole body would sink as if in water, I chose not to, deciding to save what time was left instead of taking a shortcut to the final end.

My partners returned, all shocked from the terrible helplessness that enveloped me. They could not reach me without developing the same fatal malady. My father looked at me as I had imagined, and for the first time in memory, I could see tears welling up in his eyes. He knew that he couldn't come to me or help me.

Ray, though always prepared, scolded himself for not carrying a rope. He was a true Alaskan and always had a plan.

My hunting partners were some of the most creative, inventive, and ambitious fellows one could ask for, and if anyone could get me out with nothing, they could. Even Paul, young in years, was always able to conjure up a plan. The "old man," who was always able to perform the impossible task at unbelievable odds, could surely come up with something. We discussed trying to ease the airboat up the soon filling channel and my breathing through a shotgun barrel until the boat could reach me, both very real possibilities.

Ray took off looking for wood to build a bridge or platform for me to crawl on. But he returned empty-handed. That's when we all came up with the idea of using my gun and vest as a bridge.

I mentioned to them my earlier attempt to free myself. All agreed that another attempt was in order. No longer alone, I felt better about another attempt. The group enthusiasm, my spirits, and some strength began to build.

All my thrashing had liquefied the mud and our concern was that it wouldn't support me. But we had no alternatives. I laid my vest on the mud behind me, then placed my shotgun on top. I lay back on the two in a horizontal position. Amazingly, the silty mire in front of my legs gave way as my body weight shifted, reducing the suction and pressure on my legs.

An emotional swing swept through my mind as a glimmer of hope surfaced. Moving the portable dock to the front, I then lay on my belly. A large portion of both legs reappeared from the gripping underworld. As I battled the suction and pulled slowly, one leg became bootless, then slipped from the jaws of that muddy monster as the wader gave in, disappearing in the softened slop. Every advance gave us more and more enthusiasm.

I returned once more to a horizontal position on my back, and my thighs acted like a crowbar or fulcrum, allowing my legs to move upward. The suction reduced, and with amazing ease, I suddenly pulled the booted leg from the hole and out onto what seemed a hard surface. My legs were finally free. I felt somewhat like a seal when it crawls onto an ice floe.

The men on the bank above cheered loudly. My only emotions were of complete relief and disbelief. The distance from my would-be grave to the safety of high ground seemed like miles. I cautiously crawled on hands and knees from the miry pit up the hardened slope to drier ground and safety.

One more gully lay between me and the safety of the boat. Having to wade down into that muck and wondering if I would repeat my last crossing tore at my heart and gut. Forcing myself into that gully is one of the toughest things I've ever done. But I reached the other side safely.

A light snow had fallen the night before and melted and the ground was still quite cold. As we walked back to the boat, the unbooted and stretched sock flopped comically. I don't remember ever being cold until I was on my way back to the boat through the ice and snow. I knew there was no wood for a fire and that we were marooned until the tide refloated our boat, but that didn't matter. That I was safe made the cold almost unnoticeable. Dad offered to cut up part of his pride and joy to build a fire, but I refused. The boat was sorry enough on a good day. I could endure the slight inconvenience until we returned to our vehicle.

Because we couldn't leave until the tide changed, the others continued hunting while I stayed near the boat. Even though I was covered from head to toe with drying mud, my upper body was warm. I pulled the sock off, got into the boat and wrapped my coat around my feet to warm them. Being alone did not bother me as I felt safe at the boat. While I waited, I mentally replayed my close call: "How lucky can one be?"

The tide arrived in its usual gliding fashion, slithering across the low spots like a snake, cautiously examining the bottoms with its watery tongue, then reaching for the higher spots in increasing impatience, unstoppable by mortal man.

When my partners returned, the water grasped the boat and lifted it free. Not long after, we departed in a speedy retreat, each of us thankful to be returning to our homes and families alive.

On a hunt several years later, Ray Uhl died when his canoe capsized in the Knik River, near where I was mired in the mud years before. He had dropped his companion off to hunt the flats while Ray sought ducks in the island areas of the river. Upon noticing Ray's predicament, his partner did all he could to reach the highway and help. Though he fought his way through the mud-trap-infested flats, filled with swamps and deep creeks, his gallant, almost impossible task was in vain. Ray was not found until later that week, after surfacing somewhere near Anchorage.

Paul Wood still lives in Anchorage, owns his own construction-related business, and is busy with his family.

Sadly for all who knew him, the "old man" succumbed to the ravages of cancer in 1994 after a long, hard-fought battle.

To this day, when I pass the glass case where the new gun has sat since that cold, frightening fall day long ago, the nightmare returns, as it does every time someone is saved from or killed by the many dangers of the tidal areas of Cook Inlet.

Afterword

Some things to consider:

Never go into silt-laden tidal flats.

If you go, stay out of the gullies and tidal reaches.

Travel on foot just after high tide to allow some time for rescue in the event of a problem.

Wear a flotation device to use for crawling to safety.

If you become stuck, lie down immediately. Distribute your body weight evenly. More leverage is also available from a seated or lying position.

Cook Inlet tides move rapidly, so don't kid yourself about outrunning the water.

None of these methods are 100 percent tried-and-true, except the first one . . . so use the first one—it's guaranteed.

Whereas Bill Zeddies fought to free himself from the mudflats, Mike Legler faced the fear of not being found.

MISTAKES CAN KILL

AS TOLD TO THE AUTHOR BY MIKE LEGLER

I swam back to the left wing, reached down, opened the door, and groped inside for my VHF hand radio. I removed the external antenna cable and pulled the radio from its rack, stuffing the radio into the lower pocket of my float vest.

When I read about Mike Legler in the newspaper, I knew I had to meet this guy and get his story. We met at the all-American store with the big golden arches on Tudor Road near Lake Otis on January 24, 1994. Mike is not a big man, but his sparkling eyes revealed some inner strength. He handed me his typed story and proceeded to tell it to me.

Marilou Slaughter settled in for the night. She read her Bible and began her evening prayer. She thanked God for His goodness and her comfortable and warm, clean sheets and satin pillow. She immediately had a vision. She saw a cabin with a man inside. God spoke to her, "Yes, Marilou, you *are* fortunate. Look at this poor man here. He's freezing."

How was she to know that her vision was a reality? That she was seeing Mike Legler, a pilot who had been reported missing four days earlier and fought daily for survival. He was down near Seward, Alaska; and she was in Eugene, Oregon, over two thousand air miles away.

That is one of the interesting sidelights to the story Mike Legler told me.

Monday, September 13, 1993, was a sunny day in Eagle River, Alaska. Fall in our part of America usually lasts only a few short weeks. Delighting in the beauty and planning my day off while making my morning coffee, I resolved it was a great day to go flying.

I would have the entire day to enjoy before coming home to the family and fixing dinner—a family tradition on my day off. My wife, Bev, an elementary teacher, was at work. My son, Jake, and daughter, Kris, were both at Chugiak High School.

I took care of a couple of business calls, then grabbed my Thermos of coffee, lunch, and flight gear on my way out the door.

I was comfortable in my New Balance running shoes, jeans, chamois shirt, and light nylon warm-up jacket. My trusty Leatherman tool (like a Swiss Army knife) hugged my hip in its sheath on my heavy leather belt.

My Taylorcraft airplane was tied down at Fire Lake, just a few miles from our home. On the way I stopped to purchase extra aircraft fuel, filling three five-gallon, plastic containers. The lake was calm and the air a cool forty degrees Fahrenheit.

As I pulled into the lake parking lot, I noticed a Ketchum Air 206 land and taxi to the fuel dock. I wondered what the pilot was doing on Fire Lake, a small lake not used by commercial operators.

I topped off my tanks and preflighted my little BC-12D. After loading my pistol, lunch, and coffee into the plane, I turned the plane around and drifted it back between the docks (using the rope attached to the tail for that purpose). I jumped in, turned on the mags, and hit the starter.

She ran a little rough due to the cool night air and the 50-weight oil. I added primer to smooth out the idle, then taxied to the north end of the lake to warm up the engine. I checked air traffic and applied takeoff power. She quickly jumped on step and accelerated. I broke water and began a 70 mph climbout. Again I noticed Ketchum's Cessna 206 below, whose pilot was looking up at me.

At two hundred feet I discovered the reason for the pilot's gaze—ground fog covered most of Cook Inlet and Anchorage, spreading north to Palmer. "No sweat," I thought, "I'm going south up Eagle River Valley." I turned left over town and continued my climb after reducing my rpm to 2,500 and lowering the nose to hold 80 mph.

Shortly after reaching 4,200 feet I passed through Crow Creek Pass, east of Anchorage in the Chugach Mountains. I turned southeast toward the headwaters of the Twenty Mile River en route to Carmen Lake, where I wanted to check out a campsite for use on my next days off from Alaska Airlines, where I am an aircraft mechanic.

Cruising at 4,000 feet I picked out distant Prince William Sound, one of my favorite places to fly. It was clear with no fog. Climbing to 5,000 feet, I tried to raise flight service on my handheld VHF radio. I received no response on any of the frequencies they monitor. I knew I should not be flying without a flight plan, but the gorgeous day won out over my common sense, and I continued on.

A short time later I set down to wait while the ground fog burned off. After watching a couple of black bears awhile, I was airborne toward Bainbridge Passage. I flew on to Puget Bay, where the 1964 earthquake had lifted land, turning two bays into freshwater lakes—one on either side of the bay.

Deciding to land on the east lake, I made a low pass over the ocean beach and spotted several objects. *Looks like good beachcombing.*

After landing and before taking a stroll down the beach, I dumped five gallons of fuel into my tank. I picked up a nearly new crab-pot buoy and stuck it in the back of the plane. With a slight ocean breeze coming up, I sat down on one plane float and drifted to the back of the lake. I ate my sandwich, drank some coffee, and savored the thrill of being outdoors in this great setting. It was my kind of day—just drifting along without a care in the world.

After a while I decided to fire up and check the west lake across the bay before heading home. After an uneventful takeoff, I crossed the five miles of bay to the lake. It has no name and is well hidden and separated from the ocean by a two-hundred-yard stretch of gravel and driftwood.

I flew past the lake and made a descending 180-degree turn. The lake was glassy smooth without a whisper of wind and surrounded by a steep mountain ridge on three sides. Tall fir trees covered the last fifteen hundred feet, reflecting back into the lake, making depth perception difficult.

Lining up on the southwest corner of the mile-and-a-half approach, I set up for a glassy water landing and began a long, slow descent. Several seconds passed as I noticed small ripples on the lake off to my left. My altimeter read two hundred feet. My rpm read 1,800. Since my plane wasn't equipped with a vertical-speed indicator, I thought, "I'll just correct a little left; I should then see the ocean and the horizon, which will enhance my depth perception. Now a little left rudder, a little aileron—"

Bang! There was a tremendously loud crash. I had slammed onto the lake without realizing I was close to touchdown. I lifted my head and could see nothing out of my right eye. I put my right palm to my eye and pulled it back covered with blood. I looked down to discover I was chest deep in ice-cold water.

Crashed aircraft often have jammed doors, so I was surprised when my door opened freely. I pulled the release on my seat belt and swam out under the left wing, which rode on the water. I pulled the auto-inflation handle on my float vest, but nothing happened. Panic and confusion grabbed me. One more try and I felt the vest inflate. I was reminded and glad that Gary McDaniel, my float instructor, had taught me never to fly floats without a Stearn flotation jacket (which contained my survival gear).

I swam to the tail of the plane and grabbed the tail rope. My only thought was, *You're not going to sink on me; you're my only way out of here.*

Trying to pull the plane, I held the rope in my left hand and kicked my feet and swam with my right arm for quite a while before realizing I was wasting my energy. The plane hardly moved in relation to the quarter mile I was from shore.

Letting go of the rope, I swam back to the left wing, reached down, opened the door, and groped inside for my VHF hand radio. I removed the external antenna cable and pulled the radio from its rack, stuffing the radio into the lower pocket of my float vest.

My next action was to retrieve my ELT. I moved around the tail to the right side. Thinking I might break the Plexiglas, I beat against the submerged rear window with my fist. The ELT was only inches away, but I could not break the window to retrieve it.

My plane was sinking fast. As long as I pulled down on the tail with the rope, trapped air seemed to keep her up. But as I released the rope, the tail rose (because of the engine's weight), and air escaped from the wings' trailing-edge drain grommets.

Water entered my mouth and shocked me. The vest was trying to come off over my head. My head went below the surface, and I realized that something held my right leg. Bracing my right hand against the top of the wing and my left against the top of the fuselage, I pushed up as hard as I could. I felt my pants rip, and I swam free.

With my heart pounding, I started for shore. Near the tail I encountered my empty gas can, which must have floated out of the large hole in the left side of the plane made by the heel of the float when it ripped off. I stopped briefly, tied it to the tail rope, and swam away. (Anyone in his right mind would have used it as a float to reach safety rather than a locator to find the aircraft later.)

The rest was like a movie. Once the wings were well beneath the water, the tail rose to near vertical and quietly slipped out of sight below the surface of the lake.

I forced myself to keep swimming without resting because I knew that time spent in cold water has catastrophic effects on people. I don't know how long I swam. It seemed like an eternity. I was able to stand about six feet from the shore, which was covered by a few small trees and weeds.

My first few steps were wobbly. My legs kept giving out and I fell several times. Seventy-five yards up the beach a breeze hit me, and I began shaking. I took cover from the wind behind a three-by-eight-foot log. My jaw quivered and my teeth chattered. I had trouble using my fingers.

I gathered a few small sticks and some dry grass tops for a fire. But my lighter wouldn't work. I blew the water away from the flint and got a small flame, but the materials were too damp to burn. Blood running from my head and dripping onto the pile didn't help matters.

I pulled out my flare gun, thinking of firing it into the sticks, but thought better of it as I envisioned the projectile bouncing off the pile, hitting the log, and ricocheting into me.

Emptying my pockets I found a pack of small cigars. I removed the cellophane wrapper, shook the water from it, and slid it under the sticks. I lit it. Thank God it burned long enough for the grass and sticks to catch fire. I built the fire up slowly by blowing on it.

I removed my clothes, wrung out the water, and hung them over the log as close to the fire as possible. I made a bandage of my handkerchief and tied it over my bleeding forehead with my left shoelace. The bandage stopped the flow of blood.

Several hours passed before I stopped shaking and my clothes were dry enough to put back on.

I walked the beach checking for anything I could use and hoping I'd find visqueen* for shelter. But I found nothing. Spotting a large fishing boat on the horizon, I fired a flare. The boat continued on until it was out of sight.

It would be dark soon, and no one would be looking for me. I stacked wood near the fire and pulled some larger logs around to form sides to my small bunker in case the wind changed during the night. Removing as many of the larger rocks as I could, I made an area between the logs and the fire to lie down. I was surprised at how weak I was, possibly from shock or hypothermia.

Just before dark I used the cross-point drive on the Leatherman tool to remove the back cover of my Icom VHF radio. An ounce of water trickled out. The inside cover and circuit board were wet. I put the radio back together and tried it an hour or so later, but it did not work.

Well, Mike, this is a fine mess you're in. The family will be worried sick and not a soul knows where you are. Emergency locator transmitters don't work underwater. Worst of all, you dare not fall asleep. If that fire burns out on this cold, clear night, you'll never get it started in the dark.

God must protect fools like me because the wood burned with water and steam coming out both ends.

The night went by slowly at first. I could hear land otters while I watched satellites passing overhead. I dozed off around 3 A.M. and was awakened just before dawn by a wolf's howling.

I arose in the calm, cool morning air, my back and hips aching from my discomfort on the rocks. I had difficulty getting the fire going. It was a clear day, and I was full of hope expecting someone to find me. *Perhaps my ELT sounded long enough for the FCC to investigate.* I knew that was unlikely from my earlier visit to an FCC station where officials explained the satellite passes Alaska every 102 minutes. If the satellite picks up a hit on passing, a second hit must register 102 minutes later or the first hit is erased.

Another possibility was for the Ketchum pilot to tell search officials the direction he'd seen me depart the lake—that would narrow the search effort somewhat. *Maybe someone will look down here in a few days.*

Since there was nothing to keep me at the crash site, I started west down the beach, determined to walk out. Before leaving, I scanned the lake for anything that might have floated free of the plane and drank some lake water.

Even though *beach* conjures up notions of white sand, North Gulf Coast beaches are rocky. Some of the boulders are car-sized. Wave action has worn them smooth except in areas of recent rock slides, where the boulders are jagged.

I hiked five miles before encountering a rock slide two hundred feet high that blocked my path. Knowing I would need my shoelace, I soaked the handkerchief with water to loosen it from my wound. I replaced the boot lace and started up the slide. At the top I viewed another slide barrier two miles down the beach; it was at least five hundred feet high. Discouraged, I climbed back down to decide my course of action.

---

*Plastic sheeting.

Do I go on and try to make it to Johnstone Bay, if Johnstone Bay is the next bay? A friend has a cabin at little Johnstone Bay where wheel planes practice beach landings. There is a salmon stream connecting its lake to the ocean. But do salmon run this late in the year? Are my chances of rescue better there or where the plane crashed?

I decided to return to the crash-site beach.

At the crash site the tide was just starting to come in. I noticed some black mussels on the rocks and walked closer. Most of the mussels were half the size of my little finger or smaller. I pulled one loose and split it open with my knife. I picked at it with the tip of my knife, cut off part that looked inedible, and popped the meat into my mouth. It was salty but not too fishy tasting.

I pulled more from the rocks and ate them until the tide covered the rocks. I picked up some kelp and chewed it. It was stringy and hard to chew but not bad tasting.

Near the tree line I sat and watched several boats five miles distant—on a line between Cape Resurrection and Bainbridge Passage. I flashed them with my signal mirror. No response.

Discouraged, I turned and looked toward the lake. It was concealed by dense brush. Walking toward the woods, I discovered a path. Following it deeper into the woods where it was cooler, I stopped and stared at what appeared to be a makeshift outhouse. Just beyond the outbuilding was a cabin. That was an emotional surge. I walked to the front door and pushed it open.

The plywood cabin was six by ten feet. There was no stove or windows. Two bunks were built along the back wall with a counter extending from the bunks and wrapping the corner nearly to the door. A well-used brown and tan carpet covered the floor.

My eyes darted about for food. Other than a bag of moldy, inedible peanuts, there were two rolls of toilet paper, a box of stick matches in a plastic baggy, a pan of rusty nails, an old hatchet, a rusted and dull ax, a Coleman lantern, three-quarters of a gallon of fuel, some Styrofoam cups, a Fish and Game area goat-permit map, and two ink pens.

Now I have a map. Little Johnstone Bay is twenty-two miles by beach. It is the next bay west around the corner north. If I go overland, I'll have to climb to thirty-four hundred feet and cross a glacier . . . not impossible. This cabin will be my shelter while I'm deciding my options.

I cut some of the carpet and formed it into an envelope the size of a sleeping bag. I cut another piece to lay over the bag as an extra layer. Using a chunk of wood and some nails, I nailed the bottom to the bunk as a seal. *Maybe I'll be warm tonight.*

Afternoon found me back at the ocean beach. I saw two large commercial fishing boats about six miles across the mouth of the bay. I flashed at them with the mirror with no response. *Should I use another flare?* Depression began to set in as I watched.

To my right I heard rustling in the dry leaves and saw a large, brown, sleek

A picture of the little shack that most likely saved Mike Legler's life.
CREDIT: Mike Legler

land otter bounding over logs and leaves. He stopped long enough to study me before disappearing into the woods.

To keep my mind occupied I took the radio, attached the antenna, and turned it on. Parts of the LCD display appeared for the first time. I removed the back cover and the circuit board to expose another board. I set the radio in the sunlight to dry and walked east down the beach in search of anything I might have missed earlier.

Large, puffy clouds half filled the sky. In the distance I heard an airplane. As its engine noise increased, I saw it break from behind a cloud. It was a C-130 military plane heading south at about eight thousand to nine thousand feet. It disappeared into the cloud directly above me and reappeared going east. *Rescue plane on a search . . . maybe listening for weak ELT signals. But they won't hear mine. Man, I wish that radio worked!*

I started for the lake to get a drink of water. I saw my floats across the lake, washed up against the bank. About a hundred yards beyond the floats was a person standing near the bank, apparently fishing. Next to him in the brush was a backpack. I yelled to him, but he did not reply. *Maybe it's a hunter who just came down from the mountains. He may be at his pickup point.* Halfway between the hunter and the floats was a rowboat. I waved my arms and hollered to the hunter, but he did not respond. *Maybe he just doesn't want company!*

Walking to the corner of the lake, I found an old metal float with fifteen to twenty feet of line on it. I removed the line and took it along toward the hunter. There was no lakeshore, just trees to the water's edge punctuated by rock out-croppings. I walked fifty yards into the woods and paralleled the lake.

Six-foot-high devil's club and thorn bushes covered the entire area making it difficult to walk. I stopped often to eat blueberries and black currants that grew in abundance. At length I reached the area where I'd last seen the hunter.

I made my way to the shore and found the hunter—"he" was an oddly shaped tree trunk. The "rowboat" was two fallen tree trunks; and the "backpack" was reddish wood from a tree a bear had ripped open. Tired and frustrated, I sat down to rest. *I must have hit my head harder than I thought. I have no energy for chasing illusions.*

I wished I hadn't removed the emergency lightweight survival food I'd always carried in my floats in an aft compartment. Thinking I might find something I'd left in the floats, I used the line I'd brought as a lasso. On the third try my line plopped over the water rudder on the left float. It was half-sunken and difficult to maneuver. I tired quickly while trying to free the float. A remaining portion of the spreader bar hung up on a half-sunken log near shore.

In frustration I tied it off to a tree. The right float was twenty-five feet out and too far for the rope to reach.

After resting I began my trip to the cabin. Depression set in as I walked. My legs were shaky and I tripped a few times on the rocks. *A concussion, no sleep last night, my attempt to walk out, and the hike through the brush chasing illusions have taken their toll.*

Back at the ocean beach the tide was out. I filled a large Styrofoam cup with mussels, eating some, and pulled some of the larger kelp leaves off a half-submerged rock, placing them in another cup.

Walking back to the cabin in the twilight, I heard the turbine whine and blades of a helicopter. Dropping the cups on the beach, I pulled out the flare gun. On the southwest horizon flew an Alaska Guard Rescue Blackhawk. It was on a line between Cape Junken and Resurrection Bay, five to eight miles out.

I didn't think the helicopter would get any closer, so I fired a flare. *Surely they'll see it against this dark backdrop; they are only fifteen hundred feet off the water.* Oh, how I wanted that chopper to turn. Then a part of me seemed to die as I listened and watched it disappear beyond the cliffs to the west.

In total despair I walked to the cabin and put the cups of mussels and kelp away. I had no appetite. Things seemed as hopeless as ever. It was getting dark so I tried the Coleman lantern. It seemed to work fine without its glass shield, even producing a little heat. I closed the door, took off my shoes, and slipped into the carpet sleeping bag. Words could not describe the depths of my depression and emptiness.

Heavy rain woke me early the next morning. I got up and opened the door. The ceiling was down to five hundred feet. I turned off the lantern and the mantle crumbled to powder. *No more night-light!* I returned to the carpet bag and slept till 9 A.M.

I awoke and ate some mussels. I planned to get two cups of water from the lake. However, it was raining so hard that I feared getting wet and cold and being unable to dry out. I decided not to go.

Having nothing to do in the cabin played on my mind. I'm an active person, and sitting and listening to my own head was depressing. I chose to make a vest of the remaining carpet. I cut another piece of carpet about two feet wide and left it the full length, about six feet. I folded it in half lengthwise and used some wire as a needle and fishing line for thread, sewing the sides together.

It was entertaining trying different stitches, pulling the wire needle through jute backing with the Leatherman (tool) pliers. I cut out a side hole for each arm and one in the top for my head. I cut an opening up the front. I put it on and tied a rope around the middle to keep it closed. *Not too bad, and warm, too.* Best of all it took most of the day to complete. I went to bed early using my new vest as a pillow.

It was still raining on day four. Some choice I thought: *Stay in and starve or go out to find food and die of exposure.* At 10 A.M. the rain let up a little, allowing me to go to the beach for more shellfish and kelp. I decided to store a lot of kelp in the cabin in case the next storm was longer. The kelp seemed to keep well when not exposed to the sun or air.

Wandering around the cabin, I noticed mushrooms, most of which had started to decay. I picked a couple of small ones from logs and ate them. *Hope they're not poisonous.* Behind the cabin was debris from an old cabin. Then I saw something white under one of the logs. *Oh, jeez, it's a propane bottle.* It felt as if it was half-full.

I rigged the percolation tube from an old camp coffeepot to the tank with plastic from the Styrofoam-cup bag. I opened the valve slightly and lit the flared end of the coffeepot tube. Flame shot out two feet. At least now I'd have heat. I carried it into the cabin knowing that it had the potential of becoming a bomb. But I figured, *Who cares? The most it could do is put an end to this miserable existence out here.*

I thought about ending it all. I could swing a rope over a rafter in the cabin and jump off a bucket. I was on a mental roller coaster, very unhealthy.

Back on the beach I found three fishing floats and a piece of driftwood wrapped in pink surveyor's tape. I unwrapped the tape and laid it on the beach in the shape of a six-foot arrow pointing toward the cabin. I set the buoys in a triangle around the arrow. Above the buoys I tied a red, four-foot-square piece of cloth to a six-foot stick and wedged it between two logs. I sat on the logs and watched till dark. Nothing!

In the cabin I lit my propane heater and closed the door. The cabin warmed up quickly but something was wrong. It seemed to be getting darker in the cabin. I opened the door and detected from the minimal light coming into the cabin that the air was filled with soot. I'd have to closely monitor my use of the propane tank.

Friday was nice and sunny. But still there were no boats or planes. I thought that strange. *I'm getting weaker by the day.* Finding a spot out of the wind, I lay on the rocks in the sun until my body warmed up completely. By now I was eating beach plants—most were bitter and I spit them out, but one type had a long, white runner root that tasted a little like celery.

When I saw the land otter again, I followed it to a slide in the woods above the cabin and figured a way to snare him. *Some meat protein might give me the strength to walk out of here.*

In the afternoon when the cabin area was in shadows and getting cooler, I walked the mile to the far side of the lake and ate berries. Warmth and something in my stomach reduced my suicidal thoughts.

Day six dawned as another nice day. Still no boats or planes. *Hard to believe no one is looking for me.* Then I noticed standing lenticular clouds drifting south out of Prince William Sound. *I'll bet it's blowing hard out of the north over Anchorage and in the Chugach Mountains. No one would risk his plane and life in that kind of turbulence.*

It was noon before I got warm in the sun. *It's too late to walk out today. I'm too weak anyway. My tennis shoes could prove fatal if I break an ankle or leg. I'll have to do something different tomorrow or I'll die here!*

I experienced more suicidal thoughts. They were most prevalent in the late afternoon and into dusk. The thoughts may have been caused from watching another day slip by with no sign of rescue . . . or by the thought of another cold night. My reasoning was affected by lack of food. Another factor was the thought of the plane I'd rebuilt with my own hands. I recalled a favorite picture of it taken at Togiak Lake. Every time I looked at it, I was reminded that we'd been over most of the state; I got teary eyed.

I sat on the beach all morning and most of the afternoon on Sunday. It was my seventh day. It was a little windy but sunny. I gathered more mussels and kelp when the tide was out. I saw one boat way in the distance. Still no planes!

Depression returned. Being cold with no one to talk to made it hard to focus on the big picture—I constantly thought about short-term things. Near the cabin I found a white paper plate that was fairly dry. I set out to write my last will and testament on it. What I wrote turned out to be more of a personal good-bye to my wife and children. I ran out of room quickly, so I closed with "To all my friends and relatives, may God keep you in peace till we meet in the hereafter."

I put the plate in a plastic baggy and hung it on the wall in the cabin. I was so ovewhelmed with grief that I began to sob like a baby. The feeling of absolute hopelessness made me feel even weaker. I closed the cabin door, took off my shoes, and slid down into the carpet covering. A heavy rain pounded the cabin.

My sleep was restless that night. My shaking from the cold continually awakened me. The air inside the cabin was damp and colder than it had been the previous nights. In the darkness of the cabin I distinguished a doglike animal calling my name. "Are you hungry, Mikey? Are you cold enough yet, Mikey? No one will ever find you here alive, Mikey!

"I can help you, Mikey! What's your God doing for you now, Mikey? Let me help you."

The creature looked like a drooling rottweiler. I spoke to it: "I should have known you were part of this—you can leave. I will never renounce God, even if it's His will that I die here."

Within thirty seconds the creature left and the cabin seemed to warm up. It suddenly wasn't as dark. The rest of the night I slept like a baby and was never cold again.

I was experiencing a battle between good and evil. I was really being watched out for. Too many things happened that convinced me that my experience was not a coincidence.

On the twentieth, rain continued. The afternoon before I had written on my daily notes on the back of the map, "Left for Johnstone Bay Sept. 20th." I crossed it out now because it was still raining hard. From the doorway I could see the lake had risen about three feet. The wind had blown leaves and bark to my corner of the lake, making it impossible to get clean water. I sat in the cabin and ate kelp I'd gathered the day before.

The rain eased up around 10 A.M. and I headed for the beach. It was windy and the clouds started breaking up. In between waves I dashed toward the surf and snatched mussels from the rocks. On one trip I slipped on the rocks, fell, and almost broke the flare gun, which I had tied on a cord around my neck so I wouldn't be without it. I accepted the injury with little concern—by now I felt that it didn't matter anyway since my chances of surviving were nil.

The next day was my ninth day since leaving home. It was clear and windy. I headed for the beach in my routine search for food. My state of mind made computing low tide difficult. The mussel-covered rocks never showed because the seas were ten to twelve feet and pushed by strong winds. The winds never let the tide go out as it had the previous eight days.

Is it possible I've been here eight days! One minute it seems the time has gone quickly, the next minute it's been an eternity. I might be here for a long time. My calorie intake is low because my jeans are loose and the vest is getting larger. I may be losing my sanity. The signs are all there, lighthearted and giddy one moment, too depressed to get up and move the next. I wonder if I'll still be alive when the first snowfall comes.

I slept late on Wednesday the twenty-second. I had little energy. I ambled to the beach around 9 A.M. The tide was still in, but the surf was smaller than on Tuesday. It was nice and sunny with a light northeast wind. I ate some roots and tried some new ones, which I spit out because they were bitter.

I sat on a log to renew my daily vigil for boats and planes, ready to signal with my mirror and flare gun. Nothing. It was almost 11 A.M. before the large rocks with mussels began to appear. I gathered all the mussels I could find and put them into a plastic bag. I ate half, storing the remainder in the cabin along with some kelp.

At noon I climbed up the hill to assess my chances of crossing the glacier. It was difficult going because of the deadfalls and moss-covered ground. One step was solid, the next I sank up to my waist. I stopped every fifteen minutes to rest. It took two hours to get above the tree line at fifteen hundred feet. The next five hundred feet was easier, but the view was discouraging.

The top of the ridge was another thousand feet. I didn't have the energy to go straight up. A rock slide blocked my way around the mountain. I saw Montague Island, Day Harbor, and Cape Resurrection; but not a boat was in sight. *Maybe tomorrow . . . if the weather's good and I eat lots today and I get a good night's rest, I'll have the strength to walk it.* I returned to the cabin.

At 4 P.M. I sat on the cabin steps eating my remaining mussels. I heard an airplane and thought, *Well, there it is again. My mind at work.* There was an instant roar as the plane passed over the cabin.

I dropped the mussels and ran to the beach, watching the tail of the Cessna five hundred feet above the ground and flying away from me. *Why weren't you out on the beach watching?* My heart pounded as I watched the plane bank right and head southeast across the bay. *Dang! If he'll only turn back this way, I'll shoot a flare and maybe, just maybe, he'll see it.* He disappeared up a canyon, but his engine's rpm were constant, indicating he was not set up for a landing.

I ran a hundred feet to the base of a cliff in the shadows thinking it provided a dark backdrop for the flare.

Here he comes! He's over the beach now on the far side of the bay, maybe three miles away. He's turning a little. He's pointing straight at me. Now! With the flare gun pointed up as vertical as possible, I fired. *Please see it!* He seemed to come at me for a second, then turned left flying out toward the head of the bay.

I reloaded the gun. Suddenly he turned my way again. *This time I have to wait until he's closer. He must not have seen the first flare with the sun in his eyes.* When he was halfway across the bay, I could wait no longer. I fired again. I heard the power come back on the engine and saw his flaps come down.

Holy smoke! He's gonna land! I ran to the cabin to get my last two flares. Standing at the corner of the lake, I watched him land near the far shore. I reloaded the flare gun and when he taxied toward me, I fired the flare in an arc along the woods on my side of the lake.

The plane was now out of my view because of the trees and sounded as if he was taxiing to the beach I'd spent my first night on. I ran up the trail, stumbling several times and falling. I couldn't let him get out of here without me! Winded, I reached the beach. But there was no plane!

I listened closely for his engine. My blood pressure was pounding so loudly in my ears I could hardly hear it. *Now he's heading toward the cabin.* I turned and retraced my steps. Even with adrenaline pumping I had difficulty picking up my feet. I fell a few more times, gashing my forearms and shins.

I crashed through the trees and finally saw the plane. I heard a shout: "If you're a person, you had better speak up." A man standing onshore reached for a rifle. I stopped and opened my mouth but nothing came out. I was totally winded. He looked up, saw me, put down the rifle, and resumed unloading supplies.

I stumbled to the plane, which was tailed into the bank, and I grabbed the stabilizer. Three men unloaded gear. The closest one looked at me and asked, "Oh, are you hunting here?"

"No, I've been stranded here nine days."

He then asked, "Oh, where's your plane?"

"At the bottom of the lake."

The pilot standing on the float looked at me, walked over, grabbed me, and said, "Man, sit down. I'll get you some food." When I didn't move, he said, "You can let go of my plane. I promise I won't leave without you."

The two hunters began opening boxes and handing me food. I was almost in tears. I ate one small roll and was stuffed. As I told them what had happened to me one kept saying, "Praise God, you're all right."

The pilot, Willie Allen with Scenic Mountain Air at Trail Lakes, got me into his plane. It was a white knuckler as we were on a downwind takeoff. Willie added flaps and forced the 206 off the water and the stall-warning horn came on. *Did I survive nine days lost to die now?* Fortunately, the plane continued on.

Willie flew the coast to Seward, pointing out sheer six-hundred-foot cliffs that barred my way up the beach and asked, "So you were going to walk this, huh?"

We touched down at Trail Lake, twenty-five miles north of Seward, and Willie's boss, Vern Kinfsford, met us with a handheld radio in one hand and a portable phone in the other. He'd been trying to call my wife, Bev, for twenty minutes; but it was busy. As I stepped off the float onto the dock, he hit redial, got a signal, and handed me the phone.

Balancing there with the phone two feet from my ear, I heard Bev's voice: "Hello." Suddenly I couldn't talk. After her third hello I managed to say, "Bev." There was a long pause, then a scream. "Mike. Mike, is that you!" I started to cry. Vern and Willie were staring at their shoes.

Before Vern could tell Bev he'd bring me to Eagle River "on the house," she hung up and was on her way with her mother and our daughter, Kris, to pick me up (a 130-mile drive). Meanwhile Vern's phone started ringing off the hook. He had three lines into his flight service and received calls from Anchorage television news channels, the FAA, NTSB. He screened calls, asking me which ones I wanted to take.

(Left) *Mike Legler one hour after his rescue.* (Right) *Mike at a "Welcome Back" party given in his honor several months after he was found.*
CREDIT: *Beverly Legler*

When Bev arrived, it was quite a reunion. We started back for Anchorage. We had a lot to talk about . . . and a lot to be thankful for.

Epilogue

A couple of days after I was rescued, I received a call from a lady who told me she had had a vision about me. She had been in Oregon during my adventure. One night at bedtime during her Bible-reading/prayer time, she thanked God for her warm bed, clean sheets, and satin pillows. God "transported" her to a cabin and said, "Yes, you are fortunate. Look at this poor man here. He's going to die."

She described items in the cabin and their location; and I had never told anyone about these things.

As Mike and I later discussed his experience, he said, "I was talking with a Lutheran minister friend who has a theory about illusions. His theory is that when you have an illusion or vision, your brain finally gets quiet enough for God to send you a message.

"I had a pretty good faith in God before my accident. During the event, I cussed him and I threw rocks and asked, 'Why are You doing this to me?' I can remember being so angry for two or three days and then finally kinda giving up. Then it slowly came around to, 'Okay, what am I supposed to learn out of this?'

"I finally surrendered and said, 'Okay, whatever You're going to do, let's do it. I'm okay with it now.' When I finally surrendered, I was at perfect peace with whatever my fate was gonna be."

As you can see from Mike Legler's story, flying gets man into trouble, but depending on the situation, *not* flying can get him into more . . . as Carl McCunn discovered.

NO SIGN OF LIFE

BY LARRY KANIUT

"ALL OK . . . DO NOT WAIT!"

The lure of the wilderness may be inescapable. For decades men have left home and country to venture into Alaska's untamed wilds. Some have come back; some haven't. The three following stories depict three young men who loved nature and went into the woods alone. They ranged in age from twenty-four to thirty-five.

Their venturing into the wilderness was spread out over nearly sixty years—1935, 1981, and 1992. All went . . . but only one returned. Perhaps these stories will cause you to wonder about the men and their activities. At the end I will share my thoughts about these three with you.

They all faced the same enemy. Some call that enemy death . . . I call it idealism.

Captivated by the raw, natural beauty around him, the lone figure gazed in awe into the night sky for several minutes with a renewed appreciation for life. Shades of red spread across the vast canopy of space. Pulsating fingers of color intensified in both breadth and brilliance as they blazed thousands of feet upward before trailing off in rainbow arcs or flowing like banners blowing in the breeze. Like a herd of wild-eyed horses, nostrils flaring and sides heaving, carrying men onto the battlefield in a galloping cavalry charge—guidons flapping, bugles blaring, guns spitting lead, and sabers slashing—the bright rose fingers swept in waves above the naked snow . . . only to retreat, regroup, then charge again.

The hissing, glistening northern lights capped his exciting day in the wild as they waved good-night to Carl McCunn.

The next day had hardly begun when excitement gripped him. He heard a sound he'd only hoped for these past several days. The sound grew louder. Before long he saw the source. It *was* an airplane! He grabbed his orange sleeping-bag cover and frantically waved at the plane that flew low over his camp.

Not once, but three times the light plane passed overhead. Even though the plane was equipped with wheels and could not safely land on the lake's frozen, snow-covered surface, the man excitedly picked up things and prepared to break camp. He assumed the pilot would alert another pilot with a ski-equipped plane to come for him.

But it was not to be. Carl McCunn was destined to remain on the ground. Things were not going according to his plans, which included leaving his solitary lake prior to winter.

Carl McCunn loved the outdoors. He wanted to spend time alone with the denizens of the forest, tundra, and mountains. He had done so in 1976 when he enjoyed five months in the Brooks Range of northern Alaska. Friends and family believed he was "woods wise" and could take care of himself, as evidenced by his Brooks trip.

Topped by curly, reddish blond hair, the strapping, six-foot-two-inch-tall, 240-pound McCunn had the size to take care of himself. His friend Randall Robinson described McCunn as "bush-qualified" saying, "If anybody would survive out in the bush for any length of time, it would be Carl because he had done that before."(2)

Carl was an amateur photographer and a well-liked Fairbanks teamster. He had talked extensively with a local trapper before making his trip. The trapper tried to talk McCunn into going somewhere else because the valley he had chosen to reside in was devoid of migrating game.

In March 1981, Carl set out to an isolated valley seventy-five miles northeast of Fort Yukon His fourteen hundred pounds of gear consisted of photo equipment and camera gear (including five hundred rolls of film), five-gallon buckets of rice, wheat, and beans, a .30-30 rifle, a shotgun, and other staples.

Pilot Roger Mayer of Arctic Circle Air Service in Fairbanks dropped McCunn in a nameless valley, on a nameless lake forty miles west of the Coleen River. Carl's campsite was fifty miles from a regular air-traffic route, which meant any air support he received would be either planned or happenstance. It would be six weeks before breakup.

Mayer helped McCunn mark his campsite on three maps, which were subsequently mailed to three friends in Fairbanks. Before leaving for the trip, McCunn had mailed a map and a letter to his father in Texas. Carl instructed his father "not to be too upset if he didn't hear from him for a while because he was considering staying the winter and coming out in the spring if things went well for him."(2)

Carl expected his friend Rory Cruikshank to pick him up. Carl had spent so much money on his outfit he wouldn't be able to pay an air taxi service to come get him. Rory was his only hope; however, Rory had told Carl not to count on him as he would likely be in Anchorage. Carl had paid Rory money to make airplane repairs that would allow Rory to fly Carl into the bush, not out. Adding to the problem of Carl's return was that he had never told Rory that he'd flown in with another pilot; and Carl left no word as to his whereabouts or a pickup date.

For the next several weeks Carl chronicled his activities in a hundred-page loose-leaf notebook. He built a duck blind from which to observe and photograph wildlife. He marveled at the wonder of emerging summer. Echoing his love of nature were descriptions of waterfowl returning from their southern migration. He loved and wondered at the cry of the loon. Swans and other waterfowl returning to their summer nesting grounds captivated him.

Carl supplemented his diet of starchy foods with ducks and grayling, using his shotgun and a fishnet he'd designed. One day while sitting in his duck blind, he heard splashing water. He looked and saw a caribou thrashing in the lake before it died. He didn't know what caused its death but welcomed the prospect of eating it.

Thinking he could wade out to the 'bou if the wind failed to bring it to shore, he was inspired and filled with renewed hope with this newfound mother lode of meat. He eventually waded into the frigid, chest-deep water and retrieved the dead animal. Carl skinned, gutted, and cached the caribou underwater in the lake. That evening he relished the liver and heart, daydreaming about a home-cooked meal on his return to Fairbanks. For a few days he gorged on caribou meat, one day claiming to have eaten seven pounds. The meat boosted his spirits.

Carl contemplated a festival in the Market Basket. His thoughts resembled those of the gold prospectors of old; it wasn't so much getting the gold as it was searching for it. Carl salivated over the mere thought of checking out the milk cooler . . . wandering through the fruit section . . . hitting the bakery . . . ogling the ice cream freezer . . . sampling the chocolate products . . . and best of all, relishing peanut butter and jelly.

Carl constructed a drying rack for the caribou meat, planning to smoke it for preservation and later use. As the days went on, he did preserve the caribou.

McCunn expected to be picked up in August, but he's the only one who expected it. For some unknown reason he had never finalized a pickup date with a pilot. The "arrangement" to be picked up was spoken about but never confirmed.

By the middle of August food was getting harder to come by. He constantly went to the nearby creek to check the fishnet he'd set. He had attached links of chain to weight down one side in the water.

He battled the birds for rose hips. These budlike growths were rich in vitamin C and remained on wild rosebushes after the flower blossoms dropped off. Another food item he added to his list was muskrats, the little ratlike water fur-bearer.

Flies, gnats, and mosquitoes persistently plagued Carl, attacking in swarms. He'd heard about these pests driving caribou and moose mad while swarming into their ears and nostrils. To combat these pests he concocted a paste of water and red pepper that he applied generously as an ointment. The bites and constant buzzing deprived him of sleep. At times the stress was so intense that Carl nearly cried. Through it all he tried to adjust. Ever the utilitarian, Carl sewed a new zipper in his canvas mukluk.

One day he shot three green-winged teal, managing to kill them with one shot. It was a time of plenty, and he roasted them.

As time went on, he went to sleep late and arose late. Sleeping in was often necessary because the big, raucous ravens that flew around his camp constantly irritated him.

Even though Carl planned to use his bed frame for firewood and to build a new bed, he didn't want to cut down any trees near camp because they were pretty and he wanted to leave the land the way he had found it.

One day he shot and ate a hawk. Later when game became more scarce, Carl began taking partially eaten kills from hawks.

He awoke in the dark one night when he heard a moose splashing in the lake. Carl fetched his rifle and went to investigate. The animal promptly put distance between them. Unable to see any horns, Carl chose not to shoot it because he didn't want to shoot a cow.

By late summer concerned friends of Carl's asked the Alaska State Troopers to check on him. On a flight from Fort Yukon to Old Crow, Trooper David Hamilton flew toward McCunn's camp.

The day he heard the airplane fly over, Carl was almost beside himself with excitement. He ran out into the open near his tent and waved his hand in a sort of sports gesture of victory. He realized right away that the aircraft was wheel-equipped, which meant it would not be able to land on the lake, but that did not bother him as he assumed the plane's pilot would return to Fairbanks and send out a float equipped plane to pick him up.

Hamilton overflew McCunn's camp two hundred feet above the ground. He and his passenger saw Carl wave a red bag. Hamilton noticed a large quantity of firewood covered with visqueen. He circled the camp a second time. He said later that McCunn "waved in a casual manner and watched us fly by. On the third pass he turned and walked back towards the tent slowly, casually. No wave, no nothing. We surmised there was no immediate danger or need for emergency aid and proceeded to Old Crow."(1)

What appeared to be a cavalier attitude on Carl's part was actually his determination to break camp and await the float plane he assumed would be coming for him shortly.

But after the plane disappeared and no other one showed up, McCunn wrote in his diary, "I recall raising my right hand, shoulder high, and shaking my fist on the plane's second pass. It was a little cheer—like when your team scored a touchdown or something. Turns out that's the signal (or very similar, because you don't close your fist, you have your palm facing away with your fingers straight up) for 'ALL OK . . . DO NOT WAIT!' They probably blew me off as a weirdo. . . . Man, I can't believe it!"(1)

Assuming no plane would return for him and with the continuing cold nights, Carl determined to dig a four-foot hole in the ground as a foundation for his tent. He figured winterizing his tent was not only worth it but also necessary for his survival. It would help provide warmth and stability.

Digging the hole four feet deep and in the shape of his tent floor took him two days. In the process he found a jar with candle pieces, rabbit snares, and soggy tobacco and cigarette papers.

On his return to Fairbanks, Trooper Hamilton advised Carl's friend Randall Robinson to proceed with plans to pick up McCunn. In the meantime a rumor claimed Carl was back in town.

While working at his camp, Carl noticed the fall nights becoming colder and the north winds increasing. Before long, snow blanketed the land and the lake froze over.

Carl saw a wolf, made a new bed and frame, and determined his next project would be to construct a floor from birch logs.

He was snaring rabbits frequently until foxes and wolves discovered McCunn's catches (at one time he had twenty rabbits stored, what he figured was a two-week supply of food). The four-legged predators seriously impacted his food source and supplies.

One day Carl wrote, "I keep thinking of all the shotgun shells I threw away about two months ago. Had five boxes and when I kept seeing them sitting there I felt rather silly for having brought so many. (Felt like a warmonger.) So I threw all away . . . into the lake . . . but about a dozen . . . real bright. Who would have known I might need them just to keep from starving."(1)

At length Carl burned the wood floor from his tent and ended up scooping fifteen gallons of water from under his bed. He constructed an emergency marker to attract aircraft attention. Carl arranged three bushy, ten-foot spruce trees in a triangle and tied an orange (international distress color) rucksack around the top of the tallest one, finalizing it by wrapping orange tape around the trees.

One day while returning from his trapline he discovered tracks of four wolves that had followed him.

Eight and a half months into his stay he was fighting a feeling of abandonment. He was hobbled by frostbite and fighting with predators for food. Carl forlornly faced each day in hopes that rescue would materialize. Entries from his diary later revealed he vacillated between blaming himself and his friends for his dilemma. One entry read, "I think I should have used more foresight about arranging my departure. I'll soon find out. Am down to beans now . . . just over a gallon. That may not last two weeks. Finished off the rice yesterday."(1)

Although it was twenty-five degrees above zero in November, the days to come and the cold they bore would test McCunn's tenacity.

For weeks cold assaulted McCunn, weakening him more emotionally than physically. Toward the end his hands and feet felt like icicles. His anguish compounded itself when he wrote that his friends in Fairbanks should have figured out by now that he was in trouble, and he wondered why he had given them the maps. He admitted he was scared.

"Come on, please . . . don't leave me hangin' and frettin' like this. I didn't come out here for that."(1)

The waning hours of daylight meant longer and colder winter nights, which caused McCunn's hope to fade, his fear and despair to increase.

Toward the end he wrote in his diary, "Fell to my knees today on the lake and begged God's help and mercy. I'm sure he heard me but don't know if He should have any reason to want to help. Tonight in my prayer I made a commitment to God. If He helps me out of this jam, I pray for His help for the strength to keep it."(6)

The next day he shot a fox and made two meals of it, eating the tongue, heart, kidneys, and liver as well as the normal body parts.

Dejected by failures at snaring, Carl wrote one night, "It's been quite a terrible day for me and I won't go into it. Hands getting more frostbitten every day . . . fingertips and edges of hands numb and stinging. Feet as well. It's only minus five degrees on the thermometer but seems colder. Nose runs from the minute I get out of bed till a fire gets going and then once outside it starts again and runs till my night fire. . . . I'm scared for my life. I don't feel there's much hope I'll even be alive in a week. But I won't give up."

With food depleted, McCunn turned to his remaining seasonings, ingesting ground red pepper, thyme, and salt "to let my stomach know I'm still here."(7)

Weakness and dizziness worked on him.

Should rescue not materialize, he considered his rifle as a last resort. Carl felt contrite as he'd never contemplated suicide. He didn't want to give up, but he was at the end of his rope, miserable, cold, weak, starving. "I'm starting not to care to live. Can't stop thinkin' about doin' myself in. Everything seems like it'll be okay when the fire's goin' and I'm warm (even though I'm as hungry as h—) but when I'm cold and shivering and feeling helpless and miserable . . . I just want to end it.

"It's weird to feel on death's threshold. When's it going to end? One way or the other, I keep telling myself, 'Hang in there, man . . . somebody will fly over!' But I'm beginning to believe I'm just lying to myself.

"It's so tempting to squeeze the trigger just to keep from suffering any more . . . but not yet."(7)

His hunger caused him to turn to peeling spruce saplings and eating the bark.

He regretted not shooting at the moose in the lake in the dark . . . and regretted his casual attitude when the trooper's plane circled his camp.

He was chilled three mornings in a row and mentioned his frostbitten hand was tender where the blisters were.

"My nose stings soooo bad, my fingers a little less, my toes hurt, my feet are swollen, my heart is truly broken, no spirit. . . . I feel no hope of help being on the way. . . . Dear God in Heaven, please forgive my weakness and my sins. Please look over my family."(7)

Exhausted from the struggle of survival and agonizing with the thought of no heat, no food, and no hope, Carl took his rifle and terminated his pain

*   *   *

When no one had seen Carl after the first of the year, urgency dictated another check on him.

Troopers were asked on January 19 to check on Carl. Bad weather hampered the search. The mercury hovered at minus forty-six when Hamilton flew over Carl's camp on January 26. He saw no sign of life.

Hamilton returned to Fairbanks for a ski-equipped plane. When he returned to McCunn's camp on February 2, the only sign of human habitation was the tent. Hamilton landed, walked to the tent, and discovered it zipped shut. He stuck a knife into the canvas, sliced through the icy wall, and saw Carl on his homemade bed, his emaciated body frozen. Carl's .30-30 rifle lay nearby.

Hamilton and his partner found a note requesting that Carl's father receive his personal items. Carl suggested that whoever found him should take his .30-30 and shotgun for their trouble.

Carl agonized over the pain his situation would cause his family. Not wanting them to suffer any longer by seeing him in his condition, he wrote, "If my body has been eaten on or if it turns out I take my own life . . . just put me under a tree so I can at least make a decent meal for some critter."(7)

In the end his own words provided his epitaph, "Humans are so out of their 'modern-day' element in a place like this."(1)

Carl McCunn died in the Arctic, alone but not forgotten. Rather than face the toothless death of starvation, he chose a rifle bullet for himself. With the hunger pains of starvation and the chilled fingers of frostbite mocking him at every turn, he laughed at these twin killers when he pulled the trigger.

Carl McCunn's death was ruled a suicide . . . but long before he pulled the trigger on the rifle, he slipped a live round into the chamber by failing to solidify arrangements for his return to civilization. Roger Mayer, the pilot who dropped Carl off, said, "We had instructions he was to be picked up by a friend of his before winter set in, with a float plane."(2)

Friends and family testified at a coroner's inquest—as did McCunn's diary—that he had failed to arrange for his pickup.

McCunn knew about a trapper's cabin four miles from his camp but made no effort to reach it.

McCunn's reason for going into the woods is not nearly as puzzling as his failure to arrange to come out of it.

Another romantic ventured into Alaska's bush alone. In 1992, Chris McCandless left civilization and his worldly possessions and headed into the hills.

THE LAST ADVENTURE

BY LARRY KANIUT

*This is the law of the Yukon, and ever she makes it plain: "Send not
your foolish and feeble; send me your strong and your sane—"*

—Robert Service, "The Law of the Yukon"

When I read about Chris McCandless's Alaskan adventure, I was shocked to
think that someone in the 1990s would do such a thing. It amazed me. As you
read about Chris, maybe you will be amazed also.

People who know someone well can often determine what he will say or do.
When Paul Harvey went on the air on September 13, 1992, and broadcast the
discovery of a starving victim's body in Alaska, some people immediately thought
they knew the victim. Wayne Westerberg of South Dakota was following the
grain harvest when an employee radioed to tell him he'd heard about a guy
starving in the Alaskan boonies . . . that the victim sounded like a friend of theirs.

Westerberg called the Alaska State Troopers and they faxed him a picture of
the victim. Wayne told them the photo resembled his friend Chris McCandless.
Identifying the deceased, whose body was badly decomposed, required dental
records. Troopers received permission to see the records from McCandless's
parents and identified the dead man as their son.

From time immemorial man has had a love-hate relationship with the unknown . . . the sea, the land, and outer space. Americans love romance . . . and
mystery. And they love speculating.

After the discovery of Chris McCandless's body on the Stampede Trail near
Healy, Alaskans and Americans alike had a field day with the why of the event:
Why did he die? Why did he go into the wild? Why was he unable to survive?
Theories ran the gamut.

The event spawned at least one book that was on the *New York Times*' best-
seller list for over a year. The headlines of the McCandless mishap drew international attention. Many portrayed him as a modern Henry David Thoreau, a
visionary in search of himself and life's truths. Others, especially woods-wise
Alaskans and those experienced with hostile environments, had a different view.

It is hard to accept a man's going into the woods in a careless manner. But Chris McCandless wasn't the first to do so in Alaska.

A popular Fairbanks teamster named Carl McCunn followed the rose-tinted trail to starvation. He died and left a diary of his midwinter 1981 activities. Eleven years later Chris McCandless followed McCunn's example and went into the woods, eyes aglow with wonder and enthusiastic plans to become one with his universe.

By all outward appearances Christopher McCandless and his siblings grew up on the East Coast in a friendly environment. Since early childhood Chris had marched to a different drummer. He participated in high school cross-country running where as team captain he led his teammates on grueling runs designed to get them lost so they'd have to push themselves to their outer limits. According to his close friend from those days, Gordy Cucullu, "That's how Chris lived his entire life."(13)

A quixotic jouster of windmills, Chris spent weekends wandering Washington, D.C., streets talking with pimps, hookers, and homeless people . . . even going so far as to bring home a bum to his parents' Airstream vacation trailer unbeknownst to them.

He was so good at nearly everything he did that he developed an aura of overconfidence.

Right out of high school he set out on a pilgrimage in his Datsun B210, promising his parents to contact them every three days. He returned only two days before college began. His parents grew increasingly concerned about his risk-taking. He constantly engaged in programs to save the suffering—the homeless in America and Africa's starving.

Chris liked to do things his way. When others offered advice, he usually thanked them, then continued without altering his plans. Once he made up his mind, there was no changing it.

For some reason he alienated himself from his former life; he seemed ambivalent toward his family. Chris had a strong, almost hostile, attitude toward money—perhaps he felt guilt over his family's economic status. Perhaps his actions regarding money were an effort to distance himself from it and the situations that money exploited.

The summer before his senior year at Emory University in Atlanta, Georgia, he was lost in the Mojave Desert. He shed thirty pounds and nearly succumbed to dehydration.

When Chris graduated from college with his degree in history, a $20,000 balance was in the fund his parents had established for his education. They assumed he would use it for law school; however, he donated the entire amount to the Oxford Famine Relief Fund. Without further adieu, and contrary to his promise to drive to his parents' before leaving, he packed his belongings in his Datsun and departed for the West. (The next time his parents heard from him, it was in a phone call that all parents dread.)

When his car broke down in 120-degree heat, he abandoned it in the Arizona desert in July 1990. He then buried his valuables and burned his money, which amounted to $160. The next few months he took up riding the rails and living as a tramp, moving around the West.

From July 29 through August 9, 1990, he worked for "Crazy Ernie" with "six other tramps" in California. When he realized they weren't going to get paid, Chris stole a ten-speed from Ernie and escaped to Chico.

From there he continued north and on September 4 was run out of Astoria, Oregon, by the police. He wore his run-ins with the law as badges of courage.

Eventually he determined to paddle the Colorado River to the Gulf of California, and on November 2 he bought a canoe, started down the river, and entered Mexico illegally on the second of December. Failing to reach the Gulf, he pulled his craft through reeds and mud. After traveling in circles hopelessly lost, frustrated, and demoralized, he lay in the canoe and wept. In the end a duck-hunting guide rescued him and told him there was no outlet to the sea. The guide towed Chris's canoe to base camp, then drove Chris and his canoe to the ocean.

Narrowly avoiding being swept to sea by the wind and waves, Chris abandoned his canoe January 16. He had spoken to no one for more than a month.

By February Chris was extremely uncomfortable in society and wished to return to the road. This apparent self-absorption had begun years before and manifested itself at different times and in different ways, such as when he refused to participate in social activities with friends and chose to be alone.

He buried his camera and later, when digging it up, discovered it was useless for taking pictures.

Sometime during this wandering, Chris nicknamed himself Alex Supertramp.

Chris was homeless for several weeks, living on the Las Vegas streets before working his way back to Carthage, South Dakota. He told Wayne Westerberg that he needed enough money for a grubstake to purchase minimal supplies for his trip to Alaska. He wanted to visit Alaska as close to the end of April as possible in order to return to help Westerberg with the fall harvest. And Chris always grew restless in the spring.

Since Westerberg was shorthanded and needed Chris's help, he offered to buy him a plane ticket to Alaska if he'd stay an extra ten days. But Chris felt that he had to hitchhike, that to journey into the unknown any other way would be cheating. And he was eager to get on his final and greatest adventure before settling down.

McCandless left Carthage on April 15, and Westerberg received a postcard from him in early May (postmarked April 27) stating, "Greetings from Fairbanks. This is the last you shall hear from me, Wayne. . . . Please return all mail I receive to the sender. It might be a very long time before I return south. If this adventure proves fatal and you don't ever hear from me again, I want you to know you're a great man. I now walk into the wild."(10)

From Fairbanks, Chris planned to enter the wilderness and live off the land.

He chose to explore the country at the edge of Denali National Park, a huge tract of wilderness and wildlife about halfway between Anchorage and Fairbanks.

On Tuesday, April 28, Anchorage motorist James Gallien was five miles outside Fairbanks when he spotted a hitchhiker and pulled over to give him a ride. When the man entered Gallien's truck, he introduced himself as Alex. When Gallien asked "Alex . . . ?" Chris replied, "Just Alex."(13)

Alaska is the repository of many people running from a past or trying to establish a future, many being youthful dreamers clinging to the fabric of some Jack London fantasy. Gallien wondered if his passenger was one of those as he drove McCandless to the head of the Stampede Trail.

An outdoorsman himself, Gallien expressed concern over McCandless's gear, knowing it was woefully inadequate. He asked Chris if he'd at least allow him to drive him to Anchorage to purchase some better gear. Chris thanked him, told him no one knew of his plans, and shrugged him off, telling James he hadn't spoken with any family members for three years. No doubt reflecting the attitude of superconfidence he'd developed over the years, Chris said, "I'll be fine with what I've got."(13)

Gallien knew Chris's tennis shoes weren't up to the challenge of the country he'd be hiking and gave his rubber boots to McCandless. Expressing concern for Chris's safety Gallien begged him, "Don't do this."(6)

When McCandless got out of the 4×4, he left the road map he'd been carrying and gave Gallien all his money, a total of eighty-five cents. Chris told Gallien, "I don't want to know what time it is . . . what day it is, or where I am. None of that matters."

McCandless's gear consisted of a backpack and books (*The Terminal Man, Education of a Wandering Man,* and *Doctor Zhivago* by Boris Pasternak). No doubt Chris was greatly affected by Tolstoy, who had rejected his wealth to live with the downtrodden. Chris carried an inexpensive sleeping bag, a .22-caliber rifle and ammunition, a fishing pole, a ten-pound bag of rice, and a 35-mm camera.

Perhaps Chris McCandless didn't know that the harsh environment of Alaska is nothing to fool with. Perhaps he thought his former outdoor experiences qualified him for his outing. Perhaps he thought the temperature and the terrain would not affect him. Perhaps he didn't know that when you challenge Alaska's rugged terrain and terribly cold temperatures, you'd better have your ducks in a row if you plan to return to civilization . . . because nature ain't fooled.

Chris waded the Savage and Teklanicka Rivers and a large beaver pond less than twenty miles from the popular 8 Mile Lake. Several miles into his hike he stumbled onto an old International, a Fairbanks city-transit bus from the 1940s that had been skidded in and parked near the Shushana River years earlier. Local hunters used the bus as a shelter, which is precisely the use Chris put it to.

It was at this shelter that Butch Killian, a firefighter, found Chris over three months later on September 6, 1992. Butch and five others including Ken Thompson, Gordon Samel, and Ferdie Swanson ended up at the bus about the same time. Butch had been hunting and decided to spend the night in the bus. When he approached the bus, he was almost overcome by an overpowering smell, what he thought might be a trapper's bait. Butch spotted a pair of boots and a backpack on the floor of the bus, then the sleeping bag with a lump in it, and knew immediately that something was wrong. He retreated and used his two-way radio to contact the Alaska State Troopers.

Ken Thompson said when they arrived, they saw "a guy and a girl from Anchorage standing fifty feet away looking kinda spooked. A real bad smell was coming from inside the bus, and there was this weird note tacked by the door."(13)

Ken Thompson and Gordon Samel edged closer to the bus and hazarded a look inside. They saw some books and clothing, a .22 rifle and box of shells, backpack, bunk, and blue sleeping bag, which appeared to have something in it. Samel said, "I stood on a stump, reached through the [broken-out] back window, and gave the bag a shake. There was definitely something in it, but whatever it was didn't weigh much. It wasn't until I walked around to the other side and saw a head sticking out that I knew for certain what it was."(13)

When the troopers arrived, they discovered a help sign scrawled on a book page and taped on the bus window that read, "Attention possible visitors. SOS. I need your help. I am injured and near death and too weak to hike out of here. I am all alone. This is no joke. In the name of God please remain to save me. I am out collecting berries close by and shall return this evening. Thank you."(1)

Troopers found a note in the camera that read: "I have had a happy life and thank the Lord. Good-bye and may God bless all!"(2)

The troopers had a body. The next step was to determine the body's identity.

While investigating they found a handwritten log, detailing McCandless's 113-day ordeal. The diary consisted largely of one- and two-word entries in back of a book about Athabascan Indian plant-food usage called *Tanaina Plantlore*. Because of the abbreviated nature of the entries, it is difficult to decipher McCandless's meaning and actual events.

During McCandless's stay in the bush he fell through the ice, scrounged for food, hiked a three-thousand-foot ridge, and wondered about his chances of survival. In the beginning Chris had eaten berries and small game. Since he detested killing, it is troubling to consider how Chris killed to eat. The bulk of his food consisted of small game (three dozen squirrels; a dozen birds including jays, spruce hens, and woodpeckers; a couple of frogs; and a porcupine) and vegetation (wild rhubarb, berries, mushrooms, and wild potatoes).

On day nine he experienced weakness and on day twenty-two indicated some disaster had befallen him. From days forty-three to forty-eight he shot what he thought was moose and then butchered it. Bugs and flies appeared, and evidently maggots infected the meat, most of which rotted.

McCandless wrote that his attempt to smoke the meat to preserve it was ineffectual and that he wished he'd never shot it. He considered his shooting the moose "one of the greatest tragedies of my life."(4) (Gordon Samel, the Anchorage auto-body repairman who was with the group that found McCandless, observed caribou legs—not moose—outside the bus.)

On day sixty-seven McCandless left the bus and on the sixty-eighth he indicated "disaster," but he did not go into detail. The next day he wrote, "Rained in, river look impossible. Lonely, Scared."(5)

More than likely he had attempted to hike out to the highway and encountered the rain-swollen Teklanicka River, whose chest-deep, seventy-five-foot channel turned him back.

On day ninety-four he wrote, "Much trouble just to stand up. Starving. Great Jeopardy."(4)

Nearly a week later, on day one hundred, McCandless wrote, "Death Looms as serious threat, too weak to walk out, have literally become trapped in the wild."(4)

On a board in the bus he had scrawled, "No phone. No pool. No pets. No cigarettes. Ultimate freedom . . . No longer to be poisoned by civilization, he flees, and walks alone upon the land to become Lost in the Wild."(12)

Afterword . . . Advice

To say that Chris McCandless was unprepared for his trek into the timber is a gross understatement. To think that he knew what he was doing is unthinkable. To expect his survival based on his preparation and actions stretches the bounds of hope, expresses absurdity, and screams stupidity.

Some say he didn't plan to die. I say he failed to plan. Solo survival demands preparation. Without experience and necessary preparation, success afield is limited if not impossible. Chris McCandless, though apparently motivated by a love of the land and a desire to challenge the wild, came up short in his bid to return to civilization.

Although there is no law against going into the woods, there should be some measure of common sense attached to such an undertaking.

It is understandable that we sometimes unintentionally bring pain, grief, and suffering into the lives of others. But to do so intentionally, as a result of limited knowledge or the complete lack of it, compounds that grief almost beyond understanding.

By all outward appearances that's exactly what Chris McCandless did. He chose to walk into the wilderness with total disregard for the survival skills necessary for his safe return to civilization. To survive Alaska's extreme weather in the bush requires extreme care and no little amount of planning.

Whether McCandless was a modern Henry David Thoreau, a visionary on a spiritual journey trying to reinvent the wheel of compassion and solve the world's problems, or an escapee from a past he couldn't outrun, he was ill prepared. McCandless had no business going into the woods alone and without sufficient preparation.

More fundamental to the speculation as to why McCandless went into the wilderness and died there is the question of why he went unprepared. Had he properly prepared, he would have stayed his execution at the hands of Mother Nature, the very force that wooed him to his death.

Several cabins, both government and private, were located within seven miles of the bus—some were stocked with food and stoves. He was less than ten miles from a Denali National Park ranger station. Within a quarter mile of the bus was a hand-powered tram to cross the river. Numerous cabins stocked with food were within walking distance. Had he taken the time to learn of any one of these facts, he could have lived.

Friends admit that McCandless's determination to be self-reliant would have kept him from using the hand-powered tram downstream a quarter mile from the bus, the cabins, or any other outside help offered him.

Chris McCandless committed a major error in playing by his rules instead of nature's. His overconfident attitude toward proper preparation killed him. He would have lived if he'd arranged for someone to check on him . . .

. . . if he had taken a dependable partner . . .

. . . if he'd familiarized himself with the area by studying or carrying a topographical map . . .

. . . if he had asked for more detailed advice on how to survive that setting . . .

. . . or if he had taken an ELT or handheld radio—even Butch Killian had a radio on his four-wheeler.

Captain John Myers of the Alaska State Troopers said that McCandless could have started a fire in the forest to attract a search party.

Another consideration is the responsibility of those who enabled Chris. How could they have helped him grasp the enormity of his undertaking? James Gallien tried to dissuade Chris.

Perhaps the greatest grief of all was suffered by Chris McCandless's parents, Walt and Billie McCandless. They were baffled by his behavior. Walt asked, "How is it that a kid with so much compassion could cause his parents so much pain?"(13)

The third man in this series entered the bowels of the wilderness over fifty years before McCandless and his predecessor McCunn. Ben White, however, had a plan.

MUGGED BY A ROGUE

AS TOLD TO THE AUTHOR BY BEN WHITE

George can't possibly live, but he's in such terrible pain. . . . You'll do George a great justice if you put him out of his misery.

In the spring of 1998 I received a phone call from Jay Stafford. He wondered if I'd be interested in going to the hospital with him to meet and visit with his friend Ben White, an old-time guide, pilot, trapper, and prospector. I jumped at the opportunity and met Jay at Providence Hospital in Anchorage. After we spoke with Ben, Jay loaned me a cassette-tape container filled with nearly a dozen of Ben's taped stories. I transcribed the following story, which reflects a young man's desire to go into Alaska's bush and the maturity level he'd attained at a young age.

In 1935, after drifting down the Yukon River four hundred miles in a canoe, I landed at a small native village called Ruby. That's where I met George Pitka, an old Eskimo. George was one of the finest men I ever met, and one who meant an awful lot to me. He turned out to be more than just a friend; he was something special in my life.

I wanted to get into the Noatak country to trap and to prospect for gold. The farther north you go, the coarser the gold is—it's called jewelry gold. The coarse gold is in the Noatak country. A miner is severely limited in production because permafrost, the frozen ground, only allows him about thirty days a year to work the creek and the muck that has the gold in it.

The fur was good in those days up in that country. You could get more than a hundred dollars for one white-fox hide. Marten brought thirty dollars apiece. They were easy to trap. You catch them in the wintertime when they climb upon the trees. You set your traps on the limbs, and when he runs out on the limbs, he hits a trap and falls out where he hangs up off the ground where the mice and shrews can't chew on the bottom side, which damages the fur.

I told old George Pitka where and why I wanted to go. He took a long look at me and said, "Young man, you're a greenhorn, what we call a cheechako in this country. It's an Eskimo word meaning newcomer. You'd better go some-place close for your first winter until you get used to mushing dogs and setting your traps."

He couldn't talk me out of it as I had my mind set on going into that country. Knowing the dangers of such a task, especially for someone alone, George constantly told me the problems I would be faced with.

He helped me to build a dog sled and said, "I'll tell you what I'll do. I'm gonna give you my best dog team." He had two dog teams, as most trappers do in case they lose one for some reason. He gave me the finest team that any trapper could ever go out into the woods with. They were half to three-quarter wolf that he had crossed his dogs with.

The purpose of having wolf-dog blood in your dog team in the early days was because it makes for a much hardier dog. Their feet are much better. A wolf has a good foot. Most dogs' feet go tender pretty easy. The wolf can stand the hardship and pull a heavier load.

In the north country where I went, it was nothing to have sixty-to-seventy-below chill factor when the wind was blowing. When it's cold, the wolf dogs curl up in the snow and lay their bushy tails over their noses and the wind will blow the snow right over them and cover them until they almost start to suffocate. They get up and shake and lie right back down in that impression.

But a dog suffers too much from the cold. Dogs require kennels, a lot of dry grass, branches, and whatnot to get them up off the ground. Although I never loaded them that heavy, a good wolf will pull 350 pounds.

A freighting or trapper's sled in the early days would weigh close to three hundred pounds and was close to fifteen feet long. It takes a lot of sled room to haul freight, fur, and camp supplies. Those Iditarod dogs that you see on television today would have been useless to an early-day trapper or prospector. They only weigh forty to forty-five pounds. They're fast and they run a long ways, but their feet are not good and they can't take the extreme cold weather when you get up north of the Arctic Circle.

When we bred our wolves in the early days with our dogs, we were coming out with wolves that weighed from 90 to 110 pounds. It made a good husky dog that could haul a good load, had good feet, and they were very, very rugged.

George gave me a real good dog team.

When I got my sled all done and was ready to go, I bought my supplies. A bean peddler in Ruby sold just about anything a trapper or prospector would want, all the way from a dog collar up to half soles to wear on your shoes . . . you name it, he had it. In those days we called the trading post operators bean peddlers. His name was Karl Boehn. He was a little short, stocky German.

George went with me and knew about what I needed in the way of grub. That one thing was beans. I bought 150 pounds of dried beans. I had 50 pounds of limas, 100 pounds of red beans. You need something in the backcountry to keep away from scurvy, which is caused from meat diet without vitamin C. You need meat in the backcountry, you couldn't go without it. You've got to get a moose or several caribou. Where I was going, there were plenty of sheep. You also have to get on a creek that has whitefish, which run all year around in the streams up north. You need them not only for yourself but also for your dogs.

You feed the dogs on a fish diet, using just a small amount of red meat. If a wolf dog gets too much red meat, he becomes savage and not trustworthy.

Speaking of trustworthiness, I had two dogs among my eleven dogs that were three-quarter wolf. They were not trustworthy. They hated me because I had taken them out of their natural habitat, put them in a harness, and made slaves out of them. They had to take orders from me. They didn't have a free life anymore. They were dangerous animals. I had to watch them when I harnessed them. I had to keep a club in one hand and harness them with the other hand. They had a great deal of respect for that club.

If it looked like they were going to come for me, I hit them across the nose just forward of the eyes to knock them out. That doesn't hurt them. After a while they came to and worked. These two were the best pullers in my dog team. Many times out on the trail the wind would blow and the trail would be drifted full of snow. The pulling was awful hard. The dogs got tired after twelve or fourteen hours on the trail. I always noticed when the other dogs were slacking off from playing out, these two vicious dogs would still be pulling the load.

Before I left Ruby and had all my stuff loaded into my sled, I made arrangements for a bush pilot to fly my traps and a number of things to my proposed camp. But I wanted to be gone about thirty days before he came in to drop it from the air. Or if he could land on skis, he would do that.

When I pulled out of Ruby, Old George Pitka reached over and shook hands with me and looked me right in the eye. He said, "Ben, if you don't make it back, I won't bother to come look for you." That cut me just like a knife in my heart. He was a good friend of mine, and he said he wouldn't come to look for me. But as time passed and I knew what George was talking about, I understood.

I went in with the dogs and got the cabin ready. I built my cabin by a creek so I'd have plenty of water and could catch all the whitefish I needed. But it was on the back side of the mountain. We had very little sun—by November the sun was gone for the winter. We didn't get any sun until clear over into the month of April when the sun was rising higher.

When the pilot came in and unloaded my gear, he had a worried look on his face and said, "Ben, are you gonna stay in here? You're going to go through this winter and the next summer prospecting and go into the next winter before you come out to Ruby?"

I said, "Yes, that's what I'm going to do. Don't look for me until early spring of the following year."

He shook his head and said, "I don't know."

He got in his airplane and I watched him fly away until the plane changed into a little black dot in the sky before it disappeared. I knew that that was my last contact with any human being for a year and a half.

The trapping was good that winter. My main cabin was where I kept my fur and my food stored. I ran my dogs twenty to twenty-five miles a day. I strung out my trapline about a hundred to a hundred and fifty miles. I built my overnight cabins every twenty-five miles. It's a hard day's work to go from one to another. I built four overnight cabins. It took me a week to ten days to make the rounds before coming back to the main cabin. That's where I brought all the carcasses and did the skinning, stretching, and drying of the skins.

I got my camp pretty well set and had to be careful not to injure myself. I knew that if I injured myself, nobody would come to help me. If I broke a leg, I'd have to make the most of it. I'd have to make a splint and get along until it healed up. If a dog bit me, I'd have a lot of trouble trying to keep the wound from getting infected. I had to be thinking twenty-four hours a day, always thinking ahead and not allowing anything to happen to me. If something happened to my dogs, I'd never make it back to Ruby. I'd have to put things on my back and travel on snowshoes, which would be difficult. It would be doubtful I'd make it out in the cold temperature.

We were more than a hundred miles north of the Arctic Circle.

Dogs are company to you, and you're company to your dogs. You learn your dogs, and your dogs will learn you. Old George told me one time, "Ben, there's going to be a time when you have to let the dogs make the decision. You're going to have to recognize that part by the ways your dogs are. You'll have to back down and say, 'The dogs know more than I.'

"But the rest of the time you'll have to be in command. If you're timid and don't have the pressure on the dogs, they'll take advantage of you." That advice meant a lot to me, and the day came when the dogs saved my life. If I'd overruled my dogs, both the dogs and I would have been buried under deep snow.

One day we came around the foot of a mountain heading for our main camp. It was getting along toward spring. The snow was getting a little bit sticky. The trail was good, and when we came to a certain point, the dogs refused to go.

I couldn't force the dogs to go. They lay down and wouldn't get up. I remembered what Old George told me about recognizing these places.

When I realized the dogs wouldn't take the trail, I knew I'd have to go in front of them on the snowshoes and cut a new trail down to the river. That meant we'd have to break trail for a little more than three miles. I was grumbling about it and trying to figure out why the dogs wouldn't go.

We had traveled about mile and a half when all of a sudden I heard one of the biggest roars that you could imagine. It was a snowslide coming down the side of that mountain right across the trail that we would have been traveling. The snow was sixty to seventy feet deep. The avalanche pushed the brush, boulders, and some ground with it, cleansing the ground on its way.

If I had forced the dogs on and gone ahead like I wanted to, we would have been buried under that snowslide, and we'd still be there today. The snow comes down and packs so hard that it turns into a glacier, it's more ice than anything else.

Another time I let the leader have his head in a whiteout. I could barely see the lead dog through the blowing snow. But the lead dog ran on weaving back and forth, sniffing the ground. It had been over a year since I'd been over the trail, but the leader was able to find it.

In those days we didn't have telephones or radio equipment, but when some-one saw you, they passed the word along that you were coming. Finally the word got back to the village of Ruby that "Ben White was returning after this long trip into the Noatak country."

After I'd been out for a year all by myself, I looked back on it and discovered there was no day I was lonesome. When I made it back out after the fourteen months, I'd never spent one hour of being lonesome. I never saw another human being during the entire time. Lonesomeness is something you bring upon your-self. It's the same as sadness. You can be happy if you want to be. You can smile instead of having a frown on your face.

When I pulled up at the trading post, I could see Karl Boehn standing out in front of his store. Right there I tied the dogs and walked up to Karl. I expected George to greet me with open arms and tell me he was real glad that I'd made it back. But he didn't.

When I first approached Karl, he had an awful worried look on his face. He said nothing other than, "Ben, we're sure glad that you came back at this par-ticular time. We've got a real problem here."

I said, "Karl, tell me what the problem is, and I hope that I can be of some help."

"You know George Pitka, don't you?"

"I know him well. He's the man who helped me get my dogs and the dog sled."

"Well, George came in the day before yesterday, and he's in real bad shape. He's been torn up by a bear, and the man is suffering something terrible. We can't do anything for him. George can't possibly live, but he's in such terrible pain. We were hoping that you could come and take charge of this. I'll take all the men in the back room out so there won't be any witnesses. You'll do George a great justice if you put him out of his misery."

I looked Karl straight in the eye and asked, "Karl, are you asking me to kill George?"

"That's pretty much what I meant, but I didn't want to put it in those words. You'd be doing him a favor if you put him out of his misery."

"Karl, you're going about this whole thing in the wrong way. I never killed a man in my life, and I'm not starting now. If you'll show me Old George, I'll see what I can do for him."

Karl hesitated before he said, "No, Ben, you can't do anything for him." He finally opened the plank door of his store and I went in to see George in the back room. There were probably thirty men in there walking around doing absolutely nothing but wringing their hands and feeling sorry for George.

George lay on the cot. They hadn't even removed his clothes. He *was* in bad shape. He was suffering tremendous pain. Being as he was such a dear friend of mine, I'm glad that I went to George without thinking, otherwise I don't know if I could have done it or not.

I asked the men to remove their hats. I don't know if any of them had ever heard anybody pray before. I asked the Lord either to take Old George home or to heal him and to stop his suffering.

I told them to get some hot water going on the stove. "We need some hot water and some bandages." In those days there wasn't much in the way of first-aid equipment.

The bear had torn up George, raked the left side of his face from his forehead scraping clear to the skull, taking out the side of his nose and tearing the upper lip. George's lower lip was torn clear to the jawbone, and his right eye was knocked completely out of the socket. It was just hanging down on his cheek.

George was covered with dirt that was packed into his wounds. The bear had tried to cover him up. Nobody thought anything about cleaning George up, patching him up, and helping him because they thought he was going to die.

We undressed George to remove his blood-soaked clothes. We didn't have much in the way of bandages or tape. We took some electrical tape from a man's toolbox and a small roll of gauze. One man went home and came back with a laundered shirt that we tore up to use as a bandage.

We washed out the eye on his cheek, and I forced it back into the socket. I put a bandage on it and taped it on so the eye would stay where it belonged. We closed his eyelids and taped them shut.

George's left shoulder had been bitten clear to the bone. I continued removing the dirt from his wounds.

I couldn't understand the reason for the heavy bleeding coming from his face until I discovered it was coming from his throat.

George couldn't talk or swallow. When I washed all the dirt off, I found that a claw had gone through the esophagus and caused a lot of damage in the throat.

That was the first and last time in my life I ever heard of dirt saving somebody's life. Because the bear had tried to cover George with the dirt, it caked his throat and caused a plaster that kept him from bleeding.

The only medicine we had was aspirin tablets, so I had the men mash them into a powder with a hammer. Once I got him cleaned and patched up, we took about ten of them and put them with a little water. We took a teaspoon and tried to get some to go down George's throat. Finally we got all ten in him.

The men said he hadn't had anything to eat for a long time, and I said, "We need some moose broth." We took some rye tack and pounded it into a powder and mixed it in with the moose broth and fed a little bit at a time down his throat. He wasn't able to swallow well, and we didn't want to choke him.

I'd been on the trail sixteen hours before I got into Ruby. I worked on Old George for six hours and was exhausted. I told the men there was nothing more we could do but have three volunteers to stay and spend the rest of the night to see that the fire didn't go out. There was plenty of wood to keep the room warm for George's comfort. I rolled out my sleeping bag on the floor in the corner and told them, "If George stirs at all, be sure and wake me. But I'll be hard to waken because I'm exhausted."

George was starting to relax a little bit. As we watched him a few moments before the men left, his arm dropped down to one side. All indications were that George just passed away.

I took his arm and felt his throat. He had a normal pulse. His heart was still beating. I told the men that he'd gone into a deep sleep, which was the best thing for him so he could get some rest.

The men went on home. George lay there. When they woke me in the morning, they heard a low hum coming. As I listened and got up, I recognized the sound as the approaching mail plane.

Oscar Winchell flew the mail up and down the Yukon River. It sounded like he was coming into Ruby. We raced out onto the river ice where he landed.

I told him that George had a real crisis, torn up the way he was. I asked him, "Could you possibly unload your mail and fly George into Fairbanks? There may be a little chance that George can live."

Oscar unloaded all his mailbags. We removed the copilot seat from the Stinson, picked up this little cot George lay on, and loaded him into the plane. There was room alongside the pilot.

He took off and I watched that airplane as it disappeared over the horizon. I knew that George couldn't live more than fifteen or twenty minutes and said, "The man can't make it. His body will be taken care of in Fairbanks."

The wind was blowing slightly, filling the air with dust. I knew it would be an awfully miserable ride in the Gullwing Stinson, an hour and a half to get into Fairbanks—those planes only flew about eighty, eighty-five miles an hour.

George was gone, and I told Karl, "I'm going to take my dog team to George's trapline to see if I can find out what happened down there." It seemed like a big mystery to me. The whole thing didn't sound right. The claw marks on Old George were definitely those of a bear, and I wanted to get to the bottom of it. It was too early for bear to be out, so it had to be a rogue bear, a killer.

I left at daylight and started down the Yukon River to its junction with the Yuki River. George had a line about twenty-five miles up the Yuki.

I pulled into George's place and put the dogs away in George's kennels. I went into his cabin. I knew that George had not intended to go to Ruby at that time. His fur was not bundled. Water was on the stove. His water bucket hadn't been emptied. There weren't any notes.

I was pretty tired so I went to sleep. Just about daylight the dogs stirred up a big fuss. I knew by the way the dogs were acting that something was moving. I got up. It was still dark and I couldn't see well. The dogs were all looking in one direction, so I knew that something was moving in from that part of the river.

I hurried up and put on my warm clothes and checked my rifle to be sure that all the ammunition was in the proper place. I stepped outdoors, still unable to see much. As I continued to look upriver to where the dogs were looking, I saw a dark object moving through the brush on the riverbank.

I felt that must be the killer. He was coming back. As the object moved closer, I recognized it as a grizzly bear. It hung to the brush along the riverbank, a sign that it was constantly making a little progress. The best way to handle a bear like that is to get out in the open and let the bear spot you so you can bring on a charge by the bear. That's what I was aiming for.

I walked out onto the river, which was normally twelve feet wide, but with the overflow it was sixty to seventy feet wide. I wanted to be on the center so I could have a good vantage of whatever came for me. I didn't want the bear to get to the dogs and kill them.

The bear continued in the brush until he reached the end of it. He was only about fifty feet from me. I moved a couple of steps to the side and spoke to the bear so he couldn't mistake my location. He stopped for a moment, assuring me that he was fixing me as his target and preparing to attack me.

I knew he would be coming any moment. His leaps would be twelve, fifteen feet. There would only be about three jumps between me and that bear.

I talked to the bear and said, "I'll give you what you gave my best friend."

The bear made that first leap; a bear will always keep its head low in a charge. You can't shoot under them into the lung area. I didn't want to shoot there anyway. I wanted to shoot him in the neck to put him out of commission.

The first shot went between the shoulder blades a little bit high. The second shot put him on the ground for good, but he wasn't dead yet. He was trying to get back up. I put the third shot into him, which proved fatal.

This is not an easy story for me to tell. George was more than just an ordinary friend. He was something special in my life. I felt that George was dead.

I started skinning out the bear, going through it piece by piece to find out what caused this bear to be a rogue, what made a killer out of him. I didn't find too much in his body. There wasn't much in his stomach and no fat on the bear at all. His stomach contents indicated that he had lived mostly on roots. When I removed the skull and cleaned all the meat from it, I found what had brought on this whole thing.

The bear had been shot twice, both times from the side. One shot had gone through the jawbone on the right side and come out on the left side. The jawbone on the left side was broken and some of the teeth were missing. Some broken teeth had nerves exposed. One bullet had gone through a little higher, through the nose. That one caused the bear problems, forcing it to breathe through its mouth.

He'd been chewing, eating, and living for a little more than two years under these conditions. The infected jawbone managed to heal back, though it still had to be painful. A bear like that would have to find a younger bear with a kill and chase it off to eat its kill.

Somebody had shot this bear but the bear had escaped. If a bear smells a man who shoots him, and the bear heals up and gets away, he'll never forget that man's smell. When he smells that man again, he comes in to settle the old score.

I took George's furs and loaded them on the sled. I closed up his cabin and put things away for the year. I took the skull and went back to Ruby.

When I arrived in Ruby, I called in six mature men that I knew, who had been raised on the back end of a dog sled since childhood as had generations ahead of them. They were men with good judgment. We set the skull on the table on Karl Boehn's store, sitting around the table going over it.

I told them the complete story at George's cabin and the actions of the bear. After I'd gone through it all, we went back to the beginning of the story and pieced it together bit by bit. It was so loaded with mystery that we could never come up with the proper answer.

We couldn't figure out how George ever got onto his dog sled, why his dogs were in the harness aiming for Ruby instead of off to his trapline. The season wasn't over. George hadn't pulled his traps yet.

The dogs were fed better during the trapping season than in the summer when they got fed only twice a week, just enough to keep them alive. In the winter you're working your dogs hard and feed them good. A dog doesn't want to leave the trapline. But these dogs left.

I found where the bear had dragged George over to the edge of the riverbank and tried to cover him up with dirt. The edge of the riverbank is always dry dirt. The overburden, the roots, and the moss overhang; and underneath is dry dirt. That's where the bear scooped out the dirt intending to bury George.

Thinking George was dead, the bear decided to leave.

We couldn't figure out how an unconscious man, covered with dirt, could get to his sled, get on it, and go to Ruby. This is a mystery that will never be uncovered.

At breakup I caught the riverboat to Fairbanks, satisfied that George had died long before he got to Fairbanks.

We had some sheep hunters coming, a fellow by the name of Gene Effler. He asked me if I'd give his hunters a hand. I agreed to take the men into the Noatak where there were five thousand sheep. Today you can't find five hundred because the wolves have cleaned them out.

We went on a successful hunt. Gene went back to Fairbanks and I cut back through Ruby to see some old friends, and I needed gas for the airplane. When I landed on the beach, word got around that "Ben White has come back."

Everybody in that village turned out to see me. Everybody was talking fast and asking questions. A boy about twelve kept pulling on my sleeve. Finally I looked around and asked what he wanted.

He said, "Grandpa wants to see you."

I didn't know many grandpas around there but said, "If you'll lead the way, I'll go see your grandpa."

He took me up a little boardwalk and up to a cabin. We went in, and lo and behold, who did I meet there? It was little Old George Pitka. He hadn't died after all.

We were both glad to see each other and hugged one another. He had as many questions as did I.

I asked him what had happened and how much of the experience he remembered. He'd heard from others how I'd patched him up in the store and got him onto the airplane and on to Fairbanks.

We talked a great deal.

After I told him about the two bullets in the bear, George revealed that he had shot at a bear about two and a half years before his mauling. He had fired two rounds at the bear and thought they were both misses. I'm satisfied that those two shots hit the bear. And the bear almost killed him.

I asked George about the eye that was knocked out of the socket and told him I didn't understand how that had happened. George told me, "When they got me to Fairbanks, they knocked me out with drugs and fed me through my veins. The doctor didn't think I'd live. For two days I lay there. When the doctors saw that I had a chance, they started x-raying me. On the back of my head the skull was like a hard-boiled egg dropped on the table, it was cracked all over. When the bear hit me on the back of my head, that's what knocked the eye out of the socket."

I told him, "I tried to see if you had any broken bones and couldn't find any."

"I did have. My collarbone was broken in two or three places from the bear's teeth. I had two broken ribs on the left side. I didn't lose an arm. I lost the eye that was out of the socket; the doctor's couldn't save it."

They sewed him up and he looked real good. This is the first time I have ever revealed this story because it was too hard to deal with . . . when you have a good friend and special person in your life, feeling that he was dead, yet he lived, it was very touching.

Epilogue

So Ben White returned from the wilderness, saved a friend, and killed the bear that had inflicted the damage. Ben, Carl McCunn, and Chris McCandless—romantics all—ventured into the wilderness to face the adventure of life on the edge. Although experience coupled with preparation and common sense provide a solid foundation, even these could not guarantee the men's safe return.

To die or not to die is not the question. But rather, to think or not to think. Both Carl McCunn and Chris McCandless could and should have lived. All that life required was for them to prepare. The parallels between them are staggering: they were young; they shared the same initials; they were unrealistic, romantic, and ill informed.

On the other hand, another idealist, Ben White, traveled to the Great Beyond north of Alaska's Arctic Circle and returned.

Ben was nearly the same age as McCandless. Ben had it in his head that he was going to trap and prospect two hundred miles away, spending fifteen months without seeing another human, making a solo trip by dog team. At first, he didn't even have a team much less know-how to run one.

But Ben "sat at the feet" of an old Eskimo, learning about the country, the game, and the prospecting. He learned what he'd have to do to come back. He did not have modern aids such as radio, aircraft travel, ELT, PLB, or GPS, yet he lived. Ben lived because he was prepared, took care of himself, and adjusted.

Ben's friend was attacked by a bear, but Don Frantz was "beat up" by a tree.

WHAT HAPPENED?

AS TOLD TO THE AUTHOR BY DON FRANTZ

A series of fortunate things happened after the unfortunate.

In March (or April) of 1996 I heard that my former coaching mentor and teaching colleague Don Frantz had been in an accident and was hanging on to life by the skin of his teeth. I was shocked and called Don to see if I could visit. Thinking stories of people's life-and-death struggles might inspire him, I took him a copy of my book *Cheating Death*. As Don lay in his recliner, ashen-faced, he told me his story. I told him that when he got well, I'd like to get his story on tape for a future book.

Time flew by and suddenly it was the second week in February 1999. I sat in Don's office taping his experience. He was the same old Don, a little grayer, but he still had that twinkle in his eye and his sense of humor. When he told me he'd recovered from his physical injuries, he couldn't help poking fun at himself: "However, I've needed mental therapy all my life."

It is great to see Don up and about and in good spirits. Here's his story.

A tree-cutting project took me to my cabin in March 1996. I flew my Aeronica Sedan, single-engine plane fifty miles northwest of Anchorage to No Name Lake, an oblong body of water a mile long and half a mile wide. When I taxied to the cabin, it was really too late to get started, so I just goofed off that night. My good friend and neighbor Greg Gullickson volunteered to fly his plane out the next day to help me and to spend some time ice fishing and snowmachining. Although I didn't really need Greg's help, I went to bed anticipating his arrival.

I got up the next morning, March 23, and decided to put off work until Greg and his son Berndt arrived. I wanted to enhance the view out the front of my cabin 150 feet from the lake. I was cutting it all down and had previously thinned out a number of various-sized trees, including two or three spruce trees over a hundred feet tall. I had half a dozen trees to finish.

Before long Greg landed his Aeronica Sedan, exactly like mine. I got the boy lined up with a snowmachine and some fishin' gear, then Greg and I went out to work, using my two twenty-five-year-old Homelite chain saws.

Greg started cutting up the trees I had cut the previous weekend while I went to cut down a big two-foot-diameter birch. The tree was on the edge of the clearing I'd cut and stood by itself, leaning toward the lake. It was about thirty degrees off vertical, so I didn't have to worry about which way it was going to fall.

I've been cutting trees most of my life and know about widow makers, trees hanging up, and all that. This one was a giveaway because there was nothing around it. I had cut other trees close to it before and this was almost the last one that I had to do on the project. I cut it down.

I stood beside the stump and the next thing I knew I was beat down in the snow. If I was knocked unconscious, it was just momentary. All I knew was that something had hit me on the head. I have always read the cartoons that show stars when people get hit on the head. Now I know where that thought comes from because I saw flashes of light and stars in my eyes. The wind was knocked out of me.

I grabbed the stump and straightened myself up so I could breathe and sat there in the snow.

I knew immediately that something was wrong with my right leg. I figured my leg was broken because it didn't work, but it didn't hurt. I had absolutely no idea what in the heck had happened.

Even though I wore snow pants and boots and it was relatively warm (in the twenties), I was immediately cold. I didn't have a coat but wore a flannel shirt. My stocking cap and safety goggles were gone. I was thinkin', "What in the world happened?"

I got a breath. Greg was runnin' the chain saw, so I knew he couldn't hear anything. When the chain saw stopped a few minutes later, I hollered for him.

Greg came up and asked, "What happened?"

I said, "Man, I don't know. Somethin' hit me in the head. And I'm freezin' to death. Go up to the cabin and get the sled and get me into the cabin."

He knew what had happened, and he looked at me and said, "Ah, I think we better get you to town."

"I'll be all right. I'm soakin' wet." I was startin' to sweat.

"I'll get a sleeping bag and get you down on the lake."

"All right."

"How do you want to go?"

"There's something wrong with my leg, so just grab me and pull me down the hill . . . get me down on the lake."

About that time his boy came back and Greg sent Berndt over to his plane to get a sleeping bag.

Greg grabbed my arm, pulled me down the hill, and got me on the sleepin' bag. Berndt came over and Greg told him, "Stay here and help Don." Then Greg got his parka and put it over me.

Berndt was scared to death.

Twice I had a little trouble talkin' and I asked Greg, "Hey, are my eyes dilated? Is blood runnin' out of my ears or anything?"

He got down and said, "No, your earplugs are still in."

That explained why I was having trouble hearing.

He said, "There's no blood. You have a little tiny cut on your face."

That's the only cut I had. When I got knocked down, I hit the chain on the saw, which wasn't turnin'. A tooth took a chunk of skin and hide out. Fortunately it wasn't runnin' 'cause the facial cut could have taken my eye.

He said, "Your eyes and ears and everything look good."

Since it had been there less than an hour since he'd arrived, his plane was warmed up and ready to go. He said, "Look, I'll go over and get the plane and taxi over here and we'll get you to town."

Because I was havin' more trouble breathin' and thinkin' maybe I had a brain injury, I said, "Yeah, I think that's a good idea." I was getting really concerned because it was getting harder to breathe. Then I became deathly afraid of passing out . . . *if you pass out, you're out of here, you're history.*

I was still cold and asked Berndt to go up and find my hat. He went and got my stocking cap, shook it off, and brought it back. It was about fifteen, twenty feet away from where I'd felled the tree. He was tryin' to help me and put it on me.

Greg taxied over, turned his engine off, got out of his plane, came over to me, and asked, "How we gonna get you in?"

"I think if you stand me up, I'll hold on to the strut and you can get around and slide me in backwards."

So he did, and as soon as he turned me loose, I fell. He said, "That's not gonna work."

"Just pick me up and poke me in the back."

He had a sleeping bag, a little nest built in the back compartment. So he picked me up under the arms and laid me in over the doorsill headfirst on my chest and stomach. Then he went over to the other side and pulled me across, then came back around and stuffed me into the back, grabbed his son, and off we went. Within ten or fifteen minutes of the accident I was in Greg's plane.

It became more difficult to breathe. I started talkin' to myself and singin' . . . anything I could do to maintain consciousness.

It's only a half-hour flight from my cabin to Anchorage. By the time we got to Lake Hood, I started to hurt. My back, chest, and especially my leg were tearin' me up. Even though Greg had called ahead, we had a little trouble connecting with the ambulance when we landed. But when we finally met the ambulance, I was glad to see one of the drivers was Mark Nokelby, an EMT and a friend I've known for years.

When I told them I'd been hit on the head, they protected my head and neck. They got me out of the plane kind of the reverse of the way I got in except I was on my back. They transported me to Providence Hospital.

The doctor on call was a man I've known for years. He said, "Don, what happened?"

"Oh, man, I was cuttin' trees down and somethin' hit me in the head."

I was restrained from the head and neck. I'd been movin' my head and neck.

By the time I got to the hospital, I was in serious pain. They don't like to give you anything for pain because they want to poke you: "Does it hurt here? Does it hurt there?"—this sort of thing.

They started x-rayin', and of course my blood pressure was rapidly falling. My symptoms weren't congruent with what I was tellin' 'em.

I was really hurting. Finally one of the X rays they shot from my neck across the top of my chest cavity showed my inside was black. Then they said, "Hey, you've got some problems." And they started checkin' farther down.

The worst thing they discovered was a ruptured aorta. After all was said and done, they figured I had had about a half hour to go until I would have died from lack of blood. I had two crushed vertebrae and every rib was either broken, cracked, or separated. My right leg was fractured in five places.

They got with it.

I was fortunate in that people were there, the plane was warm, I got to the hospital, and of the two people in the state who were capable of doing the kind of surgery that I needed, one was available. He was there within twenty minutes. They got all the medical stuff goin', dopin' me up, and I went on the operating table. I was in surgery a little over five hours, and they repaired my aorta. They gave me three units of blood.

That afternoon Greg, two other friends—Walt Kephart and neighbor Don Hoshaw—and my son Dowell decided they'd fly out, close up the cabin, and bring back my plane, but fog prevented them.

If my accident had been a little later, I couldn't have flown out and no rescue helicopter would have had time to save me due to the fog.

The next morning they returned and spent two hours removing the three-hundred-pound stove from my airplane and taking it up to the cabin on a sled (I had help loadin' it and knew Greg was going to be there to unload). They put everything away and took a bunch of pictures. Walt and Dowell flew my plane back while Don and Greg flew their own.

The next day, Sunday afternoon, they came to the hospital after Kephart got the film developed and showed me some pictures. Apparently when I cut that tree down and it hit the ground, the vibrations caused a standing dead birch tree thirty feet away to fall. It was dead and rotten but wasn't tangled up and had nothing to do with the one I cut down.

It was about fourteen inches in diameter where it broke across my back. I got a glancing blow to the back of my head before it knocked my head over against the stump that I had cut. I'm sure the blow on the head stung me and kept my attention from the hurt of my back, chest, and leg injuries.

A series of fortunate things happened after the unfortunate. One was that I didn't have to sit there for months and think that I did something stupid or careless. It was almost like being struck by lightning; if you're in the wrong place at the wrong time, it's going to happen.

It was the first time in my life since I was little that I've been totally dependent upon people. It makes you appreciate people being able to help you. My wife,

A photo of the fourteen-inch-diameter birch tree that broke over Don Frantz's back. It was sixty to seventy feet long. To the right is the stump of the tree he was cutting at the time of his accident.
CREDIT: *Walt Kephart*

Georgette, provided twenty-four-hour-a-day care for several weeks and made my fantastic recovery possible.

I've always tried to take reasonable care of myself, and the healing went miraculously. I'm happy I was in reasonable shape and good health. Now almost three years later, I have some aches and pains but I'm doing everything that I ever did, and the only residual effect is that I'm exactly two inches shorter than I was because of the crushed vertebrae.

I had two primary MDs; one was the surgeon John Broda, and the other was the bone doctor Michael Eaton. My constant concern was nerve damage. The doctors conferred and decided that I had a bunch of potential problems but no nerve impairment. They decided that I wasn't goin' to go dancin' and hoppin' around anyway, so they didn't set a cast on anything.

That leg caused me more grief than everything else combined. One of the breaks was in my fibula, and it's not a major weight-bearing bone, so they didn't set it.

I was up after surgery within three or four hours. I was up several times a day thereafter, and their attitude was, "If it hurts, don't do it." I was x-rayed every two or three days and the vertebrae were monitored. I was only in the hospital seven days.

The surgeon knew from experience that the most comfortable place a person can be is in a recliner. So he kept pushin' to get me home. He's correct. When I got home, I virtually lived in that recliner for three months—I wasn't able to lie down on a bed or anything until July.

The crushed vertebrae were healing well. About a month after the accident my doctors referred me to a spine specialist, who came in cold. He couldn't believe that I had walked into his office . . . very slowly. After he had assessed the X rays and the damage to the worst vertebrae he said, "When those heal, it may fuse those vertebrae. If it does, that's the best thing that will happen because as badly crushed as it is, if it doesn't, you'll have to have surgery to fuse those vertebrae."

The ribs healed and fused the bad vertebrae to one on each side, so I've got three fused vertebrae in the thoracic region of my back. That's a pretty rigid part of your back, so I don't really suffer from inflexibility. It doesn't appear that I'll have to go back under the knife.

The other vertebra wasn't as badly crushed.

The spine doctor wanted to measure me, but at that time I couldn't stand up straight. I said, "Nah, I don't even want to know now. When I can stand up straight and stretch and do all that, I'll worry about it."

He said, "Get yourself ready because you're going to be considerably shorter than you were."

When I had a physical in February '95, I was five-ten, and when I went back in February '97, I was five-eight.

Epilogue

I was fortunate. First, the tree was rotten or it would have crushed me like a bug, killing me instantly. I never thought about dead trees when I was cutting. That's changed now. When I hunt or walk through the woods, it seems that I see every dead tree. It's funny how your perception changes.

Second, my aorta had torn in a spiral shape a little over halfway around. The sheath around the artery also tore, but off the line of the vessel rupture. Instead of going *spurt, spurt, spurt,* which would have caused me to bleed to death in a minute, it was leaking. Every time my heart beat, the aorta leaked, but obviously not huge volumes. The surgeon explained later that many people who die of accidental injuries have ruptured aortas and bleed to death very quickly.

Then there was Greg. He was severely disturbed because he knew what had happened when he walked up to me. I'm sure I didn't look any too good. He was just petrified. Greg's a big man and very strong. It took a man like Greg to get me into the plane because there's no way I could have done it on my own. It may seem that he was a little hasty, dragging me off the hill and pulling me into his plane in my condition but if he hadn't, we wouldn't be conducting this interview. You gotta do what you've gotta do.

Helping hands rallied to save Don, just as many searchers rose to the call to find Dr. Paul McCord.

GONE WITHOUT A TRACE

BY LARRY KANIUT

The ocean never gives up its dead.

A few years ago I picked up the newspaper and was saddened to read about a snowmachine mishap. A severe weather front had lashed the land with a fury of wind and snow. Visibility was nearly nonexistent. The mercury hovered below zero and the windchill sliced to the bone at forty-three below.

A well-known and respected Barrow doctor left his home village to keep an appointment. Later that evening a signaling device indicated he was in trouble. A summary of his known experience follows.

An emergency distress signal from a personal locator beacon (PLB) was picked up by officials in Wainwright, Alaska, at 9:50 P.M. on October 27, 1996. Usually whenever a distress signal is received, a helicopter is dispatched; however, the weather was too severe that night.

Ground searchers left Wainwright immediately. Hampered by the blowing snow and with visibility limited to twenty feet, the searchers reached the doctor's PLB's last reported location, but he was not there.

Paul McCord and his wife, Amy, had arrived in Barrow in 1994 and loved it from the outset. Paul had grown up in the Midwest, the son of a minister. The couple met in 1989 on the Northwestern University campus in Evanston, Illinois. Three years later they married.

Paul fulfilled his residency in Cook County Hospital in Chicago—an inner-city hospital, which may have fanned his interest in public health, to which he dedicated his life. During his final year at Cook he was offered the opportunity to go to Kotzebue for six weeks. That experience planted the seed for Paul's return to Alaska. On his return to Illinois from Kotzebue, he asked Amy if she'd like to live in Alaska.

They chose Barrow because it represented the extremes—it was at the top of the nation; incoming ice from the Arctic Ocean was beautiful; Barrow possessed a peacefulness; the sky was immense, the area was both powerful and captivating.

The curly-haired, thirty-four-year-old adventurer had always loved the outdoors—he was a triathlete, rock climber, hiker, mountain biker, marathoner, and kayaker. When the couple arrived in Barrow, Paul purchased two new Polaris snowmachines.

Because of the extreme weather, the lack of roads or any "normal" transportation, and the threat of death or injury any day on the winter trail, Paul took an arctic-survival course. He prepared for the outdoor experience judiciously, buying maps, compasses, handheld GPS (global positioning system). He regularly read his Polaris repair manual. Amy said he often retrieved it from his bedstand to read at night.

One spring he broadened his experience by riding with friends on a two-thousand-plus-mile loop, visiting Bettles, Kotzebue, Teller, and Point Hope. Paul's survival skills continued to expand. He had been stranded twice—once his snowmachine had broken down on a trip to Bettles; another time, on the way to Wainwright, he was stranded and built a snow house while awaiting rescue.

But he was soon to face his most difficult test.

At the end of October 1996 a winter storm blew in. It raged so severely that schools were closed—only the second time in twenty years. Hunters returned home or to camp where they holed up to wait out the raging weather. Barrow villagers were encouraged to stay home.

But Doc McCord had patients to see. On Sunday, October 27, around 2 P.M. he pointed his snowmachine toward Wainwright and zipped out of Barrow on the well-used, hard-packed trail. Wainwright was nearly one hundred miles distant to the southwest (around the crook of Peard Bay). He was scheduled for and planned to meet patients on the twenty-eighth at the village clinic.

Amy expected to hear from Paul Sunday night around 10 P.M., telling her of his safe arrival. But a call came from a friend in Wainwright, not her husband. Her friend informed her that Paul had not shown up. Amy then called Barrow's Search and Rescue. They told her that they had received a distress call at 9:50 P.M. from Wainwright where visibility was zero. An emergency personal locator beacon (PLB) signaled from twenty-five miles away. It was McCord's.

Knowing her husband's experience and confident of his survival skills, Amy said, "I wasn't real worried at that point. A real bad storm had broke out. There was no visibility and I figured everybody had to hold tight until the morning."(1)

However, Amy slept that night with the phone in her hand.

The day before Paul had left Barrow the National Weather Service had issued warnings about an approaching storm, one that would sweep the Seward Peninsula. By Sunday morning, before McCord left Barrow, the storm neared Wainwright with wind gusts of fifty-two miles per hour, pushing fresh snow and dropping visibility to zero.

The Search and Rescue office in Barrow loans personal locator beacons to interested travelers. McCord had checked one out. Users are instructed to turn on the beacon only if their situation is a matter of life and death. Once activated the beacon signals map coordinates and triggers a search from the closest village.

Paul was warmly dressed and carried a Thermos, tarp, shovel, water, extra fuel, and lots of candy bars. McCord had encountered polar bears on previous outings so he also carried a pistol in his pocket and a rifle on his sled.

Arnold Brower Jr., the coordinator for the Barrow search office, said he thought McCord was "confident he could get there and there was no way to get lost. He had a [personal locator beacon]. I don't think he expected the storm."(1)

Amy said, "I had a lot of confidence. I thought he had dug himself in a snow cave, or he had made a shelter with his sled and tarp. But as the search continued and visibility improved, there was nothing."(1)

In the meantime officials in Wainwright received readings in different locations. From 9:50 P.M. to 4:59 A.M. his PLB indicated ten different locations. But the officials had no way to relay that information to the ground searchers because their radio communication works only in clear weather.

Apparently Paul had no mechanical problems and continued, searching for an area cabin. At one point he was within two hundred yards of a cabin but didn't know it. Some speculated that, although a calm person, he was adversely affected by vertigo, which affects judgment. Perhaps he pushed on thinking he'd find the cabin soon.

Later the readings stopped and officials in Wainwright thought searchers had found McCord and that he had turned off his PLB.

Monday morning, however, the searchers returned to Wainwright without McCord. More searchers departed. Skies began to clear and air support responded.

At one of the beacon-reading sites footprints were discovered. The last three beacon-reading sites were on the ice pack, meaning McCord had left the land and was on sea ice. Because of the flatness of the coastline near Wainwright, it is not uncommon to wonder off land to sea ice.

Paul's parents flew from Illinois into Barrow along with some of his best friends. His sister flew from New York City and his in-laws came from Massachusetts. All joined Amy . . . waiting and hoping.

After the storm had blown through the area and the skies cleared allowing air travel, searching pilots indicated that they could see the storm had broken and pushed the shore ice to sea and against the arctic pack ice. They found no trace of the missing medical doctor.

Over the next six days dozens of search and rescue crews—some from neighboring villages, others from elsewhere—responded with fixed-wing aircraft, helicopters, and a Coast Guard C-130.

Even though the search continued nearly a week, after day three Amy McCord had little hope of finding her husband alive. She said, "Missing people can't say anything, so we will just never know. . . . I'm happy his life didn't end with him sitting in a rocking chair dying of cancer."(1)

Searchers discovered a set of tracks that led out onto the sea ice . . . ending abruptly. Fifty-mile-per-hour wind gusts had pushed the ice out to sea, opening and exposing the thirty-two-degree Arctic Ocean seawater.

What was Paul's experience? Was he warm and determined as he pushed along looking for a cabin or shelter? Had his eight hours on his machine over-heated him, causing him to perspire and chill? Was he thinking properly?

What exactly happened on the ice? Did he have any knowledge of the ice's breaking? Did he actually run off the ice and into the open sea? How long did he survive on the drifting ice or in the cold, salty seawater?

These haunting questions have no answers.

Temperatures had dropped and the windchill had reached minus forty-three degrees.

There was no trace of the missing man. Even though it was customary for search and rescue volunteers on the North Slope to respond a couple of times each month for a lost or stranded traveler, seldom is there a search where nothing or no one is found. This was one of those times.

Early in November, five-hundred people gathered at the Barrow school gym-nasium to pay their last respects and to remember Paul.

Paul McCord's tragic ending brought immeasurable pain.

Epilogue

After Paul's disappearance some people said sometimes it's impossible to save man from himself. Some theorized that his modern electronic gadgetry may have been more harmful than helpful to his safety, that he would have been better off to hole up and wait out the storm than to depend on his GPS and PLB. Even though a strong case can be made for not depending on devices, which may be detrimental, sometimes they are the difference between life and death.

Arctic seawater thickens with ice crystals in the fall. Smooth ice forms on the surface and can be six feet thick by spring. But the sea ice is not as strong as freshwater ice. It is impacted by warming temperatures, tides, currents, and winds. During the fall and winter seasons, wind can break and blow the ice to sea at any time.

Unfortunately Paul left the mainland and ventured onto the ice, probably without knowing it until it was too late.

A friend and coworker, Dr. Tim Coalwell, said Paul "was doing what he loved. . . . That's why he lived in the Arctic. He got out and he enjoyed it. That's how he made contact with people. He was willing to become one of them. He was a good doctor."(1)

When Paul first started traveling about the wilderness, Amy worried about him, as any woman would. But later she said, "Then I saw how much he knew. That he got all the maps. Plugged into the GPS and marked all the cabins on his maps. No one could have been more prepared. I always had faith. . . . Plus even in those times when I did worry, I knew that wasn't going to change anything. If you are committed to being with someone that has an adventurous spirit, that is part of it."(1)

On July 15, 1997, a teal-green Polaris snowmachine was found on a beach fifteen miles northeast of Peard Bay. The machine, missing its windshield, handlebars, and hood, was badly corroded from the salt water. However it bore the serial number of the machine McCord had been riding when he disappeared eight and a half months before.

North Slope Borough Search and Rescue deputy director Randy Crosby said a sled, an empty rifle case, and two gas cans were also found on the beach. He said, "The ocean never gives up its dead. We've never found anybody that's gone down in the ocean unless they were attached to something."(3)

Earlier in July the Alaska Academy of Family Physicians had posthumously presented Dr. McCord their Alaska Family Physician of the Year award.

The search for Dr. McCord proved tragic, as did the one for a missing child and his grandparents.

COSTLY MISTAKE

Those people are in trouble.

Imagine driving on an isolated Alaskan road in the dead of winter. The temperature inside your vehicle is sixty-five degrees; outside it's forty below. Your car stalls. You know there's a lodge nine miles ahead through the knee-deep snow. Or . . .

You're following a single set of vehicle tracks through deep snow on a desolate stretch of road in January and come to an abandoned vehicle. You and your partner notice the message "HELP" and an arrow pointing ahead stamped into the snow. Or . . .

Imagine two men knocking on your door at the Alaska State Troopers office after dark. They tell you they've just come from a stranded vehicle whose missing occupants have left a message in the snow and are in trouble.

What would you do?

Everyone in this circumstance faced that question. But not all took it seriously. And that's the tragedy of this story.

Palmer and Leah Olrun were stranded and faced death's cold chill.

Vern Rice and Marcel Kania found the Olruns' car and faced helping someone in trouble.

The Alaska State Troopers faced the decision of *when* to respond to this emergency.

When I first read about the Olruns, I was surprised to learn that our neighbor and friend Vernon Rice had found their car. I called and asked if he'd mind sharing his experience for my new book. He agreed and said, "The troopers dropped the ball on this one."

Palmer and Leah Olrun, both in their early fifties, regularly selected one of their six grandchildren to go with them for a car ride. On January 11, 1996, they left Anchorage with Ethan, their two-year-old grandson. Palmer told a family member that he planned to go ice fishing (though no ice-fishing gear was ever found in the car). Other family members thought they might drive to Lake Louise or Homer, 150 and 180 miles respectively east and south of Anchorage.

There was no specific return date. Sometime during the next few days they changed their minds about their itinerary.

It appears that they left the Parks Highway on January 14 intending to drive the Denali Highway to Paxson. Travel is possible from either end of the gravel road, as crews maintain it for some miles; however, deep snow renders the middle section unpassable for automobile traffic in the winter. Usually a fair number of snowmachiners recreate along the highway, but the year's lack of snow and recent minus-sixty-degree weather may have discouraged snowmachining.

On Monday the fifteenth, when Leah failed to appear for work, Ethan's mother, Cynthia, reported the Olruns missing.

As the Olruns continued east, they approached a hill that their car refused to clear. They rocked it back and forth in an effort to get it to move, but that was unsuccessful.

What exactly happened to them that night and the following day? Did they remain in the automobile, starting it periodically for heat? Did they remain there until they'd exhausted their fuel, then start for Maclaren River Lodge? What is it like struggling through knee-deep snow and trading a two-year-old grandson back and forth in temperatures of minus thirty to minus sixty degrees? How long would it take the couple to travel nine miles under those conditions? What must they have been thinking! Surely we can only guess about their dilemma and their thoughts.

They plodded along dressed in winter clothing, which included jackets, boots, gloves, and mittens. Hour after hour they trudged onward. Partway, they tried to start a fire, but there was insufficient wood.

They did not know it, but they covered eight and a half miles. They were less than a hundred yards from the top of a hill from which they could have seen smoke curling from a woodstove in a building at Maclaren River Lodge. But at that point they turned back.

Vern Rice and his friend and hunting partner Marcel Kania were on a caribou-hunting trip when they decided to hunt the Denali Highway. They started up the highway on the fourteenth but went back to spend the night at a motel near the Cantwell cutoff. The next morning they got an early start across the Denali Highway, driving east.

They put the pickup into four-wheel only when they entered the deeper snow on the Denali. It appeared the vehicle whose tracks they were following was following yet another set of older tracks.

The weather was clear, sunny, and cold.

They'd seen many moose and caribou along the way. Several miles back they'd passed hunters in a number of vehicles. Vern and Marcel noticed at least four places where the vehicle ahead had become stuck and the occupants had dug themselves out. At one point they'd left their ice scraper sticking out of the snow.

As the hunters drove on toward Paxson, they continued watching for caribou and talking hunter talk; Vern counted sixty-one moose in a mile. A couple of hours into their drive they encountered a red vehicle parked in the middle of the road. They were twenty-seven or twenty-eight miles beyond the lodge at milepost fifty. Marcel stopped fifty yards behind the car (to provide room for turning around). It was around 2:30 P.M.

While Marcel stayed in the pickup, Vern exited his passenger door and approached the vehicle, which turned out to be the Olruns' missing 1990 Subaru Legacy station wagon.

Vern noticed venetian-type blinds on the side and the rear windows.

The windows had no frost nor other indication of having been there long. As he walked closer, Vern shouted, " 'Is anybody in there?' And I knocked on the side window, on the passenger side, got no response. I walked in front of the car and looked back into the station wagon."(4)

He could see that no one was inside and didn't try to open the doors. He didn't see any articles in the vehicle. He felt it would be better not to walk in the footprints or touch the vehicle.

His first indication of real trouble was when "I turned around and I saw that arrow on the side on the snowbank there."(4) Next to the arrow was the word HELP stamped in the snow in capital letters four feet high and twelve feet long.

Vern then saw two sets of tracks in the snow leading eastward away from the front of car. "I thought it was a person with a small wife or a teenager, because all I saw of her tracks was just a little shoe track."(4)

Vern figured the car's occupants could have returned to the hunter's cabin back toward Cantwell. Vern felt bad about them and speculated, "If these poor people had come back, there was a . . . not a mile from there . . . was another cabin right along the road."(4)

Although it was unoccupied for the winter, they could have taken shelter and probably obtained some food. Vern realized they might not have seen the cabin in the dark.

Another possibility of helping themselves in that situation would have been to set their car tires on fire. However, when you're on an isolated road in midwinter, you don't usually expect any other traffic. And besides, they probably thought they could make Maclaren River Lodge.

Marcel's four-wheel-drive, late-model Ford pickup was not equipped with snow tires or chains. They couldn't pass the Subaru because it blocked the roadway. Although Vern and Marcel had a snowmachine in the pickup, it wouldn't start.

A layer of glare ice beneath the snow increased their chances of getting stuck. They knew if that happened, they'd be in the same jam as the missing car occupants.

Since they were the only hunters this far back, Vern told Marcel the best thing for them to do was to return to Cantwell and inform the Troopers so the occupants from the Subaru could be found. Taking turns with a round-point shovel, they dug out an area to turn around and began immediately for Cantwell, fifty miles west.

By the time they pulled into the State Trooper facility at 5 P.M., darkness had replaced the daylight. Both Marcel and Vern approached the Trooper facility, which also served as his residence. A note by the doorbell instructed persons to ring the bell after hours. Vern said, "I pushed the buzzer, and the lady says, 'Can I help you?' "

Vern assumed she was a state trooper and said, " 'Yes. Is there any place open between here and Paxson?'

"She says, 'No.'

"And I says, 'Well, there's some people in trouble. We had followed their tracks and it's a little car. Those people are in trouble.'

"To the best of my recollection, she says, 'Well, what kind of car was it?'

"Marcel spoke up and says, 'It's a Subaru.'

"She said, 'Do you remember the license number?'

"I said, 'No, ma'am, I did not.' I had no reason to take the license number down at the time." ("I wasn't worried about the license number. . . .The car was there . . . it wasn't going anywhere.")(4)

"She never asked my name, my address, nothing . . . and that struck me . . . she might have thought I was a prankster.

"What shocked me . . . I thought that she'd come downstairs and turn the light on and we'd go in, in where it's warm and talk to her, but I talked to her on that intercom. And I told her it was cold. I said, 'Those people had wrote in the snow, stomped out, ah, an arrow and a help sign.' I said, 'They're in trouble, they need help.'

"She said she would call the State Troopers in Paxson and let them know."(4)

It turned out that the lady Vern and Marcel left the message with was an individual at trooper headquarters. The trooper was laid up with an injury from a car accident. The individual did not take their names or numbers.

The report was passed along, albeit with some skepticism. The trooper called Fairbanks within a half hour after the hunters departed.

The Fairbanks dispatcher notified the Glennallen detachment, the nearest post with an available trooper. The Glennallen dispatcher contacted the off-duty trooper at Paxson Lodge and a message was left for the trooper's boss who called dispatch and informed them to have the trooper call the next morning (Tuesday) at eight-thirty. "For reasons yet to be determined, no appropriate action was taken by the Glennallen post."(2)

Tuesday passed with anxious Olrun family members worrying over the whereabouts of Palmer, Leah, and Ethan. The wheels of public safety seemed to have ground to a stop, if, in fact, they'd even begun.

On Wednesday, more than a day after the missing-person report, a C-130 aircraft and a helicopter flew over the Seward Highway between Anchorage and Homer looking for the Olrun's Subaru. The searchers came up empty. Late Wednesday the search turned north after the off-duty trooper returned to Glennallen and read the missing-persons report. He made the connection between it and the abandoned Subaru that Rice and Kania had reported two days previously.

Shortly after midnight Wednesday the Air National Guard in Anchorage launched a helicopter from Kulis. Later that morning the searchers spotted the bodies of the missing family. The Olruns had backtracked a half mile from their farthest point east. No one knows their reason for turning back, but cold affects a person's thinking. It is normal for a person in the latter stages of hypothermia to think he's hot and to take his clothes off.

And so, less than a mile from Maclaren River Lodge, where help was available, the Olruns perished in the cold.

The crew of the helicopter landed and retrieved the frozen bodies. Leah and Ethan lay side by side, just off the snow-covered roadway. About two hundred yards beyond and over two low hills lay the body of Palmer. The bodies indicated the Olruns had experienced classic hypothermia—Palmer had removed his gloves and unzipped his coat. Leah had taken her coat off. Ethan wore a sweat suit and jacket.

Later the Troopers examined the Subaru, which contained no snow removal or survival equipment, only a Thermos with frozen liquid.

Thursday, many Olrun family members gathered at the paternal home in east Anchorage. Palmer and Leah had moved to Anchorage from Bethel in 1990 following his retirement from the Army National Guard. Palmer was an accomplished mask carver of wood, ivory, and soapstone; Leah worked as a nurse's assistant in the emergency room at Alaska Native Medical Center.

Epilogue

After the recovery of the bodies of Palmer, Leah, and Ethan Olrun, a great deal of speculation surfaced . . . and a lot of finger-pointing. The Olruns were blamed; those who found their car were ridiculed; and the State Troopers were accused of mishandling the emergency.

Palmer's brother Eben speculated his brother had chosen to go to the Maclaren River Lodge, which is maintained through the winter by Rich Holmstrum, owner of Tangle Lakes Lodge, farther east.

An investigation into the handling of the case by the Alaska State Troopers resulted in a report over four hundred pages in length. Some of the findings were:

Cold weather was the reason given for not initiating a search on the day Rice and Kania found the Olruns' abandoned vehicle.

No one could contact the hunters who found the vehicle because a trooper's wife failed to get their names and numbers.

The detachment supervisor chose to wait until the next morning to follow up the emergency report.

Another trooper chose to await warmer weather before sending out a search-rescue helicopter.

Two field commanders with the Alaska State Troopers were relieved of field duties and given administrative posts, while investigators tried to determine the reason these men did not order an immediate search regarding the Olrun emergency.

It wasn't until Wednesday that the troopers made the connection between the abandoned vehicle on the Denali, reported by Rice and Kania, and the missing-persons report from Cynthia Olrun brought to the trooper's attention two days earlier.

Kari Bazzy Garber, attorney for the family, believes the family could have been saved had the Troopers responded in a timely manner: "How would they feel if their family was out there and this was how the Troopers respond? Nobody deserves to die because they've made an unfortunate choice."(3)

If the Olruns died before the vehicle was found, the delay was inconsequential. But what if the Olruns got stuck Sunday evening, periodically ran the car engine to produce heat through the night and into the next day, then left the vehicle? Rice indicated there was no frost on their vehicle's windows. If they left their car at noon or later and hiked four hours, they would have been alive at 4 P.M. or later.

The Troopers were notified at 5 P.M. Would the Olruns have still been alive? How long would it have taken a pickup to travel to the abandoned car, off-load snowmachines, and travel eight and a half miles to the Olruns?

It's something to think about.

Another consideration, which may be of even greater consequence, is that the Alaska State Troopers are woefully understaffed . . . if they had the manpower our residents deserve, perhaps the Olruns could have been found in time. In fact, had the Troopers the personnel and equipment to work so vast an area as the state of Alaska, they could routinely patrol the Denali Highway and other roads to prevent similar tragedies.

That's something to think about also.

Two and a half weeks prior to the Olruns' attempt to cross the Denali Highway, two women floundered in their vehicle and nearly lost their lives near Maclaren River Lodge.

Bruni Warrick and her friend Brenda Acton, visiting from Dover, England, drove the same road the Olruns did in a rented Jeep. As Bruni drove east, the snow-covered roadway was more difficult than she remembered it in summer.

With headlights stabbing into the black of night she pushed on through one snowdrift after another until she was at a point of no return. Getting stuck and digging themselves out twice, they used floor mats and a jacket for traction. Warrick feared stopping would doom them, so she kept moving ahead, hoping to reach Maclaren River Lodge.

Approximately ten miles shy of the lodge they had trouble discerning the roadway from the ditch. She thought it would get better and drove on.

Fortunately the women spotted the lodge beacon, parked on the Maclaren

River bridge, and walked the few hundred yards to the lodge. The two men there had seen lights in the distance and speculated they belonged to snowmachines. They'd never seen a road vehicle come so far in the winter.

The women had to be glad they had made it that far.

Some searches end with no trace; others result in finding the victim but not in time to help; still other searches end happily.

WILL THEY FIND ME?

AS TOLD TO THE AUTHOR BY DUANE AND BARBARA PERSSON

He desperately honked the horn and screamed for help but the sound of the plane grew weaker, until there was complete silence.

Having read about Duane Persson and his accident in September 1988, I wanted to learn more about it. I finally caught up with Duane through his son in December 1998, and he agreed to send me his story. The following account is a combination of his and his wife's versions which they sent me by way of audiocassette. Following their story is further comment from their son Craig of Fairbanks.

With the sun in his eyes on the uphill curve, Duane was surprised by the sudden appearance of a moose darting onto the highway in front of him. Duane swerved hard right to miss the huge animal. The car hit the embankment, launching it eighteen feet off the ground. Instantly airborne, the Chevy Cavalier rocketed through the upper branches of poplar trees before it slammed grille-first into the earth. When the vehicle came to rest, it lay on its passenger side in a patch of thick birch trees.

Duane was knocked out in the accident. When he regained consciousness, he shut off the engine and knew immediately that he was in a fix.

Duane was no stranger to tight situations.

He was born in Brainerd, Minnesota, June 9, 1936, where he lived on a farm until he went into the service in 1954. He got out of the army in 1956 and worked in a paper mill from 1958 until May of 1974, when he left for Alaska.

When he reached Alaska, he joined the Culinary Union and worked on the Trans-Alaska pipeline at Deitritch for two years. From there he went to pump station eight as a cook and eventually got promoted to camp manager. He was working camp manager for the culinary for two years and then went to Happy Valley as manager. In 1988 he got a job as a cook at Clear Air Force Base.

Duane's wife, Barbara, commented: Although we lived in Arizona, during the summer of 1988 we were house-sitting in Fairbanks. Duane commuted back and forth between Clear and Fairbanks on his days off. About the eleventh of September I left for Arizona to go back home. Duane gave the house its final touches, loaded his suitcases and briefcase and a two-gallon water container, and drove off in his 1986 Cavalier, never dreaming what was about to happen would change his whole life.

As Duane drove toward Clear that September 18, the temperature was fifty-eight degrees. He was going in a little earlier than usual because he was going to do his laundry. While driving down Parks Highway en route, he was feeling happy and content with the whole world. He had passed the halfway point where he sometimes stopped to take a break, but this time he didn't.

He was approaching a hill and a curve so he took his time. The sun was in his eyes as he came to a curve. That's when the moose ran out into the roadway in front of him. "Oh my God," he cried.

Then he left the roadway.

When Duane regained consciousness, he found himself dangling in the air, suspended from his seat belt. Fearing the car would catch fire, his first thought was to shut off the ignition key.

Next he tried repeatedly to release the safety device. It seemed like hours. Finally he succeeded.

His success, however, brought Duane new problems. He plunged onto the passenger side, landing on shards of glass. The back window had shattered on impact, and most of the glass ended up in the front of the car.

Duane knew immediately his back was broken because he couldn't move his legs and he felt that he was completely paralyzed. He tried to lift one leg with his hand and it just flopped from one side to another. There was pressure on his right hip, which rested on the hump in the middle of the car's floorboard. To help relieve the pressure he took his comb and wallet out of his back pocket.

He was calm, figuring someone would spot his car and rescue him at any time. Not wanting to look a mess when they rescued him, Duane combed his hair. However, what he didn't know was that the car was hidden amongst young birch trees and bushes thirty feet off the highway.

The car's brown color coupled with the changing color of the leaves camouflaged his car from the highway. Duane tried the horn and the radio and both worked. "Great," he thought, "now all I have to do is honk the horn when I hear a vehicle approaching."

Hours crawled slowly by. His mouth was dry. He was extremely thirsty and in pain from his back to his neck. He suddenly remembered the two-gallon Thermos that he had placed in the backseat of the car. "Just how will I get it?" he wondered. "I can't move my legs."

He thought for a few minutes and then removed his belt from his pants and made a loop with the buckle end. He tried to hook the Thermos. With each toss of the belt he prayed, "Please, God, help me." After two hours or so he finally succeeded. But only a few drops remained in the Thermos.

By now it was getting dark, and he was in a lot of pain. He heard the cars and the trucks going down the highway. He honked his horn and blinked his lights, but no one heard the sound or saw the lights. He furiously tried to get the sheepskin covers off the seats to warm his body, but he failed. With the cold and dampness penetrating his body, he prayed that God would give him strength to survive. Filling his mind with prayer and determining not to give up, he finally fell asleep.

When he woke up, he was confident that he would be missed when he failed to show up for work. He knew that his colleagues would be out there looking for him. He turned on his radio just long enough to determine whether his disappearance had been reported. Instead, he heard that the temperature had dropped to twenty-three degrees the night before.

There was moisture on the window. He took his finger and rubbed it against the window and wet his lips with it. It felt so good against his dry mouth.

He knew he had to concentrate on getting the seat covers off for warmth in case he was there another night. Getting water to quench his thirst became a primary objective. Leaves had fallen on the windshield during the night and, due to the heavy dew, began to stick, making it darker inside the car.

He figured the time would come when he would need the flashlight in the glove compartment. He struggled to open the compartment only to find the flashlight wasn't there. He did find a pencil and some envelopes, which gave him an idea for getting water. Then he prayed for rain.

His day was all planned out. He alternated between getting the sheepskin covers off and wedging a pencil into the cracked window to make a hole large enough to place the funnel he'd made from the envelope. The ashtray was clean, so he would let the water drip into it.

Removing the seat covers was a much harder task. His hands were getting sore and cut up, especially his right hand. He must have hurt it when he tried breaking the window with his fist to get out of the car.

He just couldn't give up. His mind was working all the time, figuring ways to survive. He wondered what his boss thought when he didn't show up for work that Monday morning. He wondered whether I'd been notified that he was missing.

Tuesday morning he awoke to birds' chirping on the windshield. It had rained a little during the night, and the birds were pecking at the raindrops. He checked his funnel to find that the paper had gotten soggy and wilted, but he sucked on the paper to get as much moisture as possible. It felt so good on his dry, cracking lips. He looked over to the satisfied birds and told them to fly away and get him some help, but first to get him some water. "It helped," he said, "talking to the birds. But most of all it helped talking to God." At that time he knew he wasn't alone, He was there with him.

He kept track of the days by making a slash with his pencil on the headliner of the car. Since it was Tuesday, he thought that surely someone was looking for him. Once again he turned on the radio to see if they were searching. But there was nothing. He continued to tug and pull on the seat covers using all of his strength, and then suddenly one broke loose.

A wave of relief washed over him as he thanked God. He immediately covered one side of his body and began working on the other seat cover. That one also broke loose. He named both seat covers—one was Joe and the other George. He spoke to them as friends: "Come on, guys, do your stuff."

He was so cold from wetting himself that he shivered and shook. He put his head under one side of the covers and breathed heavily to warm his body. Then he breathed on the other side. His worst fear was going into hypothermia. But now he could help prevent that or at least help prolong the situation.

Because of all the struggling to release the sheep seat covers, he started to feel a burning sensation on the right side of his body. The glass he was lying in was irritating him. He tried to lift up with one arm, but the pain in his back only left him screaming. It was getting dark, and he was getting weaker.

The pain increased. His lips were developing sores and beginning to swell. He fell asleep dreaming someone found him and said they would be right back to rescue him.

He woke up believing his dreams because he heard voices. He honked his horn, then heard someone say, "What's that?"

The other voice said, "I don't know, but let's get the hell out of here."

They just got into their car and fled as if they were scared to death.

Sleep was hard to come by. Duane was beginning to get confused as to the time of day because more and more wet leaves fell on the car making it darker and darker inside.

Even though he had very little light, he knew it was another morning. Once again he took the moisture from the window and applied it to his cracked and swollen lips that felt almost numb.

He turned on the radio. "Surely they have reported me missing by this time," he thought. The radio still carried no news of his disappearance, only that it was Wednesday and nine o'clock in the morning. Knowing the battery must be getting weak, he didn't want to leave the radio on for any length of time.

He finally realized that he must be so far off the road that nobody could see him. "But why is there no news of a search party?" he thought. "Dear God, why isn't anyone looking for me?"

Suddenly he heard a plane just above him. He couldn't see it because of the fog, but he thought, "Thank God, they are looking for me." He desperately honked the horn and screamed for help but the sound of the plane grew weaker, until there was complete silence.

It seemed like his pain intensified each day. He was so thirsty. He thought, "If only I had some water." He felt around with his hand, trying to find anything that that might help him. In the process he touched something round. It was a peanut. He reached back with his left arm. It was an awkward position to try to pick up anything, but he took his time. When he finally thought he had the peanut, he started slowly to bring it up to his mouth. But he dropped it. He never found it.

The cold and dampness grew worse. He alternated between breathing heavily under the covers and shivering with exhaustion. He continued to grow weaker and light-headed, causing him to do a lot of thinking. Periodically, Duane honked his horn and blinked his lights. But there was still no response.

The pain was increasing in his back and neck. His right side was burning like fire, and the sheep fur that filled his mouth from breathing under the covers made him feel as if he were choking. It could snow any day, the car could be completely covered, and he wouldn't be found until the spring. Light-headed again from lack of food and water, he fell asleep.

That night he was awakened by a scratching noise coming from the broken back window area. He almost stopped breathing. "It could be a bear or even a wolverine," he thought. He knew that he was helpless. It could tear him to shreds. He lay there very still. The only sound he heard was the pounding of his heart. Finally the creature went away.

Thursday morning he woke up and wanted to leave a message for me. With shaking hands he picked up a broken pencil and wrote on the headliner of the car, "I love you, Barb." Then out loud he repeated, "I love you so very much." He felt at peace now, telling himself how easy it would be to just fall asleep and all the pain would go away. That night he made his confession to God and drifted off to sleep, not knowing if he would ever see the light of day again.

He woke up on Friday morning and found it hard to believe he was still alive. Once again he turned on the radio and thought his absence would surely have been reported by this time. He thought, "My family must be worried sick." He didn't know what to think anymore. He picked up his pencil and started to write, "I don't think I will make it." He got as far as *I don't th* and his pencil broke and fell.

Then he began to pray for God to help him. He heard gunshots. He couldn't believe it. The shots were nearby. Duane immediately started honking his horn. His voice was weak but he desperately cried for help. He heard voices and kept honking and yelling.

The voices he heard belonged to hunters Phil Robertson and Tonya Artoqueta. They had shot a grouse, which fell behind Duane's car.

When Duane heard the voices, it was Phil instructing Tonya to go down and pick up the grouse. She started to retrieve the bird but ran back, saying, "I'm not going down there, it looks spooky."

Then they heard Duane's cry for help.

Phil ran down to the car. Duane asked if they had anything to drink. Phil ran back up to their car and told his girlfriend to drive to Nenana and call an ambulance. He grabbed his Pepsi and headed back to Duane.

Duane gulped it down and asked if he had any more. Phil said he did and ran back to his car to get two more. Duane thanked him kindly and then offered to pay for the soda.

The Nenana fire and rescue squad arrived. Duane told them that he knew his back was broken. They had to use the Jaws of Life to get him out of the car, and it took them about three hours. Then they transported Duane to Fairbanks Memorial Hospital.

When he arrived, the rest of his family and I were there waiting for him. It was the happiest moment of both of our lives when we saw each other. The first thing Duane said to me was, "Hi, honey. I love you, and I thought I would never see you again."

As I waited in the waiting room, Dr. George Brown came to me and showed me the X rays showing the extent of Duane's injuries. He had a broken back, L-2 fractured neck, and collapsed lung. His esophagus was all squished to the lefthand side, and he had third-degree burns on his side and his leg due to the glass that was embedded in his skin. Dr. Brown operated on Duane's back with no guarantees.

Duane remained in the hospital until the end of October, then was transported to Tucson Medical Center for rehabilitation.

While doing his rehabilitation in Tucson, he started walking, but not on his own. What really helped him was the pool that they took him to every day. They first stuck him in the pool on a stretcher, and he was slowly able to move his legs.

When he left Tucson Medical, it was just before Christmas, the twenty-fourth I think. At that time he was still in a wheelchair. I took him home to Kingman, Arizona, and made arrangements for him to get therapy at Footprints in Kingman. That's where he started moving his legs more and more with the therapy they gave him.

Duane's boss called me and initially told me Duane had two years to get back to work to keep his job. Then he called back and told me Duane had a year. So with all his therapy and exercise and walking up and down the street to get his legs back in shape, I think he went back to work in October of 1989.

He worked almost four years until he developed a fracture in his back and was forced to retire in July of 1993. Duane still has severe pains in his back and in his neck, and at times he loses his balance and is unstable.

Following is a copy of a letter that Duane received from a Pat Davis in Jackson, Mississippi, on December 16, 1988.

Dear Mr. Pearson,

I was so touched by the enclosed article that appeared in my little newspaper concerning your tragic accident. I am sure you would prefer to forget this terrible time of your life, but I felt bound to send this copy to you. You will surely be an inspiration to the generations to come. I hope you have a speedy recovery and I know this will be the most wonderful Christmas ever for you and your family. Seasons Greetings.

Duane wished to thank Tonya and Phil for saving his life. He lost contact with both of them. As far as we know, Phil Robertson has left Fairbanks and Tonya went to Japan to work.

Duane and Barbara's son Craig was kind enough to send me his thoughts about his father's accident. I received his letter in late January 1999, which I've copied below:

Hello Larry,

It is about time I get back to you about my dad's ordeal.

I only have a few things to add.

At the time of my dad's accident I was out hunting moose fifty miles southeast of Kotzebue. The pilot came and picked up some of our meat and told me that something had happened to my dad, and that he was going to fly me back to Kotzebue where the Alaska Airlines jet would hold for me until I got there. This was Wednesday the twenty-first of September. I got home late Wednesday night.

Bonnie, my wife at the time, had made the original missing-person report to the State Troopers on Monday the nineteenth, as my dad did not show up to work.

On Thursday the twenty-second, Bonnie and I searched every old road and trail from Fairbanks to Skinny Dick's which is about halfway to Nenana. If we would have gone another ten miles or so, we would have found him.

The next day Jon Chapman, a coworker of mine who flies helicopters in the Army National Guard, was going to see if he could make a flight to look for my dad.

At about 10:30 A.M. on Friday I received a phone call from the airport police/fire dispatch center. I work as a police officer/firefighter at the airport. The dispatcher, whom I know, told me that they had heard from the State Troopers that someone had found my dad and that he was on his way to the hospital via ambulance.

I was so elated. I rushed to the hospital and met the ambulance there. I was never so glad to see him. As I am writing this, I am getting emotional thinking back about it.

The next day I went to the accident scene to have my dad's vehicle removed and towed back to Fairbanks. I paced the distance from the edge of the shoulder of the road to the vehicle and it was only fifty feet. It appeared as if the vehicle had flipped over a grove of twenty-to-thirty-foot-tall poplar and birch trees and they had sprung right back to normal. It was hard to see the car unless you were really looking hard for it.

I went to blow the horn of the car. No more horn was left. The battery must have been totally dead. It also started getting real cold and was snowing that afternoon.

To this day, whenever I drive down the Parks Highway by the accident site, I always remember that I am lucky to still have my dad and thank God he managed to survive the crash and can still walk.

If a man can wait for rescue six days in a car, how long can a man wait while clinging to an airplane float in freezing water?

SEVEN HOURS ON A COLD FLOAT

AS TOLD TO THE AUTHOR BY KAHREN RUDBECK

The dangerous waves smack the main rotor blades causing the helicopter to plunge into the lake! One skid strikes Bart . . . sweeping him into the stormy water.

In the summer of 1998 I received a phone call from Kahren Rudbeck, who wondered if I'd be interested in reading a story she hoped to publish. I was excited when she told me it was about the heroic efforts of Al Lee and others . . . that was a story I had planned to write, but, thanks to Kahren's great story, I could focus on other stories and include her version.

I am grateful to people like Kahren who wanted to write and made an effort to contact me. Helping others achieve publication is a wonderful feeling.

Moose and caribou hunting season was in full swing on September 10, 1995. Clarence P. Bartley, owner and operator of Alaska Airventures, an air taxi business on Snowshoe Lake, sat at the controls of his Cessna 180 float plane, running through his checklist. Known to his neighbors as Bart, the sixty-eight-year-old pilot checked the tanks' fuel levels while his two hunting clients finished coffee at his home and base forty miles west of Glennallen. The hunters boarded the plane, and Bart taxied to takeoff and lifted over the red and gold carpet of the birch and poplar trees below.

Patches of gray clouds lined the sky to the east. The temperature hung in the midforties, hinting fall's arrival. Nothing indicated a change in the weather.

Fifteen minutes later Bart reached their Tazlina Lake destination, twenty miles of glacial, gray water trailing from its namesake, Tazlina Glacier. Timbered slopes blanketed the foothills, rising to the east of the lake and melding into the rugged Chugach Mountains.

Bart circled low along the west side of the lake where choppy waters broke against the rocky shore. Turning for touchdown, Bart anticipated a rough-water landing. He reached between him and his front seat passenger for the flap lever and added full flaps. The Cessna 180 slowed to just above stall speed as Bart skillfully set the float plane onto the pounding water.

Bart taxied to shore and tailed the plane onto the rock-studded beach. Moments later, a pilot friend, Dennis Pollard, landed his 150 Super Cub near Bart. Local pilots often fly cover for one another for safety reasons.

Dennis helped the hunters unload their gear and carry it to shore while choppy water crashed against the tops of Bart's boots as he held his plane away from the rocks.

Dennis prepared to take off. Whitecaps danced on the waves as Bart steadied his friend's plane. Knowing Denny's plane was much lighter and took off quicker than his 180, Bart joked, "Hey, Dennis. I'll fly the Cub off. You take the 180."

Dennis laughed and firewalled his throttle. One bounce and the Super Cub was airborne. He circled once, and satisfied to see Bart's taxi under way, Dennis headed homeward.

Like other lakes fed by sprawling glaciers, Tazlina Lake changes dramatically and without warning with variations in temperature or wind direction. The lake chose this moment to get ugly.

Bart fed in power to his engine until it reached full throttle. The plane responded, thrusting her floats into three-foot waves. She bounced atop the waves but couldn't pull free for a takeoff. Bart aborted takeoff, fearing the tall, choppy waves might suck the float's nose down and tip him over. He decided to seek calmer waters across the lake and taxied that way.

What he did not know was that the severe bouncing had jarred three float balls out of their pockets on his left float. The nineteen-foot-long floats are divided into sections with eight balls on top of each float. These two-inch ball coverings provide the means to pump any accumulated water from the floats.

Every breaking wave spilled water through the open holes, filling the compartments and causing the plane to list to one side. Bart fought to bring his craft to safer water. He spied a sandy shore about a hundred yards ahead of him, a safe haven to beach his crippled plane.

It was not to be. As the plane limped and listed, a mighty gust surged under the cocked right wing. Suddenly the plane tilted in the huge waves. *She's going over! This can't be happening.*

In his fifty-two-year career as a pilot he'd never faced such a dilemma. *No time to radio for assistance. No time to hit the ELT [emergency locator transmitter] toggle switch in the dash that will summon help.*

Dark, cold water poured through the side window. Bart barely had time to release his shoulder straps. He fumbled unsuccessfully for the door latch. He pulled his knees up to his chest, clumsy hip boots hampering his effort to kick out the door. As the cockpit filled with murky water, he pushed free of the inverted craft. Only the floats bobbed above the water. Bart struggled along the wet metal float to the front of the plane. He pulled his 220-pound frame along the walk wire stretching between the front of the floats. Although he'd lost his trifocals, he was thankful to be alive.

Bart straddled the float like the experienced horseman he is, but instead of a comfortable saddle he rode a two-inch raised ridge keel on a cold metal tube just six inches above the water. He considered dumping water from his hip boots, but decided he needed all the warmth available: A body loses heat twenty-five times faster in water than in air. Dressed only in a jeans jacket, cotton shirt, jeans, wool socks, and camouflage life vest, he was not prepared to endure extreme conditions. Fortunately, his baseball cap stuck with him during this unexpected swim. He anguished knowing survival gear was close at hand. *If only I could reach my warm neoprene gloves, handheld radio, and extra glasses in the cockpit.*

He knew his ELT, which sends out an electronic signal to a global satellite, was useless underwater. There was no significant impact to trigger it. No one knew where he was.

Expecting Bart would beat him back, Dennis Pollard stopped at Snowshoe Lake just before noon. He was surprised Bart's plane was not docked. As he entered the Bartley home, Dennis muttered, "It's not like Bart to miss a coffee break."

It had not been a favorable year for the Bartleys. In July, Rosemary, Bart's wife of six years, had quadruple bypass surgery. Dennis knew she didn't need added stress now.

Rosemary hurried to meet her guest, asking, "Where's Bart? He should have returned by now."

Not wishing to alarm Rosemary, Dennis told her that he'd fly out to check on Bart, adding, "He's probably checking on some other group of hunters."

A hunter and friend of the family, Charles Atwood, sensed the need for action. He recruited several local pilots to start a search of the surrounding lakes.

Immediately Dennis refueled and pointed his Super Cub toward Tazlina Lake.

In his absence the lake had turned real nasty. Waves battered the shore as Pollard risked another rough-water landing. He taxied toward shore. Unable to beach the plane, Dennis shouted to the hunting party he'd left earlier. They were busy setting up camp and had had their backs to the lake when Bart taxied away. They had seen nothing. "Keep an eye out for him," Dennis yelled as he took off to look for his friend.

All he saw were three-to-four-foot waves marching resolutely across gray, stormy water. He flew southeast under adverse wind conditions through a mountain pass to check another popular lake. No luck. Knowing another set of eyes would be valuable, he flew back to Snowshoe Lake to pick up Larry Woodside, who was working that summer for the Bartleys.

At the Bartley household, concern grew. No one had seen Bart. He must be somewhere on Tazlina Lake.

The search centered there.

The wind rose as Bart tried to find a comfortable position to avoid the drenching waves. He took stock of his situation. There were no access roads to this remote lake. No lodges and no lake homes dotted the shore. He was alone, drifting on a slowly sinking plane in glacial water in a screeching wind.

Shivering and staring across the open water, Bart wondered, "Where are they?" Suddenly he heard a marvelous sound. *Airplanes!* He turned cautiously and saw two small planes. *They're searching the wrong shore. I taxied miles southeast of my original position. Got to signal them.*

But his numb fingers barely held the six-inch, waterproof sky-blazer flares he'd removed from a pocket. He blew his breath on his fingers to warm them. *Got to pull the tiny loop chains to activate the flares.* He tried to wedge a ballpoint pen into the loop.

The pen slipped from his clumsy fingers, bounced against the float, and vanished under the dark, roiling waters. Grasping for the pen, Bart knocked the three flares into the icy lake. He reached into his pocket for his reflector mirror. *One more chance to make myself seen.*

He looked at the rolling clouds and prayed for a small ray of sunlight. The clouds remained a tight blanket of gray as the plane drifted toward shore. *Maybe I can swim to shore.* But he knew his limitations. He was weak and cold, the slate gray water deceptive.

A sudden shift in the wind or lake current made his decision. The plane was forced back toward the middle of the lake. Bart's stranded spirit started to sink. He was satisfied to have had a full, adventurous life. His family was grown and self-sufficient. His concerns were for Rosemary and the anxiety she had to be feeling. *I won't give up, but I can never survive a night out here.* He considered ways to tie his body to the float.

Dennis Pollard and Larry flew low, double-checking the shoreline, still expecting to see Bart's plane pulled up onshore. Denny glanced across the lake and saw smoke rising from a cabin tucked in the trees on the eastern side. He landed in smoother water and questioned two people walking the shore. They yelled back at him, "A while ago a plane possibly flew over toward Kaina Lake."

Realizing his was the plane they'd seen earlier, Dennis thanked them. Dejected, he and Larry considered going home. He told his spotter companion, "Just one more pass along this southeast side and we'll call it quits."

Larry pressed his face against the side window, peering for Bart. "Hey, Dennis! There is some guy down there with two kayaks waving at us!"

Bart heard, then saw, a plane. He waved desperately thinking, "What if they don't see me!" It was a chilling thought. The plane banked to the left. *It's coming my way.*

Dennis was shocked to see Bart perched on the floats of the overturned plane. He studied the monster waves. *This is not Super Cub water.* But he risked a landing. He touched down, bounced toward Bart, and tried to maintain control of the lurching Cub.

As they neared Bart, he shouted over to Dennis, "Been waiting for you guys all morning!" Pollard angled his bouncing Cub alongside and tossed a rope across to Bart. Several times the rope slipped through Bart's numb fingers. It wasn't working. Bart couldn't pull himself across. Waves threatened to swamp the Cub as it drifted away.

Larry exited the Cub and stood on the floats, hands gripping the wing struts. *If Dennis can swing the plane in close enough, just maybe I can reach across and grab Bart.*

Again Pollard maneuvered the plane alongside the floats. With one hand gripping the strut, Larry leaned out, extending his other hand to Bart. Too cold and exhausted to make the connection, Bart shook his head. The planes separated.

Dennis had difficulty judging distance and coordinating the motion of the planes. Again he brought his plane into a docking position. This time the Cub nosed right against the center of the float Bart occupied. The spinning prop was dangerously close. Bart struggled out of the way. Then the plane swung in the wrong direction.

Only the passenger side opens on a Cub, and it was on the opposite side from Bart. In a desperate move, Dennis leaped out the door, ducked under the tail of his plane, and stepped across to the off-side float. Straddling water, one foot on his float and the other on Bart's submerged float, Dennis grabbed the tail of his Cub and tried to pull the bobbing crafts together.

This impossible feat almost spun Dennis into the swirling water. He was shaken. He knew that Larry couldn't fly. He theorized that if he become separated from his Cub, there would be another plane adrift. Dennis swung back to safety, urging Larry to get back into the cockpit.

Even though Bart's hand slid along the fuselage of his would-be rescuer's plane, he had no strength to pull himself across. Each second increased the danger and Bart screamed to Dennis, "Get the hell out of here and call search and rescue!"

Bart slumped onto the cold, waterlogged float, grasping the sleeping bag that Dennis tossed him.

Pollard flew to five thousand feet to radio a Mayday.

Moments later Anchorage Air Rescue received the report through Kenai Air Flight Service that a plane was down on Tazlina Lake. Kulis Air National Guard Base in Anchorage radioed an HH60 Pavehawk helicopter to divert from another mission and head directly for the scene of the mishap.

Within minutes of receiving Pollard's message Kenai Air Flight Service called the Bartley home to report the situation. Rosemary frantically called the home of air taxi pilot Al Lee. She reached Al's wife, Helen, who relayed the message to Al at Tolsona Lake, where he waited for wind conditions to improve before taking out his hunting client, Larry Ransom of Anchorage.

Al threw a life vest to his passenger and rushed to his DeHavilland Beaver, departing for Tazlina Lake. Ironically the Beaver was the same one Lee had taken in swap with Bart for the Cessna 100 now sinking in the lake. A 30 mph south wind whipped waves across the lake. Chances were slim of spotting anything below. Suddenly the clouds parted. Al caught a glimpse of reflecting metal on the water.

In a short time Dennis Pollard and another local pilot returned to the scene in separate aircraft. Knowing they couldn't land on these wild waters, they continued to circle above their downed comrade.

When Al Lee swung his plane low over the water, Bart gave him a smiling thumbs-up salute. He hoped the larger 450-horsepower Beaver could handle the waves.

Al Lee shook his head. *These conditions are beyond my plane's capabilities. I wouldn't land here for $10,000 cash!*

Twenty miles north, a 206 Bell Jet Ranger helicopter refueled at Gulkana Airport near Glennallen. Pilot Don Willey and Bureau of Land Management surveyor Ron Walter heard Pollard's call for help on their radio. They were only twenty minutes from Tazlina Lake and knew that every minute counted to a downed pilot. They radioed they were on the way.

An unknown private pilot arrived on the scene and radioed Al that a helicopter from Glennallen was fifteen minutes out. Relieved, the Beaver pilot decided to circle and watch.

As Bart watched his friends circle above him, he knew the deadly risks of battling these waves. He didn't want them to try it. The soaked sleeping bag provided him no warmth, and he let it slip into the splashing waves. As Bart hunched down to control his shivering body, he heard the thud-thudding of a hovering helicopter.

Ron Walter leaned out of the chopper using hand signals to urge Bart back from the front of the float, which was dipping underwater. The rescuers wanted him in a more favorable position for pickup. But the six long, cold hours in the wind and waves had taken their toll.

Bart's responses were slow and confused. The helicopter dropped lower until the skids rested across the rolling float. Ron Walter opened the right rear door and attempted to pull Bart aboard. Bart grabbed for the external cargo basket, creating chaos. The weight of the two struggling men tipped the chopper to the right, pulling it off-balance.

Don Willey, with seventeen years' experience, fought for control. But the dangerous waves, like tentacles of a giant squid, wrapped around the main rotor blades and hauled the chopper into the lake! One skid struck Bart on the chin before slamming into his chest and sweeping him into the stormy water.

While circling and watching from above, Dennis thought the situation was under control. As he turned his Cub homeward, Larry cried out, "The chopper is going down! It's sinking!" Stunned, they hustled to the accident scene.

Still circling above, Al Lee and Larry Ransom watched the disabled helicopter sink like a rock. The pilot and his passenger kicked out a window and struggled free of the machine. When they bobbed to the surface, they saw Bart conscious but helpless in the water. They managed to save a flotation cushion from their cockpit and forced it under Dennis.

Then they struggled to push and pull him onto his overturned float away from the pounding waves. They climbed onto the float, their weight forcing the unstable floats even lower into the cold water. With no protection from the relentless waves and the howling wind, there was little float surface left to cling to and Bart was seriously injured.

Still circling at five thousand feet, the unidentified pilot radioed Al Lee that the National Guard Air Rescue had diverted from another emergency call and was heading to Tazlina Lake. Al Lee determined there was not time to wait for additional help. The plight of those three men was desperate. Al Lee had no doubts about the danger of landing in the hungry waters, but he thought, "You do what you gotta do."

The Beaver touched down hard into the wind. As Al shut off the engine, his plane shot by his intended landing spot. He drifted with little control. The engine sputtered. *If I can't regain power, they'll be trying to rescue me.*

The seventy-one-year-old pilot cranked the switch. The engine roared to life and he angled back for a rescue attempt.

The waiting Don Willey grabbed the rope tied to the Beaver's float and successfully pulled the two planes side by side in the rolling waves. Larry Ransom carefully crawled from the Beaver onto the float. Desperate times called for desperate measures. It was going to take a lot of strength and ability to transfer an injured man under these conditions. One slip meant disaster.

Bart screamed in pain as the two helicopter men and Larry Ransom dragged him across to the floats of the rocking Beaver. He pleaded, "Don't lift me into that plane! Just let me ride on this float!"

That was not an option. No one could survive the trip to shore on a float against the battering waves. As gently as possible the three men eased Bart into safety behind the middle seat. They gladly abandoned the unstable float and squeezed aboard.

But the danger was far from over. Lee's leg muscles, cramped from holding the rudder pedals steady to hold his plane in position, screamed in pain. Al was exhausted. Knowing he couldn't lift off safely, he faced taxiing three miles to the beach, forging through four-foot waves and a stiff wind.

Dennis headed his plane toward a small, protected cove. He radioed Al that he'd start a fire to warm the drenched survivors.

Al knew the Air Rescue helicopter would need a reasonably flat place to land. He scanned the shoreline for a suitable spot and selected a cove a short distance from Pollard's plane. He taxied the Beaver to shore where he and Larry Ransom pulled the tail up on the rocks.

The unidentified pilot radioed Al that Air Rescue was twenty minutes from touchdown.

Bart dreaded the thought of being moved from the Beaver. His chest and sides burned with pain, but he knew the plane's floats would be ripped open if they continued to pound on the rocks.

When the Air Rescue crew arrived in the HH60 Pavehawk, the pilot landed the large helicopter on its skids while the companion Hercules 130 aircraft circled overhead. The skilled pararescue team, trained in cold-water rescue, had anticipated pulling the men from the lake, but they were unaware of any injuries. They hurried over to the Beaver where Pollard and Woodside had arrived.

The pararescue men removed Bart from the Beaver and worked quickly to stabilize him. They cut off his clothes. A quick examination revealed suspected broken ribs, possible punctured lungs, and severe hypothermia. Fortunately the other rescued pilot and passenger were only wet and cold.

While the rescue team worked on Bart, Al Lee pumped many gallons of water from his damaged floats. He then took off in an eddy and flew to the protected cove Pollard had found.

Bart was conscious and well aware he faced another move into the rescue helicopter. Wrapped in a warm sleeping bag, he begged, "Just let me get warm."

Dennis Pollard and Larry Ransom took turns with the pararescue men carrying Bart to the HH60 Pavehawk where the pilot had cranked up the heat. After that, Al ferried Ron Walter and Larry Ransom to Tolsona Lake.

Meanwhile, Bart's son, Bruce Bartley, hunting in the Nelchina area, was notified of the accident. He was flown to Tazlina Lake by local pilot and friend Ray McCarty. They did not land since the rescue helicopter was departing. Bruce and friend immediately returned to Snowshoe Lake where the family gathered before departing on a frantic three-hour drive to Anchorage.

Bart arrived at the Alaska Regional Hospital where his daughter-in-law, Annamarie, and her husband, Matt, greeted him. Rosemary, son Bruce, and other family members arrived and waited anxiously for the medical report. Bart's core temperature had dropped to a dangerous eighty-four degrees. He had punctured lungs, four broken ribs on one side, five on the other, three of which were broken in two places. Pararescue member Garth Lenz assured the family of one great sign of survival: "Bart was a feisty, combative patient!"

True to Mr. Lenz's prediction, Bart was out of intensive care by September twentieth and home a few weeks later. In a dramatic postscript to this adventure Bart says, "God has a purpose for everything. The intensified MRI examination revealed an aneurysm hiding in my iliac region. It was not something that would have shown on a flight physical. It could have ruptured at any time. Although definitely traumatic, this accident probably saved my life."

Al Lee and Larry Ransom were awarded the Carnegie Medal and $3,000 each. Al Lee also received the National Heroism Award.

By the spring of 1996, Clarence Bartley was flying as a spotter for the herring-roe fishery in Prince William Sound. Al Lee continues to operate his air taxi service out of Tolsona Lake by Glennallen. Dennis Pollard has changed his profession to carpenter. The Alaska Air National Guard continues on alert to serve the residents and visitors of Alaska.

During the summers of 1997 and 1998 Mr. Bartley and his wife, Rosemary, resumed their air taxi business. Bart is happily flying his Cessna 185. He carries large waterproof flares and long orange streamers that can be released and easily seen in case of emergency. He continues his search for his sunken Cessna 180, but that is another story.

Sometimes man's rescue is hastened by others; sometimes he has to rely upon himself.

RIVER GONE WILD

AS TOLD TO THE AUTHOR BY VERNON SCHMIDT

I sank below the surface. My entire body was numb.

Our good family friend Don Miller, owner of Miller's Homestead Inn of Tualatin, Oregon, told me about his hunting partner's experience on a moose hunt. I was quite happy to contact Smitty. Vernon Schmidt of Anderson Island, Washington, responded with his harrowing tale.

My three hunting partners and I were more excited than the proverbial kid with a new red wagon. Our plan called for a ten-day hunt in September 1982 on my favorite river in Alaska. We would hunt the largest member of the deer family in an area that had produced Ken Best's 1978 world-record moose.

Although my pal Don Miller wouldn't be going, I was happy to have my son Roger along. We would be hunting with another father-son combo, Hal and Jeff Stevens. My thirty-year-old son and I are partners in Muffler Shops and Rental Trucks; and Hal and Jeff are partners in a concrete-related business. We're all members of the Southwest Washington Sportsman's Association, which is sponsored by the First Church of God in Vancouver, Washington.

None of the others had been to Alaska, so they were almost as excited as I to be going to the Last Frontier. I could hardly wait to introduce them to the joys I'd experienced, knowing that we would fly over her endless rivers, swamplands, and virgin forests; see the snowcapped and rugged mountain peaks reaching to the heavens; camp along a river traveled by so few adventurers; hunt the lichen-carpeted tundra; and best of all, share the good fellowship around the campfire.

I was no stranger to moose hunting, having begun in the 1950s in British Columbia and Alberta. My Alaska hunting began in the 1970s. In 1982 I was sixty-two years old.

We would hunt moose on the Innoko River. I had made the trip many times, having done so two years previously with my wife, Carol, Don Miller, and his wife, Evelyn. We would float the river in my eighteen-foot Ridgeway rubber raft, which I had stored at my friend Jim Branscom's in McGrath.

We'd been planning our trip for over a month. Now on September 18, 1982, we were Alaska-bound. We left our Vancouver, Washington, homes and deposited a mountainous pile of gear at the International Airport in Portland,

Oregon. We gawked at wax-coated cardboard boxes full of food, a spare twelve-foot raft, sleeping bags, air mattresses, rifles, and duffel bags with cameras and personal gear.

We spent our first night in Anchorage on Saturday the eighteenth. The next day we attended the church my friend Steve McCoy pastored. After church we drove to Portage Glacier, some forty miles southeast of Anchorage, enjoying gorgeous mountain scenery and the ruggedness of Alaska.

On Monday the twentieth we flew to McGrath and spent the night with Bob Magnuson. He's considered the best all-around pilot in western Alaska (as was his father, Warren). Nightfall found us sleeping snugly in Bob's bunkhouse.

The next day Bob's pilot, Darrell Jerue, helped us stow our gear. He would fly us over the Kuskokwim Mountain range to Ophir. Hal and I would go first and wait on a little gravel strip while Darrell returned for the boys.

As we skimmed over the terrain, Hal and I were unprepared for the devastation we witnessed from a recent storm. Winds of 100 to 150 miles per hour had uprooted trees and overturned buildings. Torrential rain had turned slow streams into raging rivers.

While Darrell returned for his second trip, Hal and I unpacked the raft and hooked up foot pumps. We worked in the howling wind, bolting and taping the tubular frame, which was designed with seats for two at each end.

We walked to the Innoko River two hundred yards distant. I was shocked to see the water. What is normally a placid stream was now bank-to-bank coffee-brown water, churning downriver. I wondered how we could travel the ninety to one hundred miles downstream at a leisurely ten miles a day in that swirling water.

Not much later the boys arrived. I told the pilot, "I'll see you in ten days in Cripple." We completed loading the raft by 3 P.M. With a father-son team on each end of the raft, we pushed off. The river snatched the raft and catapulted it downstream at an alarming speed. I figured we'd reach a good stand of sheltering timber within a couple of hours and get out of the wind.

We always camp near timber, which provides firewood and tie-downs for tents, tarps, etc. Almost before we knew it, we reached a good stand of trees, made a comfortable camp, and ate dinner. After the meal the boys went off to scout. They took a .357 magnum pistol.

As darkness fell, Hal and I became concerned about the boys. We built a huge fire to assist them in finding camp. Sometime later we heard the report of their pistol and answered with a shot of our own.

The boys finally staggered into camp. They weren't used to tundra, had gotten confused about the camp's locale, and couldn't find their way back until they heard our shot.

At 3 A.M. Wednesday the howling wind was tearing our tie-down ropes loose. We rescued them, but at 5 A.M. we were awakened again. We held on to tarps to keep rain from our sleeping bags. By 7 A.M. dawn broke and we covered our gear with plastic. Uprooted trees plowed downriver, tearing apart our camp. We hurriedly finished breakfast and loaded the raft in an effort to leave for safety.

We were all dressed for the weather. We wore hip boots, heavy clothing, and cowboy hats. Although rain slickers were the order of the day, I wore a heavy mackinaw.

We pushed off amidst ominous clouds overhead. The threatening clouds released a downpour that the winds pushed horizontally. Even though the screeching wind repeatedly slammed us into the banks and drifting trees, we were amazed that the boys maneuvered the raft so well. We were glad to be alive and determined to make the most of a bad situation.

Heading northeast with the storm at our backs around noon, we entered a big bend in the river. Battered by blasts of wind, the raft, which usually draws four inches of water when loaded, now skipped across the surface completely out of control.

Partway into the bend we saw a sweeper (a tree projecting from the shore toward the far bank). Before we could adjust the raft, we were crosswise in the stream. We plowed into the tree so hard that the raft went airborne. Spontaneously it turned upside down and dumped everyone and everything out.

I went under, hitting the bottom of the river. I fought to the surface. When my head surged out of the water, I saw Roger running down the bank. He shouted encouragement to me, "Hang on, Dad. You'll make it!" I couldn't believe my situation.

The river pulled me under, and I bounced along on the bottom. I fought to the surface and gulped air. Then I was pulled under again.

I asked forgiveness, repeating over and over, "Forgive me!" I don't know whom I was asking to forgive me. Maybe I was asking forgiveness from my Father in heaven, or my wife for all the heartaches I'd caused her, or my son for bringing him on this terrible trip, or Hal and Jeff Stevens. I'll never know.

The others watched my struggles cease as I disappeared below the surface. They thought I had drowned.

My hip boots and coat were too much for me. I sank below the surface as if in a dream. My body hurled through endless water. My body was numb. I couldn't lift a finger.

Determined to wave at Roger, I struggled to the surface one last time. But no one was in sight. I'd been washed downriver out of sight of the others.

My experience became a dull, endless journey, bouncing off the bottom. I quit holding my breath. The howling wind no longer screamed at me. It was peaceful, and I quit struggling.

I thought someone was slapping my face. My body was hard against the riverbank and roots were telling me to open my eyes. I could see daylight far above me.

The next thing I knew I was on the surface grabbing for anything. But my hands were so numb I couldn't hold on to anything. The overpowering river pulled me down. The current swept me terribly fast underwater, but not for long. Next the river pushed me to the surface and flushed me onto the riverbank.

I lay there half in and half out of the water, too weak to move. My lungs screamed for air while water poured from my nostrils. I'd never been sicker.

I had given up and should by all rights have drowned. Yet here I was lying on the riverbank fighting for my life. I had experienced a miracle. By the grace of God I had been spared.

I felt guilt for the mess I'd brought the others into. I thought, "Let's see how you're going to get out of this one without your fancy high-powered rifle, raft, food, and gear. I'm supposed to be the leader and guide on this trip; and here I lie helpless, unable to even pull myself from the water."

I knew my son was safe but wondered what had happened to the others. Then above the noise of the wind I heard Roger yelling for me. I tried to see him but couldn't. Then it dawned on me that my glasses were gone, and without them I'm partly blind. Vaguely I understood Roger's yelling that Hal and Jeff were hanging on to the raft . . . somewhere along the river.

The river still tugged at me, as if reluctant to release me. It took all my strength to roll over away from the river.

Using my hands, I pounded and rubbed my body to restore feeling. My lower body felt like dead weight. My hips and legs were completely numb and without feeling. My waterlogged coat held me down. I struggled to my knees and was blown flat on my back by the hundred-mile-per-hour wind. I was instantly reminded that we were at the mercy of the elements.

Doubling over with cramps and chills, I began shaking so uncontrollably that I was unable to unbutton my coat or to stand up. I lay on the tundra, my lungs and chest afire with pain, coughing until my throat was raw and burning. Continuing to black out and regain consciousness, I began another journey. All I wanted was relief . . . to hold my stomach . . . to curl up . . . to sleep.

Sometime later I came to with Jeff bending over me. He removed my coat, wrung out the water, and put it back on me. He got me to my feet, but my knees buckled. He half carried and half dragged me to the river where Hal held the empty raft. Hal took one look at me and said, "Thank God, we thought you were gone."

I was a half mile downstream from the spot where we'd rammed the tree. Somehow Hal and Jeff had hung on to the raft and one paddle. We started for Roger on the other side of the river. Jeff managed to guide the raft across the stream, and Roger grabbed some ropes on the side of the raft as we swept by him. We were all together again.

We knelt for prayer, thanking God for sparing our lives. Then we bent to the task of surviving the remainder of the trip.

We were in for a terrible ordeal. We'd lost our food and all of our gear. All we had left was the clothes on our backs (Roger had lost his boots and socks, but never complained), the raft, one paddle, Jeff's rifle (which rusted immediately), a pole, matches, and two Bic lighters. We were out of touch with the outside world, and no one would be looking for us for another eight days.

I was in real bad shape. Someone rubbed my body continually to keep my blood circulating and to fight off hypothermia. Our immediate need was to reach a stand of timber and start a fire to dry out and warm up.

It took an hour to find timber and shelter. The others helped me from the raft and began tearing bark from trees for a fire.

None of our waterproof matches worked. However, Roger's wife, Leslie, had given us two lighters just before we'd left home. Roger's didn't work. Roger dug mine from my buttoned shirt pocket. The wind had abated, and after a few turns of the wheel, the Bic kicked out a tiny little flame. With the help of a small can of lighter fluid from Roger's pocket, we soon had a roaring fire (we safeguarded that lighter after that!).

Somewhere downstream was a party of four Texas hunters. If we could catch them, we might be able to get some food.

We were miserable the next few days as Hal and Jeff worked the raft downriver.

Later we found some of our lost items . . . the other paddle and a soggy sleeping bag. Next we recovered a grocery box on the riverbank. That find was like an early Christmas. We opened the box as if it were a gift-wrapped present, discovering dehydrated food. We exuberantly ate some, then pushed on for Cripple, hoping to catch a bush flight back to McGrath.

A couple of days later we caught up with the Texans, who loaned us food and other items we needed, plus a pair of warm boots for Roger. They had retrieved Jeff's duffle bag and dried out the contents, including clothes and quite a sum of cash. Assuming someone had experienced trouble upstream, they had awaited the arrival of that group. They returned all items and encouraged us. Sadly, I did not get home with their addresses. After thanking them we continued.

I knew that we could not go beyond the pickup point at Cripple. From there the river winds to the Yukon River, and no one would pick us up beyond Cripple.

The boys kept the raft moving at a good pace as we traveled under low-hanging clouds. We saw moose constantly, but getting off the river alive was our main concern.

At one point where I had taken a seventy-three-inch bull in past years, we saw a monster bull, one that Hal thought would equal mine. I decided to call him closer so my companions could have the thrill of seeing this animal in his mating mood. We watched him in the willows within two hundred yards of the shoreline; and I told the others I'd call.

The big bull responded immediately. He feared nothing on earth. He tore up trees and threw sod and mud into the air. We were glad we were on the water and out of his reach.

That little episode caused me to wonder if the Innoko was trying to tell me something. The year before I had stepped into a clearing when I thought my partner had shot a moose. However the moose was merely wounded and charged me immediately from ten paces. I fired my rifle from the hip and fortunately dropped the moose. We are permitted few mistakes in the unforgiving wilderness, and I began wondering if I was fast using up my quota of mistakes.

We continued down the river.

Around 3 P.M. (Thursday) we heard a small plane. We signaled for it to land. Moments later the small float plane settled in over the river, landed smoothly, and taxied across the water to us. Larry Henslee with the Alaska Department of Fish and Game climbed from his plane. We'd met before (and I'd supported his work trying to catch game thieves who hunted only for antlers and left meat to rot).

We decided I would go with Larry to McGrath to arrange for a plane to return for the others. We arrived at 5 P.M. to discover that Bob Magnuson was out with a hunting party. Since he had the only plane large enough to retrieve the others and their gear, I waited.

A couple of days later Bob flew into town, heard my story, and gassed up to go immediately for my partners. I chartered a flight to Anchorage via North Pacific Airlines. From there things worked like clockwork.

On Saturday Bob returned my companions and our gear and we departed. Within hours we were taking hot showers in Anchorage and eating a hot meal.

We caught a flight the next day and were with our families that Sunday night.

I've been asked many times if I'll return to Alaska. My response is, "Once you've been to Alaska, you will always return. Yes, I will return to Alaska, to the Last Frontier and its wild rivers. I'll have a camera in one hand, a rifle in the other, and of course, a Bic lighter . . . or two!"

Afterword

A couple of things would have enabled us to avoid our disaster. First, we should have considered waiting out the wind and water until it was safer to float (even though we thought we'd be safer downriver).

Second, I was the only experienced Alaskan hunter. I now know that when you take greenhorns into the maw of Alaska's wilderness, you expose them to death. The more experienced or well educated the partners are, the better.

Third, there are other fire-starting materials that would have helped us. For instance, we could have used a magnesium stick, which ignites even when wet.

Epilogue

Smitty and his wife, Carol, finalized this story in the spring of 1995, just prior to his departure on his last great hunt to the Happy Hunting Grounds, where the fish and game is all record class and he'll never have to fret about wild rivers!

In a letter I received from Carol in March 1995, she commented:

Even now it is hard for me to visualize the sleepy little Innoko River I drifted on with Smitty, Don, and Evelyn turning into the river that the guys described on their return. Thankfully, we have film of our hunt with the Millers. The Larry Henslee Smitty mentions in his story flew in and checked the guys' licenses and tags on that trip. I was fascinated to see the float plane land and this uniformed guy get out while Don and Smitty were hastily getting their animals tagged.

Larry said as far as he knew, Evelyn and I were the first ladies on that river in forty years.

We had such a good time and we've always thought we'd know just how to manage with half the gear the next time.

We saw a grizzly bear our first day out. He was as gold as the bush. From then on, I wore a whistle around my neck and told the guys that if I blew that whistle, all modesty was out.

We saw lots of animals, but the most fascinating were the wolves. We had a choir that could outdo the Mormon Tabernacle Choir.

Just before we left McGrath we ate dinner at the restaurant. You eat family-style there and Rick Mackey was at our table. I got real excited and jumped up and got his autograph. I think I embarrassed my poor husband, but Rick thanked me for being interested in the Iditarod Race. The year before we got to see Rick Swenson practice his dogs on sand.

I wore ski clothes and stayed pretty warm and dry. The bugs really got to me, and later Smitty introduced me to his friend Jim Branscom, saying "This is my wife, but she doesn't look like this all the time." Evelyn and I put on stocking caps when we left Ophir and removed them when we stepped into a shower back in Anchorage.

Smitty is failing pretty rapidly. The doctors keep him pain free and yet he remains himself. The medical experts are getting better all the time at pain management.

I wrote Carol for any final comments she considered appropriate, and her response August 18, 1995, was:

I look back so thankful for memories of a man who was a sportsman in every area of his life. And so Alaska and indeed the Innoko River tell me to count today's blessings. A serene, peaceful life can turn into turbulence and distress much like the river Smitty described. I remind my family we are making memories. Smitty's family have the best that life can offer. God is good.

Not only does danger stalk the wild rivers, she also frequents the mountain peaks.

PIECE A CAKE

AS TOLD TO THE AUTHOR BY JOHN CLORAN

John took off his boots to examine his feet . . . six to eight inches of flesh was ripped away from an area around the small toe on the right foot.

The gray, spitting clouds stood watch over the lone hiker as he trudged above the timberline. Fog enveloped the mountain peaks, reducing visibility. A steady drizzle turned into a downpour, and the hiker sought shelter. His leather boots encased two pairs of waterlogged socks and two feet whose condition worsened by the hour. His movement resembled that of an animated glacier as he inched along—cold, wet, and alone.

Seven days had elapsed since his departure from Anchorage, Alaska. It had been more than two days since he had eaten. His earlier doubts about his location were now a certainty . . . he was hopelessly lost.

He focused his attention on survival. He must conserve energy. He would not let the mental anguish extinguish his hope. His goal was to escape the grasp the mountains had on him. He *would* get out.

He agonized over the stark reality of his predicament. The physical part was difficult, but the mental aspects were even more devastating—this wasn't a temporary screwup but a survival trek. Even if someone had been present to encourage John Cloran, he knew that his chance of survival under these conditions was nearly impossible.

It was pouring rain. He was soaking wet. A stiff mountain breeze blew constantly. On top of all that, he was without food and lost.

Had he been familiar with this area, he would have known which trail to take—he would not have chosen the wrong pass. But John had purposely chosen this hike, confident that his skills would enable him to cross the mountains and enjoy a leisurely four-day hike.

John's current mountain location was a long way from his New England, working-class roots. Until John was eighteen he had felt no desire to hike. Subsequently he had begun taking day trips into the New England countryside. His three years as an army MP gave him an uncompromising attitude: he refused to quit on hikes, assuring himself that all he needed to do was to put one foot in front of the other.

After his stint in the military, John attended school in New Mexico to become an RN, focusing his expertise in the newborn Intensive Care Unit. John got involved with a traveling nurse program, which allowed him to contact different agencies and pick jobs and locales that appealed to him at various times of the year.

Since he'd always wanted to go to Alaska, when the opportunity presented itself, John jumped at it. Hiking figured into his decision. He had hiked in New Mexico, Colorado, and led a group up to Mt. Massive, the sixth highest peak in the United States. John's hiking experience included a twenty-miler and a fifty-miler. His twenty years of backcountry hiking and camping, combined with his continued efforts to prepare well for each situation, supplied him with invaluable experience.

After arriving in Anchorage, one of his first acquisitions was a hiker's guide book, *Fifty-five Ways to the Wilderness in Southcentral Alaska*. He decided in July 1989 to solo the Hicks Creek–Chickaloon Pass hike. It sounded very pretty, and he reasoned that an early-season hike would enable him to avoid hunters.

John was thoroughly prepared for the forty-two-mile hike which he planned to make alone. He had selected the proper food and gear. On July 13 he left his car on the Glenn Highway at Hicks Creek to complete hike number 48 (from *Fifty-five Ways*) within a five-day time frame. He reached Hicks Lake after four-and-one-half hours of minimal effort and pitched his tent for the night.

On July 14, John reached Caribou Creek, unaware of his impending problems. The trail split into three branches, and he chose the one that led him astray. John compounded his problem by not believing his compass.

He constantly referred to his two map—he had the entire route from *Fifty-five Ways* (he'd photocopied it, shrunk it, and put it on one piece of paper). He also had the area topographical map—both were laminated. The map from the book advised him to proceed two or three miles down a braided riverbank until coming to a cabin. He'd complied, but never found the cabin. He knew the book was ten years old and reasoned that cabins appear and disappear.

John hiked another two days before the trail ran out. He backed out a half mile and picked it up again but it died out on a ridge. He became increasingly concerned about his directions.

He was out of food and in an area he didn't know. It was nine o'clock. John considered his alternatives. He figured he could follow Boulder Creek down to the Chickaloon River. From there he could head directly south another mile or two to the Glenn Highway, his car, and safety—he kept extra food, clothing, and money in his car. He could retrieve his gear later. It was a piece of cake.

To expedite his trip out John left his pack, including tent and sleeping bag, then dropped off the ridge to the river. John took matches, insect repellent, a self-inflating mattress pad, two plastic bottles, a small Swiss army knife, and first-aid kit (including enough moleskin for five days), and nylon pouches for the bottles and first-aid kit.

John kept walking. What he didn't realize immediately was that he was on the wrong river. He wasn't heading west—he was heading north, walking out of an area where searchers would expect to find him, should a search be mounted.

This was July 17 and the fifth day out for John. Half a dozen hours after running out of food he had decided that things could get bad. But as it turned out, he discovered he wasn't that much more hungry day three than he had been day two. Hunger wasn't a progressive kind of thing, yet he determined to put food out of his mind.

John encountered a number of waterways that he was forced to cross. The constant immersion of his boots kept both his boots and feet wet. John wore double socks and knew that the proper care of his feet was crucial to his survival.

Another problem became increasingly apparent as John encountered more and more bear scat and bear-rubbed trees. To make bears aware of his presence he whistled as he walked through head-high grass and alder thickets (he had left his bear bell and walking stick with his pack). Although he was on the lookout for bears, he feared them less than hypothermia.

The farther John got from his pack, the more confused he became with his surroundings and the more determined he was to get out. Each day began with his resolution to find familiar terrain and enough edible materials to sustain his strength. He found berries everywhere; but they were not ripe. He put some in one plastic bottle and ate them from time to time.

He'd been having periodic pain with his feet, and on the seventeenth John took off his boots to examine them. What he saw were two whitish, wrinkled feet that looked as if they'd been in a tub of water for a week. Six to eight inches of flesh was ripped away from an area around the small toe on the right foot. After drying his feet, he covered his right foot with gauze bandages from his first-aid kit, then wrapped it up with tape. John applied patches of moleskin around both boot tops, along the sides of his feet and toes, and in the back of his heels. Finally he taped his feet up for support and continued his trek.

As the days ran together, John continued to ponder his chances for survival. *Did I tape my feet on the seventeenth or the eighteenth? What day is today? Is there a chance a search has been called for me?*

He reasoned that since he was a punctual person, his colleagues at Providence Hospital in Anchorage would note his absence and question his whereabouts. John hoped that within forty-eight hours after his failure to report to work, someone would contact his family and call the state police. He knew they'd see his car on the side of road, run a check on his plates, and send someone looking for him since he'd left word that he was going into the Chitina Pass–Hicks Creek area.

Although John hoped somebody would put that together, he assumed zero. He was determined to get himself out of there. He kept moving.

On the nineteenth, his seventh day out, the rain hit . . . and it hammered him for five consecutive days. It was a heavy, depressing weather pattern. Although he had little gear and his clothing became soaked, he managed to maintain his body heat.

Depression weighed heavily on John's mind. Sleep became a stranger to him. He knew that his survival depended upon utilizing everything he had in a variety of ways.

John wore a brand-new Gore-Tex suit under which was polypropylene underwear. He wore an army wool-rag sweater and a Gore-Tex hat. One of John's best tools was his mattress pad and its nylon container. Sometime that day he began crossing swift rivers, using his mattress and two plastic bottles for buoyancy. He wrapped the mattress around his waist beneath his coat, inflated it, put the empty bottles in the coat pockets, then floated and kicked his way across a stream.

At times he used the mattress as a tent, huddling under it with his back against a tree and holding it over his body lengthwise. If the wind was blowing with an accompanying light rain, he would deflate it and wrap his legs with the mattress to cut the windchill.

John repelled the mosquitoes with his hat and a couple of bandannas. He used his two nylon pouches (first-aid kit and bottle containers) as gloves or coverings, depending on the situation.

On the twenty-second he decided to try to start a fire to dry himself and his gear. John figured his Skin-So-Soft lotion was oil-based and should work as a fire-starter. Having placed sticks together, he squirted a couple of drops of the lotion on the wood, touched a match to it, and it whooshed into flame. He maintained his fire for thirty hours—drying his gear, warming himself, and tending his feet. He got too close to the fire and partially melted his Gore-Tex suit and caught his boots on fire.

The next day John's absence from work triggered a call to the Alaska State Troopers, who began an immediate search.

John continued to walk. He was pleased that he'd been moving as well as he had the past few days; but his strength was waning. On the twenty-fourth, the five-day downpour stopped. Also that day, John acknowledged that his lack of nutrition was affecting his mobility. He began passing out. He would walk a few steps then drop like a rock. Time was running out for him.

On the twenty-fifth, John's thirteenth day in the wilds, he stumbled onto a lake and discovered two cabins. He broke into one, found a candy bar, and wolfed it down before crashing into bed. He had more reason to hope for rescue now than he had had in two weeks.

The next day he put together a plan. Behind the cabin was an oil tank. He could build a smudge-pot fire. His earlier frustration with a smoke-producing fire had been compounded by the fact that the thick cloud cover hid any chance of discovery. Nobody could have seen him had they flown right over him. Now in addition to the smudge he could use the paint around the cabin to paint a red *SOS* on the aluminum roof. Although he was too weak to check out the second cabin down the lake, things were looking good. He could rest today.

On the twenty-seventh he was awakened from sleep by what sounded like an airplane. John looked out the window and saw a float plane taxiing on the lake.

He was out the door, waving his hands like a madman. The minute he knew the plane's occupants had seen him, John dropped to his knees and said a prayer. He admitted later, "I don't know if I'll ever be as close to God as I was on that trip. The very first thing I did was drop down and thank God for saving me. When I saw the pilot and his wife, Jack and Lynn Cole, my elation was, Jesus Christ was comin' in on the plane. That was it. I cannot, can *not*, describe the amount of emotion that I experienced—one minute wrapped up in dry clothing and trying to figure out the next game plan, and the next minute salvation.

"Jack and Lynn had come to work on their cabin. We introduced ourselves and I let them know what I was doin' there. They wrapped me up and kept me warm. They got some food, started the fire, and began heating water for tea and my feet.

"Jack took off my bandages and began my feet soaking in warm water with pHisoHex—so there would be no chance for infection. A lot of skin was hanging from my feet.

"Lynn brought me a cup of Constant hot tea with sugar for energy, and as fast as the tea would cool, she brought me more. I had three cups of tea, a couple of cups of hot apple cider, and two cups of soup. I had an immense craving for pumpernickel bread with maybe a bit of cheese and water. I asked Lynn if she had any dark bread. Eventually I ate one or two pieces of that. It was like heaven. Then I had half a turkey sandwich, which was the best thing I've ever eaten.

"I couldn't make any kind of quick moves at all. Even standing up was a real chore. I was trying to stand up, and I had to be literally held up.

"I was with the Coles for a few hours, then they flew me to Stephan Lodge about three-thirty P.M. There I had a small dish of applesauce, cheese, and saltine crackers. At Stephan Lodge I got the first look at myself. When I saw myself in the mirror—I just peeked—the first impression was horror. I looked nothing like me at all. My hair was awry and I was a mess. My whole face was hollow. I had shoulder blades and ankles and nothin' in between. I looked like I had just come out of Auschwitz. It scared the hell out of me; I gasped aloud at what I saw.

"I couldn't stop crying, and I apologized to women at the lodge. They told me not to worry and that I looked great. Big towels were wrapped around my feet with plastic bags over them. Even though I was talking okay, I was fuzzy and not myself.

"According to a survival book, all people who have been left several days may look okay and may speak okay, but in fact everybody has a certain element of shock. I felt like I was speaking to people, but I felt like the whole back third of my head was almost a separate entity—a real dizzy, light-headed feeling.

"A police helicopter picked me up at Stephan Lodge and transported me to Providence Hospital in Anchorage just before the change of shifts about eleven o'clock at night. They brought me in two plates of food, which I ate.

"I had a very good doctor at Providence. She came in and looked at me and we talked. She said straight out that I'd be okay physically but that psychologically it might be tough a week or a month later. I talked to a clinical psychologist next, who encouraged me and gave me names of people should I want to talk. All I wanted to do was get out of the hospital.

"I got back to the house here about midnight and I sent out for a twenty-six-dollar pizza! The pizza was unbelievably good. I've been eating heartily every since.

"That night I woke up in a nightmare where I'm right in the middle of a forest fire. I don't know if I ever had a dream like that before. It was a very real situation, and I was up for the rest of the night.

"A couple of days later my brother was here, and I sent him down to pick up some stuff at the store. I must have looked out of the window thirty or forty times. *Where is he?* I checked my watch constantly. He was gone no more than forty minutes, but I was frantic. I didn't want to let him out of my sight again.

"I had to keep looking out the window to make sure people were nearby. That stunned me. Coming from total isolation where I struggled with the elementary essentials for survival and coming back into town where I'm drinking a Coca-Cola, it's totally incomprehensible.

"I later spoke with three men who work extensively with search and rescue. Wayne Schrober headed up the task force for the Alaska State Troopers, Andy Scheider of Alaska Mountain Rescue, and Brian Hohner of the survival school also lent their support.

"Brian Hohner told me that fifty percent of all people who die of hypothermia will die on day one. Twenty-five percent will die on day two; and something like eighty-seven percent who are out there four days don't come back. Most people don't walk out after ten days.

"These guys work search and rescue day in and day out; their work is fascinating. They talked about how easy it is to get turned around. The state trooper pilot who picked me up was telling me that in his limited experience he has been out on three search and rescues for people who were doing the exact hike I was who have gone wrong in the exact area.

"Part of the problem was that I didn't believe what I was seeing. Looking at my map, I was not believing it. I had a compass and all the equipment I needed. The other night a lady from work was telling me that she had done the same hike a couple of years ago with two experienced hikers—able to read topos, compasses, the whole bit. All three flatly denied that they were in the position that the map indicated. They all had different opinions about where they were.

"If three experienced people are confused, you can imagine how easy it is for one person to be uncertain. It is a lot easier to become lost by yourself simply because you don't have somebody to discuss things with.

"Brian Hohner told me I should not be embarrassed about being lost. He's more impressed with the fact that I got out. Many people get into the same situation—they become disoriented, they don't necessarily believe what's going on, and that's part of the problem.

"Instead of being on Boulder Creek coming off of Chitina Pass, I ended up on the Oschetna River going north. The river I eventually hit and thought was the Chickaloon was the Susitna River. I was one hundred and eighty degrees and scores of miles in the wrong direction. My initial hike from the roadway to Chitna Pass is twenty-five miles. From where I became lost at Chitna Pass to where they picked me up, I had covered over ninety-five miles.

"Determination and the will to live pushed me on. At one point I drank my own urine. That's not something I think about all the time. There was absolutely no water available. I was completely dry. It's no big deal unless you're out of water on top of a mountain.

"My weight plummeted twenty pounds during my bout with death. My normal body size is one hundred fifty-two and just under five feet ten inches. When I came back, I was lighter than I've ever been as an adult. I've run competitively as a racer, half marathons; and when I was in my best condition, I was about one hundred forty-two, which makes me look very thin.

"I can move my toes, but I have no feeling in them. Luckily I was rescued when I was—if it had gone on several more days, gangrene would probably have started. When I'm able to hike again, I plan to retrieve my gear—top-of-the-line cameras, tent, sleeping bag, binoculars, and the pack itself, easily worth a thousand dollars.

"The fact that I was going to die was not a primary concern to me. I don't want to die. But what really, really bugged me was that I was not going to be found. I knew it would really bug my family. I didn't want to think of my family wondering what had become of me.

"I prayed constantly. Specifically I prayed, 'Whatever You find proper, let that happen.' I prayed that my family would have the strength to deal with the situation. For myself I asked only to be warm and dry. After five days of rain, I got the dry cabin.

"I don't believe the state troopers will charge me for rescuing me. I don't know what the hospital will charge me. I'm sure that at some point in time they will send me a bill. I wouldn't be shocked if I didn't get a bill either because I work for Providence, even though they have no legal obligations to give me anything free.

"Hour after hour, day after day, the only thing that mattered was my relations to family and colleagues. What matters is my overall gut reaction and how I deal with people. The minor disputes became meaningless. I'm a much, much better person today. I'll never be the same as a result of this experience.

"After fifteen days alone in the wilderness and ten days without food, fighting weather, terrain, and my internal feelings, I gained a new perspective on hiking and life. Among other things I will not hike alone. Even with all the planning and preparation there are factors which we encounter that can be life-threatening. I've learned that a simple hike is not a piece of cake."

One of the premier ingredients for survival is the refusal to quit. Many people in these stories possess that quality, especially a trapper named Jack whose tenacity is bulldog tough.

ONE TOUGH TRAPPER

AS TOLD TO THE AUTHOR BY WADE NOLAN

Jack pushed against the wolverine with his mittened hand. The wolverine was a windmill of razor-blade paws.

Ten years ago Wade Nolan and I returned to Anchorage from an ice-fishing trip. The day before we had sadly watched Andy Runyan's cabin burn to the ground near Lake Louise, Alaska. Wade spun a tale about a trapper whose innovation spoke volumes about his courage and desperation. I could never find the trapper and asked Wade to recount the story from memory.

In the early winter of 1979 or 1980 I completed six months' work in Nome. I boarded a flight out of Nome back to Anchorage, probably a two-hour flight. As I sat in my seat, this big guy, a grizzled, bearded old trapper, sat down next to me.

We both looked at magazines before and after takeoff.

After a while I looked over and noticed his hand was all scarred up. It looked like he'd stuck his hand into a bag full of razor blades. The scars were healed but they were relatively new, not ten years old. Later on I glanced over at his face. It, too, was heavily scarred as was his other hand.

As time went on, we started talking. I think his name was Jack, but I'm not positive. I'm going to call him Jack for the sake of the story.

He was a lone trapper with a line up in the Kigluaik Mountains, north and east of Nome. They are their own little mountain range, right in the middle of nowhere. They're so remote it takes forever to get to any place from there.

Jack's trapline was similar to others' in that he had a base cabin with a number of small trapline cabins. These small, often crude cabins provide overnight shelter—a place to get in out of the weather, to skin animals, to sleep. His line was circular and took several days to cover. He worked out of his home cabin and snowshoed the line checking traps and stopping at several-mile intervals at his line cabins.

One winter Jack made the rounds of his traps, clad in his parka, his backpack slung on his back, and his webs rhythmically slicing along the trail. He resembled many an old-time trapper. It was late in the afternoon when he neared the end of his line, between the last line cabin and his main cabin. Each of the many traps he'd just checked held remnants of eaten carcasses of pine marten or mink. He had recently noticed wolverine tracks and knew that pirate of the north had beaten him to his traps.

Wolverines are secretive and rarely seen by the foot traveler in the wilderness. They are sly and hold a reputation for gluttony and ferocity.

Jack reset the traps and tossed aside the animal remains. He traveled on, thinking little of the glutton but more of his main cabin and warmth and food. That's when he noticed some ptarmigan. He shouldered his .22 rifle and shot three of the pigeon-sized fowl, which would make fine table fare that evening.

Walking along with the birds in his mittened hands, Jack paid no heed to the blood occasionally dropping from the birds onto the trail. He noticed a weather front closing in on him as it started snowing. The storm built so fast he knew he couldn't reach the cabin before it reached its zenith. He decided to hole up until the storm blew over.

Knowing the country well, he hurried to a nearby hill studded with rock outcroppings. He reckoned an outcropping would provide safety away from the wind where he could back in under a ledge for protection and sit out the storm.

He left the main trail and found an appropriate ledge. Jack took off his pack and laid it down beneath the ledge. He crouched down and backed underneath the ledge—there was just enough room to sit with his knees up under his chin. He laid the ptarmigan in front of him at the mouth of the ledge.

What he didn't know was that the trap-raiding wolverine had been following him. The carcajou, knowing the rewards to be found along a trapper's trail, had keyed on the blood from the ptarmigan. It walked right up to the top of the ledge, just above the trapper's head. Spotting the ptarmigan below, the wolverine pounced down on the birds where they lay just a few feet in front of the trapper.

Startled by the blur of an object dropping in front of his face, Jack jerked back in surprise, automatically raising his hands. Instead of bounding away like most any other animal would have done, the wolverine instantly jumped onto the trapper.

Jack pushed against the wolverine with his mittened hand. The wolverine was a windmill of razor-blade paws. Even though this big, brawny trapper was doing his best to hold the wolverine away from him, the animal's claws whirled and slashed around his face. Jack repeatedly pushed the animal away, and the wolverine kept pouncing back at his face.

Moments into the attack Jack's mittens were ripped off. He pushed with his exposed hands. In short order the animal shredded Jack's hands.

Compounding Jack's efforts to free himself of the furious attack, the beast caught a claw in the hole on his parka zipper. Somewhat trapped, the wolverine went crazy. Old Jack said it felt as if the fight hadn't begun until then because the wolverine went into high gear, fighting for its life. Jack saw only whirling claws and teeth.

In spite of his cramped quarters and the animal's attachment, finally Jack shoved the wolverine back far enough to break its hold. The wolverine landed on the snow two to three feet away. The animal glanced at Jack momentarily, grabbed the ptarmigan in its mouth, and trotted off, leaving the badly bleeding trapper.

Jack had so much blood in his eyes he could hardly see. Wounds on his face, hands, and wrists were bone-deep. Jack knew his very survival dictated reaching his home cabin, even though the storm was now raging.

Picking up his pack, Jack crawled from beneath the ledge. Trailing blood, he struggled off along his trapline in the diminishing light.

Before darkness closed in on him Jack reached his cabin. His clothes were matted with blood. He shuffled through the door knowing it would be nearly as cold inside as outside. Jack's survival necessitated getting a fire going in his woodstove. Coupled with his weakened condition from the loss of blood and his injuries, finding a lantern and starting the fire was an ordeal.

His next step was to evaluate and care for his injuries. In the glow from the lantern the mirror reflected a mask of death. His only help would have to come from his own efforts. Jack found his sewing kit. He propped up the mirror in front of him next to the lantern on the table.

He fumbled for a needle and thread. Sitting there in the gathering warmth of his fire and the glowing lantern light, Jack slowly and painfully inserted the needle into his skin, pulled the thread through and tucked the wound together, one stitch at a time.

As he sewed, he blacked out. Later he came to and continued sewing. He doesn't know how many times he blacked out; but all night and into the wee hours of the morning Jack alternately stitched his wounds and passed out. Finally, exhausted, he'd closed the major wounds on his face and his hands.

He climbed into his bunk. Without a radio or any way to contact help, he had no other choice. He didn't know what he was waiting for . . . he was just trusting that something would happen. He could only wait.

As the Lord would have it, He saw fit a couple of days later to send a bush pilot. Passing low over Jack's cabin, the pilot noticed no smoke was coming from the chimney, so he landed. He entered Jack's cabin and found him in serious condition in his bunk. The pilot loaded Jack into his bush plane and flew him back to Nome, where after weeks in a hospital Jack survived.

Although we live pain-free, comfortable lives in our concrete world (wondering if the car's going to start in the cold or when *Titanic* will come out on video), in Alaska's Great Alone outside the major metropolises people involved in their regimens frequently face death.

In the Kotzebue area, for instance, out-of-town travel is accomplished by air or water. These travelers regularly ride twenty to sixty miles on water in summer by boat and on ice in winter by snowmachine. These people's journeys in their extreme winter environment place them in jeopardy every time they leave town.

Travel is crucial to survival as the following story about a disabling injury indicates.

COME BACK ALIVE

BY ANONYMOUS

*I slipped and shot down the snow. I discovered too late that the gully
was steeper than I thought.*

Tim Jordan worked on a ship off Alaska's coast in the Bering Sea a few years.
He left that job to go to Newport, Oregon. After two years in Newport he was
hired as an accountant for North Pacific Ship Supply in Dutch Harbor, Alaska,
during early March 1991. He told me his story from a hospital bed.

When I read in the newspaper about the death of a nine-year-old boy falling off
Flattop Mountain, I was shocked. (See "Death Stalked the Edge.) My first reaction was, "That's where I used to camp." It was a staging area for my hikes
back into the Chugach Range ten years ago. I set up my tent and hiked from
that point into the various peaks.

I could hike three mountains from there in a day and come back in the
evening. Starting in February when the snow melted off the ridges, I hiked every
weekend, climbing just about every peak you can see behind Anchorage. I love
hiking those beautiful Chugach Mountains in Anchorage's backyard.

To contrast the danger of the mountains with the serenity, a week after the
death of the young boy on Flattop, a string orchestra performed up there.

The boy's death reminded me that this hiking business, although it's relatively
easy and pleasurable, has inherent dangers. Ignoring that aspect can create problems.

After moving to Unalaska, I continued hiking on weekends. I planned to hike
on Friday, July 26, 1991. I followed the same pattern on every outing, incor-
porating my knowledge. It's so simple to bring the right stuff on a hike. I had a
list I'd used for years. I'd go down it every time before I went out to make sure
I had all the essentials for safety and survival. I always carried twenty pounds
on my back going into the wilderness. It was no burden at all.

The peculiarity and the advantage of Unalaska's mountains is that they are
dramatic and beautiful even though they're short. They're only fifteen hundred
to two thousand feet high. I know that sounds like absolutely nothing; but within
two thousand feet you can have some awesome, thrilling mountains.

I left work at 5 P.M. and drove to the area I planned to hike. It's called Pyramid
Valley, four or five miles from Dutch. It has mountains on three sides. I'd hiked

the other two sides and wanted to climb the middle, which has a long, gradual face. The idea was that I'd come back to town and have a great supper.

I wore a shirt, a light sweater, a heavy sweater, and my blessed Gore-Tex jacket—it's just a shell, but it works. I wore hiking boots and wool socks. And of course I had my pack with my two bananas for a snack.

I began my hike thinking, "Well, I'm going on this little couple-of-hours hike . . . it's nothing, just a cocktail-hour hike."

But that was the mistake. I was to discover that was not the case. Probably no matter what form of wilderness it is, whether it's desert or the center of the ocean, it's never casual.

I hiked the valley through this long canyon. Although there was a lot of snow, I covered a couple of miles and got almost all the way to the top walking normally. I reached the top of the mountain by seven.

After viewing the beauty from one peak, I walked to another one. Before me the mountains and water of Beaver Inlet spread out—utterly, utterly untouched, beautiful nature. Sunshine flooded that side of the island.

Next I hiked to a peak that consisted of crumbly, gray rock. I could kick the rocks with my feet and almost see them crumble. I stood on a two-foot-square platform of rock surrounded on three sides by air and a vertical drop of fifteen hundred feet or more to the water. I carefully retreated from this position and walked over to the main peak, the attractive peak of the mountain.

I got to the top of that one, which was about six by six feet of lawn grass and absolutely beautiful. Because the Aleutian Islands have no big cities, the scenery has not changed for centuries—for 360 degrees natural beauty surrounded me.

Some mountains rise up and then drop straight off. This peak had that type of jagged drop-off. I walked down from the peak, walking the knife edge of the ridge. If my wisdom had been working at all, I'd have been staying away from the edge.

A little voice was talking to me. It was saying, "This is unusual." But I wasn't listening to it. I was being careless, not in my alert-survival mode.

As I walked along, looking down over this edge into the bowl, I noticed off to one side a possible alternative way back to the car. I wondered if there was a way to get down. I was thinking, "We'll pick the best way to get down there."

That was another mistake.

I spotted a gully twelve feet to fifteen feet across. It was tight with a relatively small opening. A snowfield spanned the chute. Earlier in the year the gorge had borne a great deal of snow. The snow had a telltale line right across it, and my brain said, "That means there's ice below it." But I just ignored that.

I figured I'd slide down the snow to the rocks, stop, and continue hiking to the car. I didn't know anything about these particular kinds of rocks or the situation I was in. So I got out onto what was real soft snow and started down hand over foot.

As soon as my feet hit the ice, I couldn't dig in at all—it was solid. And my hands were useless in the snow-choked chute. I slipped and shot down the snow.

I discovered too late that the gully was steeper than I thought. It happened so quickly that before I knew it, I had tumbled another thirty feet over jumbled rock. I managed to get spread-eagled and stopped.

Excruciating pain shot up my left leg. Waves of nausea flooded my being.

I crawled off to the side and just hung on there for a while. Coached myself. *Got to keep from passing out.* I found that passing out was at times almost voluntary. I had a terrific desire to go to sleep. But I didn't do that. *I gotta hang on.*

There was really no place to hang on in this steep place. After a while I inched over and around boulders, descending from this area. I finally got to where the slope was more gradual and I wasn't going to start rolling spontaneously again.

I did something that seemed to be significant. I didn't really know what type of injuries I might have. For the first time I tried to put my weight on my left foot. I just collapsed. The blinding pain shot through my leg.

I tried to stand again. My body screamed and I collapsed, crumbling into the rocks again. I hurt like hell. My left leg was broken. I was really immobile. I wasn't going anywhere.

As Friday night approached, I knew I was is no shape to get to my vehicle and questions plagued my mind:

What are the chances of another hiker coming into the area? Will he find me?

Will I have to stay here until Monday for a search and rescue to begin when my colleagues discover I haven't returned to work?

What will the weather be like?

Can I survive the weather . . . and how strong will I be without food?

The night and the pain continued. It was not a big pain, but a bothersome pain. I was kind of lucky in some respects. A little patch of snow was six feet away, and another had melted, leaving a pool of water with a rivulet trickling downhill. So I always had access to snow and water.

The dull pain continued on through the night.

Having made it through Friday night, my big project Saturday was to slide six feet downslope to urinate, ease six feet over to gather some snow, then slither six feet back up the slope to my hide. This required great physical effort, but little mental energy.

I stayed in the same area on the side of the slope. It was all rocks. Thousands of thoughts coursed through my mind as I lay on the mountain, and periodically I pulled out a rock and pitched it downslope, making a smoother spot to recline. I pushed myself up against the rock wall, which shielded me somewhat from the rain.

Saturday turned into Saturday night. Even though I had a pretty interesting book with me, I found that living from moment to moment, just sitting there looking out, maybe not thinking anything at all, was so much more absorbing and real than reading, and it made the time seem short. I wondered for a while if perhaps I was never going to be bored the rest of my life, if something had changed and I would be incapable of boredom because the whole experience seemed totally absorbing.

I continued changing my three positions—first I lay on my back; then I rolled over onto my side; and lastly I sat up. My time was spent in one of these positions; in making my big journey of the day—my triangle to urinate, get snow, and return; in thinking about life; in sleeping or . . . talking with my family, friends, and associates.

Sometimes when I awakened, I was in a half sleep. That's when I had conversations with just about everyone I ever knew, everyone who was significant to me.

Sometimes the conversations would end abruptly and I would come back to reality. And that would be fine and it would be gone. But later I would remember it as having been a real event and that the conversation really took place. I can remember having internal arguments where I'd say, "I had this conversation." But, "No, you couldn't possibly have had that conversation 'cause you're on this mountainside."

"Maybe you didn't have any of these, but you had *that* one." I had to make sure that I didn't have at least one conversation on that mountainside. That was a really strange thing, to have the brain telling you that this thing had happened. But it's real. It must have been kind of a wish thing.

I guess the body and the brain behave in ways that I never knew they could. Totally normal things happened that really make me wonder, that impress me with just the nature of our structure that most of the time we lead reasonable lives and don't call upon it. For example, my cuts on my hands never bled much. They didn't hurt or anything. I thought they should be bleeding.

One of the things that seemed interesting to me was maneuvering my broken left leg from one position to another, trying to do it without much pain. I had to use my right leg. Quickly the right leg learned how to do it. Moving around was complex. I found that if I tried to think about it or tried to use my brain at all, I couldn't do it; I didn't even know how to do it anymore. But the right leg knew perfectly well how to do it. The only way I could do it was to ignore it and let my right leg do its thing, as if it had its own intelligence.

The weather wasn't that bad. Friday and Saturday nighttime temperatures were in the forties.

More repetition—sleep, awaken, remove rocks, rotate positions, hold conversations, complete my triangular journey. Time crawled by, yet it sped by.

I wondered whether I'd be found. I thought, "Well, first of all, it was clear, there had been helicopters coming over."

At one point and without warning a Grumman goose flew right along the ridge. I looked right into the window. I waved and thought, "They know me by now and I'll keep waving." No one ever saw me. So it was like, "Okay. I can stay here another night."

It seemed that my sound didn't get out of the bowl at all. It's like being invisible and inaudible. I thought about what it must be like for people like fishermen who get caught in the water to be rescued . . . how horrible it must be. When the sound is right over you, it's bad. But when it's far away, you're saying, "Come over here."

Dealing with my situation was a challenge mentally and physically. I experienced a progression from more pain to less pain. As Sunday progressed, I didn't know what was wrong with my body. I had thought that maybe my foot was broken because it was really painful. By Sunday night I could move my foot around, and I thought, "Hey, it's getting better."

Sunday night the rain began bothering me. It's not as if I were drinking a quart of water. I was really thirsty, and yet I wished it would stop raining.

By Sunday night I had removed most of the rocks, making my area more comfortable.

Since I'd seen choppers and a plane overpass, I had given up hope of being rescued. I was in a really camouflaged place—rocks of all shapes and sizes covered the ground everywhere. I was nearly invisible in the bowl.

I knew I couldn't survive long without food. I needed calories to stay warm. I was cold and getting wetter. I continued to debate. *Do I get into a position of discovery or devote myself to getting out?*

I figured I'd try to get out so that if they didn't find me, I'd at least have a chance of rescue on my own. *I'll maneuver toward the car and hope I'll get into terrain where I can more readily be seen.* My decision was complicated by the knowledge that if I wasn't discovered, I'd probably die on the mountain. *If I go for the helicopter and they see me as a nice smooth hump, I'll be dead.*

Sunday evening was a breakthrough for me. I decided, "I'll get up tomorrow morning, and I'll start crawling out of here. I'll rescue myself. What have I got to lose? Staying here will bring death."

So I got up at eight o'clock on Monday morning and started lifting and dragging myself over the boulders. That was a long stretch going over boulders, down into the dips. I was getting into some real water so I got down and drank a lot of water.

I tried to keep a positive attitude, but I was going down a blind alley. I knew it. There was no protection or anything. I was pretty cold and wet. I exhausted myself and burned up energy with little hope of rescue. But I refused to quit. *I'm not going to stop. If I stop, I'll get the big chill.*

Everything was awful. The bowl was a rugged cluster of rock upon rock; nothing resembling gentle terrain existed. It was jagged, multisized boulders. I kept moving more and more toward hospitable terrain, more tundralike and less jagged rock.

I don't know how much ground I covered. I was able to go only four or five pushes before resting. I dragged my body forward with my right leg and pushed with my hands at the side of my buttocks. Sometimes I went sideways. It was easier going sideways because I didn't have to use my foot to pull me. It took more energy to pull with my right leg and push with my hands.

Realistically I was a long ways from anywhere . . . *if a helicopter flies over and fails to see me, I'll keep crawling.* Eventually I would have gotten tired; and I think that would have been my final resting place. But I forced that possibility from my mind and kept on pushing and pulling.

For nearly twelve hours I inched along, periodically resting, drinking water, and wondering, *How much farther can I go? Is there really any hope?*

During one of those interminably long pauses in movement, I heard the familiar throbbing of a helicopter. I looked up.

It thundered into view. In seconds it flew over. Immediately the pilot turned the chopper. He banked ninety degrees and flashed his lights. I didn't stop waving until he was positively on the ground.

He was a neat guy. He was cool. He sounded just like a rescue helicopter guy should sound. He actually carried me to the running helicopter. He gave me a 7UP and a chocolate chip cookie.

The change of circumstances was incredible. One minute struggling to survive, the next a survivor!

That was an ongoing thing that evening. The reality shift. It was an incredible, sudden shift—as if everything that went on before it stopped, and now something entirely new had begun. It was dazzling.

Then I found out about all the community activity and effort on my behalf. At least sixty people were climbing around on that mountain. Unisea Corporation, a big business in fish-packing and boats in Unalaska, spontaneously brought out to the end of this road a whole spread of sandwiches and refreshments so that rescuers could have something to eat and drink. Westward Seafoods, which has a plant right where the dirt road meets the main road, opened up their galley for free—anybody could go in.

You've got this little island out there where the people came together. They behaved like a group of friends, a strong community of people.

Having survived a casual hike that could have dealt me a tombstone, I've learned a couple of things.

First, you need to have a survival kit, up to twenty pounds of gear. You can take a lot of stuff—a sleeping bag, a tent, food, bottle with sugar water or other liquid with nutrients. Take that kit with you every time you go into the wilderness.

Second, people should always travel with a companion. It's a sad thing because it's nice to go hiking alone. I don't feel that I have the right to do it anymore. I used up my credit as far as that goes.

If you get hurt, it's simple. If you're not going to bring a crutch with you, and who is, what are you going to do without a companion? You're not going to get out without a companion.

Third, never take your outing casually, not for one minute. There's a fine line between being cautious and being a chicken. I've been hiking with people who I felt had a foolish sense of precaution that I didn't care for. There's got to be a right way of always being cautious.

We have a sense of being bigger than life—most of the time we don't realize the danger we face. It's important to be prepared and to do everything within your power to come back alive.

Epilogue

Interestingly enough, many stories I've gathered (or attempted to gather) over the years have stories behind the stories that are as interesting or more so than the stories themselves.

For instance, in the late 1970s I called the friend of a bear-mauling victim who had been killed in the encounter. The source told me, "He was a friend of mine. I don't want to talk about it."

Another bear-mauling victim told me that I had enough stories and didn't need his. I assured him I could give him a fictitious name. He refused.

I pressed neither party further.

The foregoing story is one such tale where the contributor wished to remain anonymous. In this story I gave him my deceased father-in-law's nickname. After I completed the transcription of our July 31, 1991, interview at Humana Hospital in Anchorage and sent it to the contributor for his approval, he returned the form with the following note, dated March 6, 1993:

Dear Kaniut,

Thank you for sending me this. I prepared myself to make alterations here and there and realized I have so filtered and molded my memory of the events to suit my own sensibility that I really don't know the truth of it at all. Please be sure my name appears nowhere in the book as I suffer from shyness. I was reminded, vividly, of the feeling I had speaking with you way back then, and this is a feeling I still have, that the whole thing really is only interesting as concerns someone's psychological experience. I still feel a sense of that, at least, it's the experience of the person, not having any hope to speak of, or great concern either, watching his one leg and foot take care of the other.

As you can see, for various reasons many people prefer not being associated with a story. Those who shared their stories did so in hopes of helping others to avoid their tragedy. And that is also my hope. May the readers of these adventures learn from them, implement the positive aspects into their outings, and go safely.

Going safely is what Bob Och did on a number of occasions and what he hopes to continue doing. You'll understand when you read his upcoming story.

OVER THE EDGE

We're dead! We're dead!

A few years ago my friend Dan Hollingsworth said he'd tell me about a flying adventure for a five-dollar finder's fee. Of course, he was joking, but he had my attention and shared the tale. I tried unsuccessfully to locate one of the participants until January 1999, when I reached Bob Och on the phone.

When I met the stout, six-foot-tall, 190-pound, blue-eyed, retired fish-and-game man with a penchant for taxidermy, he invited me to his home and told me this story.

The adventure started in 1980 when I was living at Kasilof and working at the salmon hatchery. I had a couple of good hunting buddies, Jim Lawler and Dave Letzring. Jim is now a retired ARCO North Slope oil worker. Dave is a retired oil-patch worker.

Jim had a Cessna 180 and I hunted quite a bit with him. I started going to the Kodiak area to hunt deer. We had a favorite place above Tonki Bay on Afognak Island where Jim had landed his 180 a time or two on a flat spot on the mountain.

It was a neat experience. We'd leave the Kasilof airstrip in his 180, fly there, land on top of the mountain, shoot a couple of nice bucks, load 'em up, and come back home the same day. Although hunting many big game animals the same day airborne is illegal, the Alaska Department of Fish and Game allows same-day deer hunting on Kodiak Island.

Those deer were always so astounded by our landing that they'd just stand around and watch while we tied the airplane down. A couple of nice bucks were always close by and it was easy deer hunting.

However, it was kind of scary each time and treacherous. The top of the mountain was only four or five hundred feet of downhill, rocky landing, a good Cub strip but a person had no business landing a Cessna 180 on that short strip. (We found out later six other airplanes are scattered around there and none of their occupants survived.)

The first two times that I went, we damaged the airplane. On the first trip we tore the tail wheel off, which was no big deal. Came home from that trip with a couple of nice bucks and that was fine.

The next year we decided we'd go again. Jim and I landed there and we had an uneventful landing. Tied the airplane down and jumped out. We killed two nice bucks fairly close to the airplane and had a good time hunting.

I spotted a nice buck farther down the mountain, so we hiked down and killed a nice big three-point. By the time we got the deer back up to the airplane, fog had socked in. Visibility was zero-zero. The wind gusted to forty miles an hour.

In spite of the adverse weather we attempted a takeoff into the wind. A hundred yards from the end of the cliff we hit a rock pile, taking off and barely making it airborne. We tore off the tail wheel and the right front tire.

When we came back to Kasilof, Jim gravity-transferred all the fuel into the left wing to lighten up the right side. We made a one-tire landing at the Kasilof airstrip, did a nice ground loop, and slid to a stop. We just barely made it on that trip, too.

It took the sheet-metal man thirteen hours to put the gearbox back in the 180.

Time heals everything, so after another year had passed, we thought, "Let's go deer hunting to Tonki Bay again." This time we took Dave Letzring. Dave and Jim were in the front seat and I was in the back. We piled all of our gear into the aircraft and we headed for our deer spot.

Flying to Kodiak in a single-engine aircraft is possible if you have the altitude. We flew over at sixty-five hundred feet following the Barren Islands—you can land on a big beach in an emergency, not that you wouldn't bend your airplane up. From that point there's Shuyak Island and not much water to fly over. Flying over water is still taking a big risk.

It was a nice, calm day when we left Kasilof, all the way down past Homer until we got to Shelikof Strait. It looked like a giant batch of whipped cream down there—the wind smoked, the swells were huge. My word, it was a no-man's-land out there. It's a pretty scary place to go flying over the open water. If you ever had to go down in that, that would be the end of it. You'd never survive that.

When we reached our hunting area, we made a pass over the top of the mountain to determine which direction the wind was blowin', which is critical for *that* landing—it's a no-man's-landing strip.

We determined the wind wasn't quite right that direction, so we turned around and made our approach from the other direction.

When we touched down, we blew the right front tire. We were still going fairly fast. Jim saw that he wasn't going to be able to get on the brakes and stop in time before we reached the edge of the cliff, so he applied full power and flaps to get the airplane airborne again.

It didn't happen.

The aircraft drifted sideways, slammed into a rock pile, launched us back up into the sky—probably a hundred feet or more—and came right back down, almost straight in. We hit on the top of the mountain, and evidently the impact tore the engine, the gear, and one wing off.

We were right at the edge of a vertical cliff. The impact was so great that time just ceased. They say your whole life flashes before your eyes . . . I don't know if that's true. All I can remember is clenching my eyes tightly shut and thinking that I wasn't hurt too badly yet.

We went over the edge of the cliff. All you could hear was the wind whistling by, *wwssssshhhhhhh*, then we impacted the side of the cliff and tumbled for a while . . . we tumbled three or four times.

About the third time we were tumbling, Dave Letzring yelled, "We're dead! We're dead!"

I sat there with my eyes clenched tight and wondered why I wasn't hurting too bad yet. And I made a vivid statement about Dave's comment: "No, the Lord's got us in His hands." I can remember opening my eyes and Dave turned around and looked at me as if he couldn't believe I had the presence of mind to say that. And I had a real peace about this.

I opened my eyes one time when we were tumbling. The whole inside of the airplane was filled with tundra, knives, packs, guns, gasoline . . . you name it. It was as if all this stuff were in a giant washing machine sloshing around when we were tumbling.

We tumbled in all directions—sideways, end over end, sideways again. In the free-falling the plane became aerodynamic and sailed. It only tumbled when it hit the ground. You couldn't tell which direction was up. I never opened my eyes any more after that. I just shut down. There wasn't a thought that crossed my mind except after every tumbling session I thought, "I'm not hurt too bad yet." I was waiting for this intense pain.

In between impacts we'd hear the wind again, *wwssssshhhhhhhhhh*. Then the aircraft would tumble and roll some more. We did that three different times before we finally impacted the tundra upside down where the mountain started sloping a little bit, about a 60 percent grade. It was still pretty vertical. Finally ten or fifteen seconds after our ride down the mountain began, the plane came to a stop upside down.

The Cessna 180 is one of the best-built aircraft around, built bulletproof. And the fuselage stayed together.

One wing was still attached to the aircraft by the strut. It was above us glupin' gasoline on top of us, *bluk, kabluk, kabluk, kabluk*. I was afraid we were going to catch on fire so I yelled, "Get out! Get out!"

Dave and Jim were below me, so when I undid my seat belt, I immediately fell on top of them. They opened their doors and were able to slide out. Then I got out.

When Jim stood up, he was holding his back and saying, "Boys, I think I hurt my lower back."

As fast as we could, we got fifty yards away from the airplane. There was nothing left in the wreckage to burn. We didn't need to get away, but we didn't know that.

Jim went over and lay down. He knew he was hurt and we suspected a broken back.

While we were assessing our situation, Jim said, "Go get my ELT. It's under my seat. And get my survival kit." He is a real good pilot, had all kinds of good gear on board all the time.

We got the ELT out, pulled the antenna up, turned it on, and set it on a rock. In spite of the injuries, with the ELT set up you assume it's only a matter of time before rescue. Dave and I had an injured man to help. The tree line was five hundred feet straight down the hill. We were thinking maybe we could get a sleeping bag, cut some poles, make a stretcher, and get Jim down there.

Dave was bleeding pretty good from the cut over his eyebrow—a chunk of skin flapped down over his eye. We got into the first-aid kit and got a butterfly bandage. We pushed his scalp back out of his eye and bandaged him, which stopped the bleeding. Other than the headache and slight concussion, he was fine. He'd impacted the instrument panel.

I got pretty badly beat up (later when I got home, I took my shirt off and discovered all kinds of cuts and bruises). The tumbling was so violent that my belt was ripped clear off me. I had an imprint of a scoped rifle across the back of my shoulders. Even though I got whacked a few times, I don't remember any of that.

With gear scattered all over the place, we sorted things out and tried to get organized. Then, lo and behold, here comes an airplane. It looked like a Citabria. The pilot was flying for an air taxi and had a biologist on board. I believe his name was Larry Nicholson. Fortunately for us, they were surveying salmon streams that day on the southern part of Afognak.

They were probably twenty-five miles away when Larry spotted something unusual. His said to his pilot, "Hey, there's something on that hillside that wasn't there before. Let's go take a look at that."

So the Lord directed him to look our way.

They started circling over the top of us there. Next thing we knew they threw out a handheld radio wrapped up in a life jacket. We got that out, pulled out the antenna, turned it on, and communicated with them.

The pilot asked, "You guys okay?"

We told him, "We got one man who might be pretty badly hurt."

He responded, "Okay, well, your ELT's not working. I can barely hear it inside of my aircraft, just faint little beeps. I'll call the Coast Guard for you."

Meanwhile Jim's lying there thinking about his airplane. He's just spent ten thousand bucks on a motor overhaul and another fifteen hundred bucks on a new prop. Here's his airplane scattered all over the mountain.

Since he had a lot of nice electronics on board, he asked me, "Why don't you go get the headsets and stuff out of the airplane, save what you can." We knew that the Coast Guard or other rescue units on an emergency flight won't usually transport your gear.

I hiked back up the mountain to look for tools that might help. Everything from belt knives to sleeping bags cluttered the landscape. I found a screwdriver and a pair of pliers.

I returned to the airplane and looked at the instrument clusters on the instrument panel, which included quality King radio equipment. I started shearing off rivets that held compartments into the dash, like radio compartments. I wrapped radios and headsets and stuff in sleeping bags.

Meanwhile we heard the helicopter coming across the water from Kodiak, *bump, bump, bump, bump.* We hustled around, got all the gear rolled up in the bags, and moved down by Jim.

The Coast Guard showed up in a Stallion, one of their big rescue helicopters (I think, I don't want to be misquoted on that). The grade was so steep that the helicopter could not land. All he could do was touch one main gear down. The pilot sat at the controls and kept the helicopter stable.

There were two crewmen. One jumped out with a headset on, ran around the helicopter, and observed the rotors missing the mountain by three or four feet. He watched for a change in the ship's attitude and kept the pilot informed.

The other crewman jumped out and started grabbing our gear and pitching that into the helicopter (including the radio gear that was all wrapped up in sleeping bags).

One helped me and Dave on board. Then they went over with a stretcher and got Jim into it and put him on board. Then we headed back across the water to Kodiak.

The pilot took us right into the hospital where medical personnel immediately looked at Jim and determined that he probably had a fractured vertebra. They wanted to send him to Providence. Dave and I were okay, dinged up a bit. Dave had a headache, but his concussion wasn't that serious and the bleeding had stopped. We were kind of just standing by wondering about Jim.

They took Jim out to Kodiak airport and loaded him on a jet, laid down a bunch of seats, and strapped a stretcher in there, and transported him to Providence. We boarded with him and came back to Anchorage.

We left that perfectly good Cessna 180 on the mountainside. I can remember looking down the mountain and seeing the engine *waayyyy* down there. I hiked down to it before the helicopter showed up. Here's this brand-new Continental engine, just been majored, all wadded up, jugs busted off, the brand-new propeller wrapped around it like an accordion. Farther down was a lake with the landing gear, and a tire lying in it.

Quite an adventure. The bottom line of this whole story is that we never did go back there again.

Epilogue

It was less than an hour from impact till the chopper showed up. Everything happened so fast, we were on the mountain and back off the mountain.

We sustained all our serious injuries on impact when the plane initially nosed into the mountain. Dave Letzring wound up with a concussion and a cut over his eye. Jim ended up with two fractured vertebrae, the old traditional seat-belt injury. I, being in the backseat, didn't sustain any serious injuries.

As unpredictable as landing on mountaintops can be, so is the danger lurking for mountain joggers.

DANGER IGNORED

AS TOLD TO THE AUTHOR BY CHRIS NOLKE

We didn't have any ropes. We were all wearing running shoes.
We weren't prepared.

After learning about the tragedy of the young runners, I contacted Chris Nolke and asked if he'd share his experience. His sad story follows.

Temptation, Flattop, The Ramp. Suicide, O'Malley. Wolverine, Williwaw, The Wedge. Mountain peaks towering above Anchorage, Alaska, in Chugach State Park only a few miles east of Alaska's largest city. Mountain peaks enticing hikers, runners, backpackers, mountain bikers, and skiers. On July 14, 1987, these peaks lured a trio of young Anchorage runners to challenge their flanks. The three were running partners on that day. On some days they were rivals.

Chris Nolke, a junior from Service High School, was the oldest at fifteen. Andrew Lekisch and Doug Spurr were fourteen-year-old freshmen from West Anchorage High. Lifelong best friends, Andrew and Doug had grown up competing since grade school in a variety of activities. On the other hand, Chris had known the two pals only a couple of years.

Their jumping-off point was the Glen Alps parking lot at the foot of Flattop Mountain. They would jog the Powerline Pass right-of-way road on a twenty-plus-kilometer run. As they left the trailhead, they good-naturedly bantered.

Scattered mountain junipers ten to twelve feet high welcomed them as they covered the half mile to the power-line road.

The young men wore cross-country running gear—long-sleeved running shirts and running shoes. Chris Nolke wore two long-sleeved cotton shirts under a rugby top. A pair of cotton Sport Hills pants, comfortably tight, covered his lower body. His footgear consisted of his favorite Asics Tiger running shoes. Doug and Andrew wore similar gear.

They left the timberline and pushed eastward up Powerline Pass toward the distant ridgeline that separates Anchorage from the Indian Creek and Ship Creek drainages. Five-thousand-foot peaks surrounded them. Their plan was to run the road to The Ramp, a high bowl that dissected Flattop and the twin Suicide Peaks from O'Malley Peak and Mt. Williwaw. At the upper end of the bowl they would ascend The Wedge on the left and return along its spiny ridgeline. That would be a great workout.

The three figures bounced along the trail in the comfortable fifty-degree weather. They shared the joy of their sport, the freedom of summer vacation, and the enchanting landscape.

The valley was nearly a mile wide. An inch-thick layer of vegetation called tundra covered the rocky ground. A narrow stream coursed the valley floor, with tall grass lining its banks and shortening in length as it stretched ridgeward. Low willow bushes blended with the streamside grass, giving way up the slope to rock slides, ledges, and scattered snow patches in the shaded gullies. In a few short weeks the hillsides would be fired with changing ground cover dominated by reds and yellows. Whispering close behind, snow would blanket the landscape to a depth of six to eight feet. But today it was great running.

Bobbing rhythmically over the trail, they reminisced about former runs and competitions where they'd taxed their wills and spirits, each realizing this run was like many they'd learned to enjoy—that it bonded the body, mind, and spirit of each as well as bonding their friendship, while increasing their physical stamina.

Chris Nolke remembered their run:

We ran back the pass that goes up The Ramp from Powerline Pass. We noted our destination, then headed off along the grassy and rocky spots, bypassing any dangerous area. Sometimes the trail necessitated rock climbing up ten- or fifteen-foot-high areas. That doesn't sound particularly bad, but if you stacked a bunch of those areas on top of each other, you see potentials that we didn't really consider. The inherent danger in those mountains was such areas.

We had run several miles when we started up into The Wedge for our return run. That was quite a perilous climb. When it came to safety, that was one of the most dangerous parts to climb.

The danger element never occurred to us as we continued. Looking down one of the chutes, we casually joked, "What would happen if you fell off here?"

Doug said, "I'm sure you'd pretty much break your neck."

"No," I said, "you're toast. If you fall off of here, there's no way you're going to survive."

The fact that we had just climbed up that chute never gave us concern that we could fall. We didn't have any ropes. We were all wearing running shoes. We weren't prepared. What we were doing wasn't really a good idea. We were young teenagers with a sense of immortality about us. So we continued to climb.

We maneuvered along the knifelike ridge toward town, which wasn't too bad. The ridge was suddenly interrupted by a twenty-foot-square boulder. The ground supporting the boulder had eroded away with rocks having tumbled down either side of the ridgeline. It looked oddly balanced.

Since the boulder was obstructing our way, I started to climb around it to continue on the trail. The north side of the boulder stuck out over a ravine. To follow the trail, we would have to scale sideways around the boulder. Doug had determined to go down and around the other way.

Facing the boulder, I extended my hands to search for a handhold. I couldn't find one.

Even though none of us had ever done any rock climbing, I figured it wasn't that big of a deal. The terrain was steep on either side of the ridge, fifty to sixty degrees. Although you could walk on the slope, you'd slide or tumble quite a distance if you slipped. The grass-covered slope was riddled with boulders.

I said, "I'm not going to go this way. I'm going down where Doug went."

I followed Doug. I think I would have ventured out on the slope if I hadn't looked down and realized it was quite a fall. Andrew decided to go along the boulder and find a way past it. I don't think he looked down.

While Doug and I skirted the boulder, we heard Andrew yell.

Not realizing what had happened, we quickly returned to where we'd left Andrew. I figured it was nothing too bad.

We crossed a grassy area, running down below the boulder. We easily ascended the trail and returned without doing too much side-tracking.

Doug ran ahead down the mountain. I couldn't find Andrew and yelled, "Doug, where is he?"

Finally Doug found Andrew and ran to him.

When I reached Doug, he was standing by Andrew. Doug kept asking Andrew to talk to him. I was ten feet away from Andrew before I finally saw him and realized how far down the hill he had fallen. He fell straight down for quite a ways, free fall—it could have been twenty feet, it could have been three hundred. I really don't know.

For some reason I didn't even start worrying about it. Rationalism took over . . . what's going to happen now?

I said, "Okay, here we are. Out in the middle of nowhere. Probably ten kilometers from Glen Alps. One of us has to go back to alert the authorities. One of us needs to stay here with Andrew." Doug was going into shock. Having him go for help would keep his mind occupied and I could stay to assist Andrew.

So I said, "Doug, run back and call the authorities and tell them where we are. Tell them they'll need a helicopter."

Doug immediately took off.

I tried to evaluate the situation. I had never had any CPR training. I was going into a sort of mild shock, which may explain my rationalism.

Being alone with Andrew gave me a lot of time to think about our past few years. I had met Doug and Andrew when I was in the eighth grade and they were in the seventh grade. We were all part of the Junior Nordic Ski program, which allowed us to train together and provided us a tool to gain more training time than a normal school practice.

I liked training with several people because it offered better workouts for me. Junior Nordic also granted me the opportunity to train with a different group, to use a different technique, and to have a different coach.

The Junior Nordic coaches, Lynn Spencer Galanes, Bill Spencer, and Jim Galanes, all Olympic athletes, were good coaches.

By the time we were in high school, we'd met numerous coaches and others involved in Junior Nordic, including a lot of really good skiers from early-college age down through late-junior-high-school age.

It wasn't an openly devouringly competitive environment. When you're around the people you compete against, you undoubtedly want to be the first one back to the parking lot. There's a little bit of competition there, making the group quite fast. That summer session we trained a lot in the mountains because it avails diverse training. Kincaid Park offers good training, but the same terrain twice a day depletes running possibilities. The monotony of the same course caused us to look for variety in training. The mountains behind us guaranteed a limitless number of places to train, so we capitalized on that.

Runs included Goldenview to Bald Peak. McHugh Peak is a little farther, a great run. There's Flattop and Ptarmigan. Then Little Ptarmigan. All of those offer really good training opportunities because they're uphill. There's always the added incentive of an incredible view once you've reached the top of a peak.

The Saturday prior to our run we were training near The Ramp, to the left of The Wedge. Jim Galanes coached and ran with us. We went quite a ways up there and explored around.

The Wedge offered some neat-looking places to climb. Doug, Andrew, and I were ahead of the group and started toward The Wedge. We'd gone a short distance when Jim cautioned us, "You guys, I don't want you up there. Stay with the group."

We responded that it looked like a lot of fun, implying we would continue toward The Wedge.

But he said, "If you want to do it on your own time, that's fine. I'm responsible for all of us. Stay with the group."

We said, "Okay." We filed away his comments in typical teenage fashion, knowing that we would probably do it sooner or later because he was an adult and had told us not to.

A couple of days later we were looking for some place to train. Traditionally someone calls up someone who calls someone else . . . we get a phone tree going. I called Doug and said, "Hey, let's go hit that peak." We thought it had great potential, and we knew how to get to it. At least this time we wouldn't have any coaches telling us we couldn't do it.

One of the best ways to train on the mountains is to go up a valley like Powerline Pass or Rabbit Lake. If you follow the Anchorage mountain valleys to their heads, the ridges on either side intersect. By jogging up valleys to gain elevation, it's possible to return along ridges without having to climb up steep faces. When the ridge terminates, you descend either side to the valley floor.

We had never come along The Wedge because it starts farther back, and it's sitting in the middle of the valley by itself. We'd never wanted to go far enough back to get on The Wedge.

But now we had. Here we were. Doug's gone for help. Andrew's injured. I'm trying to figure out how to help him.

He didn't look that bad. I've seen people badly beat up that looked much worse. I thought, "He's gonna make it."

His head was pointed downhill with his feet uphill. I turned him so his head and feet were reversed. I gently placed him on his side and tried to take his pulse. I was holding him sideways so that he could breathe. I held him to keep him from rolling down the mountain.

I took all my stuff off, right down to my little Lycra tights, and put them all on Andrew.

Weather conditions were deteriorating, and it began to rain. It was a typical dreary, drizzly Anchorage summer day with clouds packed back into The Wedge. The falling rain chilled me. Because it was raining, my clothes were on Andrew, and I was not moving, I was going into hypothermia.

Crouching down and holding Andrew was a grueling task. During the last twenty minutes I held Andrew, all of his vital signs gradually deteriorated. I tried mouth-to-mouth resuscitation. But it didn't work. His breathing slowed down, then went away.

I kept thinking, "He's still alive," perhaps willing him to be but knowing that he wasn't. There was absolutely no sign of consciousness. As I battled my thoughts and looked at Andrew, I prayed that he would live.

I was fearful of moving him, but at length I didn't think it would matter. Gradually I realized Andrew was more than likely gone, so I moved him fifteen feet to a spot where he wouldn't roll.

My legs were cramping up, and my strength was deteriorating. I knew I needed to warm my body. My condition dictated action. I started doing jumping jacks and aerobic exercises to warm up.

My thoughts demanded the helicopter's arrival. I was getting a little bit delirious. My mind played tricks on me, and I thought I heard 130 helicopters in half an hour.

I went into minor shock, getting upset. There was something about being alone and unable to help in a situation like that. No one was anywhere near. I'd been alone for over an hour.

I thought, "What in the world happened? Where's the helicopter?" It was about a 10K run to help, so it would take Doug about forty minutes to reach a phone. After his call it would take about ten minutes for a helicopter to reach our position.

An hour and forty minutes into the accident, while I was exercising, I heard a helicopter. The pounding rotors drew closer. Then I saw the chopper coming directly at me. It hovered about a hundred feet away. I wondered if the pilot saw me. Then he flew away, which I thought was strange.

It was crucial to me that I not remain alone, and the chopper's leaving disturbed me for a moment. I needed someone with expertise to come to my aid and my comfort.

Within thirty seconds the pilot flew from behind the ridge and returned. I hadn't thought of it at the time, but obviously he was looking for a spot to land.

He landed the chopper on a little flat indentation halfway down the final ridge at the end of The Wedge. We were a hundred yards from the end of the ridge, close to having finished the run.

I hiked down to the helicopter and told them everything I could about what had happened.

A paramedic grabbed a life pack (for monitoring vital signs), a defibrillator, and a monitor and headed for the accident site. He tried everything to save Andrew. But there was nothing he could do.

The paramedics said there wasn't a pulse. Even though I had earlier thought Andrew would make it, he must have sustained internal injuries that were irreparable under the circumstances.

A lady with the crew, perhaps one of the paramedics, was to help see us through any psychological needs. She was very helpful.

Originally the authorities had planned for the helicopter to take Andrew to the hospital. A Chevrolet Blazer would transport Doug and me (Doug had shown the pilot to the scene). Realizing there was nothing that could be done for Andrew and with Doug and me in shock, the helicopter crew changed plans and took us back.

We just hopped into the helicopter and rode to Glen Alps. Authorities prepared to bring Andrew out later.

Mr. Lekisch and Mr. Spurr had been notified by the officials and were at the Glen Alps parking lot.

Doug and I had to sit in the fire truck and go over things, explaining our experience. Quite a number of emergency vehicles were there. The news media were there. I became upset with their insistence on gathering information by hounding us as well as Mr. Lekisch. My attitude went from incredulity to pure anger. I wanted to unload on the TV cameraman, but I'm glad I didn't. My attitude was affected by my condition.

After things had finally quieted down, Mr. Spurr took me home. That's the first my father knew of the accident.

A few days later, services were held for Andrew. At a funeral I envision twenty people all dressed in black standing around a hole in the ground. Not this time! There must have been two to three hundred people in attendance at the Anchorage ski center at Kincaid Park. Anchorage's mayor was there.

It was weird being involved in the memorial service since I didn't know Andrew as well as a lot of the other people did.

Andrew was involved in so many activities that his life touched a lot of others' lives. Andrew was success in sneakers, a champion in cross-country togs. He had developed quite a reputation. A few years earlier he had come to the attention of older athletes, who predicted great things for this young competitor who excelled in cross-country running and skiing, bicycle racing, triathlons, swimming, and tennis.

Doug took the accident much differently than I did because he was much better friends with Andrew. He saw him daily at school. Their friendship may best be symbolized by Doug's run for help. He covered ten kilometers in thirty minutes, an incredibly fast time. Nationally, racers cover that distance in twenty-seven or twenty-eight minutes.

Since the accident, I've learned to look more carefully at everyday situations. I recognized things in my everyday life that I'd never seen, potential disasters waiting to happen—driving down the highway, skiing, things like that. I became more aware of the number of situations in everyday life exposing one to danger. For some time after the accident I overreacted to danger.

I looked at Andrew and the fact that he had died when he was fourteen. Many people said, "He lived a full life. Even if he died at fourteen, he still had a wonderful life."

Andrew did have a positive effect on people.

Before the accident I felt I should live as fast as possible. It occurred to me after the tragedy that we only get a little time here. So, I've slowed down to a normal level of living . . . making every day count.

In the shadow of this tragedy, another befell a group of University of Alaska–Anchorage students and their instructors in 1997 . . . where heroes rose to the occasion as those in this story did.

HEROES, ONE AND ALL

BY LARRY KANIUT

I remember everything. We hit a boulder, and at that point I decided I was dead because I hit it so hard, and I knew there was more to hit. I just basically gave up at that point. It was so fast. It was so terrifying.

Basking in the sunshine near the summit of Ptarmigan Peak, fourteen mountain climbers reveled in their accomplishment, ate lunch, joked, and laughed. Several hours earlier, just after 7 A.M., June 30, 1997, two instructors and twelve students from the University of Alaska–Anchorage's Wilderness Studies Mountaineering I class, had left their base camp two thousand feet below.

The 4,880-foot peak lies fourteen miles southeast of downtown Anchorage and sits near the middle of a ridge that houses Flattop a few miles to the west and the Suicide Peaks to the east. Across the valley to the north preside O'Malley Peak, The Wedge, and Williwaw. Although thousands of recreationalists enjoy the high valley dissecting the ridges, this area has a history of tragedy, taking the lives of hikers, runners, skiers, and snowmachiners. I call the area the Valley of Doom.

Ptarmigan is roughly six miles up the Powerline Pass trail from the Glen Alps parking lot at the foot of Flattop. Natural rock from the area paves the trail that serpentines along the valley floor, and in places overhanging alder limbs narrow this abandoned road to bicycle-handlebar width.

The class experienced nothing out of the ordinary during their ascent. Some of the group went on to the false summit before returning to the others preparatory to their descent. Blue skies and seventy-five-degree weather proved a plus as they enjoyed the beauty, their success, and scanned mountain peaks miles in the distance.

Most of the climbers lived in the Anchorage area and ranged in age from fourteen to forty-three. The husband-wife team of instructors Benjamin and Deborah Greene led Steven Brown, Jay Chamberlain, Mona Eben, Mary Ellen Fogarty, Jacob Franck, Bernadino Lagasca, Andrew Murphy, Juanita Palmer, Jerilyn Pomeroy, Eric Schlemme, Kirsten Staveland, and Joshua Thomas.

The climbers divided up into teams and roped up into four groups, then began their descent of the thirty-to-forty-degree, snow-filled north couloir. As the class plunge-stepped down a gully—jamming boot heels into the snow below—there was little warning of what lay ahead. The groups were stacked in the trough separated by scores of feet.

The last team onto the snow was Joshua Thomas, twenty, Eric Schlemme, thirty, and Jacob Franck, eighteen. As Franck moved below him at the end of the rope, Thomas saw Franck slip on the slope and start down. Thomas felt confident as he jammed his ice ax into the snow as an anchor and clutched its steel pick and adze in his hands. Thomas thought things were under control.

Twenty feet of slack between Franck and Schlemme posed a potential problem, and Schlemme planted his ice ax as an anchor. When Franck hit the end of the slack, the rope tightened and jerked him, so that he was unable to help himself. The rope's pull yanked Schlemme off his anchor, and he joined Franck in the downward plunge.

Schlemme went into self-arrest hoping to stop their slide.

Realizing that he was the last line of defense, Thomas turned his face against the slope and leaned against his ice ax. The combined weight and speed of his two rope-mates peeled Thomas off his feet, and the three men rocketed toward their classmates below.

Instructor Deborah Greene shouted to them, "Self-arrest!" And they tried.

Bouncing and glissading, the trio plunged downward, each attempting to fight the speed and disjointed gyrations of their descent caused by the whipsawing rope. The jerking rope prevented them from self-arrest.

Three roped teams spread across a narrow neck of the couloir below, stacked within a hundred feet of the sliding team.

Some class members said, "Here they come." They braced themselves for the worst, and the worst embraced them. The speed of the falling team made them unstoppable.

The fallen climbers smacked into the next group and swept them into their fall.

Looking up the slope, Mona Eben had seen Franck slip. She anchored herself into the snow and hung on, watching the men rocketing toward her. She felt secure with her ax in the snow and never thought she'd be knocked off her ax. Although she hoped the falling melee would miss her third group, a body slammed into her, ripping her from her hold and adding her rope-mates to the mess. She said later, "It happened so fast, and the force was so strong, there was nothing I could do."(3)

Meanwhile Jay Chamberlain, twenty-eight, a member of the lower team, looked uphill and saw someone fall a hundred feet. "I was hoping they would catch. But one by one I saw the fall compound. I saw the bodies coming right toward me."(2). Jay buried his ax in the snow to anchor himself to the slope and held on for dear life, "but they snagged our rope, and then we were part of it."(2)

*   *   *

The entire group dominoed. As the mass churned toward the jumble of boulders below, cameras, water bottles, and mittens flew off the climbers, sunglasses and watchbands broke, and ice axes were torn from their grip, leaving a trail in their wake. As the climbers increased in speed and gyrations, so did their outcries.

Josh Thomas said, "Nobody could do anything because we were being hit from right and left by other bodies. We hit quite a few rock outcrops on the way down. I could see every rock outcropping as it came along. You could see how nasty it was, and there was no way around it."(3)

Mona Eben said, "I remember everything. We hit a boulder, and at that point I decided I was dead because I hit it so hard, and I knew there was more to hit. I just basically gave up at that point. It was so fast. It was so terrifying."(3)

They plowed down-mountain, banging over several rock bands and plunging a thousand feet onto a heap of boulders, ending up as a tangled pile of roped and fractured bodies, some on top of others, at the foot of the snowfield two hundred yards south of the Powerline Pass road. People with bloody faces and gear agonized.

At the moment of the fall, skiers Ian Sharrock, Judd Englund, and Chris Norguard hiked toward the couloir. They slugged their way uphill expecting to top the rounded hill and drop into the dip beyond, preparatory to scaling the north couloir of Ptarmigan Peak, where they planned to ski. Noticing the descending group of climbers on the snowfield far above, the three friends watched in stunned disbelief as the climbers plunged down the slope, rolling, tumbling, and screaming as the fourteen became one.

Knowing there would be serious injuries, the three skiers sprang into action— Norguard dropped his pack and skis and ran toward the Powerline Pass trail, hoping to encounter someone with a cell phone. Sharrock and Englund hurried to help the injured.

Earlier, Scott Medlock and his family, wife Maria Elena and sons, had mountain-biked toward the Pass for a picnic, passing the three backpacking skiers. Scott and his family were the first persons Norguard met on his way for help. Hearing Norguard shout from the distance, Scott said, "His cry for help was of such a nature that I knew intuitively that something major was wrong."(4)

Scott left his bike on the trail and climbed up the hill. Before long he heard the screams of the injured, realized the seriousness of the situation, and sped to his bike where he rode toward succor.

Scott passed a man and his son and sent them to help the injured. Two more bikers received similar instructions before Scott reached a man with a cell phone. Within thirty minutes of the climbers' fall Medlock spoke with Alaska State Troopers before returning to assist the injured. At 5:33 P.M. troopers contacted Providence requesting that the LifeGuard helicopter be placed on standby. Before long choppers filled the sky, five helicopters scrambling into action (two

National Guard, one Alaska State Troopers, one from LifeGuard Alaska, and one from ERA Aviation).

Sharrock and Englund increased their pace toward the fallen climbers. Sharrock said, "It was a full-on, adrenaline-rush blur." Fifteen minutes later they reached the blood-covered area of the injured, which Sharrock described as "basically a war zone. We're still in shock at what we saw."(2)

Climbers lay in disarray. Some had ropes around their necks and were choking. Others suffocated beneath classmates. Still others had difficulty breathing due to internal injuries.

Sharrock and Englund rushed to remove ropes from climbers, then assisted them into positions that would facilitate breathing. Victims screamed when moved. Some were unconscious, others completely disabled.

Englund then returned to the base camp to retrieve sleeping bags, meeting mountain bikers who had heard the moans and cries for help.

While she ran up the trail with a companion, Shawn Armstrong also heard screams for help. She grabbed a backpack from the climbers' base camp, jammed it full of sleeping bags, and scrambled up the slope to the injured. She said, "When we got there, it was pretty gruesome. It seemed so surreal, I am still reeling from it."(2)

Armstrong, her friend, and others helped comfort the victims, providing first aid.

Scott Medlock and his fourteen-year-old son, Aaron, climbed to the injured, carrying sleeping bags from the climbers' camp, and helped stabilize them.

One of the others first on the scene was J. Anderson, eighteen.

The Alaska State Troopers paged Scott Horacek, Alaska Mountain Rescue Group volunteer medical technician, and told him of an injured hiker. He drove toward the accident scene gaining more information en route. Officials initially thought there were few injuries; but the numbers grew and it turned into Alaska's most-injured-climbers incident.

Scott drove up Toilsome Hill Road toward the Glen Alps parking lot. He was waved onto the Pass trail where he sped along in his Ford Explorer, thrashing his vehicle against rocks and alder brush along the trail, until he came to the batch of mountain bikes and people directing him uphill. He parked and made his way from the trail to the injured, some two hundred yards uphill over tundra studded with boulders and up the scree slope. "It's one of those things that you can train and train and train for, but you'd never expect anything this large, particularly not in that type of an environment."(2)

As the heroic helpers scurried around assisting the injured, helicopters and aircraft thundered overhead. One Pavehawk chopper hovered near Campbell Creek while another picked its way up the high valley toward the injured. A C-130 tanker circled above, refueling the choppers, while another C-130 circled at a distance, coordinating communications of the air traffic jam below.

With the rescue under way, some climbers' family members arrived and sat at the Glen Alps parking lot awaiting news and speculating about their loved ones while the police chaplain consoled them.

Meanwhile, Dr. Ken Zafren, an emergency room physician at Columbia Alaska Regional Hospital and head of the medical arm of the Alaska Mountain Rescue Group, and Chris Flowers, Mountain Rescue volunteer, arrived via Pavehawk helicopter. The terrain was so rugged and steep the chopper could not land near the injured. The pilot managed to plant a ski on a narrow ledge five hundred feet away.

Zafren and Flowers exited and gouged footholds in the snow and scrambled to the injured, and Zafren later admitted his shock at the scene: "It was a pretty scary situation. There were so many injured people that I didn't know how many there were. It took me about five minutes to figure out who the worst ones were, but I had to continuously revise my assessments. They were all pretty conscious . . . everybody had head injuries to some extent. Several people were having trouble breathing. If I made up this situation for one of our trainings, no one would think it was very realistic. It's a rescue nightmare, and it's a triage officer's nightmare."(2)

By 8 P.M. an external code alert had been declared at Providence—calling extra physicians, nurses, and support personnel—with six operating rooms readied for severe trauma injuries, including multiple traumas and fractures (legs, lacerations, head injuries, broken hips, ribs).

In addition to the civilians, eight Mountain Rescue volunteers and nine National Guard emergency rescue specialists from Kulis and two paramedics from the Anchorage Fire Department worked on the injured. A Pavehawk helicopter hovered fifty feet out from a fifteen-hundred-foot, near-vertical rock wall while workers lowered a cable hoist.

Calm evening air enabled the chopper pilots to approach the cliff. Air National Guard colonel Terry Graybeal, commander of the second Pavehawk, said, "You couldn't have asked for better weather."

An eleven-member rescue team worked from the Pavehawks. Because the site was too steep and rugged for a landing the helicopters lowered the litters to rescuers. The downdraft from the Pavehawk's huge blades necessitated their staying as far as possible above the rescuers and injured—to reduce the chill from the cooling air and to avoid causing rock slides. Unstable rock scree on the slope compounded the rescue effort, causing rescuers difficulty in walking, and causing problems in maneuvering the injured onto litters. A couple of times the cable hoist was let out as far as it would reach, two hundred feet.

The ground personnel set up a triage station to evaluate the injured and loaded the most seriously injured first into the hovering choppers. The number of injured and the extent of injuries required more time than previously expected. Each person had to be placed on a backboard in a sleeping bag and then on a litter.

The Pavehawks ferried the injured to the waiting LifeGuard helicopter, which flew immediately to Providence Alaska Medical Center. Medical personnel treated the injured en route. The first victim, a woman, was unloaded from an Air Guard Pavehawk chopper in a covered litter at 8:39 to intensive care. By 11:45 P.M. the last person was delivered to Providence . . . seven hours after the ordeal began.

The choppers and huge number of rescuers who rallied reduced the time of rescue and the compounding of injuries. Had the injured had to wait longer because of weather or lack of transportation, more serious injury or death would have been inevitable.

Of the fourteen climbers there were two fatalities. Forty-year-old Mary Ellen Fogarty had signed up for the class to overcome her fear of heights. She was an anthropologist for the Alaska Department of Fish and Game and had a reputation for being a kind, people person. For Steven M. Brown, twenty-three, from Royal Oak, Michigan, this was his first class at UAA.

Unfortunately a misstep escalated into a tragedy and took the lives of these two and seriously injured the others. They will be missed. But may their lives and the obstacles they worked to overcome remind us to accept the challenge of life and to be adventurous but aware with every step.

Anchorage's proximity affords easy access to the wilderness, and Chugach State Park is a year-round playground. The siren song of adventure sung by Mistress Wilderness often spawns danger where fun can turn to tragedy in one misplaced step. Fortunately, Anchorage housed the support group of rescuers who responded when Ptarmigan Peak played a cruel joke on the climbers. That support group of citizens, firemen, law enforcement, military, park, and medical personnel became heroes, one and all.

This mountain tragedy is often mirrored when a person finds himself alone and lost, as did Richard Trovillo.

DEER HUNT GONE AWRY

AS TOLD TO THE AUTHOR BY RICHARD TROVILLO

*I was getting wet ... I was chilled. ... Everything was wet ...
I had no fire and no food.*

Having read about a lost deer hunter in the newspaper in September 1990, I contacted him. Richard Trovillo agreed to share his story via a telephone interview. He makes some strong points for preparation and survival gear.

Three deer hunters left Ketchikan before dawn on Tuesday morning, September 4, 1990. Excitement reigned as they departed the dock in their powerboat for a day of hunting on Gravina Island, a four-by-twelve-mile, tree-covered, foliage-choked rock jutting out of the Pacific Ocean. The deer were plentiful and they planned to hunt on the northwest side of the island in Vallenar Bay.

During the half-hour jaunt across the Tongass Narrows, Richard Trovillo, Shane Sooter, and Rusty Speck kicked around plans for the day. They would split up and hunt individual areas, then meet at the boat at 10:30 A.M.

Richard Trovillo related his experience to me:

The area we intended to hunt was one and a half square miles of timber punctuated with open meadows from sea level to five hundred feet in elevation. I hunted the benches above the bay.

After hunting all morning without seeing anything, I was on the verge of returning to our rendezvous. That's when I came across some deer tracks that looked fairly fresh. I debated pursuing the animal, knowing my buddies would be waiting at the boat.

At length I decided to pursue the animal and see what I'd come across. I took up the distinct track. A gentle drizzle continued to fall as I poked along the deer trail, meandering up and down hills and through the timber.

I kept on the track for an hour, wondering when or if I'd ultimately catch up with the deer ... or another one. I hoped I'd run across a nice, fat buck to help fill the meat supply for the winter.

I didn't think about the distance I'd come,

Finally I spotted the deer. It was a spike buck standing across a thirty-to-forty-foot-deep ravine, about fifty yards away.

I sat there for a good three or four minutes trying to decide whether to shoot.

The buck was curious, too—he didn't run. He just stood there looking at me. I didn't make any sudden moves to frighten him.

I didn't know exactly how far I was from the beach, but I presumed I'd traveled inland a good two and a half miles. I continued watching him and wondering whether I wanted to pack this guy that far out of the woods.

Since it was the first hunt of the year, I thought, "Why not. I might as well take him." And I shot him. It was around eleven-thirty in the morning, an hour after I was due to meet Shane and Rusty.

I figured I'd hurry, dress him, and carry him out. I got busy dressing the buck. I decapitated him, made a pack out of him, and threw him on my shoulders. He was an average-sized spike and weighed about ninety pounds without his head. I was forty-one years old, five feet ten inches tall, and weighed 165 pounds, so the pack wasn't anything I couldn't handle.

I started for the beach, toting my .338 rifle and the buck. The rain continued falling.

My path was riddled with little ravines and hills. Up and down. One hill turned into a dozen. Minutes turned into hours.

It seemed as if I carried that buck a hundred miles. I got so tired I had to stop every couple of hundred feet to take a little break. I don't know how far I hiked; however, somehow the fatigue and fading daylight disoriented me.

I lost my balance and fell into a small stream, drenching me and the buck. I continued on. Step followed weary step. The brush and devil's club compounded my problem. I kept wondering if I was going in the right direction. And I kept hurrying along to beat the dark.

I noticed on my watch it was getting kinda late. It was also getting pretty dark. I didn't want to walk in the dark. I decided, "Hey, it's gettin' too late to be packin' this thing. It's a whole animal." I dropped the deer.

I'd packed it from eleven-thirty till dark, probably six hours for sure. I was exhausted, and I had no idea how far I was from salt water.

I felt I was lost, but I wasn't concerned. I thought, "I'll find my way out in the morning. I'm just stuck here for the night. Tomorrow morning I'll walk outta here."

I decided to lighten my load by cutting meat from the buck. I took prime cuts of meat, slicing off the backstrap, tenderloins, rump roasts, shoulder roasts, heart, and liver. I had a plastic bag, so I threw all these choice cuts into the plastic bag.

I wanted to build a fire to warm up and dry out, but I was unable to locate anything dry enough to start a fire. Since it had been raining a couple of days, everything was wet. It was also too dark to be trying to locate anything. I tried carving a little bit of the inside of the bark off a tree. I even cut part of my rubber boot out to try to get a fire going. The rubber boot burned fine, but it wasn't able to ignite anything else that I had to burn because it was too wet.

By this time I was soaked from head to foot. I knew it was going to be a miserable night because it was still raining and the temperature was fifty degrees.

Fortunately I was wearing wool pants and a sweatshirt. My baseball cap helped keep a little of the rain off me. I had no fire and no food.

I found a couple of trees growing together that provided some shelter. I sat under the trees all night. I was still getting wet and was chilled. If I caught myself dozing off, I'd get up and walk around the area, jump up and down a little bit to get the blood circulating to keep hypothermia from setting in.

It was the first time I've ever been lost in the woods. I never expected it to happen. I grew up hunting in Ohio; I've had experience in the woods. I didn't think I was gonna be gone that long to begin with. I figured I'd only be out for a couple of hours.

During the night I realized my mistake. I thought I was heading toward Vallenar Bay. On the contrary, I was heading northeast and ended up bypassing Vallenar completely.

At the crack of dawn I got up, picked up my bag of meat and rifle, and started hiking again. I started backtracking. I was still unable to see the bay, however I started heading south and west toward the bay.

While I was working my way toward the coast, a search party was looking for me.

Shane and Rusty had waited for me until five or six o'clock the day before. When I didn't show up, Rusty radioed from his boat to the Coast Guard to report me missing. The Coast Guard turned the case over to the Alaska State Troopers.

A dozen people combed the woods and beaches for me. Beginning at 7 A.M. they searched by air and boat. They didn't know if I'd fallen down and hurt myself or what had taken place. Although we weren't that far from Ketchikan, we were in the wilderness where a man alone can have real problems, including bear confrontations, cliffs, and water hazards.

A twenty-foot Alaska Department of Fish and Wildlife Protection boat with two troopers checked the shoreline and cabins in the area. The search continued until one o'clock with no sign of me.

Temsco helicopters transported eight Ketchikan Volunteer Rescue Squad volunteers to the island. They split up into pairs to look for me.

Ken Eichner volunteered his private helicopter and flew the island looking for me.

A row of mountains on the island ranges from 1,500 to 2,100 feet high. I could have gone up to those at any time, but I decided I didn't want to climb. I reasoned if I fell and broke my leg or fell in a crevice and hurt myself, then I would be in bad shape. I didn't want to risk climbing the mountain and ending up in worse shape than I was. I decided my best bet was to stay in the valley.

I kept moving. It stopped raining.

I hiked until I reached the place I'd left from with the deer the day before. It was inland and to the west. I had bypassed Vallenar again. This was getting ridiculous.

There I was another two or three miles inland. This time I had gone too far to the west. So I turned around and started backtracking again. I just kept walking.

That day thirty people searched for me. I got a lot of support from the community.

During the day I heard airplanes and I built a fire, reasoning I could attract them with smoke. Thinking wet ferns would create a bunch of smoke, I dragged ferns through the creek and tossed them onto my fire. My fire produced a great smoke cloud, but since the creek was in a valley with high banks and trees on each side, by the time the smoke had reached the top of the trees, it had dissipated so much the planes were unable to spot any.

I saw and heard a half dozen or more planes throughout the day. At one point I rushed into a clearing and waved my shirt at a plane that was no more than a half mile away.

Later a plane flew right over me and I saw its belly.

It was disheartening to know searchers were so close, but that my rescue was thwarted.

Around five o'clock that evening I got pretty hungry and decided to build a fire. I was near a creek bed, so I went down and gathered some rocks for a fire ring. I looked for dry wood. Nearly all the wood was damp, but I found enough dry wood and some pitch from a tree to get a fire going.

At that time I realized I wasn't going to find my way out immediately. Thinking ten pounds of meat would last me until I reached the beach, I cooked that amount and discarded the rest.

It started getting near dark. I decided I'd spend the night right near the fire. I gathered a bunch of ferns and made myself a bed. I made myself as comfortable as possible and spent the night.

The next morning I decided, rather than walk around in circles anymore, I'd follow the creek out to the beach.

I started out.

Partway down the creek, I heard airplanes overhead. I knew they were searching for me and that they couldn't see me in the creek bottom, so I scambled up into a muskeg meadow to signal the pilots.

I saw a couple of planes pass by. I had my shirt off and waved it at them. I was unable to attract their attention . . . even in the clear muskeg. I actually felt rather helpless. There was even more aircraft activity that day—Cessna 185 float planes for the most part, the Coast Guard in choppers.

Since the creek was full of spawning salmon, I encountered plenty of black bear signs. I saw a couple of bears along the creek, but I didn't have any problems. There was so much feed available to them, they didn't bother me.

I followed the creek, not knowing it was Bostwick Creek, which emptied into

Bostwick Inlet. I stayed on the southeast bank until I came out to the bay about 12:15 P.M.

When I saw the bay, I thought, "This is it. This is great. I shouldn't have any problems now being spotted." Then I saw smoke. And I thought, "Well, okay, I'll hike over toward the smoke where there's likely to be some people."

I saw a couple of skiffs out in the bay, and I started yelling to them. They were unable to hear me because of the noise their motors were making.

About then I saw a Coast Guard chopper hovering low, rumbling over the drainage I had just left. They had gone up the west bank and returned along the east bank. Then they spotted me.

They sat down and picked me up. They gave me some food and checked me over. I was in good shape.

It was September 6, a happy day for this footsore hunter.

Epilogue

Needless to say, as soon as I got back to Ketchikan, I bought a hundred dollars' worth of survival gear. My gear now includes signal flares, a fire-starter stick, a tube tent kit, bouillon cubes, fishing line and hooks, twenty-five feet of duct tape, and a compass. If I'd had the signal flares, I could have been rescued the first day.

Although Richard was rescued, Bob Elstad encountered his own dilemma on his return flight to Anchorage.

NIGHTMARE IN
THE INLET

AS TOLD TO THE AUTHOR BY BOB ELSTAD

*Suddenly there was a lurch and a rending roar. The plane flipped
upside down.*

" 'I've got him . . . the downed pilot,' " screamed the headlines of the *Anchorage Daily News,* Monday, October 29, 1979. I was astounded to read about the pilot who had emerged from the fog on the New Seward Highway after having spent hours crossing the deadly mudflats of Cook Inlet in the dark of night. *I need to get his story.*

It took me a while to find Bob Elstad; however, on December 13, 1991, I ecstatically interviewed him in my English classroom at Dimond High School at 8:30 A.M. He agreed to share his story.

The plane's intense white landing light stabbed across the black waters into the nothingness of night. Kaleidoscopic green, red, and silver flashes pierced the darkness from the plane's wing and tail strobe lights. The navigation lights on the panel of the Cessna 185 leered at the lone figure standing dazed on the gravel bar. He tried to make some sense of his situation.

The combination of blackness and pulsating, colored lights created an eeriness for Bob Elstad. His red-trimmed, white Cessna N94178 lay piled at his feet, useless in Turnagain Arm on the outskirts of Anchorage, Alaska. His destination a few thousand yards to the north lay shrouded in fog. Six miles to the east, flirting headlights of passing vehicles teased him.

While contemplating his condition and gathering a few survival items from his craft, he reviewed his past few hours.

I left Lake Hood, one of Anchorage's float-plane bases, around four o'clock in the afternoon of October 28, 1979. I headed to my cabin at Lake Creek on the Yentna River, some ninety miles northeast over Cook Inlet and the Big Susitna River. I hauled four sheets of four-by-eight-foot plywood on what I figured would be my final trip of the winter. As is customary, I carried materials between my floats on spreader bars (two horizontal bars that separate the floats). I'd secured the three-quarter-inch lumber with motorcycle straps. I also had a couple of blankets and an old jacket as well as a ceramic toilet in the back baggage compartment.

Although a friend had volunteered to help me, he never showed up. So, having secured the lumber on the floats, I lifted off Lake Hood and flew out to the cabin. The weather was VFR (pilots flying according to visual flight rules) at the time. Since the river is really low at that time of the year, taxiing up to the cabin was out of the question. I parked at the mouth where Lake Creek dumps into the Yentna. After three exhausting trips with the plywood, struggling three blocks upstream along the beach to the cabin, I started my return flight.

I had about an hour's worth of fuel on board. Normally the one-way flight takes twenty-five to thirty minutes, so I wasn't concerned about my fuel supply. I figured I had more than enough fuel to make the trip safely, barring any weather problems.

On my return to Anchorage the weather was turning on me. I passed through a snow squall and continued toward town, cruising at fifteen hundred feet. When I approached Anchorage, I found it socked in—both the entire city and the Port of Anchorage were shrouded in a giant, white cloud. It looked like a silver-gold mushroom with a bright light under it that just glowed . . . in an eerie, spooky way.

Aside from the cloud it was a moonlit night. But anything in or around Anchorage was zero-zero visibility.

Lake Hood was closed so I circled around for a while. If I'd had three and a half hours of fuel, I would have climbed up ten thousand feet and flown over the mountains to Lake Louise or someplace where I could see in the moonlight and land the plane safely. I could have got up on the top and got a directional from the airport or used my compass. But I just didn't have enough fuel to make that flight.

I talked to the Anchorage International Airport tower, and they said it was socked in from Kenai to Tyonek, a thirty-five-by-seventy-mile fog bank. They asked me if I wanted to declare an emergency and land on a runway at the airport. I didn't want to mess with the FAA and make that emergency situation. It was my choice to land where I wouldn't have complications. Since my plane was equipped with floats and I could see the Inlet and land safely, I chose to forgo a runway landing. The Inlet's waters looked as smooth as glass.

I thought of making a landing down near the Port of Anchorage, but not knowing what was out there, I was afraid that I might run into a barge or ship at anchor.

I circled on the edge of the fog offshore between the Campbell Lake area and Indian. I kept looking, thinking I was going to get into Campbell Lake, which has no tower. I even dropped into the fog a little bit near Campbell Lake.

Portage Sound was VFR, so I decided since my fuel was getting lower and lower and lower, I'd better commit to a landing in the inlet offshore from Campbell Lake. The full moon enabled me to see. I'd touch down and let the rising tide float me to shore. I'd be home free.

I set up for my approach and settled down toward the shimmering waters below. The airplane eased in. Anchorage tower had advised me that the tide was on its way in. I had some fear that the big waves might get me; but there weren't any. The water was as smooth as I've ever seen the Inlet. It looked like another perfect landing.

Suddenly there was a lurch and a rending roar. The plane flipped upside down and tore the tail right off. My left float had hit a sandbar I couldn't see. It was a routine landing until I hit the sandbar.

The plane turned over so fast that I didn't even have time to think about it—one second I'm landing, the next I'm hanging upside down in my seat belt. I was just thankful that I wasn't all busted up so I could still get out of the airplane and do something to help myself.

I got out of the seat belt, opened the door, and exited the plane. Even though I wasn't knocked out, the crash had thrown me for a loop. I felt the back of my head and discovered a long, vertical cut. It had opened up so much I thought I might be touching my brains and perhaps I'd die.

Evidently the toilet bowl had come flying forward from the baggage area and hit me. The toilet had disintegrated like tempered glass. Had the toilet not shattered, the blow might have killed me. I then hit the instrument panel, banging my head and cutting myself.

Except for the moonlight and the flashing of the Christmas-colored strobe lights and the landing lights stabbing across the inky waters of the Inlet, it was pitch-black.

I could see by the light of the moon. I saw the gravel bar. The big mushroom cloud still hung over Anchorage, like an atomic-bomb cloud. As I regained my senses, I noticed the incoming tide lapping at my plane. I needed to head for shore pronto!

I looked into the plane and gathered some survival gear. Of course everything that had been on the floor was now on the roof. I put two blankets and an old jacket into a Hefty garbage sack so that I'd have some kind of life device in case I got into water. Hopefully the bag would hold enough air to float me.

With my boot heel I tried to scratch an arrow in the hard gravel bar indicating my direction of travel. But it didn't work.

I could see vehicle headlights on the Seward Highway south of Potter's Marsh, probably six miles away.

I couldn't make a straight shot to the beach because deep, water-filled channels blocked my shortest path to the highway. The gravel bar was several miles long. I started walking toward shore and that big, foggy cloud.

I was wearing hip boots, cords, a flannel shirt, and a light coat. It was between thirty and thirty-six degrees. The wet mud and water intensified the cold; however, it wasn't cold to the point that I was freezing to death.

Using the car lights as a reference, I followed the sandbar east toward Potter's Marsh. Turnagain's main body of water was on my right.

As I walked, I realized the gravel bars were as hard as concrete, like pavement. I couldn't even put a footprint in them. It amazed me.

I had wondered if the Inlet would swallow me up. I've lived here all my life, and most people who crash in the Inlet or get stuck in its mud never get out of it. From duck hunting and hooligan fishing experiences as a kid, I had realized how easy it is to get stuck.

My fear of getting stuck was not real pronounced. I knew my object was to get to shore. I just kept telling myself, "I'm going to get back to see dear old mom."

Then I began to wonder if I'd be able to get to shore before the water engulfed me . . . the silt would weigh me down . . . or I wouldn't be able to swim because of the strength of the tide. Getting to shore was my ultimate goal.

I kept walking. Finally I reached the end of the sandbar and encountered my first crossing attempt. I wondered whether the water would rise over my hip boots, forcing me to swim. That would have gotten me colder and wetter. Could I make it to the next sandbar?

I waded into the water. It rose around my waders but didn't go over them.

I felt my way along, testing the bottom of the Inlet, carefully placing one foot in front of the other. Fifteen minutes later I walked out of the water onto the next bar.

I continued east paralleling the shoreline until I came to another body of water. It was big enough to land a float plane in, three hundred feet wide and miles long. I said to myself, "If I can't make it across, I'll just have to back up, take my clothes off, put them in the Hefty bag, and try to swim that couple of blocks of slough there."

As I waded into the ebony water, it rose slowly. It was never more than thirty inches deep. As before, the water did not go over the tops of my hip boots. I waded across it to the next bar.

I walked another couple of miles until I was close to the shoreline. I'd crossed two bodies of water without having to swim.

I got to the shoreline and encountered the difficulty of the mud banks, which were too high to see over. I thought I'd be safer on top of the banks, so I started up. I ran into big, crevasselike rivulets. The mud was slick and Jell-O-like; and I kept falling. I wallowed in the gray muck. I fell and regained my footing so many times I lost count. I also discovered it was like quicksand.

The going was easier on the gravel bars below than on the slick slop above. The bottom was hard gravel covered by four or five inches of water.

Finally I managed to find my way through the goo and get to shore. I don't know what someone else does in a near death situation where the Inlet's chasing his butt, but I told myself, "I love my mother and all my friends. I will make it back to see them all." That's what I kept telling myself. For some reason that's what kept me plugging away.

It took me close to three hours to reach the highway after I left the plane. I must have looked like some hideous monster—I was caked with mud and blood.

I hit shore near the shooting-range building by Rabbit Creek Road. I saw a light in there. I wanted to get help, but I was afraid that somebody might shoot me since I looked like some kind of freak. I was a scary-looking human being—all cut up and covered with blood and mud, red and gray from head to foot.

I passed the building, got to the highway a hundred yards beyond, and tried to hitch a ride. I could see people approaching. Drivers looked at me and veered around me. It was as if they were thinking, "I'm not picking up this creature."

I said to myself, "What do I have to do to get some help here?" I was beat. When no one stopped for me, I gave up in frustration and walked uphill toward Anchorage.

Then I saw a vehicle sitting on the shoulder of the road. I approached the driver a little nervously . . . I didn't want him to think I was some kind of Peeping Tom and shoot me.

The driver got out of the car. I said, "Hey, mister, could you help me? I just wrecked my airplane in the Inlet."

He was a newspaper reporter looking for the downed pilot! He'd come out to Potter's Marsh on a hunch.

We started for Providence Hospital in Anchorage. Along the way, I said, "Hey, buddy, why don't we stop and get a beer? I need to get a cold beer, wash this mud down." He didn't stop for a drink; I think he thought I was going to die in his car. I had to show him how to get to the emergency room.

When I got to the hospital, I saw the fright on people's faces. The first thing I wanted to see was what I looked like. I knew it was like something out of a horror movie. I discovered they couldn't have dressed me up any wilder.

When the medical personnel started examining me, they couldn't understand why I wasn't suffering from hypothermia. I hadn't gotten my body totally immersed in water, which kept me from getting colder and going hypothermic.

They wanted to keep me overnight, but I talked them out of it. I told them, "I'm okay." They took seventeen stitches to sew my head up and released me.

Shortly after I got to the hospital, a dear friend of mine, Pete Potter, showed up with his wife, Jane. It was really nice to see somebody that I knew. They lived on Campbell Lake, and he had been listening to my entire radio conversation through his scanner as I circled Anchorage. Knowing and caring for me, he actually went down the highway looking for me.

Pete came over to me and said, "Bob, I tried to get a search party organized for you. I drove the highway for hours looking to see if I could find you out there."

I was grateful that he had thought of all that. Nobody else did. He had tried to get a boat to go out at the Port of Anchorage, but the weather was sour. They just didn't put together a search. I assume they figured a downed pilot in the Inlet was a goner anyway.

The next morning my buddy Potter and another guy picked me up. We flew over the Inlet looking for the plane, and we found it, swirling around in the receding tide. We hired a chopper to go out to pick it up.

An old friend of mine, Kip Kippingham, who had retrieved a lot of bush planes, told me what I would have to do to get the plane out. He said he didn't think that I'd be able to salvage anything but the engine and the floats. The silt gets into the wings and the plane is so heavy that if you try to lift it with the chopper, the pressure pulls the wings off the airplane.

The wind kicked up to sixty to seventy knots, and they had to wait for the winds to die down. After the third tide the winds abated, and we went back out. But the plane was gone. The tide had taken it out to sea.

My loss was $75,000. I had put the plane up for the winter and had just canceled my insurance coverage the week before. In the interim I'd decided I needed four sheets of plywood at the cabin. It would be easier to take it on the airplane. I rationalized, "One little last flight isn't going to hurt anything."

Thirty miles east of Elstad's accident scene, at the headwaters of Turnagain Arm, the Dickisons prepared to prospect for gold. However, their accident would be much more costly.

DEATH WOULDN'T WAIT

*The Dickisons didn't know about the treacherous tides, currents,
and mudflats.*

The local newspaper carries a great deal of tragic news during a year's time.
But one of the saddest stories I ever read involved a newlywed couple recently
moved to the Last Frontier. I couldn't help wondering a number of things as I
went over their plight.

You're mired in mud to one knee in the tide flats and unable to free yourself.
You see the malevolent waters of the incoming tide flooding toward you. Your
newlywed spouse stands nearby. What thoughts course through your mind?
What is your spouse thinking? What are rescuers arriving at the scene thinking?
What about parents, siblings, or other family members when learning your
plight? What goes through the mind of the person holding you up to stave off
your drowning . . . or his suffering the same dilemma? What about those onlookers onshore? Or the one responsible for bringing and starting the lifesaving
equipment? This whole scenario is not pleasant to consider . . . but it *is* reality.

Jay and Adeana Dickison eagerly anticipated their outing, one that offered them
the opportunity to explore their new state and possibly to provide them with
some extra money. Early that Friday morning, July 15, 1988, the newlyweds
unloaded their silver pickup truck at the head of Turnagain Arm some forty
miles southeast of Anchorage. Jay was twenty-five, Adeana was eighteen.

Nothing but excitement filled their minds. The newcomers, recently arrived
from Dayton, Nevada, had lived the past month in Eagle River, a bedroom
community a dozen air miles north of Anchorage.

Although only 5 A.M. it had been daylight several hours in these northern
climes. It was an incredibly terrific summer day.

They off-loaded their Honda, four-wheel, all-terrain vehicle and hooked up
their trailer. Once the trailer was loaded with their gold-dredging equipment,
they started off toward the creek.

Clumps of wild rye grass welcomed the young couple as they motored west
over the hard, sandy soil. Their destination, only a few miles beyond, was easily
accessible, within a thirty-minute drive on their puttering machine. Seattle

Creek sliced seaward through timber-choked mountainsides. Seattle Creek was a popular area for placer mining only four miles from the New Seward Highway.

They were unaware that the terrain they crossed is one of the most treacherous pieces of real estate in the entire state of Alaska, an area whose concretelike surface belies its Jell-O-like characteristics depending upon the tide or locale. Numerous glacier-fed streams dump fine glacial silt into Turnagain Arm. This silt settles when the tide goes out, allowing relatively safe passage as it is firm in most areas. However, when the tide turns and starts in, the silt softens.

A person standing in one spot while moving his body like a dipnetter can get stuck in the mud. The movement, along with the person's weight, pushes his feet down into the mud. Pressure builds as the feet sink until there is no pulling him free.

The Dickisons' jaunt onto the flats would not be the first . . . but would remain one of the most widely read about and tragic tales of stark terror and tragedy to surface in Alaska.

Jay and Adeana reached an empty channel and dropped over the shoulder of the tide gut. In moments they were mired in the soft underbelly of the channel. With Jay attempting to drive the four-wheeler out of the goop, Adeana pushed on the machine.

People would find it inconceivable that a person could sink in mud up to the ankle or even the knee and not be able to escape. But on the mudflats surrounding Anchorage, it happens all too often.

Although Jay was trying to help dig it out, Adeana's right leg remained firmly stuck in the mud. Jay tried for three hours with no success. At length, and knowing that the returning tide would fill the channel, he reassured Adeana that he was going for help.

Just before 8 A.M. he ran the half mile to the highway and asked a couple of Minnesotans to help. One departed immediately for the Tidewater Café at Portage, half dozen miles en route to Anchorage; the other returned with him to the machine and Adeana.

Alaska state trooper Mike Opalka related later, "I got the call about seven fifty-two. I called the fire department and told them to get on down there. I walked on ahead to see what kind of situation we had."(1)

Opalka arrived and saw Jay and one of the tourists trying to dislodge Adeana from the mud. While the men tugged at Adeana's limbs and torso, a few men pulled on a rope that had been tied around her body. But there was no dislodging the woman.

The water's thirty-eight-degree temperature sapped everyone's strength, sucking the heat right out of their bodies. And Adeana had been there for over three hours. Imagine her thoughts and fears. Her agony.

Riverlike, the brown-gray water roared into the channel, rapidly covering everything in sight. By the time Opalka reached Adeana, the murky, frigid water had risen to her chest. He said, "I talked to her, told her everything was going to be all right, we were going to get her out of there."(1)

By this time the firemen were arriving with their water-pressure porta-pump that was designed to force water through a pipe and out the various holes along its length, reducing or offsetting the pressure so that a person could be freed.

When Opalka saw the firemen coming with their equipment, he left Adeana only long enough to run a hundred yards across the flats to help them haul the pump and fire hose to her.

By the time he reached her again, water was covering her head. The water was too swift and too high for the equipment to be used successfully.

Opalka knew it was a dire emergency. Mike grabbed a piece of hose from the mining equipment and handed it to her, hoping the frightened woman could use it as a breathing tube while the firemen tried to start their pump to free her.

With his hands beneath her armpits, Trooper Opalka held on to Adeana. As she screamed in panic, the water rose over her head.

Someone on the bank said, "She's under." Fireman Mike Polzin got to the stone-faced Opalka, who said, "she's been under awhile." Mike dived down and grabbed a leg. It was Opalka's. Mike came to the surface and went under again, but Adeana's leg was cemented in.

Hope dwindled with the rising tide and Adeana lost the tube.

Mike Opalka lost his strength.

Mike Polzin said, "I couldn't believe Mike's stamina out there. My hands turned white. I could barely get a rope around her. I pulled on her with all my might. Mother Nature had her."(1)

Later Opalka said, "I was holding on to her as she drowned. I'm hanging on to her and I had to let go. I had no feeling in my arms. I just had to let go. She was alive, conscious. There was nothing that we could do."(1)

Jay Dickison stood helplessly by.

For twenty minutes after the water covered Adeana, the men continued trying to free her. At length and with water around their necks, they were forced to leave her behind and haul themselves up the rope to the beach. Her lifeline became theirs.

The men left the water cold, exhausted, frustrated, and with pockets full of the heavy silt that claims so many people's lives in glacial waters.

The rescuers stood by helplessly as the mud of the arm held Adeana fast and the roaring incoming tide covered her like a liquid shroud. Nothing more could be done for her except to grieve.

Thirty-three feet of water poured into the area, forcing all to leave for their safety.

A backup emergency team that included divers arrived from Anchorage an hour later. Tragically, it was too late.

Had the firemen and troopers been contacted sooner, they could have rescued Adeana, and none of the papers or the news media would have had a story. No stories are the best stories.

The tide ebbed, and six hours later the channel was all but dry. The firemen accepted their gruesome task of hauling their equipment onto the flats and releasing Adeana's trapped leg and thus her body.

Having wondered what it would be like to have someone die in your arms when there is virtually nothing you can do about it, I wanted to hear Mike Opalka's version of this tragedy. After several days of telephone tag I met him. When he opened the door and welcomed me into his home, I realized immediately that Mike is a man's man—at six feet four inches and 280 pounds with military-style, graying hair. He told me he'd been in law enforcement thirty-five years since his MP days in Vietnam prior to working for the Denver Police Department and in Alaska. I asked him to share his thoughts and he does below.

It was a nice day. I remember vividly because I have a routine. I get up between five-thirty and six-thirty, go out, get the paper, drink a cup of coffee before I get ready to go to work.

I had a forwarding device so whenever a phone call came in for the State Troopers, it would automatically redial to the dispatch in Anchorage. It had a speaker on it, so I could hear the conversation back and forth.

I'd just started reading the paper and I heard the guy say, "My wife's stuck in the mudflats," and he gave the location. I got into a pair of coveralls. Then I had the dispatcher call the fire department here in Girdwood for a mudflat rescue. I headed south to see what was goin' on.

I left here and headed toward Ingram Creek, about a fifteen, twenty minute drive. I expedited, but I didn't go crazy. I got there, saw a car, and saw what was going on.

It was about a quarter of a mile at least from my vehicle to the girl. You had to walk down a trail and over a bank. There was no way she was visible from the road, and besides that she was down in the gully.

When I first made contact with the lady, she was scared spitless, but there was nothing critical. I was convinced we were going to get her out. Nobody's gonna drown; I'm not going to let anybody die in my arms.

I went down there and talked to her, held her hand, calmed her down. I assessed the situation. By that time the fire department had arrived back up on the road. So I ran back up to the road and grabbed a shovel and waited for them. I don't know what in the world I was going to do with a shovel because it was worthless.

You don't dig that stuff, and besides that, water was rushing in. That's like trying to go out into the middle of Eagle River to dig in that sand. You just don't dig in it, period. Even if there's no water around. You just don't dig that mud.

We started back down and they were bringing a porta-pump, a device to pump water in to relieve the suction.

By the time I got back down, the tide had started to come in. It was in the gut, a fifteen foot-wide and six-foot-high channel. It was a significant current, and it was rising fast. That's when I started gettin' worried.

I stuck the shovel in the water right beside me and grabbed her under the arms and started liftin' on her to see if I could jerk her out. By this time a couple of other firemen had come down without the pump and gotten in the water with me. We were workin' on her to get her out.

It was apparent things were not going to go well, and she was starting to scream. We were trying to calm her down and get her out of the water. All we could do was tug on her.

It finally got to the point where I couldn't hold her up because she was underwater and that water's so cold I had no control whatsoever of my arms and my hands. It's a shock that renders you helpless. I'd been in the water fifteen to twenty minutes. I couldn't do anything or grasp anything.

One of the firemen had tied a rope around her. Mike Polzin was in the water with me. We thought if the force of the water was able to get her out, we wouldn't lose the body. I think she was already dead then, but we weren't willing to admit it.

After I got everybody else out, I started to get out of the water. I said, "I'm coming out." I had to put the rope underneath my arm between my elbow and body and kind of inch myself along, then they helped me to get out.

Thinking about the danger never entered my mind. None of us thought of that at the time. I was convinced that we were gonna effect a rescue and go away fat, dumb, and happy.

The husband was there and everybody was kind of numb to the situation. The fire department started loading up to leave and I said, "No, guys, we've got to get a dive team down here, we've got to wait because when the tide goes out, we're going to have a body recovery, we're still going to need you."

So they hung around and I got the dive team from the Anchorage fire department to come down in case I needed them, too. Between the time we came out of the water and the time the tide started goin' out, hordes of people started showing up.

There were helicopters. I was on the handheld radio screaming to my dispatcher, "I need a helicopter!" If you need something urgent, my standard procedure is to call my dispatcher, they call the Anchorage tower, and if there's a helicopter in the area, they'll see if they can divert that guy to come down.

Our helicopter takes an hour to get going if he's not in the air, or the 210th Air Rescue at Kulis takes an hour and a half with a crew.

One helicopter was operating that morning so they diverted it to come down. I don't know which company, ERA or Alaska Helicopters or Temsco. By the time he got down there, it was over with.

A helicopter would have done no good, none at all. I was going to tie a rope on her and have the helicopter pull her out. Well, the helicopter couldn't have pulled her out.

On the way down I passed a military bus from Fort Richardson going to Seward for recreation. It was about up here to Girdwood when I passed. Later

I thought, "If I could get somebody up at the road, I'd have somebody flag that bus down and have all those guys come down here and help." But that didn't work out. We just didn't have the time. That's all there was to it.

If there had been enough time, we could have saved her. She'd gotten both feet stuck from pushing on the ATV. Her husband had started his gold-prospecting suction dredge and sucked up the mud from one foot. He started on the other one, but the dredge quit. Finally when he realized it wasn't working, tide's starting in, he went for help. At that point if a bunch of people had been right there, it would have turned out all right.

But we had no time.

It took a long time for it to set in, I couldn't believe it actually happened . . . that somebody actually died in my arms and I couldn't get them out. But after the tide went back out . . . another six hours, we got the body out. When all the hype was over, the news media was gone, all the hardware was gone, the helicopters, the buses and the press, the people and the investigators, all that was over with . . . I was in the car returning to Girdwood, yes, I cried . . . for her, for the situation, for myself. I was not happy with it. It was not something I expected to go that way, and then I had time to think about it. I didn't go to pieces on it, I didn't go sobbing, but it was a situation where I broke down and cried.

Afterward there was critical-stress debriefing done. The chaplain came down and talked with a few people. I don't know what the fire department did in detail with their people, but I know they did some follow-up. I don't remember exactly what the procedure was.

At that time it was just starting to become a situation that the organization recognized had to be dealt with. They recognized that maybe people weren't coping too well, but they pretty much let the person come forward and ask for assistance. If somebody needed help, wanted to talk with them, they would provide something.

It's been more refined since then. Now it's almost a mandatory thing with a psychologist, it's written into the policy that you will go through this, et cetera, et cetera.

I don't think you ever get over it; people deal with it in their own ways just like I deal with it. In this line of work and the training that comes with this job, you either deal with it and cope with it and develop an attitude that "I feel sorry for these people, but I'm glad that it didn't happen to me," or you can't do the job. If in each and every situation where these deaths come about or these tragic situations arise and you're not able to deal with it, if you internalize it and take it home with you, your life will go to hell in a handbag real fast. You'll end up getting divorced, you'll have mental breakdowns and stuff, or you better quit the job. One of the two. That's all there is to it . . . you probably become cold to it, and that doesn't sound like the proper word, but, yes, you become cold to it and you suppress it. Otherwise you can't do the job.

With all the traffic-related deaths . . . the worst ones, of course, are kids and children, infants and stuff. I cannot take those. I do them, but I can't take them. A fifty-year-old guy out there on the highway who dies, while I don't like it, I can deal with it. When the car went over the guardrail and into the inlet two years ago and the father emerged from the vehicle and the infant couldn't be reached, that was difficult for me. I had to extricate the infant, get him out of the car, put him in a body bag, cover him up still in the car seat. I think about my own kid that way. That's when I lose it.

Our department has been so decimated by budget cuts that we can't do the job we want to do.

As the force of the moon caused the ebb and flow of the tide, the hands of the clock would not slow long enough for a group of gallant men to save a lady in distress. Truly a tragic footnote as to the price of going afield in a hazardous area.

Hopefully Trooper Opalka's work in providing the Girdwood Fire Department with equipment through grants and donations will help prevent future deaths in the Arm.

Parallel Story

In September 1998 a duck hunter was trapped in the mud not far from the area where Adeana Dickison lost her life. His good fortune was in having a companion who could alert rescue personnel, who in turn had time to respond before the tide came in.

Kirk Holdburg and his nine-year-old son, Frank, and Justin Wells, sixteen, were crossing the mudflats about a half mile off the Seward Highway near Ingram Creek. Frank sank into the mud and his father freed him but became stuck in the process, sinking into the mud to his knees.

Frank remained with his father and was concerned for his safety while Justin ran in his hip waders the half mile to Holdburg's pickup and used a cellular phone to call for help around 7:30 P.M.

Girdwood's volunteer fire department responded. They arrived on the scene and placed boards around Holdburg to provide themselves firm footing. With the use of their portable pump they had him out of the mud within an hour of their arrival.

Fire Chief Bill Chadwick said, "If he would have been alone, he would have been dead."(4)

Danger and death walk hand in hand . . . often the difference between them is measured in the tiniest degrees.

ESCAPE FROM THE PIT

AS TOLD TO THE AUTHOR BY C. D. TUGGLE

Having your emotions ripped out can hurt worse than having your face shot off.

Although this story did not take place in Alaska, the hunt and ensuing trauma could have. This is a story that I tracked down through the publisher of a magazine. I knew only the essentials of the story, the magazine editor's name, and the city where C. D. Tuggle attended church. I contacted the publisher, Arlo Newell, at *Vital Christianity* and he sent me a copy of the article.

I mailed a query letter to C. D. Tuggle's pastor in care of the First Church of God in Great Bend, Kansas. The pastor hand-carried my letter to C. D. and was shocked to learn it was from me. Stranger than fiction, truth marches on—the pastor was Dick Ogle, my pastor when I grew up in Clarkston, Washington, in the late 1950s. Small world. God *does* work in mysterious ways.

C. D. wrote me and later called. He was a wonderful man with a love of life. I was grateful for his kindness in sending his story and being my friend.

It started out as a great morning—from the hot coffee, camaraderie in the duck shack, walk to the blind, and the bone-chilling sunrise. Everything was perfect ... until the shotgun blast. Believe me, I've had lots of time to remember and review my life before and after the accident.

I was born August 10, 1912, in Deerfield, Kansas, where my father worked as a section foreman for the Santa Fe Railroad. Later we moved to Scott City where I attended grade school and high school. I pursued tennis and basketball, winning the state singles tennis title just prior to graduation from high school. Oklahoma University, Nebraska University, and Emporia State approached me about a tennis scholarship, and I chose Emporia State because it was closer and provided better benefits.

While in college, I won the Kansas singles title two years, but the biggest thrill in my tennis career was winning the Canal Zone Open in Panama later, during my military tour of duty.

I was anxious to do some traveling after returning to our home in Ottawa, Kansas. My wife, Dorothy, had no objection to a vacation in California.

Luanne was our only daughter at the time. We toured places we had always wanted to see. It was fun, but I knew I had to find work even though I had no idea what I'd do.

We returned to set up housekeeping. In a few days I was contacted by the district manager for the Travelers Insurance Company in Kansas City, Missouri. Al Calaw, a former New York Yankee, was looking for a man to be trained as an agent. Selling insurance was the furthest occupation from my mind, and I jokingly told him I did not have many relatives to call on.

He worked with me until I qualified as an agent. What a deep feeling of satisfaction it was to have a title and the possibility of effectively producing a decent living. Mr. Calaw made arrangements with the Travelers for me to draw $50 a week against my commissions or meals could have been slim around the Tuggle household. We struggled along making ends meet with a two-year-old daughter.

Word got around that I was in town, and I was offered the position of head tennis coach of the Ottawa University squad. I accepted, met the tennis players, and realized immediately there was some real raw talent. These were men any coach loves to work with, and we worked hard.

The school had never won a conference title, but Bill Schmitz and Gayle Twyman won the doubles title. I was proud of the team and built for the next season by recruiting Ray Robbins, the state junior-college singles state titleholder. We wanted both the doubles and singles titles and achieved them the next year. The town and school were proud of my work.

Travelers transferred me to Great Bend, so I told the school and my players. It was emotional leaving the school and city.

We moved in January 1951, set up an office, and I began to do real well with the slogan "No struggle—C Tuggle." I achieved my goal of being a million-dollar producer.

Since my three brothers and I enjoyed hunting, we built a hunting club and lodge. We purchased 185 acres of land and excavated two hunting lakes and a one-acre fish pond and built a modern cabin. We installed two irrigation wells to flood the lakes and pond, knowing that the water supply would always be there. Our south lake was twenty-one acres and the north lake was twelve acres.

We had locations for ten blinds—six on the north lake, four on the south. The blinds were six by eight feet and designed to fit in the ground like a pit four feet eight inches deep. They were open at the front and the roof was three feet above the ground.

Our Sand Hills Gun Club, sandwiched between the Cheyenne Bottoms and the Quivira National Reserve, was well known statewide. These two reserves were developed as a resting area for migrating waterfowl and accommodate 250,000 ducks and geese. Men from eastern states are frequent hunters to our area on the central flyway. We rented out to twelve men to cover our light and fuel bills. Hunting was good.

C. D. Tuggle (second from right) before the accident with his brothers and nephew.
CREDIT: *Picture taken by one of the Sand Hill Club members in 1974, and is part of*
C. D. Tuggle's photo collection.

It's been a privilege to hunt with Kansas's former governor Robert Docking; Tony Schartz, a leader in the State House; and Ralph Terry, former pitcher with the New York Yankees. I met Mickey Mantle.

Our area brags many excellent hunters, and I hunt with two of the best, local businessman Bob Rowland, and Chuck Carper, a credit manager for a large trucking company. Both are quality men. Chuck Carper is Kansas duck-calling champion. Since he is nationally known, he is often invited to other cities for a demonstration of his duck-calling ability.

Hunting was my favorite pastime. It always gave me a break from my busy schedule. I wanted to go hunting Thanksgiving week of 1975, but I was swamped with new insurance accounts. All week the television reported a winter storm approaching. Finally I decided to go. It was too late to call one of my buddies, so I went alone. Mainly, I just wanted to relax and enjoy myself.

I set my alarm and got up at 4 A.M. on November 25, 1975. I didn't want to awaken my wife so I quietly scurried about, checking my shells and getting my shotgun. I had only eighteen shells, but with only four allowable ducks, that was enough. I decided on my three-inch shotgun and reached into my gun case. I looked outside. The weather was a duck hunter's dream—the sky was hard and gray with wind at twenty miles per hour from the west. With only a twenty-minute drive to the club I was anxious to go. I slipped out the door and picked up thirty-six decoys from the garage. I stowed them in my pickup and headed south.

As I neared the club, I could see the yard light was on, so I knew other friends were there. It was a warm sight as I reached the cabin. I could smell the aroma of fresh coffee the minute I climbed out of my pickup. Ed Schonhoff, our president, and Bob Law, an oilman, were in the kitchen. We swapped a few stories and emptied a pot of coffee as we waited for the sunrise.

I was as excited as a kid on Christmas morning. I told myself, "This hunt should be a dandy. Ducks and geese will be moving."

With only 125 yards to my blind, I drove down to unload my decoys. I took my gun and shells to the blind. Relying on the beam of light my truck's headlights cast across the water, I set my decoys. I like two sets—a small bunch of ten to twelve and a second group, perhaps twenty-five yards away, with a couple of dozen decs in it.

I returned the pickup to the cabin and walked back to the blind. The sharp winds forced me to pull my earflaps down from my cap.

Secure inside the blind, I watched the snow melt off my green chest waders and form little puddles of water on the floor. My heater kept my bottom and legs warm. I was snug in my heavy hunting shirt and blue insulated jacket. With my gloved left hand on my left thigh and my ungloved right hand in my pocket (for warmth, safety, and instant use), I awaited first light.

I marveled at the beauty around me. Dime-sized snowflakes whispered from the sky, covering the ground in a soft, white layer. Distant, leafless trees pointed their rigid fingers skyward. The freshness of a new day dawned.

Soon I saw a couple of teal fly by. Five redheads rocketed into view and skidded down onto the water. The ducks were moving. It wouldn't be long till larger ducks would fly in.

"There they are," I thought, "all mallards, probably twenty-five." They were flying by the lake. I gave them a quick feed call. They turned and with whistling wings shot toward me. Adrenaline surged through my body. I jumped up, reaching for my shotgun. My right foot slipped on the wet floor, knocking the gun against the blind. Although it was on safety, the sear spring was broken. A blast of red-orange flame exploded from the muzzle into my face.

The blast ripped my face apart. I was in total shock. I knew I was hurt bad. I tried to collect my senses. I had to get out of that blind and hope someone would see me. I could not yell, I had no tongue. I could hardly see; one eye was shot out and blood was flooding the other. I kept trying to get out of that cold, wet blind but always fell back. I had no strength in my arms or legs.

"Help me! Help me!" I cried out to the Lord. Instantly He responded. I was zoomed out of the blind. I was alive. Men at the cabin heard the shot and looked out. They saw me stumbling around and assumed I was having a heart attack. Ed Schonhoff came running to my side. Seeing my condition, he shouted to Bob to radio for an ambulance.

They kept me outside on the screened-in porch (the cold helped clot my blood) and positioned me so I would not choke on my blood. The flesh on my face hung in masses.

Within minutes I heard sirens screaming through the storm. Trooper Larry Werner, Stafford County sheriff Ed Miller, and his officers arrived with the ambulance. I knew I was in good hands as I lapsed into unconsciousness.

I was rushed to our local hospital and later to a Wichita hospital with more extensive facilities.

At the time, my daughter Luanne did not realize that her favorite scripture (Proverbs 3:5–6) was working in her life (and that I was being rushed to the hospital). She and her husband were going to Wichita to Christmas shop. After dropping the children off at school they were on their way. They stopped at Wesley Hospital to visit a friend, Bill, who had been in an accident.

They arrived and went directly to Bill's room. Bill's wife took my daughter's husband aside and told him I was being transferred to Wesley with a gunshot wound. They went to the emergency room, where Luanne waited about thirty minutes for me to reach the hospital.

When I arrived, I was surrounded by ten to twelve policemen and hospital personnel. Luanne was not allowed to get close. My blood pressure registered 50 over 0 instead of the usual 100 over 80. They took my family to a waiting room. The doctor told them the extent of my injuries and that they would be taking me to surgery to stop the bleeding. He then told them I would never make it through the night.

While I was in surgery, Luanne spent the majority of the time in the chapel. My wife went to the motel to rest, and Luanne's husband went to Hutchinson to take care of the children. After surgery the doctor continued to tell my family I would not survive the night as my blood pressure was 50/0.

Luanne continued to come to my bedside and read scriptures and pray. When she tried to rest, she felt strengthened by the Lord and returned to my bedside. Every time she was in my room, my blood pressure rose; when she left, it dropped.

The doctor returned the next day and, much to his surprise, found me still alive. Six days later I woke up with a minister holding my hand and reciting the Twenty-third Psalm. (I learned later that my daughter had spent many days and nights reading scriptures to me and praying for my healing.)

I spent nearly two weeks at Wesley before being transferred to Great Bend Hospital for a month. I was a happy man the day I left Wesley to return to Great Bend. Plans were then set in operation for my continued treatment. We chose the Mayo Clinic as the treatment facility.

Dorothy and Luanne cared for me until January 1976, when we began the first of many, many trips to the Mayo Clinic in Rochester, Minnesota.

Although I had been happy the day of my release from Wesley, how could I know then that my hurts had only begun. I remember one evening I went into the bathroom and for the first time realized the extent of the massive injuries I had sustained. Even though I had looked in a mirror many times previously, this time I saw what I looked like. I went to the den where Luanne was and we cried together like babies.

Surgeries continued over the next six years—most of these at the Mayo Clinic. (Many famous doctors and physicians hunted at our duck facility while I was going through my surgeries at the clinic.) I had several tongue operations and can now speak, although some people have a difficult time understanding me. I can make no lip words (*b, p,* etc.). It is hard to be a salesman and not be able to carry on a decent conversation. However, people are patient while I try to explain situations with my pencil.

My injury seriously affected my insurance sales. I had been a consistent million-dollar life producer for the Travelers for years, being in the upper 1 percent of all agents in the company.

C. D. after the accident with two Canadian honkers.
CREDIT: *Taken in December 1991 by a friend, and is a part of C. D. Tuggle's photo collection.*

It is disheartening to see fear and pain in others' eyes, and even though I wear a mask over my lower face to cover my deformity, I get discouraged when children look at me and cry in fright and run to a parent's protection. I become bored eating all of my meals through a syringe. I fondly remember candlelight steak dinners, and I feel so alone when I can't eat in public. I wish I had been more thankful for little things before the accident. Now I can't even smile. But I am grateful for my children's understanding.

Thirty-five surgeries later, I can tell you there is a living God. I could not have survived all of this alone. I am active in my church, where I chair some morning worship services, lead the congregation in prayer, serve on the board of trustees, and receive my Communion through a syringe at the public altar.

Through all of this, I thank God for my life. My burdens have allowed me to live closer to God. It has become absolutely impossible for me to turn my heart away from anyone in need. Because I lend money to widows, newly marrieds, and the hungry, my family has protected my income by placing my assets in a trust. They claim I do not have good judgment when it comes to helping others. They are right. God has tenderized my heart as I have battled my way through these trials. He has given me new priorities that others do not understand.

I agree with the author who wrote, "I expect to pass through this world but once; any good thing therefore that I can do, or any kindness that I can show to any fellow creature, let me do it now; let me not defer or neglect it, for I shall not pass this way again."

SURVIVAL APPENDIX

While reading adventure stories over the years, I have always been interested in the indomitable human spirit and the improvisation of people to overcome their adversity. Having lived in the outdoors and read about adventures afield for five decades, I would be remiss in submitting this book if I failed to offer specific principles for survival in the outdoors, hopefully enabling you to avoid consequences others suffered "out there."

I believe an outing is a pleasant and memorable experience. I define an adventure as an outing gone bad. We should be able to enjoy an outing without having it become an adventure.

Although this is by no means a comprehensive commentary, most of the necessary principles for surviving an adventure are listed below under the acronym CAMP SAFE:

C— Choose to survive—it's a choice most of the time
　　Common sense
　　Communication
　　Clothes—pants, rain gear, helmet, footgear, poncho
　　Conditioning—physical, mental, spiritual
A— Attitude—stay calm; refuse to quit; improvise (utilize whatever's available)
M—Mental
　　Mobile (keep self able to be mobile); don't move if you're lost unless you know for a certainty that your survival rests squarely on your shoulders
P— Preparation
　　Partner
　　Protection (take care of yourself against the elements, animals, and environment)
　　Practice
S— Self (care of yourself and your competence)
　　Shelter (from the elements)
　　Signaling device
A— Anticipation—don't take things for granted; anticipate things
　　Alcohol—discretion is essential regarding alcohol and other drugs afield
F— Fire
　　Food and water
　　Fuel
　　First aid
E— Experience (know self, partner, environment)

Equipment (brain, see list end of this chapter):
Fire starter
Compass
Signaling device—ELT, PLT, cell phone, handheld radio

Ingredients for Survival

Four items that top my survival list are (1) personal accountability, (2) common sense and proper mental attitude, (3) a fire starter, and (4) experience.

First and most importantly, the survivor must take care of himself. You are responsible for doing everything you can to improve your situation. Obviously one's chances of surviving are affected by the extent of one's injuries. If the survivor fails to take care of himself, he compounds his situation. He needs to keep warm and dry, maintain a positive attitude, and avail himself of food and water.

Second, common sense, mental attitude, and use of his brain top the list of items necessary for a man to survive. The more positive his attitude, the greater his chances of survival. Refuse to give up. And keep your mind alert to your situation. Choose to survive. Will to live. Control the situation rather than be controlled by it. Don't let anything break your spirit.

Third, a guaranteed fire starter is essential for heat and mental health. My preference in fire starters is a magnesium stick with a built-in spark strip. The magnesium is scraped into a pile and the spark stick scraped to produce a spark, which ignites the magnesium. Cold is master in winter—to ignore or disobey the rules of survival is to invite certain hardship, frostbite, or death. Weather often dictates man's schedule.

Fourth, there is no substitute for experience. The more experience a person gathers, the better he can face different situations with confidence. However, experience is no guarantee against mishap, as many experienced woodsmen have had misadventures. If outdoorsmen with years of experience have had close calls with the grim reaper, how important is it for the inexperienced to apprise himself of the dangers "out there" and to prepare properly?

Your expertise should reflect your knowledge of yourself, your partner, your equipment, and your environment.

Know yourself: What is your experience? Can you handle the expedition you're undertaking? Don't rely upon yourself entirely. Your survival gear may save you . . . but not if you leave it at home. Know survival skills and have first-aid knowledge including CPR and the Heimlich maneuver.

Know your partner: Is he someone you can depend on in a critical situation?

Know your equipment: A person can survive nearly all outdoor catastrophes with a minimum of equipment. The outdoorsman's survival kit is a must. The more items a person has, the greater his chances of survival. Survival equipment varies with the type of environment (see end list).

Know your environment: If you're in strange country, familiarize yourself with the use of topographical maps and others' input in order to successfully confront your environment, find proper edibles, and get out to civilization. We are often captives of our environment and must act appropriately.

To attempt to educate the inexperienced about the wilderness is a poor substitute for actual face-to-face involvement. Only by going into the hinterlands can a greenhorn experience firsthand the horizontal sheets of rain hammering a flimsy, ill-designed tent, or a one-day goat hunt bathed in early-morning sunlight that turns to snowfall on the peak endangering descent, etc.

Don't be hamstrung by ignorance . . . because it could kill.

A number of other principles apply to survival.

Preparation for the outing is important. As in the saying "I didn't plan to fail; I failed to plan," preparation is essential. The survivor must take everything about his outing into consideration—transportation, weather, clothing, equipment, and health and condition of each person in the party. Be prepared to provide first aid for various injuries, including not breathing, bleeding, broken bones, and shock.

It is essential to *communicate*—before you leave, during the outing, and while seeking rescue. Tell someone where you're going and when you plan to return. Do not change your planned destination. Leave a map of the locale or the latitude and longitude. Make sure someone will check on you at least once a week. You need to tell more than one reliable person your plans and to leave word that if you're not back within a certain time frame, to start a search immediately.

A person needs a signaling device, be it a personal locator transmitter (PLT), emergency locator transmitter (ELT), cell phone, handheld radio, flare, mirror, or other device to get someone's attention. Often the best signal is the smoke from a fire or during night hours the fire's flames. After your return, notify the necessary officials or others of your safe arrival. If you encounter severe conditions or a marauding animal, leave a note at a trailhead or inform officials.

While afield, make sure you and your partners have a thorough understanding of plans and any signals—which direction each person plans to take, destination, times to meet, and alternative plans.

If you become lost, stop—sit down, think, observe, and plan. It is nearly always best to stay where you are.

In many ways the "old" Alaska differs from the "new," but some things, like communication, never change.

Many outings are just that. The experience is nothing unusual—people return from their wilderness trip with pleasant memories. However, some outings are far more than that. They are adventures—an outing gone bad. Although it is unintended, countless outings evolve into full-blown adventures. In many instances one day leads to another, new wrinkles unfold, extending the outing into a horrible event that nearly always results in life-changing circumstances.

Frequently trouble is undetected until it's too late—overflow water on ice, soft ice, thin ice, partially covered chasm (snow bridge), camouflaged hole, sweeper on river, icing conditions, mudflats, poisonous and water reptiles such as rattlesnakes and alligators, water levels, animal "sign" or other calamity, travel in diverse terrain such as bayous, swamps, desert, or mountains. It is important to educate yourself and gain experience to deal with myriad problems:

- know the dangers outside our temperature-controlled wombs in vehicles . . . the outdoors;
- never travel an isolated roadway with no knowledge of its dangers and never forge ahead through deep snow;
- know how to read "signs"—be they weather conditions, road, or animal; and
- never fly without acknowledging the vacillating waves on a lake's surface (microburst activity) and never continue into a storm (the same applies to piloting a boat).   The following anecdotes provide insight into some survival situations that you may encounter.

Communication/Oversight

Most outdoor emergencies are the result of some oversight.

In the case of two Kodiak brown-bear hunters—David Embry and his friend Marty—a little miscommunication nearly proved their undoing. They had been dropped off by an air taxi in October 1987 in Deadman Bay, to be picked up by the pilot ten days later.

They were dropped at Horse Marine canyon and enjoyed the early part of the hunt in this beautiful fjord. From their beach campsite, the landscape oozed upward, covered by thick alder patches and backdropped by sheer, snow-covered mountain slopes. Eagles wheeled overhead, seagulls shrieked, and waves rhythmically washed the beach.

Dave shot his bear and wrestled the wet hide back to camp. A blizzard kept Marty from filling his tag. As the day of their pickup arrived, they were enthused about the prospect of returning to civilization. But the plane never showed.

The hunters were not prepared for the weather they faced—hurricane-force winds, rain turning to snow, temperatures near zero. Their tent was designed for warmer climates. Snow mugged their tent and condensation covered the inside, wetting their sleeping bags. To further complicate their dilemma, their inexperience kept them from living off the sea's bounty.

They grew weaker with each passing day. Deteriorating weather conditions and their need for warmth and food dictated they seek shelter elsewhere.

Dave recalled having read about Hal Waugh, legendary early-day Alaskan guide, who had built cabins at the head of the bay. Dave believed their only hope for survival was to find the cabins. The men picked up a flare gun, one rifle, and their frozen sleeping bags and started up the beach.

Their misery-plagued journey found them across the bay from the cabins . . . a solitary stream barring their way. They waded into the cold water, which reached shoulder depth, before they gained the opposite bank. They found wood in abundance, built a fire, and warmed up. Their next order of business was to construct an SOS and await rescue—never realizing that thirty-two days would pass before a pilot spotted them.

The aviator, having retrieved their gear and bear hide earlier, landed and transported the hunters back to Kodiak, where they learned the cause of their belated pickup.

The young pilot who had dropped them off a month earlier had returned to Kodiak, marked the pickup date on the calendar, then left on a month's vacation. On October 29, the pickup date, Kodiak's normally unpredictable weather proved worse than usual, negating flying. On the last day of the month an unobservant worker ripped the page from the calendar and tossed it into the garbage . . . without transferring the pickup date to the first day of November!

Clothing/Communication

Two other hunters gained a great deal of experience and respect for preparation while on a casual hunt. It is not likely that they will repeat their hurriedly planned outing (Bill Corning and Wally Gunderson, "We Felt Ourselves Freezing," *Alaska Sportsman,* April 1967).

Nightfall on January 28, 1967, found Bill Corning and Wally Gunderson contemplating their situation. They were pinned on a four-by-six-foot ledge at the 1,250-foot level of a mountain. Earlier in the day they and their skipper, Gary Cobbin, had pulled crab pots from Chugach Bay near Portlock. Rough seas had forced them into a sheltered harbor. Three hundred yards from shore, while waiting for the water to calm, they spotted goats on the mountains.

All three men agreed they could use a break and went ashore in their skiff (with rifle, camera, and binoculars) to pursue the majestic animals.

The skipper went off to scout a valley while Bill and Wally took a direct route up through the spruce forest at the foot of the mountains. Halfway to the 1,850-foot summit, the pair ran out of timber and encountered a near vertical wall. The next three hundred feet required cutting hand- and footholds in the snow. They mounted a ledge only to discover that they were trapped . . . descending would be impossible without endangering their lives.

Below them, their ship, the *Violet,* rode at anchor. Gary soon appeared. The hunters fired off the universal three-shot signal; however, Gary could not locate them.

Accompanying the fading light was a drop in the temperature. The wind picked up to twenty-five to thirty-five miles per hour—making the windchill forty degrees below zero. The wind's increasing velocity escalated the men's concern.

Their clothing was woefully inadequate for a night on the mountain, consisting of rubber boots, light socks, short underwear, pants, T-shirts, coats, and gloves (holes in Wally's exposed his fingers). In addition, Bill wore a wool shirt and thermal-underwear bottoms.

Although they had cigarettes and lighters, they had no food and no fuel.

As night set in, they huddled together for warmth, taking turns rubbing each other's arms and back to stimulate warmth. Limited to the small area, they kept moving their feet and arms to maintain circulation. With a half dozen goats nearby the men took turns napping, both shivering the night away.

Sunday brought daylight and another boat to the bay. Search planes circled. By noon the men had run out of cigarettes. The men fired their rifle and shouted, but no one saw or heard them. They knew the danger of freezing and kept moving their hands and feet slowly to maintain circulation without inducing perspiring (which would accelerate body cooling). They periodically placed their hands beneath their armpits to warm them. They ate snow for liquid.

By Sunday afternoon they could still move their toes. Nightfall witnessed the arrival of the Coast Guard cutter *Confidence* (a helicopter on board charged their hopes).

Both men knew that time was running out—either they would be rescued or the freezing cold would claim them.

Monday morning Bill and Wally acknowledged their feet were freezing. They felt no pain, only numbness. Their urge to escape intensified; however, knowing that moving on frozen feet in their weakened condition could result in injury, they chose to stay put. They prayed for a hasty rescue.

The Coast Guard helicopter flew the mountain all day—once passing close enough for them to feel its downwash.

Wally's hands were freezing. Bill felt the freezing numbness moving up his legs, making standing difficult. By Monday night neither man had feeling in his feet.

After a gruelingly cold night, day broke on Tuesday. The men knew this was their final day of life if not rescued. The helicopter search continued.

At noon Second Class Petty Officer Richard McCoy spotted them. The pilot lowered a basket and plucked Bill off the ledge. Moments later the chopper returned. McCoy dropped on a line to assist Wally.

The helicopter immediately flew the hunters to Providence Hospital in Anchorage. On arrival, Wally's temperature was eighty degrees and Bill's was ninety. They were given the whirlpool treatment developed by world frostbite authority Dr. William J. Mills Jr. Most of the men's feet and hands were saved.

And they saved a lesson from their experience—dress accordingly (with extra dry clothes); retain the safest location; conserve energy; don't panic.

Mental Preparation

Often while experiencing a misadventure people give up (or at least consider giving up). Causes vary but include discomfort (we're not used to extreme cold, swimming in cold water, climbing on ice, etc., and would rather not deal with it); our inability or frustration in dealing with the misadventure, isolation from aid, improper equipment, uncooperative weather, or lack of survival skills.

Often it is easier to give up and give in—a friend who was trapped underwater in his Super Cub airplane felt he'd done all he could and thought, "This is what it's like to die." In "Look for a Corpse," Fred Easley felt it would be easier to quit digging himself out of the avalanche and just surrender to the numbness of his situation.

Partner/Anticipate the Unexpected

One can never know what will happen in an outing, however the more experience one has and gleans from others' experiences, the better prepared one is for whatever may happen. Surely as Rick Janelle departed the beach in search of Sitka blacktail deer on November 24, 1985, he had no way of surmising this hunt was nearly his last (Robert Lee Parish, *Alaska Where Only the Tough Survive* [Cordova, Alaska: Fathom Publishing Company, 1987]).

Rick was one of several hunters aboard Mark Peterson's *Connie N*. He was dropped off on the beach at South Island along with two others. The men headed into the woods, agreeing to meet on the beach by 2:30 P.M.

Rick slipped silently uphill toward a favorite hunting spot. Scattered snow patches remained from a previous snowfall. Within a mile of the beach he spotted a bedded buck. Janelle fired at the deer's head, and the animal lurched to its hooves and bounced away uphill. Disappointed and angry with himself for missing, Rick looked for signs of blood, then continued on.

Minutes later, while enjoying the surroundings, Rick detected his quarry above on the hillside and determined to redeem himself. He drew down on the buck and in nearly the same motion slipped and fell.

Landing on his back, he felt a stab of pain. Rick was momentarily stunned. While gathering his thoughts he rubbed his back and was shocked when he noticed blood on his hand. He reached back to assess the wound, slipping a finger into a hole between his lowest rib and pelvis.

Rick discovered a tree snag on the ground covered with his blood. As the urgency of rescue overcame him, he realized his only hope for survival was to stem the blood flow, keep his senses, and get to the beach immediately. He quickly removed his wool sweater and shirt, fashioning a compress. He knotted the compress over the wound, replaced his sweater, and started down the slope.

Rick slithered and slid, supporting himself by holding on to berry bushes and trees. Brush, downfalls, and treacherous footing hampered his descent. However, the foliage was only part of the barrier he faced, as psychologically it became harder and harder to go on. The farther he went, the more chest pain he experienced. Breathing was more difficult. He willed himself forward, forcing each step.

The shimmering water below seemed to mock him. Waves of nausea nearly overcame him. The struggle for each breath greatly weakened him, and he wondered if he'd make it.

Nearly three hours slipped excruciatingly past before Rick staggered onto the beach. A short distance beyond, a cabin beckoned. With his final effort Rick reached the shelter and weakly knocked on the door.

His knock was met by Ken Marlowe. Marlowe eased the injured man into a chair. Gently removing the sweater, Marlowe taped a compress over the wound. All they could do was wait for Janelle's partners to exit the woods and hope the *Connie N* would arrive soon.

Sometime later Rick's partners and the *Connie N* showed up. Gravely aware of the danger Janelle faced, skipper Mark Peterson called the Coast Guard on his radio. When a doctor arrived at the cabin and examined Rick, he discovered Rick's blood vessels had collapsed.

Janelle was immediately helicoptered to Bartlett Memorial Hospital in Juneau. Doctors determined he had a punctured lung. Blood had filled his chest cavity and deflated his lung, causing the difficulty in his breathing. The blood was siphoned out, relieving the pressure and allowing him to breathe more freely. Five days later he left the hospital with a new appreciation for life and respect for the unexpected.

Communication and Thorough Preparation

One tragic event that transpired before Alaska's statehood could have been avoided.

Two men, Dr. Allberry, who was about fifty years old, and a young man went to Montague Island, to prospect or beachcomb. The young chap had been a deck hand onboard the *Siren,* a famous Prince William Sound boat, for one season.

Montague Island lies one hundred miles southeast of Anchorage and separates the Gulf of Alaska from Prince William Sound. This island is fifty-four miles long and twelve miles wide at its widest point.

A boat captain dropped the men, their equipment, and enough grub for a month's stay at McLoud Harbor on Montague. A month later the captain returned for the men, but they were not to be found. There was no sign that they were anywhere near, so he assumed that another skipper had picked up the men.

A second month passed.

Then a third elapsed with no sign of the men. At that point the Moose Lodge in Nome hired Pete Nicholoff to look for the missing men. Pete was the skipper of the *Siren,* as famous as his craft and just as dependable.

Certain the men were still on the island, Pete theorized they had hiked over the island from east to west coming out at Nellie Martin River, the site of two abandoned trapper's cabins and a logical spot to be picked up by boat. Such a hike was nearly incomprehensible since the men would have to cross three mountains nearly three thousand feet high and tramp several snow-covered miles in severely cold weather.

On a cold, gray day with a knife-edged, icy wind slicing the island Pete dropped anchor in the bay. Viewing the distant cabins through the leafless alder brush, Pete dreaded what he might find in the dwellings.

Silence reigned.

No life stirred.

Mere moments later Pete spotted movement some two hundred yards up the beach. He immediately assumed it was a bear out of winter hibernation. Then it dawned on him that the figure was the shell of a man hunched over almost double. The frightful figure stopped and looked toward the boat, seemed to wipe his eyes, then shaded them. Next, in an awkward running motion, he stumbled down the beach.

The men aboard the *Siren* lowered the skiff overboard and rowed for shore.

When the men reached shore and saw Doc more closely, Pete hardly recognized the husky man he had known. Doc Allberry looked like a skeleton in a ragged parka, eyes sunk in and cheeks hollow. Doc tried to smile and told them that he had seen a boat so often he thought he was dreaming. He then reached out his hand and fell forward in a dead faint. Doc's young friend wasn't so fortunate. They found him in the second cabin frozen solid.

Later the men reached the boat and got part of Doc's story . . . the men had hiked across the island where the younger man starved within a couple of weeks. Doc managed to stay alive for eighty-three days on a few mussels he found on the beach.

This is another strong message for communication and proper preparation while experiencing Alaska's great beyond.

Attitude/Keep Your Head

Alfred Wolfe's *In Alaskan Waters* tells of Alfred's friend's tragic experience.(1)

On August 13, 1920, the schooner *Daisy* sailed out of Seattle. While it was anchored in a hundred fathoms of water on the halibut banks off the coast of British Columbia and seventy-five miles from the nearest medical facility at Albert Bay, tragedy struck.

That dismal, drizzly, foggy dawn the crew went on deck to pull the 250-pound anchor attached to a four-and-a-half-inch rope-cable. A strong swell and a deck awash with fish slime made standing difficult.

Retrieving the anchor with the use of a power winch required every man aboard to haul and coil the rope-cable. The skipper started the winch engine. While Alfred's friend O. Vanebo ran the winch, Alfred took two or three quick turns on the niggerhead and started to haul. The other men stood four or five feet apart hauling the line to assist the winch in breaking loose the anchor.

As the winch struggled against the weight of the anchor and the pull of the sea, the *Daisy* unexpectedly rolled. Vanebo stumbled and fell. In an effort to regain his balance, he threw out his right hand, which caught between the niggerhead and the taut cable.

Seeing his predicament, his shipmates froze in horror.

While the niggerhead wound the cable, those closest to Vanebo heard the bones in his fingers cracking and saw blood squirting from his hand in all directions. Next came Vanebo's wrist. Then his forearm. And finally his upper arm. At every turn the men heard more bones crunching.

Vanebo showed no sign of pain. No expression crossed his face, which was as hard and white as marble. No sound escaped his tightly clenched lips.

Everyone on board knew that the only way to stop the winch was to stop the engine. Yet no one moved.

While others stood in silent paralysis, Vanebo shouted, "Stop the engine! If you don't, I'm a goner." (1)

As if awakening from a trance, the skipper lunged to the engine and threw the switch. Vanebo's shipmates unwound the cable, which grudgingly relinquished his mangled mass of blood, shattered bones, pulpy muscles, tendons, and ligaments.

Refusing succor from his crewmates, Vanebo rose to this six-foot height, his hand dangling nearly to the deck. In a firm but weak voice he commanded, "Get a knife and cut those things so I can get a bandage on and check the bleeding."(1)

No one moved. Barely breathing, the men stood agape.

Vanebo grabbed a dull, rusty fish knife and hacked through the pulp that hung from his shoulder. Having removed it from his body, he tossed the globby mass into the sea, where it landed on floating kelp before slowly sinking into the depths.

The captain wanted to cut the anchor line to save time, but Vanebo told him that wouldn't return his arm. At length with the anchor aboard the skipper set his course for Albert Bay.

No one aboard but Vanebo believed he'd live.

He refused a tourniquet and swathed his stub with towels. Blood oozed through the towels onto the deck and out through the scuppers.

Vanebo asked for food and quaffed strong, black coffee.

Twelve and a half hours later Vanebo was hoisted onto the dock in a fish box and falteringly walked to the hospital.

The doctor said only Vanebo's will to live, his courage, his refusal to faint or sleep kept him alive.

Partner

Hardy Trefzger, an old-time prospector-trapper from southeast Alaska, made a grisly find when he and his friend Carl were on a prospecting trip in the summer of 1918.

In August they came across a six-by-six-foot cabin which they suspected was that of the "wild man of the Alsek River." There was no sign of life. Hardy looked through a hole along the stovepipe and saw the empty bunk. In the meantime Carl gingerly opened the door. Upon the bunk in the dank, dark cabin were the remains of the wild man.

It appeared wolverines had eaten the man. Carl and Hardy moved the clothes on the bunk and saw a single-action .44 revolver, a spent cartridge under the hammer. Then they found the skull, a hole in the middle of the forehead with an inch-and-a-half hole through the back. The force of the bullet lifted the top of the skull off as clearly as if by a saw.

They found and read the man's diary, which chronicled his tragic last six months: In early October he had got a cold in the lungs, which resulted in a high fever. The next week he got stronger and started building his cabin, later finishing a smoke house. He shot a number of animals including bear, goats, and wolf. In November he made bearskin pants, two pairs of moccasins, a pair of snowshoes, a fur coat, and a bear-goat-canvas sleeping bag.

Beginning in December his health worsened, which he blamed on his diet of nine-tenth meat. The entire month was very cold with much snow, the river remained open allowing poor travel, and he was low on grub. He broke through the ice. His stomach got worse.

Although most of January promised great weather, his health was very poor. He got two lynx and a goat. He subsisted on salt and tea once a day in early February. He shot a goat. By the end of the month he was eating dry meat and tallow, and his health had improved.

The trapper tried to go to Dry Bay in March, but travel was difficult, and he managed to return to his cabin after four or five days. His eyes were getting bad.

In April a wolverine came through the stovepipe and tried to run him out. He shot a goat using all but three shells because he couldn't see his rifle sights. He had more wolverine and vision problems (from the sun's glare). By midmonth he was very weak, had little grub, and spent most of the time in bed. On the twentieth he cooked his last food. His legs wouldn't support his weight. On the twenty-second his eyes were useless for hunting as was the remainder of his body. He jotted down a will. The twenty-fourth of April was crossed off on his calendar.

Hardy and Carl buried the wild man and left a hand-carved headboard with the trapper's name on it.

Experience

In *Sourdough and Swahili: A Professional Hunter on Two Continents,* Bud Branham relates his friend's winter dilemma while running his trapline. (2)

During the winter of 1940–41, Bud Branham worked his Rainy Pass trapline and mentored his friend Paul Vance. Bud thought Paul's experience trapping, driving the dog team, caring for the animals, and surviving winter conditions prepared him adequately, so he gave Paul his blessings to try the line alone.

While following the trapline twenty miles to Bud's Shirley Lake cabin the first day in minus-thirty-degree weather, Paul had no problems. He spent an uncomfortably cold night and planned to move on toward the Skwentna River the following day.

Even though more snow had accumulated during the night and Paul knew that the snow depth was greater in the lower elevations, he continued on to the Portage Creek cabin on the Skwentna. As he negotiated the steep slope, snow held the sled back, making the going easier. However, the deepening snow on the river's ice caused Paul difficulty. After traveling for some time in foot-deep snow, he donned his snowshoes to break trail for the dog team. His increased activity caused him to perspire more, a danger in cold weather.

With nearly five miles separating him from the cabin and knowing that he could make it easier without the sled, Paul abandoned it and took the dogs, his rifle, and snowshoes and headed toward the dwelling. After a while Paul reconsidered the likelihood of reaching the cabin by nightfall. He decided to spend the night in the woods, building a fire and getting as comfortable as possible until the next morning. He found a canopy of spruce deadfalls, shoveled out the snow beneath them, and gathered fresh boughs for a bed.

A short time later the snowfall stopped and with clearing skies the temperature plummeted. Paul's wet clothes began freezing. He knew he couldn't last the night and immediately set out for Portage Creek.

Before long he was too exhausted to lift the toes of his snowshoes out of the snow. Bud's lead dog, Kenai, took charge as Paul sent the dogs ahead. Removing the snowshoes, he jammed them upright in the snow and continued on as the dogs broke trail.

Slowly slogging along the river, hour upon agonizing hour dragged by while Paul witnessed daylight turn to darkness. Yet he moved on. Finally reaching the creek, he started upstream, cautiously picking his way from side to side to avoid breaking through the ice. A few miles later Paul followed the dogs across a section of thin ice. Normally the dogs would have detected the thin ice and refused to cross; however, several inches of snow disguised the danger that awaited Paul.

Just after the dogs crossed, Paul plunged through the ice over his boot tops. Lurching from the creek, he scrambled to shore, quickly removed his boots, and wrung out his soaked socks. Replacing his socks and boots, he moved out.

Fighting exhaustion and cold, Paul lurched on. After each rest stop he had more difficulty rising. When he was within a half mile of the cabin, he stopped to rest and couldn't rise until Kenai licked his face, making him more alert. He strained to his feet and staggered on, reaching the cabin around midnight. He entered and with Herculean effort built a fire.

Paul put his feet into the stove's oven to thaw his boots enough to remove them. He inspected his badly frostbitten feet. His left foot was frozen from his toes to his instep, the toes being black.

He ate and drank warm fluids and managed to keep the stove going all night.

Paul removed several blankets used as a bed mattress and covered himself with them.

The cabin contained food and Paul knew that he would not go hungry. Dog food in the form of moose meat hung from the meat pole outside.

Paul knew Bud would be worried and probably start a search for him. He knew he could not move until his feet were sufficiently healed, which would take days.

He fashioned an SOS outside the cabin, but the plane that flew over the third day did not see it. Each new day brought more snow.

Nearly two weeks later with moose meat for the dogs diminishing, Paul's strength increasing, and his feet healing, he started the eighteen miles to the Rainy Pass cabin. That morning a plane flew over the cabin and spotted Paul, giving him hope that the pilot would pass on word to Bud.

As Paul progressed up the slope, the snow depth decreased. A few miles beyond he found a candy bar tied to an upright stick in the snow. Paul realized that even though Bud didn't know where Paul was, Bud was searching and had left the candy to encourage Paul.

Descending Round Mountain and nearing Puntilla's old cabin, Paul saw open water and stopped to drink. He knew he was dehydrated and cautioned himself about drinking too much. He struggled on and was within a mile of the home cabin when he saw more open water and stopped for another drink.

Secure in his knowledge of safety nearby at the cabin, Paul succumbed to the temptation and drank too much, causing hypothermia to set in. He lost his strength. Unable to rise, he commanded Kenai to go to the cabin for Bud. The dog ran only a short distance before turning to look at Paul, then began howling.

Dogs at the cabin howled in return, alerting Bud. He gathered rescue gear and set out in search of Paul. Bud found Paul, got him to his feet, and assisted him to the cabin. Paul remained bedridden for two weeks, then slowly recovered.

Experience

Con Bunde wrote in *Alaska Sportsman* that he had been on a southeast Alaska goat hunt with friends.(3) Because of his youth and enthusiasm he took their advice with a grain of salt and took off up the mountain alone.

He spotted a billy goat and climbed a chimney. Reaching the top, he realized he faced a vertical wall with no way to continue. Because of the treacherousness of the slope and the narrow ledge he was on, he questioned his ability to descend safely—he was okay facing the wall, however his pack's thickness thrust him out away from the cliff into space whenever he tried to turn his back to the wall.

At length he remembered and retrieved a thirty-foot strand of rope from his outside pack pocket. He lowered his pack onto a rock slide below, slung his rifle around his neck, and managed to descend to safety.

*   *   *

A requisite for life is communication. Slim Williams was a young man working out of Valdez, Alaska, around 1900. He'd observed a tent for a few days, the only sign of life being some sled dogs. Curious, Slim investigated the tent. He approached the dwelling and "helloed." The tent's occupant responded weakly, bidding him enter. Slim found a sick old-timer, prepared him food and drink, nursed him a bit, and mushed him to Valdez in the man's dogsled. Grateful that Slim had intervened to save his life, the old-timer gave Slim his outfit, including his three dogs.

Anticipation

In the late 1940s Iris Warner went to bed while her husband, Al, worked the night shift at a placer mine near Atlin, British Columbia.(4) When she went to bed, the temperature was minus fifteen. During her nearly sleepless night, Iris discovered that her dog and cat had joined her in bed. She shoved them away.

Twice more they returned as she lethargically tried to understand the coldness in the room and her inability to get warm. Through the cobwebs of her mind she realized that her jaw was tightly closed, that she was unable to open her mouth.

Iris gradually realized that she needed to do something to warm up the cabin. Lurching from the bed, she discovered her hands were unbending and her foot like ice chunks. She flapped her arms about in an effort to bring feeling and use to her hands. Gradually she managed to dress. After great effort Iris lit the lantern, then stumbled to the stove and lit the fire.

Feeling a cold draft, Iris discovered the living-room window was broken. She patched up the opening, assuming the dog had broken it in the couple's absence the evening before.

At dawn Iris read the thermometer, which registered minus fifty-five. Because of an unexpected broken window, she had nearly frozen in bed.

Know Your Environment

One of the stories from Alaska's early days involved Slim Williams, an old-time Alaskan dog musher. It relates one of the dangers of glacial crevasses.

As a young man Slim arrived in Valdez, Alaska, and took a job sledding goods inland. Every day was a challenge and an adventure spiked with danger and fraught with life-threatening events, especially while crossing a glacier near town.

One day while approaching the glacier he encountered a group of men in the midst of a great commotion. He stopped and discovered that one of the group, Tom, had slid off the trail and fallen into a glacial crevasse.

Men stood on the lip of the crevasse, holding a lantern aloft, peering into the black below for their partner.

Peeling off his parka, Slim volunteered to descend to determine Tom's condition. Slim assured the men he was skinnier than they and he might be able to help their partner, who was even smaller than he. Prepared to report his findings and with a rope about him, Slim told the men to keep it tight while lowering him. Then he edged over the side.

Moments later he hailed them to stop. He'd descended twenty feet, a full six feet farther than they'd previously descended.

Slim spoke with the unseen, trapped man and ascertained that he'd shot off the main crevasse into a side crack. Slim knew rescue was hopeless and called for the men to pull him up.

Once on the rim, Slim slipped into his parka and told the men that Tom had slid into a side crevasse and sounded as if he was in a large chamber with a tiny opening. He told them that he was wedged so tight he couldn't move, and he was nowhere near Tom. Sadly he explained that rescue was futile.

Slim assured the men that Tom would get cold and go to sleep, dying a painless death. He apologized for not being able to do more and continued on his journey.

On Slim's return trip he spoke with one of the men who had stayed behind with Tom. The faithful friend told him that Tom's last words expressed his lack of pain and his desire to take a nap. Thus ended an early prospector's dreams of finding the mother lode, another victim of the danger that stalks the Great Land.

Minimal Survival Gear List

I suggest you research survival books and produce your own list for your undertaking. Then incorporate a survival preparedness checklist and evaluate it every time you leave home.

Minimal equipment should include:

Fire starter—magnesium stick, cigarette lighter, matches

Space blanket

Compass

Signal device—mirror, flares, GPS, ELT, PLB, handheld radio (or cell phone) and flashlight

Shelter material—poncho

Adequate clothing and footgear (cotton kills—I recommend wool or polypropylene)

Rain gear

Maps

Salt tablets

First-aid kit

Rope or cord

Adequate sleeping bag (that will produce warmth—down not recommended)

Nutritional food and water

Survival Preparedness Checklist

Before you leave, check yourself out to see if you're ready to go:

___ I am prepared for this activity.

___ I have the necessary equipment (in good condition) to return safely.

___ I have anticipated circumstances and will continue to do so until safely home.

___ I have left directions to my proposed destination.

___ I have also left these directions with a backup person.

___ I have given the estimated time of my return.

___ I have an infallible fire starter.

___ I have access to fuel.

___ I have my survival kit that includes Vaseline-soaked cotton balls.

___ My survival gear is accessible.

___ I have the necessary clothing and footgear to return safely.

___ My pilot/air carrier is qualified and cautious.

___ I will make sure he has enough fuel and that it is not contaminated.

___ My skipper is safe on the water.

___ I am physically capable of this task, including swimming to shore.

___ I know the characteristics of avalanches and will avoid them.

___ My partners are equally qualified to return safely.

___ I have the necessary maps, know where I'm going, and know how to reach civilization.

___ I have an adequate weapon for any circumstance (red pepper may not stop a charging bear).

___ I know the symptoms of and will avoid hypothermia.

___ My physical conditioning will enable me to help myself and my partners to safety.

___ I have chosen to survive and refuse to give up.

SOURCE NOTES

TOO LITTLE, TOO LATE
Personal interview with Lynn Puddicombe, November 1988, in his Palmer, Alaska, home.

NEVER GIVE UP
Personal interview with Randy Cazac, December 2, 1998, at his Anchorage home.

FIRE AND ICE
From *Billy Mitchell in Alaska*, excerpted in *An Alaskan Reader*, ed. Ernest Gruening (New York: Meredith Press, 1996), chap. 14.

DEATH'S COLD GRIP
Personal stay, interview, and ongoing correspondence with Jack Whitman, beginning March 1997, McGrath and Sitka, Alaska.

FAIRWEATHER NEARLY WON
Personal interview with Calvin Lauwers in my English classroom at Dimond High School, Anchorage, Alaska, October 31, 1991, 6:55 A.M., and subsequent meetings and conversations.

Personal correspondence via E-mail with Eric Peterson, Calvin's climbing partner, February and March 1999.

LOOK FOR A CORPSE
Fred Easley (as told to K. A. Taylor), "Reported Dead," *Alaska Sportsman,* June 1943, pp. 10–11, 27–29.

NEARLY TOO LATE
Denise Harris and Roger Lewis, "We Nearly Froze to Death," *Alaska Magazine,* May 1980, pp. 20–23, and June 1980, pp. 11–14.

SOLE SURVIVOR
1. "Eklutna plane crash leaves 3 dead," *Anchorage Times,* August 24, 1991, pp. B-1, B-11.
2. John Foley, "Air crash survivor stabilizes," *Anchorage Times,* August 25, 1991, pp. B-1, B-8.

3. Pamela Doto, "Long night for woman in crash," *Anchorage Daily News,* August 25, 1991, pp. B-1, B-3.

4. Phone conversation with James Michelangelo, head of National Transportation Safety Board, Anchorage office, August 26, 1991.

5. John Foley, "Woman survives air crash," *Anchorage Times,* August 26, 1991, p. B-1.

A TAIL AND A PRAYER

Personal visit with Pastor Paul Weimer, Friday, November 27, 1998, at his Dimond Boulevard Baptist Church in Anchorage. Condensation of his taped and written story.

DEATH STALKED THE ICE

Ed Fortier, "The Incredible Journey," *Alaska Sportsman,* February 1969, pp. 7–9, 46; (part II) March 1969, pp. 14–17, 53.

DEATH WORE WHITE

1. Diana Elliott, "Avalanche buries Anchorage snowmachiner," *Anchorage Times,* December 30, 1990, pp. A-1, A-7.

2. Charles Wohlforth, "Search party unable to locate avalanche victim," *Anchorage Daily News,* December 31, 1990, pp. A-1, A-10.

3. Larry Campbell, "Searchers continue probe of avalanches," *Anchorage Daily News,* January 1, 1991, pp. B-1, B-3.

4. Pamela Doto, "Searchers find man's vehicle," *Anchorage Daily News,* January 3, 1991, pp. B-1, B-3.

5. Pamela Doto, "Searchers find snowmachiner's body," *Anchorage Daily News,* January 6, 1991, p. B-3.

6. Gail Boxrud, "Body found 325 feet away from initial slide," *Anchorage Times,* January 6, 1991, pp. A-1, A-7.

7. Hugh Curran, "Avalanche kills snowmachiner," *Anchorage Daily News,* March 29, 1994, pp. A-1, A-8.

8. "Snowmachiner again cheats death in avalanche," *Anchorage Daily News,* February 10, 1996, p. D-3.

A FRIEND IS LOST

Personal interview with Jack Parret, Wednesday, January 20, 1999, at Cornerstone Church of God in Anchorage, Alaska.

WHEN A FRIEND FALLS

Phone interview and continued correspondence with Steve Hanson, Talkeetna, Alaska, January through March 1999.

MIRACLE MAN
Personal interview with Gary Franklin during the spring of 1994 and subsequent visits to his and wife Dorothy's home in Anchorage, utilization of their written account and Dorothy's journal.

Scott Weber, "The Divine Touch," *Guideposts*, April 1998, p. 46.

DEATH STALKED THE EDGE
Personal interview with Loretta Andress and Stanley Truelson story at Stan's home in Anchorage, December 6, 1998.

Personal story of Mindy Stephenson "Tragedy on the Mountain."
1. Craig Medred and Marilee Enge, "Boy hurt in fall," *Anchorage Daily News*, June 14, 1991, pp. B-1, B-4.
2. Scott Reeves and David Futch, " 'He just got away from me,' " *Anchorage Times*, June 14, 1991, pp. A-1, A-15.
3. Daniel R. Saddler and John Foley, "Nine-year-old dies after Flattop fall," *Anchorage Times*, June 15, 1991, pp. A-1, A-14.
4. Marilee Enge, "Fall victim helps others," *Anchorage Daily News*, June 15, 1991, pp. B-1, B-15.
5. "Hundreds remember Flattop victim," *Anchorage Times*, June 18, 1991, p. B-1.
6. Jay Blucher and Don Hunter, "Hiker dies on Flattop," *Anchorage Daily News*, June 8, 1992, pp. A-1, A-8.

DATE WITH DEATH
1. Craig Medred, "Kayak trip on the Sound ends in tragedy," *Anchorage Daily News*, August 23, 1989, pp. A-1, A-10.
2. Craig Medred, "Deaths on the water: Painful questions haunt survivor, writer," *Anchorage Daily News*, August 27, 1989, pp. G-1, G-5.

IT WILL NEVER HAPPEN TO ME
I met Mike Wise in Kotzebue in November 1998 and he later sent his story via E-mail.

FUNCTIONAL RELATIONSHIP WITH GOD
Personal visits with and stories from Jerry Olson since 1992, his home, my home, in between.

Personal contact with Jim Brenn, who recommended a couple of stories, and ongoing conversations since 1996.

IN THE FACE OF DEATH
1. "Bear Attacks Lone Trapper," *The Valdez Miner*, December 17, 1927, p. C-5.
2. "Injured Trapper Will Save Limbs," *The Valdez Miner*, December 24, 1927, p. C-6.

"COME QUICK! I'M BEING EATEN BY A BEAR!"
From Larry Kaniut, *Alaska Bear Tales* (Seattle, Wash.: Alaska Northwest Books, 1983).

AGAINST ALL ODDS
Personal interview with Dennis Gum and his wife, "Rocky," at Red Robin, Northway Mall, Anchorage, Alaska, fall 1997. Subsequent meetings.

A BROTHER'S LOVE
Bill Vaudrin, "Gunshot," *Alaska Sportsman*, October 1966, pp. 23–25, 54–56, 59.

MY HAUNTING NIGHTMARE
Personal correspondence and visits in my home with Bill Zeddies from 1991 to 1998.

MISTAKES CAN KILL
Personal interview with Mike Legler, January 24, 1994, at McDonald's on Tudor Road near Lake Otis in Anchorage, Alaska, and several follow-up visits.

NO SIGN OF LIFE
1. "Abandoned alone in bush, man leaves diary of despair," Associated Press, Fairbanks, fall 1982.

The following references are from copied news stories Kris Capps sent me with the comments: "The McCunn story was printed from Wednesday, Nov. 10– Saturday, Nov. 13, 1982. One of those days probably had two installments (maybe the 11th?). On Saturday, Nov. 13, in addition to the end of the story itself, there is a separate story providing an overlook of how this happened, interviews with all the players, and a story in the weekend magazine of other survival stories and why those folks survived and McCunn didn't—plus a little pep talk on how to survive if you find yourself in such a situation."

2. Kris Capps, "Jury assigned no blame but guilt lingers," *Fairbanks Daily News-Miners*, pp. 1, 2.
3. Kris Capps, "In the bush desperation turned to tragedy," *Fairbanks Daily News-Miner*, pp. 1, 7.
1. Kris Capps, "A caribou helps his spirits rise," *Fairbanks Daily News-Miner*, pp. 1, 2.

5. Kris Capps, "Hopes rose and fell as the plane came and went," *Fairbanks Daily News-Miner*, p. 1.

6. Kris Capps, "He was depressed but 'hanging in there,' " *Fairbanks Daily News-Miner*, pp. 1, 6.

7. Kris Capps, "He prayed for a moose, rabbits or a plane," *Fairbanks Daily News-Miners*, pp. 1, 2.

THE LAST ADVENTURE

1. Anna Farneski, "Hunters find body of man," *Fairbanks Daily News-Miner*, September 9, 1992.

2. Anna Farneski, "Diary tells of fatal ordeal," *Fairbanks Daily News-Miner*, September 10, 1992.

3. Kris Capps, "Hiker's fate, ID a mystery," special to the *Anchorage Daily News*, September 11, 1992, pp. 1, 3.

4. Kris Capps, "Autopsy finds hiker died of starvation," special to the *Anchorage Daily News*, September 12, 1992, p. 1 and back page.

5. "Diary documents hunting, opportunities lost, disaster," *Anchorage Daily News*, September 13, 1992.

6. "Motorist warned hiker against trip," *Anchorage Daily News*, September 15, 1992.

7. "Identity search leads to South Dakota," *Anchorage Daily News*, September 16, 1992.

8. "Troopers identify wilderness victim," *Fairbanks Daily News-Miner*, September 20, 1992.

9. Kris Capps, "Dead hiker ID'd," *Anchorage Daily News*, September 19, 1992, pp. A-1, A-12.

10. Anna Farneski, "Friend says Alex 'stepped over the edge,' " *Fairbanks Daily News-Miner*, September 20, 1992, pp. B-1, B-6.

11. "Diary, photographs reveal Alex's travels," *Fairbanks Daily News-Miner*, September 20, 1992, pp. B-1, B-6.

12. Bill Hewitt, Johnny Dodd, "End of the Trail," *People* weekly, October 5, 1992, pp. 48–51.

13. Jon Krakauer, "Death of an Innocent," *Outside*, January 1993, pp. 38–45, 90–92.

MUGGED BY A ROGUE

Transcription of Ben White's taped story of his friend George Pitka and successive visits with Ben at his home from spring 1998 through February 1999.

WHAT HAPPENED?

Personal interview with Don Frantz in his Anchorage office, February 9, 1999.

GONE WITHOUT A TRACE

1. Natalie Phillips, "Barrow mourns MD with taste for adventure," *Anchorage Daily News,* November 10, 1996, pp. A-1, A-12.
2. Craig Medred, "Our wonderful tools can be our worst enemies," *Anchorage Daily News,* November 12, 1996, pp. C-1, C-6.
3. "Missing doctor's snowmachine hits North Slope beach," *Anchorage Daily News,* July 24, 1997, p. B-6.

COSTLY MISTAKE

1. S. J. Komarnitsky, "Grandparents, child freeze to death," *Anchorage Daily News,* January 19, 1996, pp. A-1, A-12.
2. Craig Medred, "Troopers dismissed cry for help," *Anchorage Daily News,* January 20, 1996, pp. A-1, A-10.
3. S. J. Komarnitsky, "Report tracks troopers; delay on call," *Anchorage Daily News,* April 5, 1996, pp. A-1, A-12.
4. Personal interview with Vernon Rice, January 17, 1999, at his home in Anchorage, Alaska, 5 P.M. (Vern provided me with the newspaper articles and the following deposition, for which I am most grateful.)
5. Audiovisual deposition of Vernon Rice, October 25, 1998, 1031 W. Fourth Avenue, Suite 200, Anchorage, Als 99501 (for the State of Alaska, Fourth Judicial District at Bethel): *Nancy Kiokun, Personal Representative for the Estate of Palmer Olrun, the Estate of Leah Olrun, and the Estate of Ethan Olrun, and Cynthia Olrun, Plaintiffs v. The State of Alaska and State of Alaska Department of Public Safety, Defendants.* Case no.: 4BE-97-274 CIV.
6. Craig Medred, "Cold almost claims two other lives," *Anchorage Daily News,* January 26, 1996, pp. A-1, A-12.

Personal interview with Alaska state trooper Michael Opalka of Girdwood's Detachment G, in his home at 2 P.M., February 27, 1999.

WILL THEY FIND ME?

Personal communication via phone and mail with Duane Persson and wife Barbara from their Post Falls, Idaho, home between January 1, 1999, and February 12, 1999; transcription of taped story.

SEVEN HOURS ON A COLD FLOAT

Personal phone calls from Kahren Rudbeck and correspondence with her to complete her tale, August 1998 through January 9, 1999.

RIVER GONE WILD

Story based on and rewritten from Vernon Schmidt's "Almost the Last Moose Hunt," *Alaska Magazine,* July 1986. Continued correspondence with Vernon and Carol since 1994.

PIECE A CAKE
Personal interview with John Cloran at his home on East Tudor Road in Anchorage, August 3, 1989.

ONE TOUGH TRAPPER
Longtime friendship and association with Wade Nolan, who told me the story of the Nome trapper in the spring of 1989.

COME BACK ALIVE
Personal interview with contributor in his Humana Hospital room in Anchorage, Alaska, July 31, 1991, and follow-up correspondence through March 3, 1993.

OVER THE EDGE
Phone conversation followed by personal interview with Bob Och in his Anchorage home, 10 A.M., January 27, 1999. Transcription of tape and successive revisions through February 12, 1999.

DANGER IGNORED
Personal interview at Chris Nolke's family home in Anchorage, January 9, 1992.

HEROES, ONE AND ALL
1. Steve Rinehart, Craig Medred, and Rosemary Shinohara, "Chugach fall kills 2, injures 12," *Anchorage Daily News,* June 30, 1997, pp. A-1, A-12; Craig Medred, "Tragedy in 'valley of death.' "
2. Rosemary Shinohara, "Fight against fear ended in death," *Anchorage Daily News,* July 1, 1997, pp. A-1, A-8, A-9; Steve Rinehart, "Survivors recount tale of terrifying fall"; Craig Medred, "Nightmare met rescuers on peak."
3. Craig Medred, "A fast slide into disaster," *Anchorage Daily News,* July 6, 1997, pp. A-1, A-6, A-7; Richard Mauer, "UAA program passed review."
4. Craig Medred, "Rescuers quick to scene, shocked by tragedy's scope," *Anchorage Daily News,* July 7, 1977, pp. A-1, A-10.

DEER HUNT GONE AWRY
Personal correspondence followed by telephone interview with Richard Trovillo in his Ketchikan, Alaska, home, February 1, 1991.

NIGHTMARE IN THE INLET
Personal interview with Bob Elstad, December 13, 1991, at 8:30 A.M. in my English classroom at Dimond High School, Anchorage, Alaska.

DEATH WOULDN'T WAIT
Personal interview with Alaska state trooper Michael Opalka of Girdwood's Detachment G, in his home at 2 P.M., February 27, 1999.

1. Marilee Enge, "Rescuers try, but rising tide claims woman," *Anchorage Daily News*, July 16, 1988, pp. A-1, A-12.
2. Jean Lamming, "Race against tide ends in death," *Anchorage Times*, July 16, 1988, pp. A-1, A-10.
3. Letters to the editor, *Anchorage Daily News*, July 27, 1988, p. C-7.
4. Tom Bell, "Duck hunter saved from mudflats," *Anchorage Daily News*, September 12, 1998, pp. B-1, B-3.

ESCAPE FROM THE PIT
Continued personal correspondence and phone calls since fall 1992 finalizing story with C. D. Tuggle and his daughter Luanne Haddaway.

SURVIVAL APPENDIX
1. Alfred Wolfe, *In Alaskan Waters* (Caldwell, Ohio: Caxton Printers, 1943), pp. 149–53.
2. Bud Branham, *Sourdough and Swahili: A Professional Hunter on Two Continents* (Clinton, N.J.: Amwell Press, 1989), pp. 208–10.
3. Con Bunde, *Alaska Sportsman*, April 1966, pp. 10ff.
4. Iris Warner, "I Nearly Froze in Bed," *Alaska Sportsman*, July 1967, pp. 15–16.